31 July 1987

Saltwood.

Our 23rd wedding anniversary! So I said to Jane this morning "Dear Jesus, some of it in darkness and drizzle, some very gentle."

I looked up the old diaries — quite inadequate. But the portrait of Stephenson reminds me of that man, on the 3rd night of our honeymoon. A long stay, more recently one, of Hoose and the Saltdean, and the King and Andrew — satisfying I remember now, how one knew so old stay 55/00 one afternoon in Andrew and even then I left it feeling.

So here we are, barn of Saltwood and the boys fully grown. An M.P., and older, but himself (it seems) of my passing ambition that 11th year, underspeculate, harshly that I can arouse, that kept me riddled at Eton, and out of the thinking. It could be a source of strength too, if only we could get to the top.

The boys have been here entirely all summer, and it has been lovely (bar (sic) the late nights.) But alas and alack, this really is the last one; because John has got his honours scholarship, and Andrew — how rapidly broad and beautiful — will be at Southend. The result I have dreaded for 15 years will be on us, in a month. John goes to Redhill in July night, Andrew starts at Portijk on Sept 7. All of them, if he gets through, will be at at the end of October — which would be lonely.

We are both trying to do too much — and it is hardly our

DIARIES

Into Politics

London Borough of Hounslow

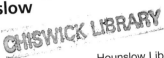

Hounslow Library Services

This item should be returned or renewed by the latest date shown. If it is not required by another reader, you may renew it in person or by telephone (twice only). Please quote your library card number. A charge will be made for items returned or renewed after that date due.

			PI0-L-2138

Weidenfeld & Nicolson

LONDON

First published in Great Britain in 2000 by
Weidenfeld & Nicolson

A CIP catalogue reference for this book is available
from the British Library

ISBN 0 297 64402 5

Typeset by Selwood Systems, Midsomer Norton

Printed in Great Britain by Butler & Tanner Ltd,
Frome and London

Weidenfeld & Nicolson

The Orion Publishing Group Ltd
Orion House
5 Upper Saint Martin's Lane
London, WC2H 9EA

'Sometimes lacking in charity; often trivial, occasionally lewd, cloyingly sentimental, repetitious, whingeing and imperfectly formed. For some readers the entries may seem to be all of these things. But they are real diaries.'

Alan Clark
Diaries, 1993

CONTENTS

ILLUSTRATIONS

A section of photographs from the Clark family albums appears between pages 198 and 199.

GLOSSARY

FAMILY

Jane

James – AC's elder son (aka 'Boy', 'Jamie')

Andrew – AC's younger son (aka 'Tip', 'Tip-book', 'Tup', 'Cin', 'Lilian')

Colette – AC's sister (aka 'Celly')

Colin – AC's brother (aka 'Col')

Lord Clark – (aka Bonny papa) – AC's father, Kenneth Clark

B'Mama (aka Bonny mama) – AC's mother, Jane Clark

Nolwen, Comtesse de Janzé – AC's stepmother

STAFF AND ESTATE

Cradduck – gardener at Saltwood

Eddie – groundsman at Saltwood

Lindley – Lord Clark's butler at the Garden House

Nanny (aka 'Greenwood') – nanny to James and Andrew, and living in a grace and favour cottage on the Saltwood estate

Gangster and Grandee – beagles

Tom – Jack Russell terrier

George – a tame jackdaw at Saltwood

Eva – Jane's Rottweiler

Angus – black labrador

OFFICE

Sue – first secretary at the House of Commons
Veronica – secretary at the House of Commons
Alison – secretary at the House of Commons

SOME CARS AND RELATED MATTERS

(Many of the cars mentioned in this volume are transitory purchases
    which AC sold on; they are usually identified within the text)

Wee Bob – mechanic to Christopher Selmes' (qv)
The Mews – composite name for various vintage car dealers'
    establishments in Queen's Gate, London
Coys – dealers in classic cars

600 – Mercedes
550 Spyder – Porsche ex von Frankenberg Mille Miglia
The black SS100 – owned by AC since his undergraduate days
The 'little white' – Mercedes 230 SL
K10 – 1979 Chevrolet
OLA – Datsun 240Z, belonging to James
Chapron – the Citroen, the *decapotable*, belonging to Jane
The Mehari – a little plastic truck with an air-cooled engine and a
    very light footprint used for clearing glass clippings and prunings
    from the garden because it does not mark the lawn.
The Locomobile – an old chain-driven racing car of 1908
THEBUS – 'the bus' – Transit van
Winter Car – 1967 Chevrolet Impala
Summer Car – 1967 Chevrolet Impala convertible
The Mickey – 2CV
Winifred – Morris 8 (see p. 343)
Bang Bang – R Type Continental (see p. 66)
Osprey and Atco – lawn mowers at Saltwood

HOUSES AND LOCATIONS

SALTWOOD CASTLE

Various rooms: the Great Library; the Tower Office; the Green Room
    (the Clarks' informal sitting room in the old staff wing)

Garden House (GH) – a large bungalow, designed by John King in the old kitchen garden in the grounds of Saltwood, for Lord and Lady Clark, when they moved out of the castle in 1971.

Sandling – the railway station for Saltwood

Gossie Bank – a steep climb at the far end of Grange Farm, Saltwood

The Seeds – a large arable field at Grange Farm, Saltwood

The Bailey (inner and outer) – the two courtyards (see also lawns)

Courtneys, sometimes Courtenays (aka the Secret Garden)

SEEND PARK

Broomhayes (aka Cherry Cottage) – near Devizes in Wiltshire; retained by the Clarks when they moved to Saltwood.

RYE

Watchbell Street – including No 11, where the Clarks lived after they married

BRATTON-CLOVELLY

Town Farm – another early home; in west Devon, about three-quarters of an hour's drive north of Plymouth

ZERMATT

Châlet Caroline – the Clarks' house in the village, which they built at the end of the 1950s

Trift – an inn at an early stage in the ascent to the Rothornhutte

ALBANY

B5 Lower/Upper – Piccadilly chambers shared at various times by AC and Lord Clark. The Upper, more an attic, had once been servants' quarters.

HOUSE OF COMMONS

Dean's Yard – mainly offices for secretaries, by Westminster Abbey

East Cloisters (or simply Cloisters) – where AC had an office from 1977

PLYMOUTH

Alma Road and Headland Park – at different times the headquarters of Sutton Conservative Association

SLANG
(Family sayings and shorthand expressions dotted about the text)

ACHAB – (lit.) 'anything can happen at backgammon', a saying originally from 'the Room' at Brooks's where games can swing at a late stage on an unpredictable run of the dice, used often as a consolation in times of depression. Adaptable in other circumstances, substituting 'politics' for 'backgammon' for instance

Ash eating – self-inflicted penance

Piccolo – a minor but telling triumph.

Thompson – defecation

Sadismoid – virtually the same as sadistically, though less *transitive* in meaning; the suffic – moid, or moidly is often attached to adjectives

Satisly – arousing satisfaction, inducing complacency

Greywater – diarrhoea

Naylor-Leylandish – named after the aquiline features of Sir Vivian Naylor-Leyland.

BHLH – a description of perfect male dress sense, right for the specific occasion. The initials were those of Basil Liddell-Hart, one of AC's heroes, who also invariably dressed immaculately.

'w' – walk, as in going for a walk

Tinky – diminutive, insignificant

ABBREVIATIONS

NAMES

AC – Alan Clark
CH – Charles, Charles Howard
CS – Christopher (aka 'Daisy') Selmes
IG – Ian Gow
RJ – Robert Rhodes James and, sometimes, Roy Jenkins
MT – Margaret Thatcher

ACRONYMS

BHLH– see Slang (above)
CGT – Capital Gains Tax
o/d – overdraft
CPC – Conservative Political Centre
EDM – Early Day Motion
F&GP– Financial and General Purposes Committee (usually of the Plymouth Sutton constituency association)
MLR – Minimum Lending Rate
OLA – see Cars (above)
PQ – Parliamentary Question
ST J – St James' Club, at Coventry House, Piccadilly until 1975, when it merged with Brooks's in St James's Street
SE – Stock Exchange
UBS – Union Bank Suisse

UCH – University College Hospital, London
TSW – Television South West
VGL – very good looking
WD – 'wet' dream

INTRODUCTION

Many begin diaries, few sustain them. Alan Clark, though, was a stayer. At his death he had been keeping his for forty-four years. Originally written without any thought of publication, in 1993 he plundered them for a volume covering his spell as a junior minister in successive Thatcher governments.[1] This contains the most authoritative – and enthralling – contemporaneous account of Margaret Thatcher's downfall.

Following the huge success of the first volume (praised and likened to 'Chips' Channon's great journals, into which he rarely failed to dip with his early morning tea),[2] Alan at first considered a sequel, to be called 'The Wilderness Years' – about what happened after he retired from the Commons at the 1992 general election, or 'Matrix Churchill and all that', as he said in a letter. By the new year of 1999 his situation had changed. He was, after all, a Member of Parliament again.[3] Far better, he argued, to go back to the moment he entered politics, which was also, for another reason, a landmark year. A further volume, which might be called 'From Wilderness to Opposition', would come later.

From the late 1960s he had been trying to gain selection as parliamentary candidate for a safe Conservative seat, an ambition finally achieved in 1972. At the same time his father gave him Saltwood Castle overlooking Hythe in Kent with the English Channel beyond.

---

[1] Titled, quite simply, *Diaries*, they start in 1983 and close in 1991.
[2] At the time of writing more than 300,000 copies have been sold.
[3] For the Kensington and Chelsea constituency, elected at the 1997 general election.

Politics absorbed Alan for the rest of his life; Saltwood would be his principal and adored home. The dye was cast.

At the time this volume opens Alan was forty-three and married with two children. The elder son of Kenneth Clark, who had been the youngest Director of the National Gallery, and his wife Jane, he had twin siblings, Colin and Colette. The family were affluent, their wealth stemming from Clark's Cotton Thread in Paisley (Kenneth Clark's great-great-grandfather invented the cotton spool). Alan was too young to serve in the Second World War (he celebrated his seventeenth birthday less than four weeks before VE-Day), but he remained proud for the rest of his life that he managed to enlist in the Household Cavalry training regiment before the war was over. His interest in military history (particularly of the twentieth century) had already been awakened.

He was educated at Eton and Oxford, where he spent three happy if hedonistic years at Christ Church reading modern history under Hugh Trevor-Roper. In his address at the memorial service for Alan at St Margaret's, Westminster, in February 2000, Euan Graham recalled their first meeting in the coffee shop opposite Balliol College in 1948, which led to his being asked by Alan to drive him to Stroud in a Buick Roadster convertible. It transpired that Alan had lost his licence for the 'relatively trivial offence' of allowing a girl to drive the car while sitting on his lap, leaving him to work the pedals. To a ripple of knowing laughter from the St Margaret's congregation, Euan Graham acknowledged that there in a single story two of Alan's pleasures were combined.

It took many years for Alan to discover his true vocation. Ten months after becoming an MP – in January 1975 – it was still something of a surprise. 'My real problem is that at the age [he was forty-six] when most people start "slowing up" I suddenly gain a job – having been in retirement from the age of twenty-seven.' After Oxford he served with the Royal Auxiliary Air Force whilst reading for the Bar and qualifying, with difficulty, as a barrister. Although he did not practise, he served briefly as judge's marshal on the south-eastern assize. He went on to augment some family money by working for a company trading in cars, particularly vintage and classic cars (an interest that he would keep up), and playing the Stock Exchange.

With a brilliant mind, this was hardly enough to keep him occupied. He inherited his father's interest and knowledge in art, but never seriously thought of following in his footsteps. He had, however, also inherited Kenneth Clark's facility for, and pleasure in, writing and by the mid-1950s was keeping a journal. In 1960 his first novel (*Bargains at Special Prices*), with its echoes of early Evelyn Waugh, was published as Number 13[1] in Hutchinson's New Authors imprint to widespread acclaim (Leonard Russell in the *Sunday Times* wrote: 'Mr Clark's very funny and instructive novel will be gulped down like a glass of champagne by the army of newcomers to stock market speculation,' V. S. Naipaul in the *New Statesman* observed that 'his dialogue is delightful' and *The Observer* critic noted that he had 'a briskly original wit.'). This was followed, less successfully, in 1963 by *Summer Season*.

By this time, writing and his interest in military matters had combined in the first of three superlative campaign histories: *The Donkeys: A History of the British Expeditionary Force in 1915*, which on its publication in 1961 was to make his reputation as a military historian, but amid torrents of controversy. 'Eloquent and painful', wrote George Malcolm Thomson in the *Evening Standard*. 'Clark leaves the impression that vanity and stupidity were the main ingredients of the massacres of 1915. He writes searingly and unforgettably.'[2] Next came *The Fall of Crete*, followed in 1965 by *Barbarossa: The Russian-German Conflict, 1941–1945*. He toyed with a number of further projects, including a history of NATO, a life of Lloyd George and a study of modern Conservatism;[3] but he failed to make the delivery dates and his long-time literary agent, Michael Sissons, would arrange the cancellation of contracts and the return of the advances. This literary life still left him unfulfilled. It was not a full-time career.

Whereas his father's politics were firmly to the left, Alan had an intellectual affinity with the right: by 1972 this meant patriotism, the Monday Club, voicing an enthusiasm (not a reverence) for the views of Enoch Powell,[4] but a distaste for many of the political views of Edward Heath, not least firm opposition to what was then known as

---

[1] The number 13 has considerable significance within the Clark family: not only was AC himself born on 13 April 1928, his elder son James on 13 February 1960, and his grandson Angus on 13 November 1997, but his father's birthday was on 13 July 1903.

[2] Even more than a quarter of a century later, in 1989, when AC was hoping for ministerial preferment from Trade to Defence, as Armed Forces Minister, he knew that the 'Army brass won't have me because of *The Donkeys*' (24 July 1989).

[3] Eventually written and published in 1998 as *The Tories: Conservatives and the Nation State 1922–1997*, it was also the basis of a television series.

[4] Was AC ever a 'Powellite'? In a letter to David Butler, who was compiling his study of the February 1974 election, AC admits that at the time he was looking for a seat he was 'much more closely identified with Monday Club/Powellite sympathies' than he was to become once at Westminster.

the 'Common Market'; he was, though, also a member of the Bow Group. He had started looking for a parliamentary seat in the late 1960s: a litany of constituency names sprinkles his notebooks: Norwood, Swindon, Ashchurch, Weston, Havant, Langstone among many others. Early in 1972 a new name emerges: Plymouth Sutton.

By then Alan had been married for fourteen years. He had met Jane Beuttler when he was twenty-eight and she was fourteen. They wed two years later. Their honeymoon ranged wide: on the train to Switzerland he continually worried that she might not like one of his favourite landscapes; they toured the battlefields of the First World War as he was already researching *The Donkeys* (to which she contributed the maps, her interwined initials in the corner being the only clue to their origins); and they visited old haunts along the Mediterranean, where they met Alan's oldest friend, John Pollock, and his patronne, Constance Mappin.[1] Back in England they bought a cob farmhouse at Bratton-Clovelly in west Devon, about three-quarters of an hour's drive to the north of Plymouth. Its position would prove significant politically. Their other early homes included Alan's bachelor house in Watchbell Street, Rye, not far along the south coast from Saltwood, and several properties at Seend in Wiltshire. Their elder son James was born in 1960, followed by Andrew in 1962.

Alan need not have worried about Jane's feelings for Switzerland and together they soon built a chalet in Zermatt, the Châlet Caroline (Jane's first name). In London Alan shared with his father the use of a set at Albany in Piccadilly.

In 1951 Kenneth Clark had moved to Saltwood. He and his wife knew this part of Kent from before the war when they owned a country house close to Philip Sassoon's Port Lympne, where they were frequent visitors. He bought the castle and its grounds from the estate of Lady Conway of Allington, who had restored it with the help of a distinguished medieval architect, Philip Tilden. A previous owner was the father of W. F. (Bill) Deedes, MP, who had been a Minister in Harold Macmillan's second government, and during much of the currency of these diaries was editor of the *Daily Telegraph* and

---

[1] 'Jane and I stayed with them at Positano,' AC recalled (*Diaries*, 16 February 1985). 'Christina [a girl friend who had been living in AC's house when he became engaged to Jane] turned up, and a farcical triangular sub-plot developed with Milo Cripps's [later the 4th Baron Parmoor] boyfriend 'Barry' falling for her, and tears shed all round.'

a valued patron for Alan's journalism. Kenneth Clark had continued Lady Conway's restoration, adding, in particular, the bookcases to the Great Library, and it was in the adjoining study that he wrote his later books, including *Civilisation* (the television series of the same name led to him being known informally, but affectionately, as 'Lord Clark of Civilisation'). Alan recalled in a 1980 diary entry the peak days of his parents' occupation 'when it was teeming with staff and beautiful meals arrived on cue.' In 1971, and approaching seventy, Kenneth Clark decided to hand over the castle to his elder son and move to the Garden House, a bungalow he had built in the Saltwood grounds. He took Lindley, his butler, with him, but he and Lady Clark found it difficult to sever the Saltwood knot, and as Alan also relates in his journals, tensions often ran high.

Following Alan's death there was much speculation that no further volumes of his diaries could be published, because his handwriting was said to be impossible to read. The publication of this present volume is testament to the unreliability of such speculation. Much depended on how tired, or how stressed Alan was at the time of writing, as well as the quality of paper on which he wrote, whether he used fountain pen, ballpoint, feltnib or pencil and where he did his writing (train journeys, for instance, do not lend themselves to legibility). And once he had started regularly taking the current volume with him to Westminster he deliberately chose what he called 'a crabbed hand' just in case it was mislaid (indeed later volumes carry the firm injunction on the front cover – REWARD IF FOUND).

Many fans of the published *Diaries* have, though, wondered what all the fuss was about, citing the endpapers printed in the hardback edition, which reproduce entries in an elegant and readable hand. As his editor and publisher for the first volume of *Diaries* in 1993, maybe this is the place to make a confession. Although the content of those endpapers was taken from actual journals of the period, the reproductions were precisely that. Alan made fair copies of a number of entries, and took considerable pleasure in ensuring that each entry appeared to end with an unresolved cliff-hanger at the foot of the page. Of the reviewers, as Alan himself recorded with glee, it was Robert Harris (author of *Enigma*) who first noticed that these entries were a bonus as they do not appear in the published *Diaries* themselves.

Early in 1972 Alan neared the end of his current manuscript volume and was concerned to discover that 'those useful, blue cloth-bound plain-sheeted loose-leaf binders', which he had been using since the beginning – what we might today call an A5 ringbinder – were, *of course*, 'no longer being made.' Rummaging around in the library at Saltwood he turned up a barely used visitors book, bound in crimson-lake leather with 'Katoomba' stamped in gold leaf on the front. Katoomba was the name given by his grandfather to his yachts, and – particularly pleasing to Alan, who enjoyed the symmetry – the few signatures this volume contained started in the year of his father's birth (1903).

'It seems appropriate enough [he wrote] for the new set of journals – Katoomba has long been an evocative name for me[1] and I have all the models: it is good quality paper and there is plenty of space – heaven knows what the pages will (fore) tell or even if I will live to complete them.'

'Katoomba' lasted until 1975, to be followed by a large hardback 'legal' notebook left over from his law studies. With lined paper, it was identified by him, thanks to its binding, as 'the black book'. Through the 1980s he used government-issue hardback A4 note-books. The paper was appalling – 'horrible "austerity" book', he called the first one – and, on the whole, his writing was worse.

Even in the earliest days of keeping a diary – the first volume begins in 1955 – he rarely let more than a couple of weeks go by without making an entry. More usually he would write once a week, a review of the past seven days. By the 1980s – particularly when Parliament was in session – he was often writing daily. Over the decade covered by this second volume I estimate that I have drawn from approximately 500,000 words of the original. The style of his writing evolved, as can be seen in this volume: there is the note (with verb and personal pronoun noticeable by their absence), the simple narrative record, and, finally, the more elaborate set-piece, often with substantial quantities of dialogue, where the sheer pleasure in writing is very apparent. In content the diary was also a confessional and the fact that he kept it going over the best part of five decades demonstrates how important it was to him, no matter the pressures.

During his first election campaign – in February 1974 – he used a

---

[1] As Kenneth Clark relates in the first volume of his autobiography, *Another Part of the Wood*, the name came from Australia's Blue Mountains, which his father had visited in his teens.

W. H. Smith appointments diary – a page a day – which also became
the journal for the October 1974 election. In the helter-skelter of
campaigning these entries are often little more than brief notes, and
on his arrival at Westminster, to judge from the content, he rarely
took 'Katoomba' to the Commons or to the Dean's Yard office by
Westminster Abbey, where his secretary was lodged. The trusty 'W. H.
Smith' (being A5 in size and therefore more portable) continued to
do occasional double-duty and includes a short account of his maiden
speech on 30 April. But his Westminster journal keeping is haphazard.
He has, for instance, not left us with his thoughts on the overthrowing
of Edward Heath, following the Tories' defeat at the second 1974
election, and the arrival of Margaret Thatcher as the Conservative
leader. However his appreciation of the uncertain future of Heath
may be read in his account of a telephone conversation during that
election campaign with Bernard (Jack) Weatherill, the Tories' deputy
chief whip. Thatcher as possible leader had been mentioned as early
as March.

Occasionally, though, he felt compelled to seize the minute, writing
on House of Commons notepaper before slipping or stapling the page
into the appropriate spot; sometimes entries were even jotted into his
engagement diary and later transcribed. The 1975 Common Market
debate is one such. But the 1974–79 Labour government – although
it had its moments, particularly towards its close – demonstrated to
Alan that, with a social life being regularly reduced to tatters as a result
of a tedious number of all-night sittings, being a junior back-bench
opposition MP was not much fun. He craved power, power for a Tory
government, and advancement for himself.

Throughout this period his writing continued, but more often at
weekends, when he would retire to the Great Hall at Saltwood or to
the garden, perhaps, at Bratton. We may have less politics than in
the later journals, but away from Westminster his days are rich and
complicated. He gives us life as he experiences it: he is insatiably
attracted to a pretty face, he suffers chronic hypochondria (like his
father), can't resist dealing in cars (or on the Stock Exchange), is close
to bankruptcy and experiences gambling disasters at backgammon
that show an addictive streak. But when he strays it is always to Jane,
to his sons and to Saltwood that he returns.

Much was to change in 1979. The general election in May – Alan
again dragged out the 'W. H. Smith' as his election journal – saw
Alan's majority double, to 11,000, and the Tories returned to gov-

ernment, with Margaret Thatcher as Prime Minister. Even as a back-bencher, some of Alan's hopes were fulfilled and the tone of his diaries changed: he realised how much he enjoyed being of the party in government, reporting what he saw, heard and was increasingly part of, as well as musing on his own hopes and ambitions. And by the autumn he had devised a solution for his diary. The manuscript book continued, but he also started dictating Westminster entries to his secretary, which considerably increased the political content. For this volume I have drawn on both.

The published *Diaries* began with the death of his father, the general election of 1983 and Alan's elevation to ministerial rank. Appropriately this current volume concludes the previous year with the political event that secured Margaret Thatcher's position – the victorious Falklands campaign, which through his military interest and knowledge gave Alan lasting political prominence and presaged his long-desired advancement. At Saltwood, too, life was about to change with the first major sign of his father's mortality, a stroke that immobilised him in the summer of 1982. But, as Alan planned before his death, this volume begins ten years before: Plymouth beckons politically and Saltwood is the new family home.

Ion Trewin
July 2000

EDITOR'S NOTE

Footnotes give the present and past — but rarely future — positions of individuals, usually at their first appearance. Nor is an MP's political allegiance listed except where this may be unclear from the text.

AC's occasional inconsistencies in style, dates, capitalisation and even English grammar, have sometimes been left as written. I have followed his own practice and where appropriate silently edited passages.

IT

1972

Centre of gravity moving inexorably to Saltwood. Only pause for thought – where the hell do the years go? Cradduck[1] (naturally) can't get possession of his cottage – and there is nowhere else – *quelle est la solution? . . . averme?* (Gamelin with Churchill May 1940 . . . *'ou est la masse de manoeuvre?'*) Very heavy expenditure looking at interior. Hence dilemma. How far to go? What degree of compromise, or not, between having it as a sort of show-place for summer and occasional smart weekends and living at Broomhayes?[2] Or living there with the whole caboosh, cars, trading, dogs, peacocks. And then, even while we are there I think it might be more 'sensible' in the Victorian part, keeping the medieval part as a show area. Real thing is, it's lovely with the boys, but when they are away, then I rather dread the *existence solitaire* (just) the two of us. If only we could have another baby!

On the financial front, still trading like crazy, though taking profits too soon I don't doubt. Periodic waves of 'panic' at my gearing cause me to shorten the line. 'Garaging' (huh!) a lot of the profits by putting them in cars (Isotta, 540U, Ferrari 375, D-Type), but could well have a car sale in October. The objective must be ELIMINATION OF ALL DEBTS.

Had this concept of a bank (Central Line Investment Management and Banking) charging $1\frac{1}{4}$ per account. Charles[3] very keen on the idea. I think this might be something (big) to go for – but very hard work, capital expenditure, office in the City.

'Daisy'[4] on the phone, ill, in Paris. 'I'm terribly worried that you're going to waste all that money (from the field) Alan . . .' So am I.[5] I

---

[1] Head gardener at Saltwood from 1951–1980.
[2] The house at Seend where the Clarks were living before the move to Saltwood.
[3] Charles Howard, a motoring friend who also regularly played backgammon with AC.
[4] Christopher (aka 'Daisy') Selmes, a friend of many years standing, who had made a fortune in the City.
[5] AC was selling the cricket field to the south of Saltwood, and houses were planned on part of it, but the builders went bankrupt. The cricket club bought its corner. A quarter of a century later, in 1998, AC was able to buy back the field as a wedding anniversary present for Jane.

am resorting to the primitive technique, *caching* it in different hollow trees like a squirrel and his nuts; the other school is concentrate, Rommel, turn it into 500[1] this year.

Politics too, that spurious sense of activity (without achievement). Plymouth Sutton – sounds promising and a spy in the camp who told me already more than I ever got out of that shower at Ashchurch. But I've seen too much of those constituency fixings to be sanguine about my own prospects.

As for Langstone, incredibly the tables have *again* turned; poor old Lloyd really looks done for now, having lost all his 'list' at the AGM and slightly gone off his rocker, discussing the agent, stopping surgeries etc.[2] But will they wear me? The bulk of the Executive – no; imprisoned, I should say, by their own guilt. Pity because I do want to get in.

Saltwood   *Saturday, 6 May*

Still not properly unpacked here, many things not 'come to hand' as yet, packing cases in the upper hall etc. *Absolutely* no decoration at all (to my parents' puzzlement ... 'is Al just going to sell the whole thing to an institution?' etc), but, in fact, adjusting 'quite well' to the change; boys seem reasonably all right at school though dear Cin a bit lonely in break which is giving him light anxiety-asthma.

Plymouth Sutton is a situation of considerable promise. My spy (Graham Butland[3]) has leaked all the questions so I am dutifully preparing fluent, moving answers. He has given me the names of the others short-listed and will meet me on Saturday morning to disclose how Friday's interviewees fared and see if there are any questions I want posed! Still Langstone to fall back on, but I am no longer sanguine there.

Went to Bratton on Wednesday of last week prior to going on to Plymouth. How lovely and soft and restful the West Country is! And

---

[1] Throughout his diaries, when referring to financial sums, AC often leaves off the final '000'. In this case he means £500,000.

[2] AC was being intemperate: Sir Ian Lloyd (Kt 1986) may have had problems with the Portsmouth Langstone constituency association, but it wasn't long before he was selected by nearby Havant in 1974, which he represented until 1992.

[3] A member of the Plymouth Sutton Conservative Association committee.

how evocative of those early distant happy days with Jane and the babies and the blue Oldsmobile. Now we hardly have time to breathe, but I can still get a great draught of peace when I am at Bratton-Clovelly. Whether it would still be the same if I was an MP down there, I don't know.

Duke of Cornwall Hotel, Plymouth   *Friday, 12 May*

I sit at a table in the bay window of a comfortable room in this old-fashioned hotel. Tomorrow I have a preliminary interview for the 'safest' of the three Plymouth seats. This afternoon I have been in reconnaissance.

I first visited Plymouth ten years ago, when I collected Jane and new-born Andrew from the maternity ward at Freedom Fields hospital whither she had been rushed by ambulance from Bratton in the bitter winter of 1962. There are some fine buildings in a hard grey stone, almost granite; especially along the Hoe where Nancy Astor[1] had a grand house. Also tracts of rubble-covered wasteland where the planners have not yet built over the bomb damage.

Hard to understand, this, as it is more than thirty years since the great Luftwaffe raids of April 1941 when the whole population would, at nightfall, trek out on the Yelverton road and camp on Dartmoor. My father, who sometimes comes up with strange, but usually accurate, pieces of useless information told me quite some time ago that Plymouth was 'the most corrupt city in Britain' – which may explain it.

There are now three parliamentary divisions. I had been advised by the Central Office list of 'Drake', a marginal, and applied. A short while afterward I was gratified to receive a telephone call from two complete strangers, who were on the Executive Council of the third seat, entitled 'Sutton' by the Boundaries Commission, out of homage to Nancy, but in fact taking in a large swathe of Heseltine's former

---

[1] Nancy Astor (wife of the 2nd Viscount Astor) and her husband had a lengthy association with the city. She became the first woman to take her seat in the House of Commons when she was elected MP for the Sutton division in 1919 (a seat her husband had previously held). She retired in 1945.

Tavistock constituency[1] and thus, putatively, very Conservative. 'Forget Drake' they said, 'it's a marginal. Go for Sutton.'

Apparently, but unsurprisingly, Central Office have their eye on the place and wish to make sure that it ends up in 'the right hands'. But there are some on the Executive of the new seat who don't like this idea.

As the preliminary interviews, which started at 4pm, are taking place in this actual building there is much to observe. I have been sitting with a tea tray in front of me since half past three. I am clean-shirted and in a light tweed suit. My features are composed, set you could say, into an expression at the same time fresh and obliging.

A big chap, fifty-ish, balding, spectacles, sat about three tables away. He too appeared to be waiting. Was he the Chairman? Practically anybody could be the chairman at this stage, it seemed. Or at least the Treasurer, or the Vice-chairman. Silently ingratiating, I endeavoured to radiate good will.

Several times I caught him looking at me. Curiously, but *cholerically*. Finally he lumbered over – 'Mr Fowler?'

'No.' Some sixth sense told me not to identify myself.

Just before four o'clock he shambled off up the main staircase – clearly to attend, in all probability to supervise, the selection process.

Scattered about the room sat other candidates. Two of them greeted each other with braying declarations, plainly false, of affection and respect. Standard Party Conference templates; i.e. not very big, not very masculine. Spectacles, new-looking suits, tightly-knotted ties. For much of the time I looked at the ceiling – but *intelligently*, like Richthofen's dog, Moritz.

Only one of these characters was actually seen back down stairs by an escorting bigwig. I recognised Michael Howard, much plugged in the broadsheet press as *thrusting*, a barrister, a high-flyer certain to enter the new Parliament, etc.[2]

The bigwig held him in 'politician's grip'; one hand holding his, the other on Howard's elbow. Not necessarily a good sign, more

---

[1] Michael Heseltine, MP for Tavistock since 1966. Rather than fight one of the reorganised seats in west or south-west Devon, he took the opportunity presented by the changes in constituency boundaries to find a seat nearer London. At the February 1974 election he was elected MP for Henley.

[2] Michael Howard had unsuccessfully fought Liverpool Edgehill in 1966 and 1970. In fact AC was wrong in his forecast. Howard did not finally enter the Commons until 1983, when he won the Folkestone and Hythe seat, thereby becoming the Clarks' Member of Parliament, as Saltwood is in the constituency.

usually an indicator of impending betrayal of some kind.

However – 'Well done', I overheard. 'You'll be hearing from us very shortly . . .'

That's that, then. All sewn up. Except, who the hell is 'Mr Fowler'[1]?

Saltwood   *Saturday, 27 May*

The Plymouth interview was a great success.

Graham Butland and David Holmes[2] brought the crib of the set questions to my germ –, as opposed to smoke-filled room. Euphoria and might even have carried the whole thing on the spot – but (according to Graham) a serious decline set in over the weekend; certainly I took an instant dislike to that little 'christian' sub-agent,[3] with his long, but grey-streaked hair – and he reciprocated and spread it round. Apparently 'nigger in the woodpile' was Betty Easton[4] – curious as I should have thought she would be a push-over; I answered her question (about tactics) at greater length than any other. Only explanation I can think of is she now wants Fowler (ex Adley, adopted somewhere else[5]) and sees me as a threat. Next step is a 'cocktail party' for wives, the speech and Q&A session – the very idea makes my stomach turn over. My chances rated low. But anything-can-happen-in backgammon/politics. Throw 4x4, 1x1, 6x6; Fowler gets adopted elsewhere etc. I must press on – that special elation I felt on the Plymouth train after the interview, one is quite charged. Else I am just doomed to sit here, grumblingly reading about those dreadful appeasement collapses of our society (just like 1937–39, with the mass of the party appallingly disreputable in their private complacency) and declining. Lines all over my face. Girls don't even look twice.

---

[1] Norman Fowler, MP for Nottingham South since 1970, but his seat would be disappearing at the next general election as a result of the boundary revisions.

[2] Like Butland a leading light in the Sutton Conservative Association.

[3] P.J. Latimer, the Sutton association agent.

[4] Mrs R.M. Easton, a pillar in Plymouth Conservative circles, who later became the city's Lord Mayor; married to Rodney Easton.

[5] Robert Adley had been MP for Bristol North-East since 1970, but with boundary revisions needed a new seat. The Sutton favourite until selected for Christchurch and Lymington.

Saltwood   *Wednesday, 14 June*

Went to Plymouth for the 'lives' after some shrewd publicity in *The Times*[1] and a huddled but productive conference in mid-week in Horrabridge with my contacts. The previous days had been consumed by incredible driving sagas (*ae?*), picking up the Cadillac at Soton, bringing it to Saltwood, down to Broomhayes, to Bratton (stopped twice by police), then over to Plymouth and back.

That evening I was dead flat. The speech a flop, response tepid. We went to bed early, in daylight, and slept 'more tired than I have been before or since . . .'

But next day, the good news. Voting was 10. 11. 9 for Fowler, Hunt, Clark. Final stage now scheduled for Friday, 30 June at Duke of Cornwall Hotel. For a few hours thought I am going to make it. All the Devon-Bratton-Tuppish-Colwyn Bay pent-up magic must be activated to bring it about. But by now losing confidence. Key element, the speech.

Saltwood   *Wednesday, 21 June*

Poor night following refusal of planning permission on field – tho' almost with relief I thought . . . 'now no obligation to try to be an MP'.

Darling 'Boy' upstairs with bad chickenpox – 'outside' possibility of encephalitis, which has reduced me to a total jelly.

Alan Cleverley rang to say that it was being put about that [Alan was] 'throwing his money around trying to buy the Constituency . . .'

---

[1] As early as 1968 *The Times* Diary column had revealed AC's political ambitions (the offer of an unnamed seat which failed to materialise); on 2 June 1972, under the heading 'Sutton hoo-hah', it disclosed that the Sutton association had upset Tory Central Office by proposing that candidates be invited to show their paces at a dinner or dance. Instead they substituted the 'lives', informal get-togethers with their spouses. AC was in a shortlist of five that also included two future Cabinet ministers: Norman Fowler and David Hunt, national chairman of the Young Conservatives. Fowler, thanks in part to being an MP already, was seen as the front-runner, AC as 'the most obvious alternative', although, said *The Times*, 'he seems to be suffering from his Monday Club tag at a time when he is viewed in the Monday Club as soft on Rhodesia.'

Bad augury. If God inspires me that evening I can go between them (Fowler & Hunt) that I know.

Saltwood　　　　　　　　　　　　　　　　　*Thursday, 22 June*

'Mounting' opposition to development of the cricket field, a like-lihood of council throwing it out; sale of Woodfall Street[1] fallen through; heavily overbought in SE with 'climate' moving against me. Obviously heading for a bad trough – hold tight, stay calm and systematic and try to see it through. Nothing really matters if dear Boy is preserved OK.

Saltwood　　　　　　　　　　　　　　　　　*Saturday, 1 July*

Yesterday was the most memorable of my life with the exception of James being born on 13 II 60.

Of course it is easy enough now to look back and say that I knew I'd get it – all the Bratton magic, the fore-ordained aspect of it all. I can only say that the moment when Tom Bridges[2] gestured to Doc Mac and Howard Davies to console the other two – well! Like a Miss World contestant for a few minutes I couldn't believe it was actually happening to me, and didn't what you might call 'come to' until the Press were taking pictures and data. Then there was the 'repeat convivial' down in the bar. I was on air. Talking to Tom about how 'fairly' the election had been done; slit-eyedly warning M (what's-his-name?); sincerely agreeing with the Macmillans;[3] then a final post-mortem in the street with David Holmes and Graham Butland. At last up to darling Jane who received one in triumph, a *nuit guise* from *sheer elation*.

The next day the early train, and off at Westbury to pick up the

---

[1] London property in SW3, originally owned by Jane Clark, its sale is a running saga through these pages.
[2] The Sutton association chairman.
[3] Dr John Macmillan [Doc Mac] and his wife Pat, members of the Sutton committee, became the Clarks' closest constituency friends.

Bira.[1] It broke down outside Marlborough and I walked for about two miles to a phone box, stumbling in my buckled candidate shoes on the hot (though intermittently cloudy) July day. I didn't mind at all; my mind just went over and over the wonderful fabulous fact that I had been adopted for a safe seat. Confidence totally restored in myself and in God's help – if you deserve it. It was the God question that won it for me, that clinched it. Before I had my turn, on arrival in room 24, I had opened the bible for a snap quotation, got the miracle of the loaves and fishes.[2]

There is a long road ahead, if I am to do everything I wish, I am still a little late – but Oh! I have got two months – the adoption not till September. Get everything tidied and sorted, build up strength, regenerate.

Saltwood   *Wednesday, 19 July*

Last night during the great summer storm that woke us three times I felt a strange, but powerful sense of depression, an impossibility of looking forward, almost as if there was a death imminent (like Jason's[3]). This may be a reaction from the intense happiness of the last 2½ weeks (it seems an age) which I can still rekindle in all its intensity by reading that item in *The Times* of July 3[4].

At least the new series[5] can open with an achievement, a *real* turning point. I was worried that we were going to run out of paper and book and things still the same – purposeless, frustrating, impossibility of getting interviewed while all the good seats were slowly absorbed by the huge demand. Jane, I know, was if not losing heart then at last

---

[1] Bentley, originally owned by and named after Prince Bira.

[2] Norman Fowler was eventually selected for Sutton Coldfield, which he won in the February 1974 general election. David Hunt had a rockier road: chosen not long after as Tory candidate at the neighbouring – and more marginal – Plymouth Drake constituency, he was rejected at his adoption meeting after criticising Enoch Powell at the party conference two weeks before. He did not finally become a Tory MP (for the Wirral) until a by-election in 1976.

[3] Jane Clark's yellow labrador. The day he was run over and killed by a milk lorry she had a premonition that something terrible was going to happen.

[4] Announcing AC's selection.

[5] As described in the Introduction, AC had just started using the 'Katoomba' volume in which to keep his diary.

questioning (and not always silently) the whole waste of time. And so much better than getting Langstone with a permanent bad taste in the air: qv Peter Rees[1] (intoned solemnly at dinner), '. . . if you have a marginal seat your enemies are the Socialists. But in a safe seat – your enemies are Conservatives.'

Saltwood   *Thursday, 3 August*

Somewhat depressed – what's it all in aid of? Just want to be civilised and scholarly and mean in these surroundings, 'working' the place for cash, a little lechery, keeping fit, some b'gammon in London, a little trading in the Mews. Key thing to protect the boys (Tip worryingly asthmatic lately, in spite of visit to quiet-spoken homeopathic doctor). In fact now faced with massive prospects of 'commitment' building up to crazy level after election.

Zermatt   *Friday, 25 August*

One of those days when just everything is falling in at once. Incredibly hot and sunny – yet no point in it really, it took too much yesterday going to the Schönbuhl Hut. Today sitting about disconsolate. ('Daisy' here and plying one with drink in between *ludicrous* deep blaspheming.) Depressed, shaken by Correlli Barnett's *The Collapse of British Power*.[2] Lilian so pale and round-shouldered. He *must* do his exercises daily. 'Daisy' successfully jeering at what I am making on the stock market. Jane crying because the children are so rude. I was briefly hysterical in response this morning in the hall, after a bad night in the dressing room; absurd, unbelievable how I am losing money at backgammon against 'Daisy'. And finally of course, and most ominous, being de-gazumped over the cricket field. A fitting little problem

---

[1] Peter Rees, QC, MP for Dover since 1970 and a sounding board for AC's political ambitions.

[2] This disturbing study of the decline of British influence between the two world wars by a leading British historian had just been published.

(BUT REMEMBER SUTTON! Although plenty of time for that to
go sour before the adoption meeting.)

Saltwood   *Sunday, 17 September*

A note of my adoption meeting at the Duke on Friday (15th):

We had spent the previous two days at Carlyon Bay, delightful,
evocative, appropriate. I had done the traditional clamber along the
rocks to my old sunbathing place of 1947, and walked down the road
to the 'Riviera Club' which I so well remember when I used to go
up and down in the black SS100 and that woman, greyish, semi-crazy
in her big Buick cabriolet. At high tide I rolled up my trousers and
walked about that hard, granulated sand. I stood first on the long rock
at the western end that one never notices at low tide and watched the
waves come streaming in, and felt Carlyon Bay's momentous evocation. Nearly thirty years ago – but it could have been five – the
burgeoning sexual desire, the endless hot days, the happy certainty
that the future could only hold excellence and pleasure.

Left the speech-making/learning a little late and had a demi-panic
at lunch in the hot enclosed front lawn at Bratton. However recovered,
washed my hair and did my stuff in the Duke ball-room. First mike
since Havant dinner way back – and I got a hang-up half way through.
Lesson, don't get slack about prepositions. Link passages *must* be
learned by heart.

Speech centred on violence, but all the publicity went to my
answers on the Asians afterwards.[1] Gloom by many on the platform,
Latimer, Easton, Bridges among them, but *response* from the hall;
stayed till the bitter end beer drinking. A good feeling. Afterwards
Peter Latimer reproached me for a 'Monday Club speech' instead of
a political generality.

---

[1] 'The Tory Party should capitalise on the public outcry against the coming influx of
Ugandan Asians and ban all further coloured immigration', was how the *Western
Morning News* reported AC's remarks next morning.

Zermatt   *Tuesday, 3 October*

Over here for a couple of days to ruminate. I had been looking forward to this, hoping for some lovely high walks with the rocks dark against navy-blue sky, but my peace of mind somewhat spoiled by the sad death on Saturday evening walk with Col,[1] of dear Grandee.[2] Evidently he had a stroke (similar to that attack of paralysis which he suffered about three weeks ago in the kitchen) and drowned in the stream in the far valley, the one I am trying to get from Ann, but she is resisting.

I didn't give it a thought at first when they started a slight hue and cry, he has so often been lost before and the last I had seen of him, quite close to home, with his nose to the ground picking up a scent. But when dinner-time came and he still hadn't turned up I knew, secretly, the worst. We had walked the full round of the Wakefield Trust that evening, and at the top of the crest I had lifted the fence for the beagles to go underneath. Gangster went straight through, but Grandee stopped and thanked me – he *always* thanked one, but this was something special, quite soppy, he put both his paws up and almost looked unhappy (as I now realise looking back). Then he went on seemingly jolly as ever. But he had been saying good-bye. I am so glad he did.

Jane looked for him by the lights of the Mehari, while I was watching *The Two Ronnies* (mediocre), then after a silent supper we went out again and I found him in the stream, very near where I had last seen him with his fine glossy coat quite dry, rigid in the 'show' position, but his poor little muzzle choked and jammed with mud and grass. I do hope he didn't struggle for too long, didn't feel abandoned. We brought him back, and dug the grave straight away, by the Barbican where he can keep an eye on the comings and goings.

How I hate that moment when the earth goes down on the body (he was shrouded in his red blanket with his steel dish and dinner buried beside him). One must have faith, but haunting me is the endless journey, faster than the speed of light, of the soul into infinity.

Anyhow the death of the beagle reminded me very forcibly (and Heaven knows, it is never very far below the surface) of how very vulnerable we all are; those lovely boys and, just lately, the old-head-

---

[1] AC's brother, Colin.
[2] Grandee and Gangster, the beagles.

of-the-house has been somewhat breathless and suffering from back
pain and potential dizziness. Hope not heading for a great bleak
autumn and winter of hypochondria like '63. Yet, looking back, just
as today's 'appeasement' of violence etc is nothing as bad as that of
the '30s (vide Correlli Barnett) so one forgets how awful that Bratton
hypochondriac effect was, how concerned I was that I was punished.
Ah well.[1]

Saltwood   *Saturday, 21 October*

Back after a very wearing week. Monday Truro (on night train) for
driving disqualification. Six months. Bah! Tuesday up again plus Jane
for night at the Howards (lose £120 to Charles), early train to
Plymouth for WAC[2] lunch. Had sudden late thought, tribute to Dame
Joan,[3] paid it fulsomely and rewarded by excellent quote in *Western
Morning News*. Friday down to Plymouth for Girls School speech in
afternoon. They universally hostile and brainwashed into a whole
series of 'progressive' clichés. The fattish, not unattractive one (Sally)
questioned one tenaciously about colour and then the dark one raving
on about general Tory principles, continuing with tea and cakes in
the common room afterwards. The dark one had done the vote-
of-thanks, very prettily, as she stood, and I had warmed to her
acknowledging our mutual hostility; but that night in the sleeper back
I nearly had a WD playing around with her and getting increasingly
'hot'. This has made me very keen to see her again. I wonder if she
felt it at all?

Then on to Bratton, and a momentary *crise* because Jane locked the
Bentley doors with the keys inside, entailing scrabbling with knives
and copper wires; hair wash, change and in to Lewtrenchard (dinner

---

[1] AC's father wrote in his memoirs about his own experiences of hypochondria, which
had their origins, he suggests, in what the French call '*accidie, maladie des moines*': 'For
some years I believed intermittently, but with absolute conviction, that I was dying of
paralysis. Like the greatest of my fellow sufferers, Dr Johnson, I went for immensely
long walks, in the hope that the fatigue would comfort me ... but nothing could get
the idea out of my head. My own hypochondria was deep rooted enough to reappear
two or three times in later life.' (*Another Part of the Wood*.)
[2] Women's Advisory Committees of the three Plymouth constituency Conservative
associations.
[3] Joan Vickers, MP for Devonport since 1955 (DBE, 1964).

dance). Not a *great* success, eg I wasn't introduced properly (if at all), my speech (by Jane's account) lacked 'punch', and I did only one dance to two-step rhythm – it, in fact, being a waltz. Was somewhat depressed – people at Crownhill totally clueless, one of them saying it was 'a dicey seat' etc; but particularly by universal hostility at Plymouth High. Are the young really like this?

A girl, a slim dedicated Marxist, asked me why I was like I was, what motivated me. 'Because I am British,' I said, 'because I want to advance and protect the British people.' 'So what's so special about the British?' she answered, 'what makes them so different from everybody else?' Well I could have answered that what makes them different from anyone else, is the capacity they seem to have for producing at every level of society, people like yourself who ask a question like that. But I get a dark foreboding, sometimes; I feel it at Saltwood as people encroach more and more, with higher sense of justification, on the boundaries and fences – 'it's not right that something so important/ beautiful/interesting/historic should belong to one man ...' There are the boys with their patriotic instincts quite natural, also the sense of privilege and assurance – but will they be able to hold it or will they be crushed before they get an innate strength and cunning such as I have? And what does the future hold for me? How far will I go? Will I be assassinated, or die venerated and venerable, or crabbed and embittered? I don't want to die anyway, at all, and hope it's a long way off.

Must not neglect the physical by the way. This bloody back of mine always lurking inhibiting me from doing all the exercises I need. Stomach at last weakening, ravaged lines (in some lights) on face. On Thursday last week went for a run along the front in my new track suit, did 3km+ by the 2CV speedo and plunged in the sea – felt marvellous. Now the week has changed course. High winds and drizzle, pool temperature 52°.

Saltwood   *Thursday, 26 October*

Extremely depressed. Compounded by fatigue (down to Seend, then London and backgammon – inc tournament – financially disastrous of course). The autumn, the late autumn nearly always affects me like this – another bright beautiful happy year gone; can another ever be the same, is it the decline from now on? Terrible weakness of arms and shoulders, also less spring going upstairs, must have some way round the back trouble so as to try and build up a little 'peck' and shape.

Poor Gangster now terribly slow and creaky and stumbly on the walks. It doesn't seem so long ago that he had that beautiful galloping movement, so much better than poor dear Grandee's Beatrix-Potter lollop. It is so depressing, the inevitable, inexorable decline of physical healing and prowess – the most obvious, the most implacable evidence of the slowly approaching grave imminently closer with each turn of the globe.

Also lowered by Ann refusing to sell the valley, blast her. I think of that beautiful romantic hidden valley, and it lowers me that it should be owned by someone who is only holding on for 'Chunnel' appreciation.[1]

Also, *inevitably*, complications on the sale of the cricket pitch. Now apparent (2 days before completion) that C. Club lease must be surrendered. Club secretary on holiday. Also doubted on whether partial completion desirable, to gain benefit of selling on. Absolutely stretched to the limit with Hoare & Co and expensive cars (Campbell Mercedes etc) coming in on Monday. Gloomy.

Saltwood   *Friday, 17 November*

Just back, very tired and drawn (lines really gone cataclysmically into the face this year, one of those deep seismic coups that alter one's appearance, like their first onset in 1951) from the candidates' conference at St Stephen's Club.

Turned up at the Conference. Status (political majority) of course important – tho' I believe probably not so much, if at all, once one is in the House. Francis Pym[2] gave first lecture. V formidable, somewhat humourless, a particularly exhausted face. A giver of 'short shrift'. I asked him a question and he barked his answer (it related to inexperience and loyalty, hm!). 'I don't know you. I expect I will know

[1] AC's suspicion about the Channel Tunnel proved quite untrue. The stone that marks his grave came from the valley.
[2] Francis Pym, MP for Cambridgeshire since 1961 and Chief Whip since 1970.

you ...' Then we had Terence Higgins,[1] cheeky, bright little expert on VAT. Drinks in the bar and I chatted up Webster;[2] he even offered me a cigar. Hard to tell what he was thinking. I may have given too much away, about the Monday Club, Sutton's desire for independence etc. After lunch I dozed in an armchair at the back.

In the evening, drinks and dinner, the PM spoke.[3] Excellent, fluent, tho' obviously tired. Occasional flashes of dry wit. A bit political with the questions – particularly that on strikers' benefits. Afterwards caught the eye of that little piece and she asked 'what sort of seat' Sutton was. 'Winnable' said Doreen, who was with her – quite put me out and I left the St Stephen's rather depressed and tired.

Saltwood											*Sunday, 26 November*

Gloomily contemplating collapsing looks and physique; derelict sex-life; continuing state of flux on field hence total standstill on such things as decorating, improving, protecting Saltwood. Purchase of the great 38/250 ex Malcolm Campbell, a most important car, means must rationalise down to eight in the collection, plus a few favourites (such as the XK) plus trading oddments. Can get by with a bit of scratching, sell about 20,000 worth of cars, possibly Woodfall. Still a whole list of the outgoings: the shop for little Mrs Clarke,[4] various bills on cars, overdrafts. Only consolation, Zermatt almost eliminated so 'v'-sign to UBS[5] at last; they even have security somewhat diminished by expiring of permits etc. Thinking of death, disease, famine and bankers' orders.

---

[1] Terence Higgins, MP for Worthing since 1964, he had not long been Financial Secretary to Treasury.
[2] Sir Richard Webster, Director of Organisation, Conservative Central Office since 1966.
[3] Edward Heath, MP for Bexley since 1950, Leader of the Conservative Party since 1965 and Prime Minister since 1970.
[4] The Clarks were buying the shop in Saltwood village.
[5] Union Bank Suisse, which had loaned money to AC to build the Clarks' Zermatt chalet.

All Souls, Oxford   *[No date] November*

John's[1] Scout has brought me tea and digestive biscuits. The room is comfortable, but not warm.

Yesterday I was in confident form. I had been invited to address a Bow Group dinner, black tie, good claret (or so I would assume), F.E. Smith in his early days. My apotheosis. But the Bow Group are just a bunch of arse-lickers really. Creepy little aspirant candidates who tremble at the thought, still less the sound of someone Right Wing. And they have one other thing in common, namely that they all want to enter Parliament. In the past they used to shun me, probably on instruction from Central Office, but now here I am with, having been adopted for Plymouth Sutton, something of an *edge*. Plus the delight of being based in the Warden's lodging. Plus with a black Bentley convertible parked in the quad.

Dear John. I remember walking with his affectionate arm draped around me in Brewer Street on a summer evening in 1948, when I was a clever but *extremely* feckless undergraduate, and his saying that perhaps I really 'ought' to have a shot at becoming a Fellow. It was rather lovely, this diffident homosexual advance, and I was complimented, like I used to be at Eton; though not, of course, in the slightest bit 'aroused'. At the time I didn't like the sound of All Souls. No girls and no racy company. But quite soon afterwards I regretted having done nothing. I'm sure John could have fixed, or demi-fixed, it for me. Although his advice on preparing for the exam – '*Re*-(sic)-read Ranke's *History of the Popes*' – was a little daunting.

John had always, though, a certain private sense of mischief for which he was notorious and of which his guests expected at least one ritual demo. This time it took me completely by surprise. Freshly bathed and in a black tie I had meandered into the Warden's drawing room, hoping for a *firm* gin and tonic before going down to Hall and meeting the (presumably mixed) Bow Groupers. There, standing by the piano looking quite beautifully bouffed and powdered, was Harold Macmillan,[2] an old friend of John (John had worked for him against

---

[1] John Sparrow, Warden of All Souls College, Oxford, whom AC had known since his childhood.

[2] Harold Macmillan, now aged seventy-eight, had been Chancellor of Oxford University since 1960. He was Prime Minister for six years from 1957 and retired from active politics at the 1964 general election.

Rab[1] when the question of succession had arisen in 1956) and clearly the guest of honour that evening at high table (a grander dinner than the one I was to attend).

'Ah,' said John. 'Here's Alan Clark. He is proposing to stand for Parliament . . .'

I simpered, deferentially offered my hand.

'. . . on a platform that advocates denying the franchise to persons of the Jewish persuasion.'

Macmillan neither smiled nor frowned. Very, very briefly he looked at me. Pale hooded eyes. No point, I judged, in saying anything, although it was so monstrous that I got a short *fou-rire*. 'I'm talking to the Bow Group,' I offered weakly.

Saltwood   *Sunday, 3 December*

Now the 'prophet's' visit. Powell[2] down for the day to chat, advise and hold forth! He was benevolent, articulate, by no means cagey, but somehow impenetrable. I *really* don't know what he thought of me – though clearly 'raw', naïve, inexperienced etc were among them. He cautioned me against too high a degree of personal commitment to the Conservatives in Sutton; also against saying things outside the Party line prior to the election . . . 'as a candidate you have no constitutional position'. Would not say how he hoped to attain power, '. . . the Lord will provide.' Right, he often is, clever he undoubtedly is, but whether he has that sheer finishing touch which Conservatives have to have to get to the top I don't know.

At least I started his car for him, forcing him (to everyone's amazement) to give up the driving seat after many ineffectual yur-yurrings (vet with *chien méchant*) and it fired second time.

---

[1] R.A. ['Rab'] Butler had twice hoped to become leader of the Conservative Party: in 1956 when Anthony Eden resigned from ill-health in the aftermath of Suez; and in 1963, when Macmillan resigned (ill-health again, but prematurely as it turned out) and Lord Home was chosen. Home renounced his peerage and as Sir Alec Douglas-Home became Prime Minister. Butler was now Master of Trinity College, Cambridge.
[2] Enoch Powell, MP for Wolverhampton SW since 1950. AC shared many of his views, particularly on immigration.

Zermatt   *Thursday, 14 December*

Poor James *again* broke his leg today – allegedly green stick, but low down in the ankle and causing him a lot of pain. His fault – he had been skiing *beautifully* on the Rothorn and Tuftern, then full of confidence on his new Atomics, but led, far too fast, on the road and fell just before Patrilav. I came round the corner and he was howling. When I noticed, I broke down, and cried, screamed, blamed poor Tip, who, it turned out wasn't really (much) to blame as James was miles ahead.

Tip and I left Jane with him and skied down, self crying out loud – 'it seems an age', telephoned from Sunegga, up again, skied down just as they were loading him on, terribly pale and shaking. Apparently it won't be so long as the last one, but bang goes the training session, the session that was going to get him really set up and boost his confidence and health. Yesterday he was so languid that I bawled him out in the evening, and today dear little chap he was good as gold, starting by calling up with our tea.

I was in a filthy temper yesterday – no proper lunch, low-grade intercourse with banks, brokers etc. Still, no right to grizzle the way I did, and was still grumpy (until tight) at the Tenne that evening.

Still, all one can say is it *could* have been worse; I thought it was, much worse and prayed – but hopelessly – to God let it be all right and he did as well as we could expect. Don't know when you are well off, Clark. Be conservative, orderly, don't over-reach. Must follow through, get everything set up so that if I go boys will have ready-made structure waiting to take-over.

1973

A month gone by. 'Daisy' came for Christmas and it went as well as could be expected, he not so glittering and effervescent as formerly and so less attractive. Kindly gave me a PIII catalogue[1] (bought from Charles Howard), but a little too homosexual now, less interesting, more boasting. Christmas itself quite good. Got Jane a gold-bar in her stocking. Then two set-backs. My back briefly popped when bending down to undo my shoes leaving me crazily twisted and immobilised. I caught a short, sharp cold from the silly, titty little masseuse.

We decided to go home early, and the day before our departure James went to have his confirmatory x-ray which revealed that the bone had slipped a bit and should be reset under a general anaesthetic. We returned to the surgery later that night (he had to wait some hours for the food, water to be digested). Naturally he was apprehensive. The hall of Gentinettas's[2] was dimly lit, noone was about. Slowly the personnel gathered, junior actors first, and a nurse gave him an Atropine injection in the behind – unheralded and unwelcome. Then it deteriorated fast: the two specialists wrenched the plaster off, muttering imprecations at their predecessor who had put it on so tightly. James – horrified – gasped and groaned with pain and simulated pain. Madame Gentinetta played her part in the 'you-must-be-brave' role as she prepared the gas. When they finally put James under we retired, Jane broke down in the waiting-room and I couldn't stand it, but took our things back to the chalet where Tip had already retired (he was incubating flu).

The next day we travelled.

Tremendous longueurs in Brig where we had four hours to wait because I had to catch Previdoli before the UBS closed.

Tip was drowsy and flushed. Boy drawn and apprehensive. That waitress came over, she really waits in the 2ieme classe, but she recognised me, *still* (although, as is the way, she seemed much altered and aged and only her aura identified her). I took a walk, and my footsteps led me, although in the dark, out of the town and up the hill to where, so suddenly, it becomes the Simplon Pass. My mind worked freely back to that first time in the middle fifties – the XK, the brown Dienst (what a sturdy little car that was), the grey,

---

[1] Rolls-Royce Phantom.
[2] The Zermatt doctors.

honeymoon Dienst, the Citroen Safari, the blue 220, the silver
Porsche, the '600'. In the early days that sudden happy realisation, on
the return journey, that one was back in the clear air of beloved
Switzerland; good-looking, seething with youth in the Buffet at Brig,
but, as she said, 'bourgeois devil'. No need of company to reassure
me (all that finally extinguished by the enforced solitary 'messing' at
Eton).

The rest of the journey was a misery as Tip ran a high temperature
and deteriorated at nightmare speed so that one had to give penicillin
from the emergency pack. Once arrived, he made an amazing recovery – but what a reversal! Jane got flu, then I got it; or was/is it flu?
A highly violent upper respiratory infection, leading to at least one
day of feverish coma, but had it to shake-off. Got horribly depressed,
achingly so, as I contemplated the scene. Rung up by Graham Butland
this evening with news that 'some disgust' in the constituency at my
non-publicity/attendances. All bound up with life pattern for this
year.

Saltwood   *Wednesday, 14 February*

Dreadful blustery day, cold snow showers whip-lashing. Tip back in
bed, very peaky and lost weight with those strange evening temperatures – could be a hang-over from his 2nd dose of flu, but both
boys (telepathically) questioned one closely about TB last night. Oh
dear. James now out of plaster, but much scarred by his experiences –
said yesterday at breakfast 'I am giving up skiing'. I suppose he will
recover once he gets the feel of it again, I remember it took me years
to get over my fear of soft snow after cracking my ankle at Wengen.

Now here I am at a chaotic desk, having given up my intention of
a five-day break in Zermatt, and determined to restore some order in
a 'Mens Sana' 4 days here. I cannot decide whether to go forward or
backward on either cars or property, ie do I buy from Danny the
Blower $4\frac{1}{2}$ and the 3 litre on BE tyres or do I retrench, take my money
on the Benz and just keep the small collection? Do I press forward
and buy the nursery and the Payne site in Prospect Road and offer
the whole (ie plus Newmans and Baileys) for 120? Or do I just take
the 35 for Newmans and back of Baileys and de-escalate?

Had a fairly beastly exchange with Hoare's over stumping up for the Benz. Change of attitude on their part, made me feel uncomfortable, has the cricket field money been dissipated quite so quickly?

All these things have generated massive decision-headaches. Also, fairly heavy political activity (not before time). Fortunately had a piccolo success at the Bickleigh Down meeting on the eve of the Western Area Conference. The food, though, was terrible. Feminine company negligible except for the young daughter of that ridiculous ego-woman from Tavistock who boldly hung about – were we establishing a rapport? In the lift she said (2nd day) 'This can't hold eight people, surely?' 'Bags I stand next to you if it does,' I said. From that time on our relations improved.

Am prepared to buy the Constituency the East End club, but Graham Butland went slit-eyed. 'Association wouldn't want to be tied to a candidate through the Club.' Of course one major flaw does hang over one – *actually losing the seat!*

Saltwood   *Saturday, 31 March*

Glorious day (as usual) emphasising deep gloom and malaise. Indigestion night (first for years) and today Andrew – who has been very well until just recently in one of his pale, prowling listlessly, hanging-around-and-trying-to-catch-my-eye conditions which are obviously pre-temperature. This to give 'full house' of troubles and complicate – or indeed abort – Spanish trip itself desperately close in the is-it-quite-reliable '600' following an incomplete rushed job at Mercedes, a mad drive to Plymouth and back for Papa's Romney lecture and canvassing. Am going through disappointing phase at Plymouth, not seen enough, enough publicity etc; people openly saying they will vote Liberal. Finally broken with Valeri/Ali.[1]

---

[1] Variously described as 'the coven', the 'blondes', and the 'i's' – three girls (the third was Joei) related to each other by blood whom AC knew for many years.

Benalmadena   *Sunday, 8 April*

Arrived last night after wearing drive – hands blistered from holding
the big white plastic wheel (of the '600') for hour after hour. Beuttler[1]
villa very nice, marvellous growth – wisteria etc. Interior improved by
decent English furniture. Spain revolting, though individual Spaniards
reasonably anxious to please. Architecture, pollution, simply awful.

Journey out was plagued by blocked fuel filters. Changed at Paris,
inspected at Bordeaux, packed up in Madrid rush-hour. Total nightmare sequence supervened (memorable land-mark in horror
experience) no tools, no language, no *garages*, 7.30pm and sweating,
no map (so no idea where we were etc etc). Pleasant shop-owner,
obliging taximan etc brought apparent relief in due time, though
further intervening horrors (mechanic trying to butcher the '600', me
wondering where Jane and the children had got to – after blithely
packing them into taxi and saying 'Excelsior', calling on totally strange
man's flat and asking for telephone directory etc.) before at last oasis
of Ifa Hotel.

Here money insulation worked. Food, service (Mercedes mechanic
came out next day, changed filter etc). Back on the road at 11am and
great heat drive. Andrew had been sick the day before but gamely
pulled round. James however incredibly stressed and puffy-looking,
slit-eyed and soft-spoken. I have worried on so many holidays about
him and it 'turning out all right', but this time seems even worse,
with this morning him just listlessly reading, looking terrible with
recurrence of watch allergy spot on his wrist. We shared a room in
the Ifa and I thought how much I loved him, just getting pleasure
from looking at his little top notch of hair showing above the sheets.

Talking about air-travel (I had postulated different planes for the
return journey) he said touchingly but alarmingly, that he rather we
all die together; he was near to tears. The next morning I tried to
explain that the line must go on, that one day one of us must do
something for his country that merited a column as high as Nelson's.

While writing weather has deteriorated. Now totally overcast and
windy. Grey-watered twice, feeling sickish. Lost God-knows-how-
much weight, sunken cheeks, match-stick forearms. Query cancer?
How are we going to get home?[2]

---

[1] The home in Spain of Jane Clark's parents.
[2] AC provided the answer (written in December from memory) in what he called 'The
Sequel': 'In fact we devised a route using entirely trains and sleepers; spending a day

Saltwood   *Wednesday, 16 May*

Nothing done, everything growing like crazy, tho' Cradduck still keeping garden looking fabulous. No drive, car parks, toilets, signs, garages *or any decoration at all* – visits start on May 28. American party on June 11. Headache.

I am concerned that relations with my parents may be deteriorating.

They were standing on the lower terrace. My mama *exceedingly* dreamy, of both tone and deportment. She swayed at a lavender bush. Then, turning to Jane, 'I never told Cradduck to cut that back'.

'But I employ Cradduck now, Mama.' I spoke very gently. In fact the shrub had barely been cut back at all.

'It's all wrong; all wrong.' Pulling at my father's cardigan (it was a very hot afternoon but he was wearing a cardigan) she set off back towards the bridge. He, sensing this was something not to be drawn into, smiled and mumbled.

That was yesterday. This morning we were in Canterbury. When we returned Mrs Yeo[1] said that they had both been over and 'gone upstairs'.

This has happened a great many times since my parents moved out. They lie awake in the Garden House and brood on the various items of 'contents' that they left behind. I think, but cannot be sure, that there was even a sort of verbal protocol agreed at the time of the conveyance that they should reserve a right of selection for items for which a 'need' became apparent. At the time it would have been graceless, as well as ill-judged, for me to turn this down. Already quite a few things, mainly books, they have retrieved.

Sometimes Lindley[2] (who fancies himself as an *antiquaiere manqué*) is sent over in the car to collect objects, which whenever practicable, he does without referring to us.

Anyway, this morning my father apparently made off with a very nice early XIXc whalebone box about a foot in diameter which carried charming ink-engraved Eskimo drawings of seals and hunters.

(again) at the Ifa – already forgotten by the staff in spite of being tipped massively. Memorable was the old-fashioned dining-car out of Madrid to Paris via Bordeaux. The great brown mountainsides in the failing light and the small station halts with their oil-lamp interiors and Goya-like attendants in upturned coat collars. How wonderful travel must have been when restricted to the few – the Grand Tour!'

[1] Mrs Yeo, housekeeper, who came with the Clarks from Seend.

[2] Lindley, the butler at the Garden House.

Jane loved this box, and was very upset. I found myself getting cross. I telephoned to the Garden House. My mother answered.

'So sorry we missed you this morning.'

'Papa had to come over and find a book.'

'He appears also to have taken the whalebone box which was in the dressing room.'

'Papa has always *loved* that box.'

'In that case why did he leave it behind when you made over the contents?'

My father took over. 'Oh God, God, don't say you are really making a fuss about the box?'

'No of course I'm not making a fuss. If you want the box, you must have the box. Jane is in tears, that doesn't matter at all. But ...' (I must *not* be so icy in tone, it's only one stage off bellowing in rage.) '... mightn't it be a good idea if we worked out exactly what is left here which still belongs to you ...?'

'I'll bring it straight back; I'll bring it back over now, immediately. Take, take, take ...'

Then Mama came on. 'How can you do this to Papa? All he wanted was that box ...'

'Keep the bloody box. I just would like to know what else he must have ...'

I went for a walk around the garden. An exquisitely beautiful evening, and all the birds singing goodnight.

Bratton   *Friday, 1 June*

'Prowling' about, came across the blue and white push-chair, Jolly's and almost wept as I recalled 'More Run' and the oggley-oggley noise 'Boy' made going round past Dick's hens. What did I feel so sad about? Would I was back then, I suppose, to play it again – yet I have been incredibly lucky, the inability to have more children the only blight.

Saltwood   *Saturday, 16 June*

Randily tired after a glorious hot day – about the fifteenth in succession – spent lounging around the pool, sneaking lecherous looks
at Andy, swimming nude, playing backgammon with Charles (won
£66) and admiring the incredible beauty of the place with the peacocks and the full foliage of the trees with the roses just about to burst.
An exquisite *douceur-de-vivre*. Also calm at having got out of the way
of three parties – US drinks here on Tues, Sutton 'workers' on Wed,
a R-R Enthusiasts send-off last night.

The Americans were 'numerous'; they strayed over the walls etc,
'most gracious of you' ... mumbled 'Doc' Goodman in his white
dinner jacket; some thought I was an Earl; they were uncertain of
how to address Jane. The Sutton workers were divine as always, my
speech started well, but got a bit guccky.

Shot at some intruders last night. Now over to office for 1½ (if I'm
lucky) hours on the telephone.

Broomhayes   *Sunday, 5 August*

Here on the way back from Bratton/Plymouth. Wet weekend and
winds; everyone rather pale. First, reasons for being low. Back, after
apparently slightly improving, very painful as both 'low back pain' *and*
no deviation of tightening down R. side and buttocks which makes
it agony in bed by about 5am. Apparently this is an osteo-arthritic
symptom and (I suspect) irreversible. My father in his memoirs says
that growing old (like growing up) is the progress from one *shelf* to
another, not a gradual ascent or descent, and with this new variant of
my back 'trouble' I have now descended another shelf. Another
reason, worried, in a kind of hopeless way, about the boys – particularly
James – being so sort of rotten and anarchic, languidly lacking in
initiative and yet very ready to take offence. In fact, noticeably poorer
in quality than one or even two years ago. James 'gets away with
things' (being quick and fly in retort) too easily and that coupled with
natural laziness leads him to dodge anything in the slightest bit arduous.
Yet without nourishment his intelligence, initiative, eagerness will all
wither. He's such a dear, I do hope it 'turns out all right'. I don't
quite know what I ought to do.

Third reason: the 'Liberal revival'. They are simply picking off the safe seats in the by-elections. Ludicrous. May be different in a General Election,[1] although at present so much momentum that looks bad – certainly Sutton no longer a cake-walk, a three-corner marginal that needs a lot of work. Very fortunately Banks[2] a little pimple of a candidate really, chosen when the whole thing was just a joke, and now they are lumbered with him, hair-lip and all – 'sympathy vote' John Miller[3] quietly asserted during dinner. I've lost quite a bit of money playing b'gammon lately. Suppose I'm all-square, having been nearly £1,500 up at one stage this year.

Saltwood   *Saturday, 26 August*

Sitting in the Great Hall with 'low back pain' and stiffness (following some fairly severe am-I-dying?-panics earlier this week including 'numb-foot' bringing the Citroen – dear Citroen – back from Wee Bob heavily laden with Derby spares at night. Depressed about endless *pressures on time*. So much to do on so many fronts – would really like three-week holiday at the Corte just slumped in the deck-chair with a series of good books – but not a hope. Plymouth always lurking, not to mention Castle openings.

The fine weather proceeds, endlessly. Lounging (discontentedly) by the pool this afternoon I started grousing to Jane about my plight and, with her usual combination of wit and good sense, she tried to sort me out. First rightly pointing to how much I already had, that to most men was just greedy. Quite right, I must connect within my own parameters. Then said – think how much 'time' spend sunbathing, no wonder you're short of it.

Rightly pointed out that I am: (a) Relaxed millionaire and superimposing on that; (b) Gov. St Thomas' Hospital;[4] (c) Parliamentary

---

[1] The previous Thursday the Liberals won by-elections in two hitherto safe Conservative seats: Isle of Ely (Clement Freud overturned a Conservative majority of 9,606 to win by 1,470) and Ripon (where the Conservative majority of 12,064 became a Liberal majority of 690 for David Austick). At the February 1974 general election Freud retained his seat; Austick lost his.

[2] Simon Banks, Liberal candidate, who fought the seat in two elections.

[3] John Miller, a member of the St James' Club.

[4] AC had been a Governor of London's St Thomas's Hospital (opposite the Palace of Westminster on the south bank of the Thames) since 1969.

candidate for distant seat; (d) stately-home-owner; (e) car-dealer; (f) fighting single-handed battles with Council, developing property etc.

And yet if I was your (c) and (d), with just a little of (e) thrown in, there would be nothing creative going back; nothing in value for all that God has given one. I still think I should go flat out, go for the Monday Club choice, take in the whole lot, National Front and all.

I suppose it is this that really fills me with gloom – the prospect of sacrificing probably for ever, certainly until I am too old to enjoy it, the happy celebration of a secure and lazy family life for the unrelenting grind of a mission. Yet, I suppose I must do it. I checked on 'Boy', wanting to help him, but only realising too late that he was now ready to board and to stand on his own. Perhaps my back/leg is to show me the same here.

Zermatt   *Thursday, 6 September*

End of nice therapeutic week here enjoying the lovely air, sunshine and hill walks. *Just* managing the latter tho' back really no better, especially that frightful tightening down the R-side, and morning pains. But did achieve at least one memorable, and new, expedition to the Spitzflüh col while accompanied by dear, active, and incredibly fit young Tip. I could look down both the Tasch and Findeln valleys. I remember Euan[1] and I had turned back on this one some five or so years back when one came to the rock fall and the huge stones through which dear Tip guided me like a little goat by ably spotting the cairns. Otherwise fittish, tho' waist definitely showing first signs now as ability to do exercises virtually non-existent (even the mildest course of week one yoga makes me feel totally battered/supine). For the first time in my life, totally brown all over, buttocks, crotch, everything. Now somewhat apprehensive of 'next stage'.

Returning to financial problems – purchase of Newton Farm [in Cornwall] at 101 has used up whole P2 reserve[2] and at a time when pressed by grotesquely high interest rates (16%) and building 'improvements' at the Castle, both internal and external, and building of garages. Toy with idea of selling all flash cars, being left just with 'enthusiasts' stable – although somewhat of a pity just after beautiful

---

[1] Euan Graham, a friend since Oxford.
[2] A reserve fund from the sale of a Rolls-Royce P2 and other cars.

garages built. Might raise 100 that way. Also somewhat depressed prospect of work/boredom/reproaches in constituency; will my health return to being '100 per cent'; and, quite deeply, by James's failure to get into Eton.[1] Definitely in decline, visibly no new interests and the old ones being pursued less energetically. Tonight he is in disgrace after spilling – disastrously – bottle of unwashable ink in the sitting-room. Somehow I feel that second breaking of the leg was an important watershed, and release, for us all, and for him in particular.

What can I do about this? Should I send them to boarding school? How can I help both to excel and develop their interests and their sense of responsibility?

Bratton   *Monday, 17 September*

Good and bad. Back quite suddenly seems to have 'turned the corner' due, I suspect, to yoga. But generally seem to be hitting little (hopefully not about to be big) bad patch. Cradduck ill, allegedly glandular fever, and unlikely to be back in harness this year, if ever. Finance light, while the works accumulate around the castle, and my parents make comments on the telephone [which] seep back to me. Poor little darling Jane holding the fort at Saltwood (and opening *alone* tomorrow). I fear somehow that yet more blows will fall.

Been working very hard (for me) these last 10 days in the constituency. Did heavy canvassing this afternoon in the rain, scoring (I think) a good mark with Betty [Easton]. Also improving relations with Piggy Williams.[2]

Great Library, Saltwood   *Saturday, 13 October*

In my father's study and maudlin on an empty stomach with suspected latent salmonella – result of one mouthful of an appalling 'steak sandwich' at a road-side pub in Preston on the way back from the Blackpool conference.

---

[1] He had been accepted, but ploughed Common Entrance.
[2] Lyndon Williams, known as 'Piggy', the current Sutton agent.

Isn't Blackpool appalling, loathsome . . .? Impossible to get even a
piece of bread and cheese, or a decent cup of tea; dirt, squalor, shanty-
town broken pavements with pools of water lying in them – on the
Promenade – vulgar common 'primitives' drifting about in groups or
standing, loitering, prominently. The conference, not a specially happy
one. Bullying of the Right by the Heathites (self again not called; fifth
conference in a row). Heseltine, Peter Walker[1] wouldn't speak to
me; Sara Morrison[2] and Richard Webster chilly; even Ian Gilmour[3]
amusingly changing the subject. I *suppose* it will be all right on the
night. Williams has arranged a sequence of open-air meetings at which
I will have to perform. Apprehensive as to (a) my complete ignorance
of the 'answers' – ie all those balls statistics about the 'over eighties',
and the standard of living, and (b) letting down the Sutton crowd.
Their usual delegates came to Blackpool, but the dinner was more
subdued, fortunately the presence of the Turners (ie Osborne-
Turners) plus Williams and Mary-Rose offered lightning-conductors.

Went on television for *Points West* BBC and hope did some good,
though not plugging the Party line. Valeri there plus usual accoutre-
ments of regularised intimacy which make me so jealous (in this case
a geriatric Great-Uncle in Holy Orders who is presumably being
cultivated for a hand-out). Really, too much. If one could paraphrase
Haig's epigram on Derby – the only good thing, incidentally, that the
F-M ever did – 'she is like a feather cushion, carrying the imprint of
the last person to roll on her.'[4]

Various other matters conspire to prevent me looking as smooth
and relaxed as, say, Heseltine: Tip still gets a lot of asthma, inc. *every*
Sunday without fail; crazy expenditure with three different contractors
now going full blast on the interior. We can *just* carry it, but long-
term prosperity heavily dependent on sale at a profit of Newton Farm

---

[1] Peter Walker, MP for Worcester since 1961, now Secretary of State for Trade and
Industry.

[2] The Morrisons were at this time a powerhouse within the Conservative Party. The
Hon. Sara Morrison, whose husband Charles had been MP for Devizes since 1964,
was in her second year as chairman of the party organisation; her father-in-law, Lord
Margadale, was, before being elevated to the Lords as a Baron, MP for Salisbury 1942–
64; she herself was the daughter of Viscount Long and Laura, Duchess of Marlborough;
and her brother-in-law, Peter Morrison, had been personal assistant to Peter Walker
and had just been selected as candidate for Chester.

[3] Ian Gilmour, MP for Norfolk Central since 1962, had been rising fast through the
junior ministerial ranks at Defence since 1970. Edited *The Spectator* (1954–59).

[4] Haig wrote to his wife in January 1918: that Derby bore 'the marks of the last person
who sat on him.'

(allegedly people still interested 'from the leisure aspect, Mr Clark' – who want to turn it into a golf course). Another heavy blow would be disqualification following the unsuccessful chase by PC James of the 550 Spyder on the Oxford bypass. 'That'll cut your capers' said Valeri, which it will; it will also make canvassing, and visiting much more exhausting, not to mention the strain of (2) school runs and life for Jane.

Saltwood   *Sunday, 11 November*

On top of all the crazy expenditure, just bought a beautiful Alma-Tadema at Sotheby's for £9,000 – suddenly got a demand for £28,000 to pay my father's Capital Gains Tax on the transfer of Saltwood.

Saltwood   *Wednesday, 14 November*

I have now been the prospective Parliamentary candidate in Plymouth for more than a year. I suppose it's all going to be ok. People, not just in Plymouth but at various kinds of political function keep saying 'You'll be all right'; by which, I suppose, they mean 'you will win the seat'. But I don't like the word 'safe'. Perhaps because I am super-stitious, or just wary of hubris. When Brian Somebody, a tiresome left-wing Fellow at All Souls, told [John Sparrow] that he wanted a 'long sabbatical' to go into Parliament and John inquired as to the putative constituency ... said ... 'It's a safe seat, of course.'

   To which John retorted, 'Safe? Safe ...? Oh, you mean *unopposed?*'

   But I've got this feeling I'm not absolutely a billion percent welcome in this outfit; not, at least, in its present 'configuration'.

   Heigh ho. More fool them, I say.

Zermatt   *Wednesday, 19 December*

Lower than ever, after quite a good day yesterday. Had taken pain-killing drug (Distalgesic – sinisterly indicated for 'malignant conditions … allowing the administration of morphine to be postponed') the previous night, after much intermittent waking at 5.50am and was puffily creased that morning, but after lunch, bathed, took evening walk and thought perhaps really getting better. Night virtually pain free (including 3.50am) until just before 6 when agony. However, fought through without Distal. Pain wouldn't go on pre-breakfast walk for papers and persisted until mid-day. After tea new site in side/hip coupled with pins-and-needles even while breathless walking. Now miserably sitting, with lowest Christmas since 1963 in prospect – only want to return to England, start serious medical treatment – Rowntree [family doctor] or homeopathy.

On my walk this morning looked with real longing at the perfect snow and piste of the little 'Home National'. It is a real deprivation for me not to be able to ski. All my fitness 'program' jeopardised. I must be in shape when I return at Easter – for the Election tone-up.

Zermatt   *Wednesday, Boxing Day*

A very good Christmas. Skied on the last day at Zermatt, and not such a disaster as might have been (though awful moment of side slipping – virtually didn't turn to the R at all). Back quite 'good' on the return journey. And since then have been almost too busy to 'dwell' on it although being very light or walks with Col and on the first of these I thought maybe I was going to be struck down with paralysis – like my poor mother, post-stroke in UCH with her left side paralysed and hopelessly depressed. She returns tomorrow by ambulance to the Hythe nursing home and then (putatively) to the Garden House and a regime with special beds, chairs and apparatus that can only end when she dies, but may project into the future for a very long time. My feeling – what a loss, ie 'loss' = 'nuisance' to us. But Jane, with her real *goodness* of nature, said quite naturally and spontaneously that we must all look after her as well as we can and hope that she never feels discarded or neglected before she dies.

1974

Low and grumpy and self-pitying after a late night, punishment at Aspinalls[1] losing £460 and bringing up my total losses to £820 certain. So now have 'given up b'gammon' following a self-denial chucking (or being chucked) by the 'i's and superimposing a certain amount of pure masochism – 'not drinking again until I have paid off all the money I owe . . .' etc.

Prospect is gloomy, and not enhanced by my poor back: skiing being so handicapped; also the prospect of my poor Mama fading away in the nursing home though with her mind still beautifully clear and wittily cynical in the best style. What an irony that she so often feigned, for reasons of convenience, slurred speech and detachment – should now be quite literally stricken with it. What a cautionary tale for us all!

1974 is not going to be good – though how bad remains to be seen.

In tremendous form yesterday morning at prospect of election(!) on anti-union platform – v. good for Sutton prospects. Now total reversal; Heath lost his nerve at the last moment that afternoon, morale shattered,[2] John Miller took £96 off me at tea, I got drunk – boringly sitting between Harold Lever[3] and John Miller at Jimmy's[4] dinner and then lost £90 to Martin Summers and £570 to Harold after the cruel last 32 game when I had a 5.2 6.1 3.1 1.1 2.2 or any 4 for a certain victory. In an absolutely *furious* temper.

Jane tested me when I got back – 'you're never here' etc. We were

---

[1] John Aspinall founded a series of London clubs beginning with the Clermont in Berkeley Square. AC and Aspinall had first met at Oxford. In these diaries he is usually referred to as 'Aspers'.

[2] The Prime Minister threatened to call a general election if the miners' union, the NUM, failed to settle their pay claim.

[3] Harold Lever, Labour MP for Manchester Cheetham since 1950 (Manchester Exchange, 1945–50). Originally a barrister, he was a minister under Harold Wilson and chairman of the Public Accounts Committee in 1970.

[4] James (Jimmy) Goldsmith, a successful businessman, of Anglo-French parentage, chairman of Générale Occidentale SA Paris, and a friend of long-standing of AC's.

walking along the old railway line. Vowed to give up b'gammon.

Worried, too, naggingly, about my mother who is dying – each so-called 'good' day is so noticeably inferior to its predecessor. I'm not giving her enough time – she only really brightens up at all when I come in, and talks quite intelligently. Is irritated by my father who, in turn, can't understand her.

B5 Albany   *Friday, 25 January*

I was in Lister's[1] waiting room. One of my teeth aches periodically, and when I bend over I can feel a pulse in it. This must be bad. I have a feeling that you can get absolutely fearful, *terminal* blood poisoning from a bad tooth. Even if this is unlikely I do not want 'trouble' over the Election.

At the far end of the room an old gentleman wearing a mac was stooped over a *Times* which he rustled and page-turned in a rather ego, demonstrative, manner. Silvery hair, pebble-lens specs. Suddenly I realised who it was – *Uncle Harold!* – and walked across. I thought it more prudent not to remind him of our last meeting [see page 19] thinking in any case that mutual embarrassment and (in his case) very poor vision would occlude the recollection. 'Sir, can I introduce myself? Alan Clark, I am the prospective parliamentary candidate for Plymouth Sutton.'

'My dear boy! Well done, well done. Nancy Astor's old seat, well I never, sit down . . .' etc. He was incredible. Lucid, compos, clear and incisive of speech. Said the Election would be a disaster – 'The working class will see it as a loyalty vote . . .'; that there should be an Energy ministry with sweeping powers; that the miners had to be bought off until North Sea oil came on stream; that it should not be difficult to outmanoeuvre Len Murray;[2] that McGahey[3] wasn't popular in the TUC; that the real agitator was (*Scrimgeour* was it? – the words came thick and fast and I was transfixed[4]); that it was urgent to find

---

[1] AC's dentist.
[2] Len Murray, General Secretary of the TUC since 1973 (he had been with the TUC since 1947).
[3] Mick McGahey, Scottish miners' leader.
[4] Presumably Arthur Scargill, although, as President of the Yorkshire NUM, he was only just coming to prominence.

some way of reassuring the middle classes who were puzzled and that we ought to be talking now to the Liberal Party. Thorpe[1] was a 'show-off' and unreliable, but could probably be enlisted from flattery ...

On and on did Macmillan speak. I have never listened to anyone so compelling, and with such sense of history. Lister's nurse appeared at the door and said he was ready, but I sent her away. What has happened to the Conservatives? How could they possibly ignore this man, so sage and so authoritative? I have already received ten tons of bumf from Central Office, most of it useless and unreadable. I don't see how we can actually *lose* this Election, or at least how I can lose it, but the whole encounter was rather unsettling. I wish I had not waited so long before going into politics, and could ingratiate myself with Uncle Harold, and defend him from ambitious and scheming mediocrities. Is it really too late? I suppose so.

I had quite forgotten about my tooth, which anyway took hardly a minute. But I don't like the high-speed drill. You can sometimes smell burning, so the frictional heat must be frightful. The accompanying water jet does not cool the 'cavity' but simply sloshes around in the mouth.

Saltwood   *Saturday, 2 February*

Sitting at my desk in office with stacks of paper all round – mainly invitations to great rash of ward AGMs – with moderate wind (now blowing for over a month) rocking the towers, vacuum-extracting the contents of the cars when a door is opened, making any gardening, tidying etc, much less leisurely pottering, impossible.

Absolutely choc-a-bloc with things to do – the whole of next week pre-empted by Plymouth and still quagmire of unfinished work, decision, correspondence. Must get away to Zermatt for a few days. Noticed to my alarm that tip of penis now not so receptive to sensation even after four days.

---

[1] Jeremy Thorpe, MP for Devon North since 1959; succeeded Jo Grimond as Leader of the Liberal Party, 1967.

Bratton   *Monday, 11 February*

Pretty twitchy, let's face it. Election ON – and DON'T WANT TO
LOSE! Definitely nervous about 'Public meetings', cavalcades, school
mums, ebb of confidence at half-way stage. Back tightened right up
after securing the 3-litre Cherrybum [Bentley] last Sunday – though
not yet crippled and trying to keep at bay with yoga and bells. Already
extremely haggard and strained – though put off going to Zermatt by,
in the end perhaps fortuitously (do I mean fortunately?) loss of
passport. Not sleeping very well, waking in the middle of the night
feeling incredibly tired etc. Also worried about Jamie (strange diffused
fatigue/nervous symptoms) and Andrew, not growing.
     Heigh ho for future entries.

Bratton   *Thursday, 14 February*

The Campaign is On! With Jane to Guildhall to hand in nomination
papers; went to wrong door so kept everyone waiting, the ludicrous
stilted formality with Labour Mayor. Pouring rain. Went out to
Plympton Police to show documents. Canvassed a little in Embankment Road on way back (not bad). Saw exactly three voters, two
solid Tory and unshakeable smart-alec woman, a common-market.
Down to Ashley Drive to meet some pensioners. Some sour looks en
route as we sped by in Land-Rover, self repeating, inanely – or so it
seemed – 'Hello, everybody, this is your Conservative candidate.
Please vote for me on Feb 28, vote AC, vote Conservative.'
     Thankfully back to Bratton for pasty supper (wrong sort of pastry).

Bratton   *Friday, 22 February*

Graham seemed reasonably calm about result, but I don't like talking
about 'when you're in the House etc.' Shattering of the make-believe
too close.
     It was agreed how much of a threat the Liberals are. Actually I
think they are a threat, but don't want confirmation of this opinion.
Just as I forecast, today in the Broadway *quite different*. Instead of people

smiling and wishing good luck, pinioned by a few grumblers.

This evening, Liberals showing 20% in the polls. All those fools at Alma Road now echoing my own words: 'the whole Liberal tide flows etc.' This evening for the first time really thought perhaps am going to lose this seat after all – total disaster; struck off by Sir Richard Webster instantly etc etc The whole of that period since May 71 wasted, all that hubris . . .

I remember the exact spot where I was going to lose. I went quite faint and dry-mouthed. It was crossing the car park to that ridiculous little lady in the Club when Kay suddenly said it was 'dicey'.

Rang Saltwood and James, whom I'm missing terribly.

Bratton   *Tuesday, 26 February*

Morale improved by Graham late last night. '. . . when you wake up on Friday morning you'll be a Member of Parliament.' Straight to Alma Road where L.K.Way[1] poo-poohed idea of Liberal victory – 'see you in London, 6 March'. Confidence returned. Took many plaudits and then on to an excellent curry restaurant with Jane. Nothing to drink so lit a small Rössli cigar

11pm. Back in bed with a piece of fruit-cake and the latest *Motor Sport*. One of the best days so far.

After lunch and a short sleep (8 minutes approx) out to Lipson Gardens (couldn't find it) and some scattered calling. Knocked off too early. Piggy [Williams] approached me – 'What do you think, really,' he asked. '50/50,' I replied. Ideas totally shot, useless. Graham very Ladbroke – we're 5/4 on.

Tea at Duke. I remark saying to Jane, 'The reason I'm in such a state is because I think I actually *am* going to lose, and I'm dreading the speeches.' The thought of winning returned for a split second when the *Sunday Times* rang, said '. . . interviewing about 40 people who will be *new faces in the House* . . .' Bob now says majority 3,000 (*far* too tight).

---

[1] L.K.Way, lobby correspondent of Plymouth's daily paper, the *Western Morning News*.

Bratton   *Friday, 1 March*

Toured (very cold) in the Land-Rover, thanking people. A delicious moment, when testing my speaker, said: 'This is your Conservative *candidate* speaking ...' 'Member of Parliament, you twit,' said Graham.[1]

Zermatt   *Saturday, 2 March*

Must be reckoned the pinnacle so far.

I have always to worry about something, of course, so am now worrying about Tip who we have brought out here 'on' a fierce tetracycline (adult) dose after bronchitis in our absence in the last week of the election. He's still a bit peaky and soft-spoken and really hasn't grown at all by comparison with the pillar in our bedroom.[2] Oh dear, I do so adore the little chap, and want him to feel himself, fine and confident.

But otherwise ... Elected, with a majority that even the most optimistic had not expected, 8,104. Back seems to have virtually cleared up. I look back with amazement at those pre-Christmas entries, at here, recall those tormented hours between 5.30–8.30. Now, a real base to build on.

Must repeat (1) my conviction that I had lost, starting from that second Saturday unhappy in Plymstock, a feeling which became congenital so that the *idea* of winning became totally remote. (2) That frightful last day, twenty-eighth, going round the polling stations and committee rooms. Certainty of defeat when I looked at the Mt Gould polling day returns, all of which showed *total* vote up, Conservative vote down (what possible confirmation) and the grey, evasive looks of the Party workers. And yet one had to carry on, still on and on in the dark, so late that we missed dinner at the Duke, until after one of the longest days of my life, Graham rang to say come on over, you got 41 per cent of the total (actually it was 43 per cent). (3) Finally, the smell of victory, the moment I was in the chamber, the palpable excess of votes with the dreaded middle cross:

---

[1] Sutton result: AC, 21,649 votes; Fletcher (Labour), 13,545; Banks (Liberal),12,683.
[2] Used down the years by the Clarks to measure the growth of James and Andrew.

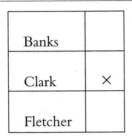

Banks	
Clark	×
Fletcher	

and the fabulous sight of the trays in the middle – the most convincing of all ways of showing it, with our blocks going up and up, and still being counted on 'our' tables.

The General Election on 28 February
  Conservative: 296; Labour: 301; Liberal: 14. Others: Ulster Unionists: 11; Scottish Nationalists: 7; Plaid Cymru: 2; others: 4

Train to Plymouth   *Thursday, 7 March*

Fabulous day of lingering euphoria and luxuriation in being MP.

Started with climb of Summerhouse Hill in glorious spring morning. Then *just* caught 11.18 from Ashford (driving there in little borrowed Triumph 1500 of my parents) still wearing anorak and check trousers/ pink shirt.

Changed and showered and to House. Collected huge bundles of (miscellaneous) mail and through to Euan's office[1] where he got me *monstrously* drunk; then drifted around the Palace of Westminster peeping and pottering, and observing massive available perks; drink in Strangers Bar and to (quite good) lunch. Hailed in Strangers dining room with incredible hurrahs by Jeremy Thorpe, more guardedly by David Steel. Then spent rest of afternoon 'walking off' drink going round various Sergeant-at-Arms type offices drawing vouchers etc.

---

[1] Euan Graham, AC's friend from Oxford days, had been Principal Clerk of Private Bills, House of Lords, since 1961.

Saltwood   *Sunday, 10 March*

After the euphoria the depression. Jane found the invitation from Ali (though fortunately not her letter) and she took it out on James – I didn't realise this at the time – and then had a very late night. Probably saved from row then by presence of Celly and, to a lesser extent Nick.[1] This morning she (and James) still in a filthy temper while Lilian pinched and pale and incredible nose-blowing coughing (which embarrasses me with Barham [doctor], against whose advice I took him to Zermatt last Saturday, which seems an age ago).

To Jane at breakfast I said 'your only real motivation, whether subconscious or conscious, the only yardstick by which you judge things, is whether I am more or less likely to get people to go to bed with me ...' and developed the theme. She cried when I tried to console her. We were interrupted by the back door bell, it was Tim, calling for James. Went and tidied around in the dressing room, with Andrew soft-spokenly helping me with my ties, then over to the Garden House, to find my mother in tears, my father his usual crotchety self, raspingly he made me 'accept' the use of Albany. Andrew deteriorating by the minute, nose-blowing etc.

Also aware on this lovely fine spring morning of the great weight of undone duties ranging from paperwork (eg Meeson[2]) to Saltwood (notices etc, garage) to bills. Financial stringency looms with disallowing of loan interest (probably), plus inevitability of Labour victory in next election.[3]

---

[1] Nick Beuttler, Jane's brother.
[2] Accountant.
[3] AC found himself at Westminster as a backbench MP for a party in opposition, with neither Conservatives nor Labour having an overall majority. Edward Heath, as 'the Prime Minister in possession' (related AC in *The Tories*) and leading a party boasting 1,200,000 more votes than Labour (but five fewer seats), had spent 'five painful days' attempting to 'form' an administration. Jeremy Thorpe, leader of the Liberals (6,000,000 votes, but only 14 seats), demanded nothing less than proportional representation to turn their future voting strength into seats; Heath offered no more than a Speaker's Conference to examine the question of electoral reform. The coalition did not happen, Heath resigned and Harold Wilson became Prime Minister leading a minority Labour government.

Plymouth train   *Friday, 15 March*

Down on the 1.30, suspect slightly flu-bound and picked up Johnny Hannam.[1] (For a few minutes he didn't know who I was.). We sat at lunch together. Self-medicating generously, talked of politics throughout the meal to the grumpy consternation of a *New Statesman*-reading geriatric opposite. Quite a nice chap, interesting and helpful. Concepted Margaret Thatcher as possible successor to Heath.

Saltwood   *Monday, 25 March*

A glorious still spring day, the sun warm – tanning if one could be out all day – and so much to do in the place if one could get down to it – fences, cutting, hedging, etc.

Been going great guns in politics: on ITN, BBC West, *This Week*, Radio 4, all arising, more or less, from the article in the *Sunday Times*.[2] Sometimes, I think, fabulous; a new face, just the right combination of attitudes, appeal etc. Rommel. Press on and on. At others I feel so far to go, such parlous resources, what a waste of the lovely weather and possessions and XVIIIc freedom. My morale suffered from mutterings at Plymouth (reported to me); Dunstone,[3] needless to say, plus letter from Sir Henry Studholme[4] in *Western Morning News*. Bloody fools had none of them read the *ST* itself, only L.K.Way's extracts.

---

[1] John Hannam, MP for Exeter since 1970.
[2] Under the heading 'Tory Party needs a rethink, but where are the thinkers?', AC was highly critical of the party machine, its reliance on the findings of opinion pollsters in formulating an image and packaging policy; he also attacked Tory Central Office for its condemnation 'amounting in the later years almost to a witch-hunt' of all expressions of dissent, particularly those who supported Enoch Powell's views. It was widely seen as a brave, if foolhardy view to voice, not least by a new MP.
[3] A Sutton constituency ward chaired by Mrs H.O'N. (Nan) Howard.
[4] Sir Henry Studholme, 1st Bt, MP for Tavistock, 1942–66, part of whose constituency was redistributed into Sutton.

Albany   *Thursday, 28 March*

Lunched with feisty old backbencher from Gillingham (Kent).[1] 'Oh, you're Alan Clark ... I've heard a lot about you.' 'All of it good, I hope,' I retorted, composing my face into a fresh, anxious-to-please expression. He then did a sort of 'Do-you-mind-old-boy' preliminary and said '... a certain amount of resentment ... don't push it too hard, lie low for a bit' etc. Crusty old cove.

Saltwood   *Sunday, 31 March*

Over in the Great Hall in somewhat melancholy and reflective frame of mind. A fine morning and the first over here this year, taking advantage of the long light and the delicious monastic atmosphere. Not as tranquil as I should have liked with interruptions (a) from my father (b) from Gangster parked in the red chinz armchair, scratching/whining periodically and then barking later.

Gloomy about constant encroachment on parkland by public, growing tendency to think 'amazing for one person to have so much land ...' actually vouchsafed by a young person whom I evicted (with three others) this afternoon. Came up by car (naturally) and went to tip of escarpment – presumably to smoke 'joints'; went off shouting leftish sentiments and slogans. Have spent huge sums in fencing and security, but still holes, fighting a losing battle; in the end will be down to the original fortified defence line of Outer and Inner Bailey. Are we (J & I and the boys) an etiolated rearguard? The French nobility in 1788? At that appalling dinner party last night every single person was 'progressive'. The good-living/thinking jealousy substitute for the deprived (sexually and materially) professional classes.

From time to time during the day – heavily persuaded by depredations on tool locker, missing funnel etc etc – thought much to do here just with the cars, the estate, *preserving* so that the boys can carry on. I just don't know what will emerge from the House, but time is terribly diminished – weekends are bliss. All the *notices*, opening decisions etc here are still undone. Yet cannot shirk. I have a debt to God who has worked my miracle for me. At least, making extra time for fitness and rest by cutting out b'gammon.

---

[1] Frederick Burden, first elected MP for Gillingham in 1950.

Albany   *Tuesday, 30 April*

Put in to do my 'maiden' today.[1] Sat in Chamber for quite a time, with 'everyone on board most helpful',[2] Spencer Le Marchant coming up and arranging my place in the order. Rose to my feet and spoke clearly and, I believe, it was appreciated once the House realised what I was doing – quite wittily. Interesting thing is both Spencer, and Tony Berry, who summed up (still slightly shaking and shimmering as of old) I knew at various stages of the education process.[3]

Saltwood   *Friday, 7 June*

A very low day. Extremely tired (did late night at Aspinalls) and awoke as unpleasant thoughts slotted into place (1) b'gammon losses last night £470; (ii) Valeri out of my life; (iii) Jimmy Goldsmith warnings about world slump. My mind was racing as to how reduce o/d and then came crashing in on top of this the recollection that CGT also (of minimum 30) is needed shortly.

My parents low; my mother now deteriorated again, although still beautifully poised and witty; talk of wealth tax, obliteration of the 'gentry', look round at the unbelievable driving up of protest sympathies by the press for the IRA and hunger strikers etc.

Given up b'gammon ... statistical analysis shows it just is too expensive.

---

[1] AC chose the debate on the Channel Tunnel, that project being so close to Saltwood (as he declared to the House), if not his constituency, but in his speech he gave a foretaste of his views from Defence, through patriotism to continental Europe, when he reminded the House that the country had always been protected from invasion by the English Channel. An attack would be by 'blitzkrieg, a lightning strike', and its most likely form would now be a parachute landing 'to seize the tunnel head and defend it for a short enough period for the invader to pass through the tunnel and completely bypass our natural protection.' And, he added, that if the tunnel went ahead a fail-safe system should be installed allowing for its instant demolition.

[2] From one of AC's favourite books, Evelyn Waugh's *The Ordeal of Gilbert Pinfold*, a copy of which he kept by his bedside in Zermatt.

[3] Spencer Le Marchant, MP for High Peak, Derbyshire since 1970, and an Opposition Whip since the election. Another Old Etonian, like Anthony Berry, MP for Southgate since 1964.

Albany   *Sunday, 9 June*

Heading for an exceptionally bad night, I should think. Great long periods just brooding – cutting out birds, drink and backgammon should have helped, but actually depression so acute that great long totally uncreative periods supervene when the mind just rambles. Also being needlessly grumpy and beastly to Jane.

Just as I was changing a mass of gawpers started pouring through the arch, re-reviving all my neuroses about the unstoppable tide (my nightmare of them all coming *down* the stairs at Saltwood with me pluckingly trying to collect a few 20p's).

H of C Library   *Wednesday, 12 June*

Low, and hot. Can't take my coat off, it seems, although I did so once before I was cowed. Walking with Tim Sainsbury[1] from the Gents to the Lobby and Margaret Thatcher[2] materialised and gushingly, 'Hello Tim we've missed you ...' etc. He dropped me like a bit of parrot shit, naturally. Then, aggravatingly, *missed a Division.* Was in committee room 13 listening with great interest to Ulster leader Willie Craig[3] telling how Heath had not replied to telegram from West[4] – 'see you at the swearing-in'. Made *no* effort to get their support and save Conservatives. (Perhaps just as well.) Anyhow the bell went, and we finally shuffled off, a terrific longueurs getting into the lobby. 'Mr Thomas'[5] suddenly yelled 'Lock the doors' – most irritating of all, to miss a vote when actually *in* the Palace, indeed *in* the Chamber!

---

[1] Hon Timothy Sainsbury, MP for Hove since November 1973.

[2] Margaret Thatcher, MP for Finchley since 1959. Secretary of State for Education from 1970 until the general election. Her name was increasingly mentioned as a possible successor to Edward Heath as party leader as Conservatives regrouped following the February defeat.

[3] William Craig, MP for East Belfast since the General Election. Leader of the Ulster Vanguard Party since 1973.

[4] Henry William West, MP for Fermanagh and South Tyrone since the general election and leader of the Ulster Unionist Party. When Heath had been trying to form a government immediately after the election, as well as parlaying with the Liberals he also had brief but abortive discussions about a pact with the Ulster Unionists.

[5] George Thomas, MP (Labour) for Cardiff West since 1950 (Cardiff Central, 1945–50), had been Deputy Speaker since the general election. His ringing Welsh tones were swiftly making their presence felt in the Chamber.

Yesterday (instead of the House), when I was lying up on the castle's terrace/battlement walk (new spot, just this side of Thorpe's[1]), did absolutely no good tan-wise, but suddenly realised the enormity of the interest charges running against me – 87 + 63 = 150 or £20,000 a year, or £500 a week. Must stop the drain and can only do so by selling cars.

Is it going to be easy to sell cars? CH very gloomy. Money drying up fast. From time to time, as I drive about in my blue Bentley – to which I am very attached, 'MP's car' – I think what a personification of Privilege I am. Silk shirts, beautiful suits, write a cheque or sign an Amex for anything you want; chambers in Albany, castle in Kent, châlet in Zermatt, credit accounts everywhere, the Parliamentary pass to flash. Press the button, the machine will respond. Total confidence. How easy to be pleasant – that calm inner assurance of superiority (like I have sometimes noticed with people who are very good at Judo, the way they move quietly and confidently in crowds). Well, could it be in jeopardy? I got the aerial photos of Saltwood today, thought God what a wonderful place, worth hanging on to, and preserving for the boys.

Bratton-Clovelly   *Thursday, 13 June*

Sitting, utterly pole-axed in the garden in a deckchair.

Seem to have had only 5/6 hours sleep every night this week, late whipping in the House, too much to drink. Incredibly, the adrenalin does keep me going during the week, but this afternoon after sleeper down, trudging around Plymouth – as Porsche in garage.

Bratton delicious, tranquil. What a place to recharge one's batteries. Chief worry is money, impossibility of selling *anything* it seems. Bonny mama not well again. Losing ground.

---

[1] Thorpe's Tower, which looks out over the Barbican Gate, the main entrance to Saltwood.

Dean's Yard   *Wednesday, 17 July*

Reflecting on most unwelcome position, the evidence of (sic) which has been building up for some time, that not only am I in a very uncomfortable financial situation – but that I totally mismanaged (from optimism, *folie de grandeur*, total lack of Scotch canniness, gross miscalculations of economic symptoms and also sheer inability, or at least unwillingness to *count*) the one last great get-out deal, namely the sale of the cricket field.

This could have got me permanently out of debt and allowed consolidation with a lot of excess assets on a well diversified earnings basis – rents, royalties, salaries, public visits. Really, after earlier reverses one would think that lesson had been learned. It *has* been learned now. Just pray I can impart it to James and Tip – one can never entirely, of course, but even *some* of it would help. Now one has to set more modest goals and they will take longer to fulfil, whereas it could have been done 'at a stroke'. Also means giving up some things I like, eg Lago-Talbot and D-type. (If – and it is a bit of an 'if' because these are days of great panic and depression – I sell them, should get my o/d down below 20.) The days of limitless cash flow are over.

Saltwood   *Sunday, 21 July*

For first time, coming back in sleeper from Plymouth, did not feel that delicious sense of relief and anticipation – the mirror-image of the towers reflected in the water as you come through the Barbican, generated anxiety instead of calming. The whole structure unchanged with absurd signs of wealth and stability but as the hot summer days (now shortening) slip by the bills accumulate, so far without *any* sales to relieve them. This has had the effect of reducing, at last, adrenalin flow (contentment must be an ingredient to get a proper flow, I think). And last night I went down with a summer cold, first cold for eighteen months. During the night an enormous chunk of the north curtain wall slid down, and will cost £12–14,000 to repair. I remember talking to my old pal Euan Graham in a bar in the House of Lords last week, and he told me how as well as being by-passed for the long-awaited promotion he had been cut out of his mother's will – 'when one thing hits you, they all do.'

Darling Jamie going to Cranwell today to RAF Camp with various
flying activities. Things could get so much worse, couldn't they? I
mean we are still painfully blessed and golden (*d'orée*). Yesterday
evening, before the cold took hold, I swam a double length of the
moat, naked, in the warm sunlight, looking up at the tower, then
drove the Ghost with Tip to Dungeness, where there's an old (but
interesting) wreck.

Saltwood   *Monday, 5 August*

Conceivably, the last day of the old regime.[1] Not impossible that by
the winter I shall be (a) wiped out and (b) lost my seat. I sometimes
seriously think of how much I could get out to Zermatt (Bavarian
Redoubt) before actually going under. A few objects and pictures
out – Degas, Bull, snuff-boxes, some Moores and Sutherlands etc. But
how would one live in the long term? On reflection, must preserve
Saltwood, so it can be run 'as a business'.

Later
Am I a Renaissance Prince, a philosopher, or a big ageing dud?
Looking back at all those lost opportunities of money-making, starting
with the waste of the first £15,000 my father gave me in 1948, like
properties in Rye (going for nothing), the Torridon Estate (£40,000
in 1964, now ½ million I suppose). And yet when I go and plump for
something like Newton it becomes a lemon at once – although I'm
sure strategically it must be right.

Fortified by two things – first how all that really matters is the boys'
health and survival and how lucky we are, second how God *did* work
his miracle for Plymouth Sutton. *That* was the real achievement, *that*
is what must be built on. Easy to recharge the batteries with Zermatt
and Bratton ... and exercise. I've learnt my lesson about financial
speculation at last having been through fire – forget it. Security you
can (still) attain. So, thank-you-God-for-any-good-luck and hold on

---

[1] The House of Commons had risen for the summer recess; everyone expected that
Harold Wilson, the Prime Minister, would call an election in the autumn in an
endeavour to get an overall working majority.

to what you've got, a happy family and fulfilment of your secret – and apparently impossible – ambition.

Charing Cross   *Thursday, 19 September*

Confident (Sutton *not* on the *Guardian* list of marginals).[1]

I went off to face Hoare's, going through the Temple. Seen in a top front room. First dear old Q. Hoare to soften me up, then 'Dick' Hoare – the head man. That was clearly his designed role, but it so happens we took an intense dislike to one another. He's determined to 'get' me, I can feel that; enjoyed bullying me to sell assets – regardless of right price or no. Made some acid quips while Q. Hoare muddled the figures from time to time. At the end (circa 5.30) dear old Q. Hoare asked me if I would like a whisky (!) Have got till 1 April next year (due to Q. Hoare's shuffling – originally in two stages with Christmas the first).[2]

Everything happening at once, ie financial collapse *and* having to fight an election. Waking early with all these worries. Fool, Clark, to have repeated your errors on such a huge scale.

Duke of Cornwall Hotel, Plymouth[3]   *Saturday, 28 September*

It was icy in (or rather on) the Land-Rover this evening. There is no proper rail along the top of the cab so I have to 'steady myself', fingers blue-numbed, by clutching at the tiny and sharp-edged guttering. As I sway about, the hand held microphone will suddenly and unpredictably emit a piercing howl. Why? It seems to have something to do with proximity to metal, at least that's my theory.

You can't talk through it, and it will suddenly cut in *while* you are talking or, even more disconcertingly, for no apparent reason whatever while one is benignly surveying a narrow street crowded with shoppers.

---

[1] The general election had been called for 11 October.
[2] Despite the severity of Hoare's stipulations, the Clarks retained accounts with the bank.
[3] As in February, AC was to use 'The Duke' as his base for the October campaign.

Some, very, very few of these folk smile or wave. Most avoid my eye, or start up conversations with each other.

Sod them, I say. What the hell are they doing shopping anyway, on a Tuesday? People who are spending money in shops ought to be Conservative, surely?

I feel myself to be getting 'out of sorts'.

'Firm Government – but Fair Government'.

Umpteen times have I called this out. A simple enough phrase. So simple, indeed, as to be devoid of meaning or even inference. Yet all too easy to get, in some perverse way, tied around one's tongue. We were driving in those streets that lead uphill from Plymstock to Hooe, there was practically no one about and Jane accelerated. The wind made my eyes water uncontrollably, and for some reason I started a longer discourse and *affected a Devonian accent.*

She jammed on the brakes. 'What *are* you doing? You just make yourself utterly ridiculous.'

Back here I ordered and consumed a lot of tea and buttered toast (both arrived tepid) in the lounge. I am depressed, irritated, suffering from exhaustion. Even in the 'good' areas the electorate are flinty-faced. What's going on?

Bratton   *Thursday, 3 October*

The dear old boy conducting me round Mt Gould – very efficiently – won my heart by suddenly saying: 'Of course you're the one, the one
. with fire in you.'

Later Jack Weatherill[1] came on the phone: 'How's it going?'

'So so, only.'

'No I mean this Coalition idea.[2] Are you getting it across?'

'They won't understand. It's far too late to start trying to sell that . . .'

[1] Bernard (Jack) Weatherill, MP for Croydon NE since 1964. A whip in government and opposition (he had been Opposition deputy chief whip since February 1974). Such were his skills with the more independent-minded Conservative members that he was known, not always affectionately, as 'the shits' whip'.

[2] At mid-point, Tory strategists, at the behest of Edward Heath, came up with the notion that to appeal 'over the heads' of the Labour Party to 'people of good will' might save a number of seats.

'Well, that's the line. Do your best.'

'Look, Jack, we're not going to get anywhere while Ted is leading us. He's had it.'

'Later. That comes later. Leave it for the moment.'

Odd. Particularly that last sentence. Actually, I think we are going to lose, again. And that will be one of the exciting things about the new House. Getting a real change.

Saltwood   *Saturday, 12 October*

Back last night after a (foreshortened) tour of Sutton with the loud-speaker (just did a 'blast' outside the Eastons' house so that they would hear me – for alibi reasons). A glance at the *Evening Standard* was enough to show that Plymouth results were *exceptionally* bad[1] – many safe seats had *increased* their majorities. Only consolation was that of course, most of Liberals had also been slashed. But undeniable bit-terness of dejection, or at least personal brush off – all those letters, all that charm. Also uncomfortably concerned that it undermines my personal activities as a right-winger and also, of course, in the Association itself. As Saltwood towers loomed up in the headlights Jane said, 'What a wonderful place.' How I agreed. But dared not say, how much in peril it is. Must take steps at virtually any price, to shift it across into the Trust, and there was that letter from Hoare's: will-you-come-in-straight-away?

Concocted a formula to get one to sleep, of selling the plot adjacent in Zermatt for 90,000 (!). I passed out in bed at 10.30 and woke at 11.20. This gave me back a bit of confidence again, a determination to concentrate on exercises, library, eschew late nights, b'gammon, the Mews etc. Clearheadedly see this through. 'No relaxation without implementation.'

The General Election on 11 October
    Conservative: 276; Labour: 319; Liberal: 13. Others: Ulster Unionists: 10; Scottish Nationalists: 11; Plaid Cymru: 3; others: 3

---

[1] Sutton result: AC, 20,457 votes; Priestley (Labour), 15,269; Banks (Liberal), 10,131. AC's majority, 5,188 (February, 8,104).

Zermatt   *Thursday, 17 October*

In Zermatt briefly, and depressed to find the old magic almost gone. Bavarian Redoubt now seems tricky, a cul-de-sac. Brought some snuff-boxes out and put them in a box in safe in back – but it's 'the addresses' isn't it? Only point as a *recuperative* tonic, a temporary refuge. Exile would be very sad. Key principle must be to SAVE SALTWOOD – still with its potential barely touched in so many ways.

Gloomy, too, about politics. Absolutely nil contact about the leadership this time, no phoning, no TV, no articles. In desperation, have sent out 53 invitations to a party at Albany as understandably all MPs long for some social contact. Can feel – perhaps with some element of paranoia – latent hostility in Association at Plymouth. They just longing to get cracking when the Chelmer rules start laying down conditions about living in the constituency, etc. (When papers interview '... at his family home, Saltwood Castle in Kent', can imagine Rodney Easton snorting and grunting and slapping his paper down.) Pine for Folkestone, and wrote to 'Albert' (who sent me a telegram, although I had veto'd sending him one).[1] Was rewarded by an instant invitation to address the AGM of their CPC (!) I don't know whether I would get Folkestone or not – the very idea of chaotic selection committee ordeal is sheer trauma – but I sometimes think I will never fight an election in Plymouth again.

Saltwood   *Thursday, 31 October*

Been in a state of considerable 'nervosity' all day. Waves of angst wash over me at the Hoare's indebtedness (wake every morning at 4am for about ¾ hr of panic). Also Lenin-stadium type cramp-angst at so much to resolve:

(1) Constantly losing and long mucked-up at b'gammon (which I love, and am addicted to)
(2) Virtually ignored in the House this time – in spite of our quite jolly and successful performances

---

[1] Albert Costain, MP for Folkestone since 1959. Now in his mid-sixties the question of when he might retire and whether AC might succeed him would recur.

(3) Rows – sic – with parents being against my advantage over possible – indeed vital – money-raising sales

(4) Feeling tired cold and looking strangely pressured with hair now degenerating in quality as well as colour and density

(5) Sick of Plymouth – will quit journeys and the sleeper etc – and their introspective minuscule horizons

(6) Badly need energy and will-power to concentrate on problems this winter

Saltwood   *Saturday, 16 November*

Filled with gloom and foreboding as market continues to slide (Coats at $\underline{26\frac{1}{2}}$), probability of yet another Arab/Israeli war with total collapse of industry, currency etc (not to mention 'Nuclear Exchange'). November is a terrible month, the equivalent of 3.10am during the night.

Desmond Corcoran[2] coming down this morning. Have prayed to God I make the right decisions.[3]

Saltwood   *Sunday, 8 December*

Reasonably randy and eating ok, but yesterday had a real shock on seeing myself on TV. Unbelievably livid, gaunt, puffy and balding – looked older than the Bishop of London who came on later. *Must* start regime *now*. Exercises, early nights, hair washes, sleep after lunch when possible, cut down on drink. Will 'report back' on this.

---

[1] A stock long-held by AC and in considerable quantities. It had been at a year high of 74. Coats had acquired the Clark Cotton Thread business many years before.

[2] Desmond Corcoran – from the Lefevre Gallery in Mayfair.

[3] AC's comment at foot of entry: 'I was very trembly to start with, but got 31,000 for nine pictures'.

1975

Have been terribly depressed these last few days. Christmas (which, thanks to Jane's efforts was as usual great fun; 'Daisy' down, and bought, among others, Phantom III from him for 8.5; thin (as usual loathsomely like at Bratton in '63) and said 'you've got a lot greyer'. Only too true, alas. Have got much more continuously tired; slowly catching one, wearing one down in the incessant pressure on time. I no longer have the capacity to extend the day indefinitely – as I used to do; getting up incredibly early to do the great long-range drive or 'missing' a night, but quickly repairing. The time in Zermatt was wonderful – though James's nerve gone, poor dear, and he hates skiing. Tip on the other hand very good potential. But I felt no oxygen boost on getting back – for the first time.

Got back today. Nanny had cleaned the place fantastically, throughout, and our fears that various vandalisms would occur proved unfounded. Even the 'No Parking' notice sensibly erect outside the Barbican, and Cradduck's stripping of the ivy from the walls over the Bailey gate most successful. Of the various anticipated disasters only one – the euthanasia of Gangster – took place as predicted. I'm sorry that I couldn't be there to bid him goodbye. But he's buried next to Grandee. And I will always remember the Beagles and their period of great physical prowess, particularly Dartmoor (that time I lost them on the twin boggy ridges that stretched out towards Meldon) and Salisbury Plain (chasing the prototype Chieftain[2]) because it coincided with the longer period of contentment and tranquillity (at Seend) in my own life.

Reasonable (and unexpected) aura of contentment in spite of letter from the Tate semi-reneging on Saltonstall.[3] Beautifully insulated here in panelled library with log fire.

But much will be decided this year. 'Survival' yes, but there must

---

[1] AC heads this page: START OF 'SURVIVAL YEAR'.
[2] The Chieftain was to become the British army's principal tank of the Cold War era.
[3] *The Saltonstall Family*, c1636–7, by David Des Granges.

also be a platform built, because if I don't get established in '76 there can be no further attainment of my goals without a miracle. Thought on the walk this evening how would really be quite content to be just stately-home-owner, dealer and b'gammon-man; last night woke in the wagon-lit feeling tired and wondered if now really too old. My age does seem to have jumped one this last year.

Dean's Yard   *Friday, 17 January*

'Punishment' phase. Lost £1320 to Goldsmith/Slater/Zilkhan at a £40 chow at Lyall Street after Aspers'(only moderate) 'talk' to Bow Group last night. Jane rightly tested me for no constituency visits, no publicity, far too much old cars. *Absolutely nothing* in the papers about me for nearly six weeks, don't open constituency letters any more, no questions tabled, no intervention, no time to work up speeches, complaints about showing my face in Plymouth – haven't even signed all the election thankyou letters yet! Now very tired indeed (7.30 train tomorrow) with cold symptoms.[1]

Saltwood   *Monday, 24 March*

Threatening position welling up in Plymouth. As I somehow suspected Larry Speare[2] undergone total personality change as chairman – head cropped, unsmilingly and *folie de grandeur*. He'd already shown incipient signs of this at the AGM with his *very* reserved compliments and injunctions to 'help the name of Sutton forward'. Then last Thursday, totally dry-minded and fatigued (I had driven down flat out that morning in the 230 SL, spurting out oil through a misplaced

---

[1] AC is silent on the change in party leadership, which was about to take place. In the first ballot of Conservative MPs on 4 February, Margaret Thatcher gained 130 votes to Edward Heath's 119, with 16 for the backbencher Hugh Fraser. Heath resigned as leader. A week later Thatcher, with 146 votes, gained an overall majority over four Shadow Cabinet colleagues: William Whitelaw (79 votes), Geoffrey Howe and James Prior (19 each) and John Peyton (11).

[2] Lawrence Speare, a significant member of the Sutton Conservative Association and sometime chairman.

filter cap) he told/warned me of possibility of not being readopted due to having been anti-Heath, anti Referendum. That evening, at the F&GP he, fortunately, 'clashed' with Rodney Easton; but if he, Easton and Speare started ganging up (Nazi-Soviet non-aggression pact) then one would be in trouble, left only with Dunstone (doubtful) and Efford and Sutton.

Saltwood   *Thursday, 10 April*

A note of the last day of the Common Market (approval) – or whatever it should be called – debates.

Entertainment, indeed History, promised with Heath, Powell *and* Heffer[1] all hoping-to-catch-the-eye. Walked up the aisle and turned right past Heath, occupying the prime position in corner seat. He bronzé in grey suit, check shirt (semi-Heseltine outfit) but rather more pinched, less ripplingly. Ugh! What a purse-mouth ('*Bonjours* ...') he made as I momentarily swished him. Humphrey Atkins[2] smiled in friendly fashion, though. Had John Stradling Thomas[3] already told him that I was going to vote anti? John himself uneasily asked me if I had 'read Margaret's speech'. Oh yes, I said, splendid stuff (I hadn't); of course if she told me to vote 'for' I would. But I welcomed the 'free' vote in order to make my little personal statement. Gloomily he accepted this.

Front bench jammed solid. 'Throng' at the Bar. Heath spoke, reasonably competent and without notes, in the 'Coningsby position' (or hand in d/b jacket pocket). For a second, when he was speaking about sovereignty, I could have interrupted him, but it passed.

'Where's Margaret?' asked nasty little Tony Nelson of Chichester.[4] 'He listened to *her* speech.'

'But wasn't very polite about it,' I said. He looked cross at this.

---

[1] Eric Heffer, MP for Liverpool Walton since 1964, and a leading left-winger.

[2] Humphrey Atkins, MP for Spelthorne since 1970 (Merton and Morden, 1955–1970) and opposition chief whip. Earlier he had a spell as secretary to the Conservative Parliamentary Defence Committee. Deputy and ultimately government chief whip, 1973–74.

[3] John Stradling Thomas, MP for Monmouth since 1970 and an opposition whip.

[4] Tony Nelson, elected MP for Chichester in October 1974, previously with N.M. Rothschild.

The Heath 5th column cheered loudly when he sat down. He was followed, immediately by Enoch! Tortured, baleful, intense, he stood only a few feet away from me, on the same row the other side of the gangway. Spoke well, gestured pointedly. Heath interrupted him three times, having to unfortunately twist his neck and his eyes round and was slightly worsted. Enoch very good and moving and made one feel *all right* about voting anti. 'That's one of the good ones', came from one of Dennis's group as I walked through afterwards and sexy little Miss Horseface (I don't recall her name, but took Dick's place at Lincoln)[1] seductively said 'I didn't know you were an anti.'[2]

Went back to St J and got into b'gammon game, and ended losing again – £226. When I collected my mail Dennis Skinner[3] was standing near. I had to give my name to an unknown PO official. 'Alan Clark'. . . 'The goal scorer,' said D. 'You scored one last night.' 'Not enough of us,' I answered. In the tea-room queue I said, 'I'd rather live in a socialist Britain than one ruled by a lot of fucking foreigners.' He seemed surprised as well as pleased.

Saltwood   *Sunday, 11 May*

An evocative date. The great German offensive across the Low Countries in 1940, Churchill gets the premiership, the die is cast in the country's fight to the death. And, five years later, VE Day, with its illusions that took so long to disperse.

And here is my own life, its 'serious', ambitious, political and however-you-like-to-call-it side so emphatically biased by those experiences, well over half-way through, even deducting the childhood years. I've got ten – *tennish* – more years active, eight as an 'active buffer', the remainder as a sage. That's always assuming freedom/deliverance from the screech of brakes, sickening thud and

---

[1] Margaret Jackson (later better known by her married name Beckett) had regained the Lincoln seat for Labour in October 1974 after the sitting MP, Dick Taverne, defected to the SDP.

[2] AC was one of a small number of Tories to vote against, but their stance was overshadowed by Eric Heffer, who was dismissed as Minister of State, Department of Industry, for not supporting the Government.

[3] Dennis Skinner, MP for Bolsover since 1970 ('good working-class mining stock', *Who's Who* entry) and already a left-winger with a reputation for parliamentary repartee.

rending of metal from the head-on crash over the brow of the hill. Now that the 550 Spyder is roadable I often take it out on fine evenings. So intoxicatingly fast and agile – but so vulnerable. Going onto the slightly blind hump-back of the A20 Sandling Bridge I visualised (as so often) that horrid impact. Have I recorded that nightmare spin in the 230 SL that night when I was unscathed? Let us hope it means that 'what is written, is written'.

Saltwood *Sunday, 18 May*

Had a relatively slack week, but precious little achieved. Tide turned at b'gammon, at last, and pulled in about £700, totally eliminating losses to Charles and producing a surplus of £100+. Also frenzied dealing in 'leaders' has produced a big surplus – but of course one false move and good deals can be undone – vide Bass, sold one hour too late at a loss of £400. Fast as one consolidates, though, past debts pile up; not only the Saltwood curtain wall and the lesser items like tidying up round the new garages etc, but a sudden 'shock' need: £2– 4,000 to pay for brochures. The brochures themselves are very good.

Tremendous long-term investment possibilities for Saltwood. My father (according to Col) now clutches his head and says 'I can't understand why one bought it ... madness.' He strangely distant and crotchety – possibly sale of Sutherlands[1] has something to do with it, but, as I said, it's now 'come and get one, Larsen'.

Dean's Yard *Tuesday, 27 May*

A certain delicious calmness – one of the first really tranquil entries for nearly a year – since the enormity of the financial crisis and the threat to Saltwood came home. Working up in my (new) 'collegiate' quarters on the quad – Abbey Garden – on a long summer evening. Sent £18,000 odd to Hoare's today, now bringing o/d to agreed April 1st limit and reductions. More to follow. The magic moment when the deeds are returned to me not so far away.

---

[1] Graham Sutherland sketched and painted a number of portraits of Kenneth Clark

What is to be the outcome of the terrible decline of the country – the total absence of leadership and inspiration in the Conservative Party? In 1939 at least we had Fighter Command and the Navy, and Winston around. Now we have nothing. My windows here are filthy, dirtier even than at Saltwood. *US News and World Report*[1] quite right – whole thing tatty, bad-tempered, lazy, in collapse. Yet of course there is no crisis; everyone flush with money. When will the recovery come? And how?

Yet even as I write this, I feel – too slack, too easygoing. In the train the other evening I thought perhaps I should go the whole way, stand as National Front candidate, a *switch* if the Plymouth Association kicks me out. Or is the very thought that I am 'waiting for the call' a concealment of my natural laziness?

After two days very successful openings, fired by the cash flow, the possibilities. One of the few 'enterprises' unlikely to be troubled even by the envy, the jealousies all around us. I also have these romantic fantasies of the besieged aristocracy. 1791. I do hope the boys will catch on in the end. James in particular is unbelievably idle about it at the moment. He has passed through girls (for the moment) and drink (largely speaking) and now is obsessed by driving. He had cleaned the Bang Bang[2] meticulously during 'garage invigilation' on the public days. Last night Tuppy suddenly cocked an ear and said, 'that's the Bang Bang engine . . .' I looked out of the door and saw it going down the drive – James was turning it prior to putting it in the garage. I waited in the shadow of the Barbican. The car came back, turned in the car park gate and then out back down the drive! I knew what would follow and sure enough an engine opened up (so like an aero-engine it sounds) and the lights clearly shone charging up Sandy Lane! I got the Land-Rover, but by then he was already returning. Oh dear, I do love 'Boy' so much, in spite of all his bolshiness of growing up. I do dread his having a motor accident. I must train and nurture him on the road. He wants to go to Lydden[3] and one might do that.

---

[1] This American news magazine had compared the Britain of the 1970s – unfavourably – with the 'swinging sixties' period.

[2] R Type Bentley Continental, the only Continental to be recorded stolen in the 1950s. Written off, it was rebodied by Bradley Brothers into a cut-down two-seater.

[3] Motor-racing track off the A2 north-west of Dover.

Saltwood   *Thursday, 29 May*

Recess. Heard dawn chorus start up after 4 struck – quite beautiful and magical – dropped back to sleep. Woke again 7am. Grey water, made tea, dressed, wakey-wakey'd boys, last minute Thompson before taking boys to Sandling. Annoyed, at Sandling, by that shirty little rotting-dog man in a white Renault who always blocks the wrong place, but did nothing. Letter from Sir Gilbert Longden in *Daily Telegraph* about me. Still mildly pleased to see myself as 'Mr Alan Clark MP'.[1]

Evening of one of the two hottest days we're likely to get this year. Absolutely cloudless, without a breath of wind. Boy out for a party at St Mary's Bay; usual mixed emotions of jealousy/frustration at the two 'maidens' (heavily-built, but one somewhat shy and lecherous I would think) and worry at his using the 1100, which has already been put in a ditch once. He is to return at 11pm so there will be a half hour of anxiety. I construct the fantasy of the Lancaster sortie in Bomber Command.

I feel 'calmer' this summer than last. The total 'apres moi le deluge' atmosphere ameliorated by velour of semi-solvency. But I also feel older, creakier. Political weaknesses remain with a dead loss situation in Parliament – no committees, no work, no activity.

Albany   *Tuesday, 29 July*

Sun pouring through windows, a.m., as this memorable summer goes on, and on and on. Ever since April have been woken (either here or at Saltwood) by squares of light moving slowly across the wall, from 5am – or whenever – and longed, with various degrees of yearning, for a few happy open-air days swimming and working out of doors to take advantage of a memorable summer that will never, in my lifetime, be repeated. Finally this morning, FED UP with still being stuck in Commons – and next week too, due to pressure of 'business'.

[1] Sir Gilbert Longden, retired in February 1974 after 24 years as MP for South West Herts. In his letter he was agreeing with AC's view that it was the duty of all Conservatives to resist socialist politics which 'opposed our liberties, prosperity and security.'

Summer will be de facto over when we are finally released as at present just mooching around in the lobbies, whips wildly inaccurate with their '... in about an hour ...' estimates. As yet plans not clear – Venice and Chalet? Or vintage rally to Lagenburg (I'm lightly sweating as I write this, by the way at 9.05 am, as in Venice.) Not much point in leaving Saltwood I don't think, until v late, end September. But then bad luck on boys' school hols. James now so grown up, still incredibly beautiful. His girl-friend shaggeable though tall. I don't know what they're doing, but they go quite 'far' as I caught them out-of-sight in the Cadillac on Sunday night. Dear Boy. Tip still tiny, it seems, and unchanged mentally or physically. I hope this isn't worrying him – it does me occasionally.

Saltwood, Great Hall (7pm)   *Saturday, 9 August*

The sun, almost horizontal now, autumn-level, slides across Courtenays, through dirty leaded panes covered with ivy leaves. The library, oppressively stuffy, the whole place ... just a few dandelions – or are they buttercups? The trees all dying on Tanners Hill. *Enfin le chef des champs!* But strangely fatigued and depressed. Can work and write over here till light fails, and much to record, but *incredibly* lethargic and sleepy. Perhaps too much sun (now pleasantly brown all over, and couldn't change colour any more like that hot summer – I suppose it was 1948 – in St John Street at Oxford), not enough protein in diet etc. Virility? Totally impotent.

Must try and sublimate, NO ALCOHOL. Had got completely conditioned by late whip nights to not needing so much sleep – could easily play b'gammon till 2 in the morning or drive down to Saltwood after midnight – but at a price of stiffness and bufferdom and receding hairline and advancing waistline when I think back to how long I kept up the early night, ultra-fit regime. That's what I owe my present condition to.

Saltwood   *Tuesday, 12 August*

By the pool, and still suffering tension in spite of rest and holidays. Derek Priston,[1] very soft-spokenly, asked if I could give *three* (!) Saturdays to attend 'flower shows' etc. Usual sort of 'people asking when your next surgery ...' type mornings turned out to be two separate women wanting to ego about women's rights/lib and Rhianon Wheeldon's 'cleaner' who'd been to Butlins where the food was very bad. Then fell back on 'pub-crawl' suggestions – GAAH! Only five days down from the House and already being pestered.

Saltwood   *Monday, 18 August*

Valeri totally disappeared; 1st phone call v. passionate; 2nd caught me at desk (impossible to talk properly); 3rd from phone box at Ritz (interrupted by Eva); 4th *missed* me by '2 minutes', given untraceable number. Since then total silence.

Zermatt   *Sunday, 7 September*

A greyish, dampish day. Queens departed – 'Daisy' now much more embittered, less effervescent, Geoffrey still splendid, but a little distant. James out here with Peter and incredibly VGL and so *tall*. He did the Mettelhorn yesterday, being dangerously late back so I contemplated getting the helicopter. Light failing and told 'only 5 minutes left' to decide, and then just as I was deciding it should go, a call, 'your son has been found and is at the Edelweiss Hotel' and the sighs of relief.

Tip looks also most pleasing now after a 'shaky' start with his blow wave and cowboy boots, whose purchase so enraged 'Boy'.

And what am I going back to?

---

[1] Derek Priston ran AC's two 1974 election campaigns; becoming full-time agent the following year.

Saltwood   *Saturday, 13 September*

More or less decided and broke the news to Jane – who took it very philosophically – to 'stand down in Sutton'. At this range, it simply isn't possible to satisfy the (insatiable) demands of the Conservative 'workers'.

Draft press release
SUTTON MP STANDS DOWN

'Mr Alan Clark, Member of Parliament for the Sutton division of Plymouth, said in a statement: It is with my great regret that ... for family reasons ... I shall not be standing for re-election for the Sutton Division ... I will of course continue to represent and defend the rights of my constituents who have so loyally supported me in two elections ...'

Cherry Cottage, Seend   *Saturday, 20 September*

Taking a couple of days 'off' here after a Plymouth session (Jane did the Gymkhana while I went to the Tory Reform Group inaugural – Peter Walker's Private Army).

As always at Seend – even when looking through the rattling windows of the train back from Plymouth – filled with an almost pleasurable melancholy. All the elms are dying – the great trees of the 'clump', or magic circle and the huge sentinels that stood beside the different gateways are absolutely stripped leaving the jackdaws puzzled and nervy. This afternoon I stripped an enormous hunk of bark off and stood it in the courtyard shed as a remembrance.

Saltwood   *Thursday, 25 September*

Last night, just before putting out the light, was talking about hypochondria with Jane. Said mine had virtually disappeared with so many other preoccupations. But morning hypochondria takes its place and comes flooding in – waking me at 3.30 (finally putting light on and peeing at 4.15). Realisation that crazy interest charges still absorbing all capital inflow this year. And now nothing left 'if Newton fails to sell'. Got about one year left before real crunch and Saltwood not yet transferred to Trust as hoping to retain under my own hand. I suppose triggered off by 'session' with Meeson in underground interview room in the deserted Commons yesterday which saw one year interest cheque on £20,000 to Hoare's due and he advised me to sell off Newton for what I could get (shades of 'Dick' Hoare). Thought no more about it at the time, didn't brood, that is to say, but sub-consciously must have been affected by TV film of my father's Edward-ian childhood, how much of those riches had gone and how I threw away the last − or at least the penultimate − chance of setting up independent solvency by letting that field money just drift away.

Dean's Yard   *Tuesday, 30 September*

Sat here doing letters feeling incredibly tired and old and Russell Fairgrieve[1] came in − he's not a specially pretty man and less so since becoming a whip. 'Had a holiday?' he barked. No. 'Why not?' − he was crazy − ' . . . not much chance of one now, none at all'. I felt very depressed. Gosh, I would like the deck-chair by the sparkling Med, I thought − now missed it for four years. Bad situation − feeling absolutely dead-beat at end of long vac before night whipping starts.

H o C Library   *Monday, 13 October*

Start of the new term. A certain sleepy tranquillity − in spite of pressures, but this to some extent induced by 'opting out'. Usual slight feeling of being useless, overlooked, passed by. That little prick Michael Latham *already* up on the screen, gabbling (presumably about

---

[1] Russell Fairgrieve, MP for West Aberdeenshire since 1974.

housing)[1] ... Loathsome, oily Leon Brittan[2] grinning nervously at everyone (but not at me; freezes up puzzledly). Speaker wouldn't call me to ask a question – gosh one's heart races after trying to get an impromptu question in. House was pleasingly crowded for Stonehouse[3] who made an appearance starting somewhat grey, portly, tho' still handsome 'at the bar' while a welter of inconclusive points of order were bandied to and fro, then withdrawn.

Multiple source of gloom/resignation, low testosterone level.

I think just *no money* is being paid out anywhere at moment. Perhaps reaction and relief after James's accident is making me less jumpy about this than I should be – but dread the long grey envelope 'Private and Confidential' from C. Hoare & Co calling me to order.. And already saddled by inability to cheque-write – that beautiful, important Hooper PI, a true Indian original. Not to mention 'hesitation' or mistiming on quite tiny items like a new pair of shoes, paying for my suits. Both Jane and I have used our 'Res' of £20 notes, and already raiding the Christie's envelope.

Second, discontented with non-schnazziness of Plymouth. Too far away, same old faces fussing and conspiring. The slow resentment at not living in will build-up and they'll try and throw me out in the end – so surely better to pre-empt and go out on a 'Dear Larry ... Dear Alan' exchange for family reasons now, rather than wait until I really am too old (ie after next election). Jim Coote[4] at Conference said: 'You've got an oily little sod as an agent, a mad gypsy as chairman and a nutter as treasurer.' Exaggerating of course, but I know what he means.

---

[1] Like AC, Michael Latham entered the Commons in February 1974 (for Melton), but unlike AC quickly became a committee man and was now a vice-chairman of the Conservative Parliamentary Housing Committee and a member of several other House committees.

[2] Leon Brittan, MP for Cleveland and Whitby since February 1974. A barrister and former chairman of the Bow Group (and editor of its magazine *Crossbow*).

[3] John Stonehouse, MP for Walsall North since February 1974 (Wednesbury 1957–74). Postmaster-General and then Minister of Posts and Telecommunications in Harold Wilson's second government, fell from grace having faked his own death (missing presumed drowned). He was eventually found in Australia, brought back to Britain and faced charges of forgery, theft and conspiracy. He died in 1988.

[4] A Conservative Party official from Central Office.

Bratton   *Saturday, 13 December*

Terribly low and depressed. Went 'to pieces' last week, ie staying up
late, working the body (and the purse), bad decisions, back failure.
Lost £140 to Charles, then £100 to Lever, then £250 to Colin Slater,
lured by 'Catto' into disastrous loss on Plessey ('rights' issue suddenly
announced 24 hours after bull position opened). Very disappointed
by failure to get elected as vice-chairman Defence Committee, so
scrapped speech on cuts; very low and disconsolate feeling while
Geoffrey Pattie[1] swept into secretary-ship.

Meanwhile down at Bratton beautiful cob barn almost beyond
repair with tin roof flapping and water running down and wasting
away the cob. I just don't have the time to spruce up Bratton – and
what's the point anyway? Broomhayes must have a higher priority. In
the defence of the empire it's like Australia – ie sentiment, but no
economic or power reasons.

Plymouth still bickering and whispering. Larry Speare now gone,
Derek Priston temporarily in the ascendant (I am going to have to say
something about this tonight at – ugh – the Plymstock Community
Centre). Apparently I was a bit 'sneery' (!) on TV and then heard a
muddled account of how someone from Drake had been asking how
I compared with, say, Peter Mills[2] – bloody cheek.

Will make one last effort to speak in economic debate on Wednesday. Try and control activities, wait for 'turnup'.

Albany, B5 Lower   *Tuesday, 23 December*

Really flying at tree-top height with only one engine at *top of the
valley* (!) Bought a beautiful SI Hooper from Charles and had to
cheque-write today (another 3+). Also ought really to get Valeri her
coat (2), plus inspected latest tax liabilities from Meeson to cripple
the New Year. Went round to the House to make a couple of free
calls.

---

[1] Geoffrey Pattie, MP for Chertsey and Walton since February 1974 and secretary of the
   Conservative Parliamentary Aviation Committee since 1974.
[2] Peter Mills, MP for Devon West since February 1974 (Torrington 1964–74).

Saltwood   *Sunday, 28 December*

Given the fact that we are all well and fine (though self oldish – more in feeling than appearance I'm happy to believe) this is the blackest post-Christmas yet. Or should I say *bleakest*; please God don't give me a really black one!

This morning up and read *Express* before breakfast – Heseltine heavily plugged in Crossbencher and talk of 'an election in '76' (thus pre-empting any move from Plymouth – and discarding 'second preference' with Costain and Folkestone). Fact is, this year has seen a steady erosion, dissipation of the position. All I have done is survive – by familiar technique of throwing pats of butter on the surface.

> Finance – worse off; o/d only minimally better. Shares all gone, plus some lovely cars.
> Politics – no progress. Original promise worn off, 'blackballed' from Defence Committee (bungled security-slip, which Pattie seized). Again 'if only' ... I should have beavered like crazy in defence field – *every* question time, badgered Defence chiefs etc etc.

One major drain this year, looking back: how unlucky I've been at b'gammon. Resolved: NO MORE THIS YEAR (ie 76), except Aspers with 1x1 and Lever on 3-tries.

Zermatt   *Wednesday, 31 December*

Year end, and gathering strength. *Very* slight improvement in health and morale. But my personal resolution for the next Christmas: I just bloody well won't have any debts at all – but of course if intention hangs fire that won't be possible. This is the one difference from last year – Newton *is* saleable.

Sitting at my desk with a heavy heart. On top: the ineradicable, obsessional worry about money. Just what am I going to do when we get back, faced with instant outgoings like mortgage on Silks cottages, school fees, stock exchange, *plus* balance to be paid Zermatt for the delightful 2-door Shadow. Immediate decision on 'culling' rest of collection to bare minimum – but will these be dissipated, when I meant to concentrate them in the Classic car a/c? One side effect of this obsession is growing identity of salvation with Hitler in 1943, that carries with it unhappy overtones of inevitability.

1976

Central Fact finally agreed today: Hoare's insisting on a reduction [of o/d] to 100 by 1st April – ie in less than two months, effectively, from 100 + 35 + 26. Reduced me to a *total* tension blubber, with slight headache, waves of fatigue and then sudden, crazy snapping-out of it, back into realisation of possible total collapse. God knows what kind of a night I'm going to have. At least I don't drink or take pills to combat this.

Need all my energy and testosterone to cope with the Central Fact. Second occurrence, which also seemed to have a kind of pre-destinational quality in forcing me to determine life pattern was the strange accidental delivery by postman of Mama's draft will (!), 1976 model, which one opened, read, took to H of C library and photo-copied and then reposted in a WC2 pillar-box (!). It was a nasty, cold document; no bequests – other than to the British Museum and to servants; Celly got the old clothes and Col and I (it said me, but clearly a mis-print for Col) got the residue after everything (including B5) to Papa. Dealt with Col at 25% of what the other gets, but as he points out, it is an ominous indication and fact is one will get *nothing* over and above what one can steal – odd bits of silver and objects ...

Back from Plymouth, and the walk on Summerhouse Hill with Col ... This will be the week of the crunch – seeing Norman Reid[1] and Evelyn Joll[2] about sales ... also had to decide about Alma-Tadema.

Incredibly tired and lined. No strength at all it seems, and back so feeble – did some 'wooding' this morning, with the Land-Rover and back semi-went almost at once.

---

[1] Sir Norman Reid, Director of the Tate Gallery since 1964.
[2] Evelyn Joll, a director of Agnew's, the Bond Street picture dealers.

Contemplate the exhausting list of sundries ... then the enormous pile of bills – just now trumped by Meeson demanding £2,700 and the Swiss return not yet sealed still less filed with Meeson – a sword of Damocles for the autumn.

Must record the visit to the Tate last Monday. Parked 'the little white', and the Indian lady at reception made me wait, before a youngish assistant appeared and took me up a spiral staircase to the Director's landing. She studied me intently at one point and I thought, somehow, like a nurse looking at a patient going to the theatre or surgeon for examination. In the curious white ultra-modernism reception room we sat down, and in a very short time I realised that Reid was expecting me to ask more money for the Saltonstall (while I was apprehensive that he might be going to renege). So, lying, that I had been offered $100,000, ie £50,000, we went through the pretence of working out what I would save in CGT by selling to the Tate and settled at £48,000. On air I descended the spiral staircase and had a wonderful dinner at Brooks's,[1] lost £170 to Kennedy and then collapsed in bed.

Since then some misgivings and still has to go to Trustees for confirmation.

Saltwood   *Wednesday, 18 February*

Ill (today) and strangely apprehensive – as if about to panic all the time – supposing N. Reid defaults on Saltonstall? ... No more gambling or b'gammon until *out of debt*. Difficult decision, but major operation justifies it.

---

[1] The St James' Club had the previous year merged with Brooks's in St James's Street. Where the St James' was 'cosmopolitan, artistic, boisterous', Brooks's was 'old-fashioned, almost Whiggish', according to the Brooks's historian.

Saltwood   *Thursday, 19 February*

Delicious spring day, first hint of warmth in the sun after fog, and absolutely still. Charles Jerdein[1] rang to say the German would *not* pay more for Alma Tadema so deal off (I had gambled on asking for 'any' increase on £11,000), took this as a bad, bad indicator. Dread the Tate trustees procrastinating. Walked round and round the battlements in an inner panic, thinking of this beautiful place, the sale, the whole collapse. Joined by Jane; didn't communicate it to her of course, but we continued to drift about absorbing the beauty of the place. This is real torture, let us hope it is the aversion therapy. Please God see me through this.

Dean's Yard   *Tuesday, 24 February*

Cleared to the extent of the Trustees confirming Saltonstall – so that will eliminate number 2 loan with Hoare's.

Albany, B5 Lower, 6am   *Friday, 5 March*

Woke early – as one does post Zurich and listened to the delight of blackbird singing. Terribly sad that with all my pressure and odious responsibilities I am cutting myself off even from nature. Got cheque for Saltonstall, but felt sick opening envelope in the Commons' phone box. Kept thinking of the quality of the painting, the shock of the blank wall – I went into the Music Room on my return. Didn't give a fuck for the rubbish I sold Desmond (though it is vitally important he bought it), but this a bad week.

---

[1] Charles Jerdein, art dealer and friend.

Albany, B5   *Friday, 19 March*

This morning woke absolutely *frantic* about being wiped out. Balance of Saltonstall consumed in serving interest charges of £8,750. Hoare's letter yesterday morning with firm refusal to release Castle deeds; and then Mr McGrath of Hoare's on the phone asking 'what about steps' being taken to reduce no 2 loan, 'partners meeting' etc. Went to bed v. tired and woke with the knowledge that unless I can get the Saltwood deeds away from them *somehow* have got exactly six months left until next demand.

H of C Library   *Tuesday, 13 April*

Birthday boy. Woke several times in the night and with the glorious Albany blackbird looked from the mattress on the floor (my father has taken all the furniture) and this reinforced the dream of being wiped out. The bailiffs had been in and taken everything.

Fact is cash run out – nothing left to live on. Also 24 light to Hoare's limit, 44 light for release of Saltwood deeds. Get intermittent waves of panic – all my means of relieving indebtedness are in goods – supposing corporate collapse and nobody (ie Desmond and co) will *buy* goods?

Going to see Desmond now, to see what can be raised. Tortured schemes thresh around – did I do a 'scheme of arrangement' with Barclays or Clydesdale?

Strange morning – picked up by Winston in the lobby and asked to a lunch with him 'for' Averell Harriman; I think he said 'my stepfather' so may see Pam[1] again – not since the golden days in Cannes and then once, fleetingly, in the Ritz when she was with some Greeks.

These ironies please me. But God please don't let me go right under. How my health and appearance stood up to these stresses I don't know.

---

[1] Pamela Harriman (née Digby) married first Randolph Churchill, by whom she had a son, Winston, MP for Stretford since 1970. She later married the American theatrical and film producer, Leland Hayward, and, following his death in 1971, the American statesman, Averell Harriman. She became a leading light in the Democratic Party and a legendary Washington hostess.

Saltwood   *Tuesday, 20 April*

What could have been a grotesque weekend was lightened by Desmond agreeing to take another 34 of pictures and then, on Thursday eve, came a call to say Newton had sold for 40!

Friday night however strange waking with minuscule pee and faintly peppermint throat. Thought nothing of it, though frightfully tired and stiff the next day. However kept busy as we are 'opening' for the first time – though took two hours off for intensive sun bathing by greenhouse. Blushingly, at supper, I said I had 'sunstroke' temp 99.8. Poorish night. Next day struggled on gamely in 'Hadleigh'[1] clothes for public – a little Italianish girl I gave a peacock feather to – and feeling rotten. Went to bed in 'summer double', awaking intermittently with progressive deterioration – or so it seemed – 100 at 2.30am.

Saltwood   *Saturday, 24 April*

'On the mend' physically, after really awful nights of muck-sweat, minute tortured dribblings, and fear of galloping prostate cancer.

Great Hall, Saltwood   *Saturday, 1 May*

Back on the night train after the usual crowded surgery, fluffing of constituency opportunities and late, late curry dinner. Also talk of early election, *the whole bloody time*. Must write to Albert (difficult letter to compose) about Folkestone possibility.

A fine, but cold day with no disasters in the waiting post (Smiler etc), but by now feeling *incredibly tired*, it swept on me about 4pm while I was polishing the Dienst. God, what a lot of polishing there is to do on the cars. If I just polished and gardened the whole day would go by. Even so, 'much better'.

---

[1] The Clarks had been much taken by an ITV television series of that title, starring Gerald Harper as an immaculately-dressed country squire, with a Monteverdi 375L sports car and living at the stately if at times expensive to keep up Melford Park.

Albany, B5   *Tuesday, 4 May*

Another glorious morning. Does London have the finest weather in England? Always look out of that little lavatory window behind the Corinthian columns of the R.A.[1]

I had walked into Chamber last night for a minute and stood by Chair as Joel Barnett[2] was saying that 'Heritage Houses' can now also have a fund to protect them, ie if only I can do my bit, Saltwood Estate can be a candidate and passed on in perpetuity. Rushed out and phoned Jane who said '. . . it makes it all seem worthwhile'.

Later

For first time starting to feel *really* on the run. Not even getting *anything* done in politics, never going into the Chamber, cancelling three engagements in a week. Obsessed with fall of the Reich. This is 1944, one year left.

H o C Library   *Monday, 10 May*

Incredibly hot and stuffy, though sitting by open window. Today (actually took place on Saturday) one of those lucky breaks – tipped by George Hutchinson[3] for instant inclusion in 'shadow cabinet'. Suddenly felt fine, burgeoning.

Port Lympne   *Thursday, 3 June*

Drove over here to my favourite spot in the whole of E Kent – one of the most evocative in the world – and shortly to vanish for ever. I sit on the terrace where one would occasionally get tea <u>limone</u>, and indescribably thin cucumber sandwiches before being sent back up to

---

[1] The Clark apartment at Albany backs onto the Royal Academy.

[2] Joel Barnett, MP for Heywood and Royton since 1964, Chief Secretary to the Treasury since 1974.

[3] George Hutchinson, political columnist in *The Times*.

'Bellers'.[1] Can still look through the glass doors at that marbled, Moorish interior, black and white floors and arched ceilings. Totally still outside, but trees now grown enormously, hemming it in, better even than in Philip's heyday. The place has *slept* for 30 years, noone lived in it since Philip died, nothing disturbed. At any moment Philip could come out and call – to this day I can hear his drawl. And in time it will be over-run, damaged irretrievably by the tramping public with their toffee papers and the Kleenexes.[2]

As I pottered about at Saltwood this morning, realised hadn't been up to London for a week – so hadn't needed any cash. Yet cash dribbling in from public – if only 'indebtedness eliminated', could submit very happily. Will I ever emerge? I remember calmly going to Hoare's when it was 190 and trying to borrow *another* 20 to buy Selmes' car and business! Have got until October – or possibly till next April (2nd half year interest) then – explosion. Unless 'House in order' first.

H o C Library   *Monday, 14 June*

Best part of the evening was chat on terrace with Tom Swain[3] and (leftish) little northerner. This latter chappie had come up and said to Tom: 'Ah, thee's courting with the storm-troopers, eh?' That pleased me.

---

[1] Bellers, a house used by AC's family in the 1930s, was close to Port Lympne, the magnificent country home of Sir Philip Sassoon, MP for Hythe and for much of the 1930s the highly influential Under-Secretary of State for Air and chairman of the board of the National Gallery (hence his original links with the Clark family). His mother was a Rothschild. To the designs of Sir Herbert Baker, he started building Port Lympne just before the First World War, lavishing upon it his enormous knowledge of art, furniture, china and old silver. He died in 1939 after a short illness and not yet sixty. Port Lympne was commandeered by the RAF during the Second World War.

[2] AC, happily, was proved wrong. He recommended Port Lympne to John Aspinall who bought it and its 275 acres for £360,000. Aspinall restored the house and used the grounds for a zoo park to complement his original zoo near Canterbury.

[3] Tom Swain, MP for Derbyshire NE since 1959, a former miner.

Another glorious evening – every day has been fine, Friesian weather, except needless to say the two days of the weekend.

Sitting in a new perch I've discovered, theoretically allocated to a member of the staff and (tidily) congested with his gear, it is pleasingly situated in a corner, the last one before the non-smoking room, beside no fewer than three open windows, so that the lazy fresh river smells of wet varnish and tidal aromas come in together with the sounds of the chuggy engines of tugs and pleasure craft and the occasional guffaw from the terrace below.

Apparently now heading for two filthy nights of intermittent voting on Land Tax committee stage. Had a very late night last night at the Clermont after late 11.45ish 2nd vote. Ran into Benson and after shocking start 'took command' and relieved him of £160. This gave me palpable pleasure. But they do drain one, these late nights. I went home for a couple of hours and, as I lay by the pool, thought how diminished (by earlier standards) was my sexuality. Always in the past I would get erotic sensations lying out after a 'dip'. Short of food and sleep of course – that strange affliction at Easter (exactly two months ago), had something to do with it. And strange after effects, practically off alcohol for virtually six weeks.

Just a note from dinner at Saltwood for Norman Tebbit: 'Many would like you as Folkestone's next MP ...', one woman said. Jane, with her usual good sense just replied flatly: '... many wouldn't.' And certainly balance of that number hasn't necessarily shifted in my favour since being in 'Parly'.

Sitting, at 8.14pm, at the end of the long table, with only a towel around my waist. What a wonderful room this is! A college library, a castle library all to oneself. For the first time for at least a year (and then it was only for a few brief weeks) I do not wake early each morning and worry about money.

H of C Library   *Tuesday, 29 June*

Absolutely dead whacked by heat, swimming and commuting.
Chucked a city lunch to hang on at Saltwood (drove down last night
after the vote in the Bira with the windscreen flat and got 'stye' in
right eye).

'Daisy' came over on his way to Boulogne/St Trop with a good-
looking (G Peck, Anthony Perkins) American student. I said to him
'... God if I was that age, and looked like that *and* an MP you
wouldn't see me for steam.'

Zermatt   *Saturday, 4 September*

Out here in poor shape. Really *alarmed* at appearance last night. Yet
again trying the Zapata moustache, which adds to haggardness. What's
the point? On arrival got letter from UBS in the C. Hoare & Co style
wanting Sw FR 17,000 immediately, and this morning opened (quite
by chance) something from La Suisse apparently noticing that house
had not been insured since April and premium of 1,200 Sw overdue.

Also a little depressed about leaving James at home – as he is
himself. Going through one of those phases – only gets excited when
talking about aeroplanes – of which he is incredibly knowledgeable,
better even than I was in 1939. Mercedes 300 car ran badly, roughly
at best (though no Mercedes is ever completely perfect to drive). Sad?
Next year will probably be in Citroen convertible. James rather
gloomily said 'our cars get shabbier and shabbier'.

Zermatt   *Monday, 6 September*

Politically an autumn of application. Allotted three committees:
finance, home affairs, defence. Work required in constituency
minimum to keep it in play until April/May – ie unlikely actually
wanting to sack me before next election or, slightly less easy, seeking
to give a reasonable reference. If APC[1] quits [Folkestone] in January

---

[1] AC's journal code for Albert Costain.

will put in, the die is cast. If he fights next election so will I – he can't
fight on after that, so the question of the new boundaries doesn't
really apply anyway.

Genuinely excited and keen to get back to the House. Ladbroke
apparently giving *evens* on a coalition by 1st Jan. I *must* lay against that.
Tories all chattering and yearning about an early election. Personally
I don't see it. Why? How can it come about? PMs' call elections
when they think they are going to win, not in order to commit hari
kari. But the gossip and *jockeying* will be fun.

Albany   *Wednesday, 13 October*

Was sipping my EMT and reading *Chips* (for 3rdor 4th time) and got
to bit when – 4 November 52 – he recalled Eisenhower's victory in
US Presidential Election. Remember on that same 'box-spring', on
which I have entertained Pam, Drew, Renny, Marge etc, hearing the
news on that same day in '52 with feelings of disgust (was I more
Liberal in those days?).[1] Reflected really that my life style hardly
altered, I mean still chasing girls and still in debt.

Back at the House, usual cock-up on voting. Whipped at 3.30, but
first vote at 7.45pm. As a result lost £96 to Charles at Coys.

Dined with Robin Cooke,[2] sparkling, in the Harcourt Room.
Good food, interesting – although younger than me he has been in
the House with Mac and Chips.[3] Seemed sanguine enough about his
chances to move on to South Dorset, but Associations are such shits.[4]
Little chat with APC in the lobby – he enigmatically withholding as
always – said my 'image' is against me, among locals etc. New Association elections in March and 'clean sweep' coming. 'Lucky him!'
Jane brightly quipped, 'people will just play musical chairs.' Robin

---

[1] In an entry for 4 November 1980, AC adds: 'at the time I was a Stevenson supporter,
faintly rebellious and reading, not very successfully, bar finals.'
[2] Robert [Robin] Cooke, MP for Bristol West, since 1957.
[3] Harold Macmillan retired as Bromley's MP in 1964; Sir Henry ('Chips') Channon died
in 1958 while MP for Southend West.
[4] AC showed prescience in this entry; Cooke was not selected for S. Dorset, even though
the retiring MP was his father-in-law, Evelyn King. He only returned to Parliament
as Special Advisor on the Palace of Westminster to the Secretary of State for the
Environment. S. Dorset chose Lord Cranborne as its candidate.

Cooke said: 'In a summer of a bygone age ... and so even you, if it comes to that.'

Yes, and so soon after the excitement of returning feel totally flat and neglected. Nobody speaks to me, no invitations, people seem to avoid my eye in the lobby.

Perhaps all that Robin said to me and what Chips wrote about England dying.[1] And yet ... I think of James and Andrew, the young who could still be taken. What is the key?

H of C Library   *Wednesday, 10 November*

Still feeling incredibly tired – constantly having to catch breath. Aftermath of heavy head-cold over weekend; late nights – H Lever last night £100 – travelling, missing meals etc.

Yesterday filthy nadir (hopefully). (1) Took deadly dose of Rontgens at fucking Panoramachest x-ray. Wanted to get up and go when bloody titty nurse in immaculate white overalls put on huge lead caps and went behind screen, but was already too tired to do so. (2) letter telling me of F&GP [at Sutton]: trouble about not answering letters and Nan Howard[2] took this up (! Groan). (3) Great 'out' as Desoutter collapsed and either lose £3000 or take them up – UGH!

Plymouth: my God! With memory of Robin Cooke in my mind, must wait until after AGM and then systematically court Folkestone officers. If 'snap' election would get in for Plymouth, if not then Folkestone option must be taken. Total shits they are – no purpose in life other than to bicker and backbite – degrade everything above a certain level of mediocrity.

---

[1] 8 May 1952: 'The England I wooed and won and love still, is dying; thus I am determined to enjoy what remains to me of it and of life here: the few declining years, the few rapidly diminishing thousands of pounds; if I survive the collapse of the country or of my personal fortune, I shall slip off to some remote part of sun-lit California to die – on my American income, so far untouched, or rather unimpaired. Perhaps I can look for another five years.' (*Chips: The Diaries of Sir Henry Channon.*)

[2] Mrs H.O'N. Howard, chairman of Sutton's Dunstone ward.

Saltwood   *Sunday, 14 November*

Very nice last night and woken this morning about 8am by banging noises at main door. 'Lady Clark died last night'. Jane and I dressed quickly, hoping to beat Col. Found my father 'in tremendous form' wiping mouth with back of hand, having just eaten brown egg and grapefruit, little tray in library.

Spoke briefly and inconclusively, then next went in to see Mama, signalling to Jane *not* to come. Apprehensive about pulling back the sheet, but found her face composed, determined, rather beautiful, not in any way distorted (my father had quite unnecessarily, and alarmingly, said, ' ... the body does undergo certain changes by now ... etc') Jane came in, and as we agreed about her expression – Jane said 'she hasn't given up' – I started briefly crying and she also.

Went back to breakfast. Rang Celly and put her mind at rest about Mama's appearance. Then Col – he wouldn't come over. Changed into black and went up to Cenotaph on green where Jane meant to be laying wreath. Small crowd expected. Jane did her stuff quite well and I spoke to a few (prospective) constituents. Back, briefly to GH, where Father turned up, looking like death warmed up.

After spaghetti lunch snoozed on upright sofa in green room while Jane went over to GH to keep Celly company and (apparently) go through the jewellery. She ran back after an hour – I had woken, washed my face – with a few very insignificant items. We took a walk, much plagued as usual on Sundays by ogling, loutish public who won't say 'Good afternoon' even. After a good tea, Col arrived. We chatted a bit and I walked him up and down, explaining that he won't get anything, as my Father will block my mother's estate and leave his own to his new wife.[1] This made Col very gloomy (later that evening he rang and said he had spoken to Celly about the will and it was a c1971 model!).[2]

My father came over for dinner, shuffling but compos. Only drank 'a little claret', talked, but without much warmth. Wonder how long he will last? Rang Jamie late. He was a bit low, and made lower by news of Granny. Dear Boy, how I love him. God please protect us.

---

[1] AC was in no doubt that his father would remarry and soon.

[2] In a later note he added that he had just read his mother's last will (sent by the Clydesdale): 'She did leave everything to me ... the fact that she did so is a tremendous liberation for me ... the way in which she died fills us with grief and affection.'

Train to Waterloo *Saturday, 20 November*

After three days feeling really awful, incredibly tired – out-of-breath (radiation disease?); utterly depressed by present condition, nullity of will, futility of H of C, losses on SE, bolshiness of Hoare & Co, and bloodiness of Plymouth constituency.

Shadow Cab 'shuffle' still giving hope, as Heseltine not promoted.

Albany, B5 *Wednesday, 8 December*

Very depressed by end-of-an-era symptom. Fucking H. Lever quite batted me to bits. I lost £350 between 6 and 9pm. I don't say I'll give the game up. But I *must* prove I'm not addicted, so will see how long I can go. Euphoria of Home Affairs Committee victory already wearing off. (Good publicity, plus photo, in *Evening Herald* will just infuriate Plymouth schemers rather than conciliate them). Really, the top priority should be devoted to politics. I'm just not being single-minded enough. I'm using the House as a kind of club/ringside seat/status enhancer, *not* as a central mission.

1977

A YEAR OF TRAVAIL

Indebtedness:	Saltwood to Trust for Jane etc
	Pension Fund
Politics:	Pamphlet on law and order as CPC booklet
B'Gammon:	REDUCED RATION (£64 a week)
Girls:	Mens (presumably) – in cupo sano. Yoga
	[mens sana in corpore sana]

Zermatt   *Saturday, 1 January 1977*

Sometimes gloomily see myself as Hemingway, 'Ernst' in Hotchner book.[1] Best years gone by etc. But at least I don't drink. Seem, in fact, strangely, suspiciously fit and non-tired compared with dragged out days at the House.

What can I do about the House? This year I must have a go. It is impossible to get called. [Speaker] Thomas simply will *not* notice me.

I must –
(a) plan questions seriously. Defence. Home. Foreign. Europe. Chancellor. PM – all got edges. Now I have no excuse for lack of confidence, or fucking sarcasm for that matter.
(b) Sit in for every Question Time until Easter Recess.

This is last chance for 'impact'. It is 1977. Pretty bullish year, three books to write, and Saltwood to improve. Something's got to give and I suppose it will be b'gammon and sex – with the blondes away.

Saltwood Library   *Sunday, 16 January*

Eight days back and peculiar 'improvements'. Are they attributable to that head or helmet that I bought at Christie's? Decided last night that it was bringing me luck following Jane recounting to me (on the phone on Tuesday night) her curious experience of hearing the Yellow

---

[1] A.E. Hotchner's *Papa Hemingway*, an account of the author's friendship with the American writer, had been widely acclaimed.

Room door opening in the middle of the night and lying frozen in terror. The next day she moved the head *into* the Yellow Room thinking (quite rightly) that it might have been trying to communicate. We both agreed how 'powerful' it is. And who knows it might – there is no reason why not that I know – have been here in the past.

What an incredible, marvellous, romantic place Saltwood is, and how I am wedded to it. I must have a little *cache* at Zermatt just in case, a few period things, a kind of mothball fleet in Northern California or Canada, but my roots are here in this glorious piece of English medieval history.

Anyhow, events: done a lot of car-trading and full of enjoyment at this. Hoping to make money by setting up a Sothebys sale and also building up of a private trading stock of mascots etc.

Had a big win off CH plus a series of little, canny ones from 'the school' so comfortably in surplus for first week (£252). And Jerdein offered 11.6 for the Alma-Tadema! On top of this a 'cunning' talk with Sam Alder and he offered 27 for Woodfall St!!

Albany, B5   *Thursday, 27 January*

There are few nicer things than sitting in bed, drinking up strong Indian tea, and reading Chips' diaries – which loosen the mind, and cause reflection. Just reached (or rather re-reached for the umpteenth time) that passage when he has been caught out, and Rab gone to Education, '. . . a bad mistake',[1] Chips thought, wrongly, and how the Commons seemed to have changed focus. But concerned to see that Chips of 44 felt himself alone and still more by his reference to Richard Wood as Halifax's 'immense auburn young subaltern'.[2]

There he was in the proportional representation debate yesterday on his gammy leg on the front bench below (my place). Don Pontificatore. 'It's all balls, isn't it?' I said to Tony Fell,[3] who was sitting on the cross-bench on the Labour side within earshot of Dennis

---

[1] 18 July 1941: 'Winston offered him the Board of Education which he accepted willingly. A mistake, I think, as he is now in a back-water.' (*Chips: The Diaries of Henry Channon*, edited by Robert Rhodes James.)

[2] 14 September 1943. Wood, MP for Bridlington since 1950, was the second son of Chamberlain's foreign secretary, Lord Halifax. He had been wounded in action later in 1943 and retired aged 23.

[3] Anthony Fell, MP for Yarmouth (Norfolk) since 1970 (also 1951–66).

Skinner. 'Yes, the most total utter bloody crap,' he answered. Both Skinner and Wood tittered.

Saltwood   *Sunday, 6 February*

Watched Enoch on TV – quite by chance. Jane spotted that he had already been on for fifteen minutes. Quite wonderful. His clarity of speech and thought, his administrative experience, his living and incomparable patriotism and they ignore him. I remember that after one of my articles in the *Telegraph* Dennis Skinner said to me – 'you'll end up in despair, like me.'

Speaking to the Folkestone YCs on Monday. Will I be able to get Folkestone? If I do, that will be the real temptation in the wilderness. Because I can either be the local squire, ringside seat, boring buffer, or go flat out with a secure base at last, having learned all my lessons from the last few years.

Billy Wallace died of cancer . . . aah.[1]

East Cloisters   *Wednesday, 9 February*

Sitting in my new desk at E. Cloisters after losing £88 to Charles at Coys (tho' still up on him this year).

Miss the blonde family[2] and being mocked on all sides. That (v. pretty) little blonde assistant to the camera team refused to be 'mistaken' and thus didn't acknowledge the dozen red roses I sent to her. Jane (Australian) said 'you're older than her Daddy.' What in hell am I going to do?

Depressed by James talking about getting his pilot's licence this summer. Oh dear! Will there never be an end to those anxieties? Quite amazingly he said: 'Grandpapa never says to *you* – '. . . you must be in by 11pm' etc.

---

[1] Billy Wallace, the millionaire son of Euan Wallace, a former MP and wartime adviser to George VI, and part of Princess Margaret's circle from the 1950s. He and AC had known each other since Eton.
[2] The coven had moved away without warning.

H o C   *Tuesday, 15 February*

Got back for Anthony's (Avon[1]) memorial service [in Westminster
Abbey]. MPs, badly treated, packed into a little side pew in the North
Lantern, while the main part was kept open until the last minute (for
whom?) then thrown open to a weird showering – mainly Palace of
Westminster staff, with a smattering of late-coming MPs, eg Pattie. I
was glad to sit next to Angus Maude in a row with Airey Neave and
Sir John Hill.[2] The old school. A few nameless slugs were there, such
as Michael Hamilton[3] who pretends (not difficult) to be very stupid.
Some days I think the Parliamentary Party is three-fifths duck-shit.
Walked back alone, aggressive, with the music of Handel's *Saul* ringing
in my ears. It's unusual, and nice, not to have heard a fine piece of
music before.

Plymouth train 7.30am   *Friday, 18 March*

Reflect on how shattered, *épuisé*, I am. It is not so long ago that with
nothing to do after tea I would go for a walk on the Hoe and do half
hour exercise in my room. My face *very* lined. Given to long periods
of lost concentration, just glazedly reflecting. Has all my physical
capital been spent? I am going through a change of life. I must not
alter. But I'm *so* low on testosterone. A beautiful new girl would put
that right – will I ever meet one?

H of C   *Wednesday, 23 March*

Appalling punishment (b'gammon) on Monday night – lost £800.
Will go and do some yoga at Albany.
    At the Bow Group dinner Heath rambled 'down memory lane'
then finally got into his theme about '... a realignment, moderate

---

[1] Anthony Eden, Earl of Avon, had not enjoyed good health since his resignation as Prime
    Minister in 1957 following Suez. He had died on 14 January.
[2] Angus Maude, MP for Stratford-upon-Avon since 1963 (Ealing South 1950–58) ; Airey
    Neave, MP for Abingdon since 1953; Sir John Hill, MP for Wycombe since 1952.
[3] Michael Hamilton, MP for Salisbury since 1965.

grouping of the centre . . .' etc. *No!* people shouted. 'Tripe!' I shouted from my traditional place at the end of the table.

Heath obviously still trying to play some cards, because I was listening to the somewhat diffuse – and halting speech by Margaret this afternoon – House v. full and she in a black suit with white collar/blouse – when Norman Lamont[1] came in and stood by me at the Bar of the House, did a 'whatsappen'd? whatsappen'd?' Apparently Steel[2] interrupted his fund-raising lunch with Heath with a desperate phone call about something. Actually Callaghan,[3] blandly in command, had clearly whipped them up. I peered down the benches, was glad to see signs of receding hairline, high spots at the temples, of the odious Heseltine.

H o C   *Tuesday, 29 March*

Policeman coming up to serve summons at Brighton with possibility of optional endorsement (!!)

Total depression. Tip going to Germany tomorrow, and will miss him. Is Boy to go to Sandhurst? I couldn't arrange the visit. The way, upperclass ADC to 'Sir Philip' or 'The General'. Who are his friends going to be?

Spoke in the House last night about Air Raid Shelters (there aren't any) and frightened myself. Sat down to deafening silence. Plymouth crumbling. Will I get Folkestone? Old and grey-looking.

To add to the burden – Stradling Thomas suggested I maintained an anti P-R group in the parliamentary party. Must start catching the eye. Breathe deeply.

---

[1] Norman Lamont, MP for Kingston-upon-Thames since 1972.
[2] David Steel, MP for Roxburgh, Selkirk and Peebles since 1965; Leader of the Liberal Party since 1976.
[3] James Callaghan, MP for Cardiff South-East since 1950 (South Cardiff, 1945–50), had succeeded Harold Wilson as Prime Minister in 1976.

Saltwood   *Monday, 4 April*

My father over last night and grumpily teasing about his will – left James 'the clock' which is in Great Hall study and belongs to me anyway!

Saltwood   *Monday, 25 April*

'Boy' going back to Le Rosey.[1] Hardly seem to have seen him these hols except briefly between biking bouts, only to shout at him for being untidy or idle. Just that one pleasing half hour at Blade's after the dentist. And, I suppose, this was his last holidays as a schoolboy as I have to arrange his Sandhurst interviews etc for the autumn and his plans to go America in the summer. Exposed all this time to more and more perils – plus the obsessive desire to 'race'.

Albany   *Thursday, 28 April*

Had interview yesterday with Margaret Thatcher for first time. She sat, china-blue. Almost *too* text-book sincere. No intimacy. The half-finished sentences, the implied assumption, that mixture of Don, Colonel-of-the-Regiment, 'Library', which one gets from almost every other member of the Shadow – Pym, Willie,[2] Gilmour – even the lower rank like Paul Channon[3] and William Clark[4] – totally absent.

Actually the *point* of my call, which at one time had looked so promising was to explain that the anti-PR strength would *not* be adequate as the Labourites would not join us in the lobby. 'Only 130,

---

[1] Le Rosey, the oldest private school in Switzerland with pupils from all over the world, and, uniquely, two campuses, at Le Rolle for spring and autumn, and at Gstaad for winter.

[2] William (Willie) Whitelaw, MP for Penrith since 1955.

[3] Paul Channon, son of 'Chips', succeeded his father as MP for Southend West in 1959; deputy leader of the Conservative delegation to the WEU and the Council of Europe since 1976.

[4] William Clark, MP for Croydon South since February 1974 (E Surrey, 1970–74), joint deputy chairman, Conservative Party Organisation since 1975.

Alan, what worries me...' 'Another 80 with you, of course,' I said and mumbled.

I also slightly fluffed it when she was talking about Callaghan's soft-centre – good for publicity, but inadequate underneath. Instead of saying 'like Heseltine', I mumbled something about 'I could mention a few like that in our party'. She looked startled. There were silences and she mentioned Defence – I half got going when we were interrupted.

H o C   *Tuesday, 21 June*

Summertime in the Library of the House; could go to bed early after some sherrys and white wine and sleep 14 hours – but instead, faced with 'until this business is concluded, which could be at a very late hour ...' so further harrowing of the body.

Still shampoo'd my hair at Albany after an All-bran box there on return from a day out to Seend. Oh how Cherry Cottage has been exposed, its character altered, by the loss of the Great Elms in the clump. I pottered about in the orchard, *recherché du temps perdu* as always at Seend, thinking of the high spots – my happiest period.

Had my triumph in the House last week – getting both sides to laugh at my 'quip' as the *Telegraph* called it about 'anyone who has been to Eton ... has already served the equivalent of five years in gaol.'[1] Actually, of course, it was really Miscampbell's[2] idea and I just moved fast enough. Miscampbell put it out during Heffer tirade; I gathered courage during Molloy's[3] follow-up and then stood – as I was close the Speaker called me, almost in surprise – it really was a piccolo triumph, *prolonged* laughter with people leaning down the benches to congratulate me, and so on. A little H of C moment.

---

[1] To which Merlyn Rees, the Home Secretary replied: 'There is one difference – in prison they learn to read and write.'
[2] Norman Miscampbell, MP for Blackpool North since 1962.
[3] William Molloy, MP for Ealing North since 1964.

Albany B5   *Tuesday, 12 July*

Ex-morning tea and reasonably euphoric – though *mouvementé*.

Must record the drive back in THEBUS, splendid on Autoroute and Alp alike, even though grossly loaded with dear 'Boy's' kit, stereo etc. The great, unusual heat of the Le Rosey garden party (certain shades of Verdon Hill in *Hemlock and After*[1]) with Boy going round getting his book signed by his chums ... 'See you ... keep in touch ... etc etc ...' The dress standard bum-boys. David Niven[2] *very* well preserved. Certain beautifully-dressed beauties.

Back at Saltwood, Le Rosey inflections already fading, though having given him, as he rightly said after going into Blades on his own, total confidence.

That week was, of course, the week of the heatwave. I say 'of course' because I was locked into the standing committee on Bill Benyon's Abortion Bill. Curtains drawn to shield us from the sun, endlessly Zombie-like, eating the occasional rock-cake in the corridor or muck-sweating making phone calls from that little, very open phone there.

At night sleeping, perhaps too much absentee sleeping, in committee room 7 where I had found a tiny curved leather armchair, and putting two others in a row could make a sort of couch. Woken in the night by muffled bangings and clatterings and at dawn found that Dr Jeremy Bray, of wealth tax fame (he appeared to be suffering from hay fever)[3] had built up a camp bed in the corner. Every two hours or so we were roused by the amiable but somewhat limited poison-dwarf Ian Campbell (Lab)[4] 'on whip' who kept going on whisky.

Saltwood, Great Hall Study   *Thursday, 11 August*

First actual day of the hols! ie weekday, fine, and *not* having to go up on the 2.52, or whatever. Did some dictating – including writing a personal letter of apology to little Mrs Williams of Bernice Terrace,

---

[1] Angus Wilson's 1952 novel.
[2] David Niven, the actor, lived in Switzerland and had daughters at the school.
[3] Jeremy Bray, MP for Motherwell since October 1974 (Middlesbrough West 1962–70).
[4] Ian Campbell, MP for Dunbartonshire West since 1970.

who I had shouted at in surgery last Friday. Then did Villa Mauresque getaway by the pool.

After tea I walked with Jane into Ann's valley. I looked at the long, burgeoning August countryside. Trees absurdly overblown, grass long and with pale brown seed pods, everything dry and felt calm – no real anxieties except 'Boy'; but just a whiff of afternoon of one's life. Stiff, energy still down, totally disenchanted. The coven disappeared, and no chance of 'getting off with' anyone else – not to that extent anyhow! And even the coven don't send one, make one's heart thump, like they used to.

Twenty years. On – I shall be 69, rising to become a sage (I do hope I have grandchildren). Back – it was 1957. The year I went bankrupt for the first time and the Clydesdale refused to cash my cheque. I was sleeping with R. (intermittently) and subsisting, no more, at 11 Watchbell Street. At some point I remember being interviewed for a job as a British Leyland salesman in Los Angeles. But of course I was hopelessly 'boyish'. Even after we were married, I used to go to Hastings and prance up and down the promenade trying to pick up girls.

At any rate, I must hold my physique now: see how much I can recover in this long recess and try not to slip back.

Saltwood   *Saturday, 27 August*

C. Hoare & Co letter this morning – always sent to spoil one's weekend. Debts now total £80,000 AGAIN.

Reading David Irving's brilliant, stylish but scholarly biography of Hitler.[1] I remember in that curious white living room of his flat with all its files and things the only time we met when he told me – 'there won't be a dry eye at the end of my next book'. Certainly I find it very unsettling.

---

[1] *Hitler's War* had just been published.

Zermatt   *Sunday, 4 September*

Returned from a great 24 hrs journey to the Mettelhorn with Cin.
He was superb (though nearly collapsed on the initial ascent last night
to Trift) – made the tent, cooked the food, supervised the fires. It was
lovely in the tent – though disappointingly ramshackle as usual. A
long, long climb to the summit – five hours and the last steps on the
Tower were torture. At the peak I twice dropped off in Rodin's
'thinking' position. Got a 'suntan' walking back across the snowfield.

Albany   *Saturday, 12 November*

Saturday morning, a pre-breakfast, post 'Chips', waiting to catch the
11.30 – is there one on a Saturday morning in winter? – for Plymouth
and 'on the spot' ego-fest by County Councillor Lake, as she calls
herself, in Cattedown followed by business-woman dinner black tie
at Duke and Armistice Service. *Oh* how these fucking Plymouth
things drain one (as Heseltine warned me they would). As I sit here
now, decided finally to make the announcement almost immediately
after the next election that will not stand again there. This should give
me three minimum more years without these pressures. Catch is,
what if Albert [Costain] makes last-minute announcement *this* time.
Personally I don't think he will, is chattily delivered to become deputy
speaker or something.[1]

On Sunday we were committed, somewhat reluctantly, to go to
the Dedication of Standards service and general ceremonies in Hythe
(British Legion). Actually it was lovely. Uplifting service – brilliant
address by new vicar of St Leonards: 'Old men dream dreams; young
men see visions', and he recited the names off the monuments and
then the battle honours. Afterwards to the new BL hall – a piece of
cake, as I said to Jane. The sort of thing one would have sat eight
hours in the Plymouth train to do and all one had to do is to climb
back into the Land-Rover and drive for five minutes!

Thursday a little House of Commons episode: I had my nomination
paper for Secretary of Home Affairs and wanted two signatures. House

---

[1] In fact Costain fought another election (1979) and only retired from Folkestone in 1983.
His successor was none other than Michael Howard (see entry 12 May 1972).

virtually deserted, but saw Mayhew, Brooke, Rhodes J and Cope[1] having a jolly dinner; wished I could have joined them instead of being stuck with Oscar Murton[2] who told me at great length about his wife's death from cancer.

Got up and interrupted them and waved my paper. Some badinage (as I thought). Cope signed reluctantly, Rho J to my amazement, actually *wouldn't*, shuffled and said something about 'I've signed so many already, I can't remember' etc, passed it to Brooke who was just preparing an excuse when Mayhew came to my rescue and signed with a flourish.

I thought I had good relations with Rho J. Two historians together in the House. Mystified. It's always hard to realise how many people hate/are jealous/turned off/by me.

'Winter Desk' East Cloisters   *Thursday, 17 November*

Last night as I was talking with Paul Channon in the lobby I noticed how strangely *shiny*, high gloss one might say, were the insides of his ears.

Short-sighted, I looked closer first one side then the other thinking he was wearing some kind of plastic, 'concealed' deaf aid. Apparently not.

Later, driving to the 10 o'clock vote I saw the aftermath of a horrible accident in Piccadilly. The ambulance parked *against* the traffic, by the dreaded St James' Club Island, where the intermittent screech of brakes would disturb one's nights in those front rooms. The stretchers and the red blankets: I was reminded of this now hearing the late night sirens of rushing police cars – that sound always makes me conscious, I ask myself 'where are the boys?'

---

[1] Patrick Mayhew, MP for Tunbridge Wells since February 1974; Peter Brooke, MP for Cities of London and Westminster since a by-election in February 1977; Robert Rhodes James, editor of AC's beloved *Chips*, and MP for Cambridge since 1976; John Cope, MP for South Gloucestershire since February 1974.

[2] Oscar Murton, MP for Poole since 1964, Deputy Speaker 1976–79. His wife had died earlier that year.

Saltwood   *Sunday, 4 December*

I took the train down to Plymouth, where it was mildly cold and was glad of the Winter Car, MoT'd by Mumford. At surgery was rung by Linda Bertram (always one of the 'never-seem-to-see-you' brigade) who said that 'they' had all been waiting at the Blue Peacock (wherever the hell *that* is) for me to turn up and do some canvassing for Eileen Smith at Efford. How was I to know? 'Oh, we thought you'd come into the office and pick up the message.' One more black spot chalked up. The constituents took up my time; then, again, Mr Johnson came in for a chat, a serious chat (I still haven't done *last* fortnightly surgery bumf!). What with Linda Bertram's phone call – she finally pinned me down to do *walkabout* – ugh!! – all next Saturday morning, and a little fireman[1] I had noticed sitting rather resentfully in the waiting room with his tall but attractive wife in her head-scarf, I was late getting to the Duke – no time for a bath – for the CPC dinner. Bought a comb from the receptionist and gloomily inspected my stubbly face – fortunately my battery razor was in the suitcase for a quick chopping for the next meeting – and went ashen-faced down to Room 31 (the original interview room for stage 1 of the Sutton Selection Committee).

I wasn't absolutely happy about it from the start. A little red wine (I drank as much as I could of this). Of course I spotted immediately the shit one – something about each ward electing a representative to liase between the Member and his constituents. I 'good-naturedly' suggested that it should be discussed at the F&GP or the Executive. The session rumbled on, after a bit getting somewhat perilously philosophical with my talking about the Conservatives being the party of appeasement, and 'declaring' for the National Front – I got *so* irritated by Kay Mansfield trying to say we were going to lose votes to the NF – 'there won't be a candidate against me,' I said. She still didn't get the point. '... because they know I'm the nearest thing they're ever likely to get to an MP.'

Little Jack Courtney made a kind of grumpy comment about not trying to ride two horses at once. However this thing had almost dragged to its close and the chairman was just about to start, did in fact mumble 'Ladies and Gentlemen ...' when Jack got up and 'straight-forwardly' said he wanted to refer to 'Question Seven' – I

---

[1] Firemen were on their first nationwide strike in support of pay claim.

couldn't believe my ears when he went much further than I thought
possible (although I knew it was going to be bad) – said I visited the
constituency 'so seldom' etc etc. Massive and flagrant. Asked for more
walkabouts. I suppose I didn't defend myself as well as I might have
done. Noone rushed to defend me from the floor, I might say. I should
have said I've been there every weekend since the recess. I had been
talking for quarter hour and all I wanted to do was scream 'fuck off
you little runt ...' and leave Plymouth never to return. That's Mt
Gould down the plug. It is probably the result of a whispering
campaign to denigrate me by comparison with Janet.[1] At first I
thought because it made it easier for Janet to shine, lately I realise so
that Janet can slide across and take my place in the redrawn boundaries.
Ha Ha! I just can't wait for the election to be over and I can bugger
home for keeps.

Fact is there isn't a single person I can trust. Even John Dobell[2]
looked slightly distant and remote, though proper and 'correct'. The
fact is, they've decided I was not getting publicity, sorry *impact*, from
the first moment, and nothing I will do will alter that. I had noticed
that little rat-skunk Courtney standing awhile on the steps of the
Duke when I arrived, and something *told* me that he was being
conspiratorial in some way. Haven't seen you for months, he kept
saying. Perhaps my irritation showed as I mocked him lightly about
catching cold. Anyway, things will never be quite the same. Will I just
be able to hold out through till the election? Yes, probably, because I
have (a) recourse to a special meeting (b) threat of standing against as
anti-common market/NF.

Albany   *Friday, 9 December*

Been v depressed these last few days. So much to do. My briefcase
goes back and forth on the train, stuffed and gasping with endless
little folded bits of paper many of them, I don't doubt, dealing with
engagements and grievances that I am missing and ducking.

---

[1] Janet Fookes, MP for Plymouth Drake since 1974 (Merton and Morden, 1970–74).
[2] John Dobell, sometime chairman of the Sutton Conservative Association and chief whip
of the Conservative group on Plymouth City Council, he had parliamentary ambitions,
trying unsuccessfully to gain the party nomination for both Drake and Devonport.

Real sadness is that some of the *taste* is going from things I like. This is a sign of age. Saltwood itself, early morning tea, the cars. Only the House retains its unique appeal, the Chamber, the tea-room, good company at dinner (as last night with Gow and Straubenzee). Left preparation of my speech on pay and conditions far too late – usual story. Margaret will be there, but entries must take priority. Actually would have been totally low, but call from the coven this morning gave nig burst of adrenalin.

Duke of Cornwall Hotel, Plymouth   *Saturday, 10 December*

Feeling (and looking) v old and creaky. Looked at old entries a year back and saw *nothing* really achieved in House (in fact lost ground, in a 'disappointment' on PR). A year gone by, and older. Still owe about 40 plus fearful Zermatt debts and no books tackled at all.

John Dobell calling for special meeting of Executive Council to 'question me about my attitude to the National Front.' Gach!

1978

Frightful pain in arm and wrist – those evening attacks are now the norm though, touch wood, nights are not so bad.

Rang 'Boy' and not too happy about him. In fact, there's a good 'Boy' scare building up: he was talking 'yeh man' to such an extent that I had to reprimand him – 'don't use that "y'know" interjection ...' etc. He was cross at the prospect of coming back to go to the Rolls-Royce school (I thought I was so clever in getting him into an early vacancy there after their putting one off until July) – but for the first time, particularly when signing off, his voice lacked that special spontaneous affection – 'God bless you too', which I can still hear him say when he was at Rosey even, and in other places.

Rang Jane immediately, and of course she remembered it too from *her* conversation with him last Sunday. The gulf had opened. 'We've become parents,' I said, instead of family, elder bro or sister. I might be wrong. He might recover, snap out of it. Oh dear I said (speaking to Jane), 'much love to Tip.' Good old Tip ... 'I know what you *mean*,' she said. 'Oh dear, let's hear no more.' God, how I wish that we could.

Perhaps I'm being punished for my total indifference to my poor father's plight (into Sister Agnes today for a prostatectomy, and still under the anaesthetic).

Just back from Oxford after talked to small – later grew larger – audience of Monday Club in upstairs room at Union. Kept thinking of Saltwood, Jane and all's well, and almost immediately the sudden pain of the realising Jane in Spain (Bertie[1] died last night), and Tip quite alone with Nanny. No warmth, no decent food then. Got to see my father tomorrow. Apparently he is 'somewhat muddled', and already overshadowed by Nolwen, who has grey water.[2]

---

[1] Jane's father.
[2] Nolwen, Countess de Janzé, who had married Lord Clark the previous year.

Saltwood   *Sunday, 29 January*

General condition no better. Concentration and creative ability much inhibited, also my *cold hand*. I love this damp new weather, don't object to it at all, but no strength to do anything.

Did at least get over the hurdle of the Executive Council meeting where Radford Ward (who else?) were to raise the question of my attitude to the National Front. It was one of those evenings that might have gone nasty if I had played along with their rules, ie let myself get into a flap and on the defensive. There was a slight – no, more than slight – atmosphere of lion-taming, if not witch-hunt. Fortunately I had got there in time to get my 'pulls' of the 'report-back' leaflet from the printer and these distributed on people's chairs so could first 'defuse' the situation by referring to these.

I noticed, throughout this earlier phase, an unknown figure *not* smiling or unbending at all and obviously in a state of extreme nervous suppressed attention. Finally he put, extremely gravely, his question about 'what is the Party's attitude to ... that disease ... the National Front?' I dodged it, by citing my election to the Home Affairs Committee, and the meeting broke up, some relieved, some thwarted.

Earlier, at my surgery, two real NF members had come in, for a chat. And I thought how good they were, and how brave is the minority, in a once great country, who still keep alive the tribal essence.

Met Boy at the station last night, and quite marvellous he looked in his belted Kardigan bought that morning at 'Drakes' and having globally travelled back by Swissair, bronzed and strong. But the fact is, he's 'gone'. This year he's suddenly discovered his independence, all in a total rush, far more than at Rosey, or more than the time we left him behind at Zermatt. He wants to go back there and then to South Africa where he thinks he will make his fortune (I have to keep stopping to hold my hand to warm it up – shades of Gavin Maxwell)[1] and so one has accepted this – I don't, can't, any longer allow myself to fuss all the time that he's out and away and so on. I mean at this moment he's driving up to London in the Datsun, and formerly I'd have been scared stiff; now I'm just numb.

---

[1] The author Gavin Maxwell (*Ring of Bright Water*) suffered endless symptoms of ill-health, including circulatory problems.

Saltwood   *Sunday, 12 February*

I just said to Jane – 'will there ever be a moment, a long lazy tranquil moment when lying in a chaise-longue (by a slip of the tongue I said wheel-chair) I can laughingly read through these terrible gloomy winter entries?'

'Not till you retire from Parliament,' she said.

'But what if I have to retire from ill-health?'

Saltwood   *Thursday, 23 February*

Had a bad night and rang Jane for Peter Morrison's 'new' osteopath – 'Johnnie Johnson' – thought, give him a try. Fighting a latent cold with Redoxon. Tracked him down at his block of flats at Peckham. He's an American (baldish) and in one of those Dr Kildare half white jackets. A very long session in which he produced every magical 'click' and a great deal of flannel. One very effective double-click of the neck side-ways. Lizard-eyes, wouldn't look one in the face.

Had a bath after the 11 o'clock vote and an intermittent night – fraught with anxiety at total seizing up again. Johnson had diffused the pain, but not reduced its intensity potential. Felt really awful this morning. Twice (once at Albany, once after getting to House) seriously thought of ringing Jane, getting her to come up to drive me down.

Later

I see my father and Nolwen taking a walk, and see myself in the main – 'waxen-facedly lying and inoperable.'

Please please God make me better soon.

Saltwood   *Wednesday, 8 March*

Tip talked to me thoughtfully about his exams. Today we had a letter from G, following his careers interview. I felt almost faint reading it, sickish. Talk of 'asthma may effect his entry into the Para Regt' etc. Don't want him to be blighted by asthma, and don't *really* want him to go into the Parachute Regt. Ideally would like him to have a marsh farm, I suppose.

Bratton   *Saturday, 18 March*

A sad melancholy – accentuated by accumulated fatigue.

I went to see Rowntree [London doctor] on Tuesday, 'You're playing your last card' said Jane, smiling; saw him at 6pm after a *very* bad day, stab pains, longish bouts of 'nerves' 99° temperature etc. He very splendid and calming, confirmed Beth's[1] diagnosis of 'bronchial nevritis' and prescribed heavily, saying if not better in 10 days – take a month off(!)

Felt better at once, of course, and went and bombed at Brooks's; two v. good days. Yesterday had to drive down from London via Plymouth on constituency matters and today very sleepy and aching and *looking awful* with the vile and ludicrous Primrose Ball hanging over us. Had felt so good that seriously contemplated Zermatt for Easter – but today not so sure, as deep, though remote, shoulder ache and cold had shown that all was not well. For the first time in the mirror, *qualitative* changes – most notably shape of body and shoulders (positively remedial) and hair at side – frizzled and sprouting, not sleek.

Depressed too, by something Rowntree said about Mama's 'awful last illness' – and suddenly realised she had committed suicide – hence all the notes and the tidy way it was done. Presumably got the medicine to do it via Kathy or what, I don't know. So even that last sneer was unjustified.

Here, barn falling down, garden neglected – though roof and interior of farmhouse still v. good. But no passage to the old 'nursery' wing and our double. Just the players, and the distant memory of 'Bubbington'[2] lying gurgling with pleasure at being called in the morning, and the dreaded change-over from Farex to orange-juice!

On Thursday in the Commons realised that I was being virtually ignored. 'Messed alone' at dinner and watched Marcus Kimball[3] being

---

[1] Beth Evans-Smith, friend and physiotherapist.
[2] Nickname for James when he was a baby.
[3] Marcus Kimball, MP for Gainsborough since 1956.

dined at Humphrey Atkins' table. That serene corporate instinct which the House unfailingly exercises acknowledged fact that since return (ie Christmas) I have done NOTHING.

Saltwood   *Thursday, 23 March*

Back this evening after a 'day trip' to Norwich to do a discussion with Neil Kinnock[1] in *Arena* (Anglia TV).

NK talked virtually non-stop on the way back. Has a high opinion of himself, but was non-specific about his views for reforming the Labour movement/party. Wants to make changes, but is, I suspect, being gradually checked by the system. Claims to have been offered office three times and contested his reaction with that of Bob Cryer.[2] Said PM was temporarily under Jay's influence,[3] and that Jay got Owen his job rather than the other way round.[4] We discussed Labour's performance. According to NK, 'in leadership contests the Right always wins' (what about Wilson?). Said if Callaghan won another term he would groom his successor – either Owen or Will Rodgers, or possibly someone called Cunningham[5] who I don't even know by sight.

Health would be steadily rising if Barham [doctor] hadn't phoned yesterday and said for insurance purposes he had to 'submit a report' to the Norwich Union – did I mind? With a sinking feeling, I said: 'I've got nothing to conceal'. 'Just that trouble with your constituents,' he reminded me. So was now gloomily waiting for either (a) refusal from Norwich or (b) request for 'fuller examination' of prostate etc.

---

[1] Neil Kinnock, Labour MP for Bedwellty since 1970. A rising young star of the party, who was about to be elected for the first time to Labour's National Executive.

[2] Robert Cryer, Labour MP for Keighley since February 1974.

[3] Peter Jay, son of Douglas Jay, Labour MP (for Battersea North since 1946) and former Minister, had been appointed British ambassador in Washington in May 1977; the Prime Minister was, coincidentally, his father-in-law.

[4] David Owen, MP for Devonport since 1974 (Sutton 1966–74) was Minister of State at Foreign and Commonwealth Office when he was surprise choice as Foreign Secretary in 1977, following the death of Anthony Crosland.

[5] David Owen, and William Rodgers, Labour MP for Stockton North, would quit the Labour Party as two of the 'Gang of Four' who founded the Social Democratic Party in 1981 (the others were Shirley Williams and Roy Jenkins); Jack Cunningham, Labour MP for Whitehaven since 1970.

Saltwood   *Saturday, 25 March*

This evening feeling not to bad 'in myself', took 2CV down to St
Leonards to see when Easter Services and if possibility of a really early
communion. Church empty, though warm and light. Walked about,
read prayers, said a brief contemplative prayer. Realised that at 50 *must*
have 'affairs in order', a conference at which I can explain whole
thing to Jane and James and Andrew. Especially <u>no o/d</u>. Why do I
still shrink from this?

Saltwood   *Friday, 7 April*

'Supervising' darling Jane clearing out the pool today. Will I ever
again bronzedly be leaping in and out?

Saltwood   *Monday, 24 April*

Yesterday quite good, and played piano in evening.
    Today Barham came, listened, pronounced 'quite clear' and now
returned to question of x-ray. We could fit it in any time this week –
so why not today! Fixed, on the spot, with Dr W at St Saviours. So,
going down there this evening. In my imagination have already
compounded his explanation – non fiction, nothing to worry about.
And my reaction – resigning, selling up, being an invalid.

Saltwood   *Tuesday, 25 April*

'Cleared' by the fresh-faced and almost smiling Dr W. As I arrived at
St Saviours, parked, went up the steps and into the hospital smells, I
realised how awful to be ill, demi-terminal or declining. Best die like
Maurice[1] in one's own bed after a jolly good dinner.

---

[1] Maurice Bowra, Warden of Wadham College, Oxford, who died in 1972.

H o C Library   *Tuesday, 2 May*

Empty stomach – this bloody syndrome of not eating when away from home (compounded by crazy yellow tongue and bilious feeling due, presumably, to being on massive penicillin). Sole substance since breakfast when felt too ill to broach a fried egg, a danish bun with the blind shop steward in the cafeteria.

Ray Mawby[1] tells me the election will be on 12 October – just as well to get it over this year; Plymouth might have become too hot – but September will not be tranquil.

Vitality so diminished. Outgoings continuing to accumulate at Saltwood. Political plan obviously nil – coming up in the Summer Car this afternoon Jane said: 'How much longer are you going to be an MP? . . . . you work frightfully hard at it, you don't really seem to be getting anything out of it.' I dissimulated. How could I confess that to give up would be to discard my perennial obsession, the vision that has been with me always, the certainty that I would be called to lead?

But when one's energy goes, *one* goes.

Jane at Saltwood, nursing Angus's wound.[2] He had his tumour removed today poor darling. Why does a tumour form? And he was so well and fine. Why have the operation? Will we be faced with this dilemma? So many decisions and commitments. And time, it seems, so terribly constrained.

Saltwood   *Sunday, 7 May*

Last night 'Boy' stayed in and played the piano and the organ. Remembered his playing the organ in the pink room at Seend. At one point woke in the night with a start and noted it was his last night and full day at home before going to South Africa.[3] Monday is a hellish day for me – when do I say goodbye to Jamie?

---

[1] Ray Mawby, Conservative MP for Totnes since 1955.
[2] Angus, the Clarks' black labrador.
[3] James was to dive on the wreck of the *Sacramento*.

East Cloisters   *Wednesday, 17 May*

'Painkilling drugs' a thing of the past. Can slump in chairs, as normal; can double-click fingers of right hand; today for the first time not cold hand first thing this morning.

House Library   *Wednesday, 14 June*

Wonderfully well-feeling; colonial appearance (weight to new 'high' of $11.6\frac{1}{2}$).

Albany   *Thursday, 22 June*

At PM's Q's John Wells,[1] unexpectedly sitting on the 'Baronets' Bench', asked me bluntly if I wanted Maidstone after he'd gone. Said yes and he replied he could fix it. Would have been on air in previous times, but now ... Especially after seeing what happened to Robin Cooke. Still it allows one a little more peace of mind.

Saltwood   *Friday, 14 July*

End of line in the Commons. First Finance Bill Committee, then Devolution, endless 3-line whips in stuffy conditions. Impossible to 'get anywhere'. Yesterday in the western constituency members committee John Peyton[2] went semi-crazy when I said I was the Anti-Common Market candidate.

---

[1] John Wells, MP for Maidstone since 1959. AC was right to take the offer sceptically as Wells did not finally resign until 1987
[2] John Peyton, MP for Yeovil since 1951, Minister of Transport 1970–74.

Plymouth train [start of recess]   *Friday, 4 August*

Really loathe Plymouth now, but can't chuck as less likely to get
Folkestone due to age, passage of time.

Trouble is I just adore the House of Commons. I am seduced by
its gossipy, club-like regimental atmosphere and love also the delicious
karate-type confidence that being an MP gives me. Last night, called
in to collect my razor and already the whole place in sepulchral
hibernating gloom – just a few dim chandeliers and 'revealed' lights.
Everything locked. Did a quick phone-call to Jane from the cheekie-
chappie phone in the twilit Members' Lobby and thought how no
life will be throbbing here until 24 October and how much I shall
miss it. Two attendants (dim flat-capped sort) emerged from the gloom
and flashed their backs on me.

Ashford train   *Wednesday, 9 August*

Going up to London in a state of 'hurry-tension' as the Americans
call it. Worried about jaw. Suddenly began to bleed in different places
when driving back in the Land-Rover around about Canterbury.

Saltwood   *Sunday, 20 August*

This was our one relaxed happy day (qv last year same date) all by the
pool, even Jane. In the evening, Jane and Boy had a row – I forget
what about – but at least it proved one could still do it.

Saltwood   *Sunday, 27 August*

Only four more days of the season left. Saltwood looking incredible,
practically never better with the new Atco definitely on top of the
lawn. Still not really *relaxing*.

Politics dead – tho' election coming in time to save my bacon. Will
probably not get a job with MT if the Tories win at all, still doubtful.

Zermatt   *Sunday, 3 September*

Early part of journey blighted by darling Jane very peaky and low about George[1] – who, I was privately convinced, must be dead – missing since breakfast the day before we left, and reported that evening down at the garage by the Military Canal! However, on arrival rang Mrs C, who said he had been brought back by 'Monty' (small world) who had a little boy called 'George' and had called for him that evening, and George had appeared!

Saltwood   *Sunday, 10 September*

Back last night after two very pleasant days driving across France. Delicious dinner in clip joint ★★ restaurant at Arbois. The Chapron went beautifully – being pressed in the last stage at continuous 160–170kph and running out of petrol, legally, in the customs shed at Calais.

Then, deterioration: missed 7 o'clock boat. Customs kept us waiting an hour and was foiled of a row by being let straight through. Arrived extremely shocked to find George [the jackdaw] had 'gone on Friday'. Greenwood white and grim. Supped on tepid tomato soup and walked into office (11.30pm), masses of useless mail. Livid with James – who was, needless to say, 'out' for the night with the Land-Rover – also I suspect not having nurtured George as he should. Paced about and ate a bit of Nan Howard's (very good) fruit cake and half a mug of hot milk. Slept poorly with Angus taking up most of the room, it seemed.

Morning wet and windy. No sign of George.

---

[1] George was a tame jackdaw, not the first, or the last, to adopt Saltwood. They were usually reared by the Clarks after falling from their nests as chicks.

Albany   *Wednesday, 20 September*

Walked through St James's Park to the House of Commons to pick up the Chev and make some phone calls. I did reflect how very lucky I am to be a member of the Privileged Classes, and how *filthily* (in Michael's[1] phrase) 90% of the rest of the population still live.

Plymouth train   *Tuesday, 3 October*

Letter from some member of the Conservative Assoc asking if Margaret T could come down and do a walkabout in Plympton St Mary's to put it on the map!

Saltwood 'winter office'   *Saturday, 14 October*

A certain delicious freedom about having forsaken b'gammon (presently owe Brooks's £888) and been chucked by the blondes.

Plymouth train   *Monday, 16 October*

Set-back when James asked me about the Cloud (in kitchen last night as I gloomily prepared to go up to London for night prior to catching 9.30 – which I'm on now – to go to 'sit-in' on council meeting about taxis). 'Sold,' I said. 'What did you get for it?' 'It went in a deal with the Bi-carb. 'You have sold the Bi-carb?' He was absolutely shattered, went quite red and eyes filled with tears. If he'd been baby James he'd have blubbed. 'Now we've got nothing to do rallies in, except the Bira.' Boy had been driving the Bira that very evening, and didn't like it – though was too polite to say so – just said it was undergeared, which it is grossly.

---

[1] Michael Briggs – old friend.

Saltwood   *Monday, 23 October*

Last night George came back via a call from the train-driver's house after he had been trying to get into their children's window (his wife, as I always suspected, being extremely pretty). Althou' sleek he is very subdued and today was hardly off his 'perch' on top of the open kitchen door all day. Incredible, though, that he is still alive and that, however torpid, he did make a bid for freedom, do hope one can rehabilitate him.

Duke of Cornwall Hotel, Plymouth   *Friday, 27 October*

Came down on the sleeper, as arrangements cocked up for the Constituency Bazaar, which I was also expected to open to the usual crowd of sullen, impatient and uncomprehending bargain-hunters, instead of, as I had agreed, doing the draw at 2.30. 'If you blew in at 4.30 (sic) the locals would feel snubbed.' Incredible. And when will it be possible to escape?

Berwick by-election result this morning[1] told me by the fierce, heavily-built sleeping-car attendant who, I reckon, stole my replica Cartier watch. So perhaps there will be another long parliament, with the constant threat of a new election.

House Library   *Tuesday, 7 November*

Woke this morning to usual 'wah' weather: ie blue sky, crisp autumn day, wind fresh. Used last bit of china in Albany (white jug) to drink my tea. Did some dictating and phoning with Veronica[2] (she looking quite attractive and pert-breasted in her silk dress yesterday). Decided to make a bolt for it and took train to Saltwood, but after an omelette

---

[1] Caused by the death of the Labour MP John P. Mackintosh, elected in October 1974. Labour hung on to the seat, despite by-election reverses elsewhere during James Callaghan's premiership, giving the new MP, John Home Robertson, a majority of 3,112.

[2] Veronica, new Westminster secretary.

lunch and in Mehari to collect wood realised *couldn't* absent myself, too much of an opting out.

Have felt somewhat ignored and 'passed over' at this return, and feel prospects gradually slipping away; talk in the papers of possible 'promotion' for Heseltine etc.

Poor old John Davies resigned today.[1] Everything lovely at Saltwood, so much to do, such glorious prospects. I could live forever doing things to the Estate, the cars, writing etc. Sadly I caught the 4.52 back up, dozing intermittently and glancing through Sedgwick's *All the Pre-war Bentleys*, a sort of *Huntingdonshire Cabmen* of '30s society.[2]

Why am I so lazy here and composition essential. I excuse b'gammon by saying I must have some relaxation – am going round to St J now. But actually it's an addiction and a destructive one.

Plymouth train   *Friday, 10 November*

Looked sadly out of the window at the beaches and rocks after Dawlish. Sun streaks down, but almost deserted. Oh for the open days with the blondes or better, even, with little children, baby sons. Has that gone from one's life for ever? Oh for those days when you realise you're going over the brow of the hill and you will never, again, set eyes on that distant, so long receding range of sunny hills and vineyards.

Saltwood   *Friday, 24 November*

Some shoulder pain and *cold hand*, but this morning a fabulous experience. Flew again with James, in the little '150' as one climbed high over Rye I could see Rye Harbour, the little boats, and the garage that used to be the 'Big' garden, and then we climbed high – into the clouds, a range of strato-cumulus like 'over Italy' from Trockener

---

[1] John Davies had been Director-General, Confederation of British Industry, before becoming an MP (for Knutsford) in 1970. He served both Heath (in government) and Thatcher (in opposition). Then suffered a brain tumour. He died in 1979.

[2] J.B.Morton ('Beachcomber' of the *Daily Express*), conceived his imaginary *The List of Huntingdonshire Cabmen* to epitomise avid scholarship.

Steg. Fantastic beautiful moving experience as great cloud valleys rushed past and towering cliffs loomed over us . . . To think that my son, whom I used to kiss goodnight in his cot in that little room, was now piloting me in this fairyland.

On the way back, my mind miles away on 'George', James suddenly said/shouted, 'Daddy, what are you doing!' and I rammed some cheeky red-coloured, but new Peugeot 104 from behind, seconds later a Yank in a blue Ford ran into us! And what's more I'm in the Chapron!!! Set-back. It must go back to Chapron that's all. Darling Jane took it very calmly, but I was shattered – old person accident – also wondered about whether I might have aggravated my 'whiplash' injury.

Saltwood   *Sunday, 10 December*

I still haven't honoured my part of the bargain with God – to acknowledge and research defence book if George came back. Only God could have sent him back in that curious indirect way that didn't quite betoken a miracle, and yet, the more one thinks of it . . .

Saltwood   *Wednesday, 27 December*

Saying goodbye to James, off to California – mislaid his passport!

1979

Heavy pain from shoulder, weak wrist etc, but still not so ghastly as last year. After a baddish night did a morning's estate work . . .

I looked round the crowded House and thought – 'in fifty years' time everyone here is going to be dead.' I looked at Hugh Fraser[1] gangling weightlossedly out of the Chamber. Then I looked at John, *Sir* John Langford-Holt[2] next to me, spare and greying, though aquiline Naylor-Leylandish features still remained in vestige. How good-looking he must have been, and charming. What unfulfilled promise when he was adopted some 30 years ago.

Will I be able to break out, either careerwise or healthwise to restore and rebuild?

Back from Plymouth. More or less decided to 'go quickly'. But at breakfast when I told Jane she didn't reply – ominous. When I tackled her with this she said: 'I thought you always said "Never resign".' Yes, quite right, I did. I think solution is try and get snap adoption at AGM. Failing that just the 'gentleman' act holding out as long as possible. Might do a deal with Larry Speare, ask him up to House.

All the same, as the prospect of losing the House re-appears I am shocked and appalled by how little I have done, how much opportunity I have wasted these last four years.

I've got £83,000 in my bag! Quite literally draft for 65 on Cézanne deal and 18 from Paymaster for NPG portraits.[3] Now we never thought we'd get here again, so the lesson of the field money must be

---

[1] Hugh Fraser, MP for Stone and Staffordshire since 1950 (Stone 1945–50) had married Lady Antonia Pakenham (better known by her married name), the daughter of Lord and Lady Longford (as they would become).
[2] Sir John Langford-Holt, MP for Shrewsbury since 1945.
[3] Portraits and sketches of AC's father by Graham Sutherland.

applied. I'm also aware that it is net figure only. Must add up liabilities/ debts and reduce all. Then work things out to see how to distribute assets.

Albany   *Wednesday, 14 March*

Savoured today the first pleasure of writing a 'surprised-not-to-have-heard-from-you' note to C. Hoare & Co who I had written to a week ago asking for exact figures with which to pay off my overdraft. Dropped it in by hand on way back from cigar-plus lunch.

Saltwood   *Monday, 26 March*

Getting deeds back from Hoare's *is* within my grasp now.

B5, Albany   *Thursday, 29 March*

Tension-headache day. Election date announced for 3 May so self building on that, also James making decision-decision on does he go to Air Corps or Cavalry, had to ring up War Office about 'buying out' etc etc. Gosh it doesn't seem so long since I was *paid* to go into Household Cavalry and then got out (we were at Lugano) in '46.

Poor dear Veronica said I '... looked terribly harassed', jarred one every time she opened her mouth.

Had tea, envying all my colleagues with good seats, hoping we don't have another hung parliament. God how I loathe the Election campaign! Back to Brooks's to get dinner, then to House to pick up papers, then to bed and catch 7.30 train to Plymouth.

Plymouth train   *Friday, 30 March*

Loathe election prospect. Slight doubt about adoption meeting, even, but presumably will be ok. Filthy to be away from the estate and dear George also will pine and whose features I want to get shining and give some fresh air to. I think a lot about George, and love the way he taps on his box when I am on the phone; he even hears my voice right down the passage and into the Green Room.

'Boy' going to Pirbright[1] on 17 April, the day the campaign 'starts in earnest'. This preferable, I think, to Army Air Corps, but involves US trip in summer (expensive and dangerous). Dear 'Boy' is so ravishing looking and maddening and engaging. Jane and I agreed on the phone that all we can do is grin-and-bear-it. Become dear old ga–gas.

Of course if I get through the election (happily with majority up) and if Cons have a good majority, then one can at last concentrate on South East, both estate and 'constituency' (will do that anyway, regardless, but less secure if majority 'teeny'). But in a sense isn't this almost dropping-out, the SE concept? Just wanting to retain the Commons as a Club? The inescapable moments of time, receding hair–line, bags under eyes (new development). But 'neck' has cured itself, a great help.

Key factor, though, is elimination of dandruff.

Saltwood   *Friday, 6 April*

Tory lead now down to 6%. Realise it will be gradually whittled away and will lose my seat or the majority halved.

Bratton   *Friday, 13 April (Birthday boy)*

Calmer than might be expected at this 'break' in the campaign, but out here, almost resigned to humiliation at polls (must admit not

---

[1] Headquarters of the army training regiment of the Brigade of Guards.

relishing the re-count!). Wouldn't mind all *that* much just being a stately-home owner.

Teeth seem to be cracking up. Also eyes still get puffy. But basically not feeling bad. A bit stiff, can get quite unpleasant twinges from shoulder if, eg, turning round while holding up phone.

Being 51 makes me feel quite lecherous.

That evening: a lovely relaxed day at Bratton – cleaning windows and paint and planning to revive it substantially, possibly to 'full Bloomsbury'.[1] Only relief in recurrent gloom, Jack the baker, saying sing-song, 'all grown up, all grown up, gone away' about the boys.

Saltwood   *Easter Sunday, 15 April*

Saltwood 'smiling'. Tortoises all woke up, tipped their box over and were released in Courtenays. My 'eye' (left-side) a little suspect. Irritated and slightly stye-borne, but otherwise fine and randy. Gloom about beloved 'Boy'. On the phone last night he recounted how his Zermatt friend in the Scots Guards had just come out of Pirbright and told him how hateful it was: '4 hours sleep, and people paid to be nasty to you ...'

This gave me a bad night. Cheered up a bit in the morning and thought 'what is written is written.' In the sunlight evening gloom of the 'formal' part of the Castle, I still get these terrible forebodings: Kipling and his son at Loos, Weld-Smith, even, of Seend Manor and his son on Blenheims.

Also filled with loathing of the Electorate. Those filthy carriages on the trip down yesterday which annoyed Jane so much, is the nation completely rotten? Yes, and has been since 1916. In the war we were saved by the middle classes who flew the Spitfires and manned the cruisers and frigates.

---

[1] The Clarks did in fact turn Bratton into a miniature Charleston. After the house was sold the Bloomsbury doors were returned to Saltwood.

Saltwood   *Easter Monday, 16 April*

In a state of *désoeuvré* apprehension. My R eye now irritating definitely; would worry over this, but must get election out of the way (very depressed about this, Labour bound to win – at least in Plymouth, it seems). Still foremost worry is darling 'Boy' going in tomorrow to the Pirbright crusher. A little soft-spoken about his coming ordeal. He may be going deliberately to 'flunk'. I don't know. It would be fabulous if he can get through and the world would be his oyster; but in a way thank God for the election to take my mind off it, otherwise I would be worrying non-stop.

This really will be the last entry until after the (re) count. Yeh yeh!

Bratton   *Sunday, 22 April*

In spite of terrible anxiety about 'Boy' plus gloom/apprehension over Polls (today showing our lead down to 5½ – ie dead heat and looking awful), am slyly, insistently *grossly* randy as one can only be at Bratton with its soft centre and lazy atmosphere. Can't ignore my fears about James – though it puts into scale one's fear about finally losing seat.

Bratton   *Sunday 29 April*

Cheered up by Graham Butland ringing on my return: the *Independent*[1] forecasting a clear sweep for Tories in West Country!

Bratton   *Monday, 30 April*

Met L.K. Way, who said (he wasn't especially friendly) that he had two 'nasty points' to put to me: (1) Large Liberal vote to be pivotal (I know); and (2) influx of 8,000 new voters (I know). Indeed I had

---

[1] West Country Sunday newspaper, published in Plymouth.

been ready to greet him with: 'Leslie, this is a Labour seat' etc. Quickly
I tried to deflect him. But feeling very anxious.

The General Election on 3 May
    Conservative: 339; Labour: 269; Liberal: 11. Others: 16

Saltwood   *Monday, 7 May*

Mrs Thatcher (or Mrs Carrington, as Papa amusingly – muddledly –
called her) has announced her Cabinet, and I'm not in, anywhere.
Don't specially mind, though resentful of Pattie being in so high up
and Hayhoe[1] (of all people) getting the Army. Wouldn't take a PPS
or couldn't take 'disabled' or 'energy'. Lovely to have freedom of the
Commons, consolidated at Plymouth,[2] and the summer before us.

But particularly bad-tempered and martyred, so in essence a little
schizophrenic, I suppose. Noone has been in touch. Where are the
blondes? Did they send the 'AC rules OK' telegram, must have? But
where are they? Sod them too.

B5, Albany   *Wednesday, 16 May*

And still the mood of euphoria persists. Waking very early. And ready
to take on anything. B'gammon – balls to it. Cars – barely interested;
quite happy with the 'gentlemanly' old SI, so reserved in its dark
green, a 2CV, and the two sports models, SG for 'recreation'. The
House consumes me and pumps me with adrenalin – like playing
game after difficult game in a major tournament.

---

[1] Geoffrey Pattie had been Parliamentary Under-Secretary of State, RAF since the general
    election; Barney Hayhoe, MP for Brentford and Isleworth since February 1974 (Heston
    and Isleworth 1970–74) the same but for the Army.
[2] Sutton result: AC, 28,892 votes; Priestley (Labour), 17,605; Scannell (Liberal), 6,225.
    AC majority: 11,287.

Dean's Yard   *Thursday, 24 May*

Didn't make '22' Exec. All PPS's and Whips now announced. Euphoria pretty well extinct. Article in *Telegraph* by Wellbeloved[1] (of all people) stating how RAF run-down. Felt I should answer this, and had brainwave of checking with Pattie: been washing the dishes after breakfast for an hour waiting for him to ring back, gloomily reflecting on contrast. There was I washing dishes. There was he (*pace* his aide) 'in conference with the chiefs of staff'.

Saltwood   *Saturday, 9 June*

One more little notch on James' separation – last night was the first ever that he has been in England and we didn't know where he was. Had a bad scare with skin condition on back, itchy, 'boils', flushes etc. Hypochondria far from dormant. Also what is to happen to 'Boy'? He appeared yesterday in his *ludicrous* spastic US uniform which he had bought at the Military Vehicle rally.

Folkestone Station   *Tuesday, 26 June*

Late for case (when it was expected I would lose my licence) as went to old court, and back to new one. In the little interview room I suddenly realised that I might lose it for a little while. However when I entered the court the Clerk of the Court said: one of the magistrates is known to you, have you any objection? . . . eh! 'None whatever,' I replied delightedly. And in due time, *very* narrowly, she declared that there were *special circumstances* which allowed them not to disqualify.

---

[1] James Wellbeloved, Labour MP for Erith and Crayford since 1965, who held the same post at Defence as Pattie until the election.

E Cloisters   *Thursday, 19 July*

So clapped out. After that one glorious 'flare-up' in June pretty girls
no longer look at me. Am drear, waxen-faced with short haircut (but
not 'boyish'). I noticed how drear, too, the whips (Newton and
Wakeham[1]) looked, and yesterday I saw Rhodes-James slumped in
that tiny niche by the phone in the tea-room corridor, his obsessively
ambitious features glazed-over. He wasn't on the phone, he wasn't
moving at all. I thought he might be stuck there indefinitely right
through the recess, and this made me grin, momentarily.

Albany   *Friday, 20 July*

Headache on side of head – right. Is it John Davies or toothache?

East Cloisters   *Monday, 22 October*

Complaining to Michael McNair-Wilson about not having a pair,
and he said – more or less – 'You've been passed finally by, why
bother, you don't need to conform ...' *Why* am I in this condition?
Immediately he tried to placate me, but as I said, they've (the Whips)
got so many candidates they want to accommodate – or rather were
accommodating – that they're only too delighted to cross someone
off their list.

Saltwood   *Sunday, 4 November*

Miss 'Boy' more than I admit.[2] Realised last night that I couldn't play
the piano until he was back (he played it – and the organ – on his last
night). Last night Col said that '... £8,000 was the size of most

---

[1] Antony (Tony) Newton, MP for Braintree since February 1974; John Wakeham, MP
for Maldon since February 1974.
[2] Off to flying-school.

people's overdraft (!)' Jane flinched, and so did I. Agreed that my father will live another five years – which puts a *totally* different complexion on everything.

House of Commons   *Thursday, 15 November*

Met the (reputedly) senior correspondent of *Pravda* in the Strangers' Lobby for lunch. I was feeling ghastly – fourth day of filthy cold – and had taken the precaution of downing a quick pink gin first. The man, Strelnikov by name, had the appearance of a standard KGB 'heavy' of mature years. He started extremely nervous (uncertainty and the prospect of having to use their own initiative always makes Soviet officials, of any rank, very apprehensive). However once he realised that I was not trying to persuade or blackmail him into defecting the atmosphere lightened. The reason I prefer the Russians to the Chinese and at some point in the conversation I even said this, is because their natural human responses – jollity, gloom etc – are never far below the surface with the exceptions of a few clam-faced Commissars, whom ordinary Russians loathe anyway.

I emphasised that this was the moment for the Soviet Union to make a real gesture of conventional disarmament as once the deployment of the new generation of 'theatre' nuclear missiles gets under away it would be more difficult. He did not demur when I said that the Brezhnev gesture of withdrawing 1,000 tanks was meaningless as we all knew they were obsolete and this was part of the normal re-equipment programme.

He fidgeted a great deal and heaved himself about in his seat starting every sentence with the words 'Mr Clark' pronounced in a curious glottal Slavic manner. From time to time I lightened the conversation by asking him about his war experiences noticing that he was both pleased and disconcerted at my accurate knowledge of fronts, Commanders and conditions (he told me that he had been invalided out after being wounded during an air attack on the Mius Front in 1943 having taken part in the great retreat across Caucasus.) Of course there may still be a file on me at the Soviet Embassy relating to my brief flirtation with Vinnikof during the time that I was writing *Barbarossa* and I may be irredeemably persona non grata as a result.

The House then got stuck into one of those days which follow

long periods of torpor and ennui that conform to Fred Hoyle's theory
of the concatenation of the Universe. For we had, more or less
simultaneously, the Chancellor's announcement of a 17 per cent bank
rate i.e. 21 per cent overdrafts and a clutch of publicity-seeking Labour
MPs each trying to beat the other to the draw (Dennis Skinner, I am
glad to say, just beat Christopher Price.[1] The two were standing
together and Skinner made it on a 'Point of Order') raising the matter
of Anthony Blunt's treachery.[2] This was a lucky break for Geoffrey
[Howe][3] because the whole Blunt affair diverted attention from the
really alarming manner in which our economy seems to be conducted.
He came to the '22' committee and the atmosphere was mildly critical.
I asked the question which, perhaps fortunately, the Speaker had not
called me to ask at the time of the statement – namely if we had really
cut public expenditure then we would not need such devastatingly
high interest rates.

   Earlier at the '22' I made an announcement on behalf of the Home
Secretary about the Immigration rules brief. I spoke clearly, slowly
and bossily and this reminded me of how I would really like to be a
Whip (*vide* Chips). This is second best from the original concept of
galloping across the countryside on a white horse, drawn sword in
hand rousing the populace, but I would settle for it, especially as it
would give me a good excuse for handing in my notice at Plymouth.

House of Commons   *Wednesday, 21 November*

Ian Gow[4] is a very assiduous attender of Committees. In the last
two days I have noticed him at the special meeting of the Finance
Committee when the Chancellor came to explain the MLR increase,
at the Legal Committee when the Attorney General was defending

[1] Christopher Price, MP for Lewisham West since February 1974 (Birmingham Perry
   Bar, 1966–70).
[2] Anthony Blunt, former Surveyor of Pictures to George VI and Queen Elizabeth II, had
   been unmasked as the 'Fourth Man' in the group of Cambridge spies (Maclean,
   Burgess, Philby etc) who betrayed Britain to the Soviet Union.
[3] Geoffrey Howe, MP for Surrey East since 1974 (Bebington, 1964–66; Reigate, 1970–
   74), Chancellor of the Exchequer since the general election after four years as opposition Treasury spokesman.
[4] Ian Gow, MP for Eastbourne since February 1974, and Parliamentary Private Secretary
   to Margaret Thatcher since May 1979.

the Protection of Information Act, at the Home Affairs Committee immediately afterwards when the Blunt affair was being discussed and tonight he was at the regular meeting of the Finance Committee when Gordon Pepper[1] addressed them.

By chance I had taken tea alone in one of the armchairs at the far end of the Members' Tea Room instead of convivially at the table. This was because I was exhausted having spent the latter part of the afternoon tramping the streets of Battersea looking for a garage 'with flat over' for the coven. I was reading the financial columns of the *Guardian,* which contained a critique of a speech made by Pepper the previous day to the Society of Investment Analysts.

It is always nice to have a crib and I decided, unusually for me, to attend the Finance Committee that evening. Forearmed (the piece was by Hamish McRae[2]) I was able to ask him a penetrating question about the way in which the recent gilt sales by the Bank had been bungled. So penetrating was it that he became flustered, asked several times if we were off-the-cuff, looked around the room in an exag-geratedly conspiratorial way etc. When it came his answer was more or less unintelligible – the only part I could understand was that Mullens, the Government broker, had spent the last month wining and dining various directors of the Clearing banks. Anyhow I noticed Ian rise from his seat and pad silently around the outer perimeter of the crowded Committee table ... I did not look round although everybody watches Ian wherever he goes because it is thought (rightly or wrongly – I suspect wrongly) that the Prime Minister confides in him and values his opinion.

He stopped behind my chair and tapped me very lightly on the shoulder bending forward and, speaking almost inaudibly, asked if I would come and have dinner. We left immediately, before the Com-mittee rose, and as everybody watched us go out I was reminded of Oliver Lyttelton's[3] story about the French broker who had done one of the Rothschilds a good turn and asked him for a tip on the Bourse. Rothschild said, 'I never give tips, but what I will do is walk across the floor in your company.' This experience was repeated when we went briefly to the Smoking Room. At the corner table by the bar

---

[1] Noted member of the monetarist priesthood. Senior partner in Greenwells and gilt-edge expert.

[2] Hamish McRae, financial editor of *The Guardian* since 1975.

[3] Oliver Lyttelton (created 1st Viscount Chandos, 1954), member of Churchill's war cabinet, industrialist and first chairman of National Theatre Board.

sat Ted Heath, bolt upright in a dinner jacket and having (apparently) had a special snow rinse on his hair which he now wears *en brosse*.

We drove to the Cavalry Club in the green Bentley and Ian ordered copious quantities of Tio Pepe, white Burgundy, Claret etc. I was soon surrounded by a number of half full glasses which I had no intention of emptying. He told me how the Prime Minister and the Treasury team were anxious that no real cuts in public spending had yet been made. He said she was out-numbered three to one in the cabinet. On her side were Howe, Biffen, Nott, Maude, Joseph.[1] The remaining 18 were mutely or vociferously hostile. (Prior[2] – whom Ian loathes – and Walker are her principal opponents.)

Later
I had a piccolo House of Commons triumph this evening. Sat through the Blunt debate (why in hell was Rhodes James called *first* from the back benches to propound his mouldy clichés). Willie Hamilton and Leadbitter[3] were the best. At 9.03pm – with everybody comfortably settled down for the wind-ups I rose – alone – and was called.

A crowded House, a *full* House! And the PM leaning forward in what Ian [Gow] calls the 'Blue Peter' position. I put my questions – none of them particularly welcome – and, regrettably, applauded more from the Labour benches. But without an exception (the – unsolicited – joke that anyone who knows anything about the KGB will verify that the Russian controllers in Kensington change every two years) I got a good feeling. The first time that Margaret T has heard me speak since she turned round and looked at me during my 'maiden'. Technique improved since then.

---

[1] John Biffen, MP for Oswestry since 1961, and now Chief Secretary to the Treasury under Howe; John Nott, MP for St Ives (Cornwall) since 1966 and now Secretary of State for Trade; Angus Maude, Paymaster-General; Sir Keith Joseph, MP for Leeds North-East since 1956 and now Secretary of State for Industry.
[2] James Prior, MP for Lowestoft since 1959, now Secretary of State for Employment.
[3] William (Willie) Hamilton, MP for Fife Central since 1974 (Fife West, 1950–74); Edward (Ted) Leadbitter, MP for the Hartlepools since 1964.

House of Commons   *Tuesday, 27 November*

I was talking to Tony Royle, eminently sensible, never seen him in a flap (ex SAS, I think).[1] But he can be very forthright, no words minced. 'Look at the people round her,' he said. 'Carrington – hates her; Prior – hates her; Gilmour – hates her; Heseltine[2] – hates her; Walker – loathes her, makes no secret of it; Willie – completely even-handed, would never support her against the old gang; Geoffrey Howe – no personal loyalties – durable politburo man, will serve under anyone. The only people committed to Margaret are Angus Maude, John Biffen and Keith Joseph and the last two are so tortured intellectually as to cast doubt on their stability in a crisis.'

I paraphrase his analysis, but it brought home to one how precarious her position is and what a disaster was the assassination of Airey Neave[3] whose subtlety and insight would have helped to out-manoeuvre these quislings. Royle pointed out that the real danger would be that a mass sacking or resignation of the old guard heavies (nominally arising out of 'attitudes' to incomes policy or enforcement of measures disciplining a recalcitrant union) would create an alternative Cabinet and one which would naturally be expected to open its doors to the ageing, sulky, shapeless but still expectant Edward Heath. And that with such weight and so many 'names' it was a danger that more than half the Parliamentary Party might be drawn off to fill their wagons. Margaret would be left with a few young (and presumably discredited) monetarists such as Nott and Lawson[4] and a rabble of African Rightists, Hastings, Winterton[5] etc and the '92'.[6]

---

[1] Anthony Royle, MP for Richmond since 1959. He had served in the Life Guards at the very end of the war, ending up in the 21st Special Air Service regiment (TA), 1948–51.

[2] Michael Heseltine had been Secretary of State for the Environment since the general election.

[3] On 30 March 1979, the day after the announcement of the general election that would bring the Conservatives back to power, the party's Northern Ireland spokesman, and a close confidant of Margaret Thatcher, was murdered in the Palace of Westminster by a car bomb; the INLA, a republican splinter group, claimed responsibility.

[4] Nigel Lawson, MP for Blaby since February 1974, and now Financial Secretary to the Treasury under Geoffrey Howe.

[5] Stephen Hastings, MP for Mid-Bedfordshire since 1960; Nicholas Winterton, MP for Macclesfield since 1971.

[6] The '92' took its name from the London home (92 Cheyne Walk) of its first chairman, Sir Patrick Wall, MP for Haltemprice since 1954, with the main aim of keeping the Conservative Party conservative. Margaret Thatcher dined with the committee in

House of Commons   *Thursday, 6 December*

Last night I spoke, again, on the protectionist theme. And intervened
to make my point. Again 'exposed' before Mrs T! These days I
interrupt with total confidence. But must be careful not to become
an Adley (ie discounted before he even opens his mouth).

1978 and in her first government she appointed six of its members as ministers, most
notably Norman Tebbit.

1980

Back a fortnight – it seems like three months!

Antony Buck[1] and John Wells down for the weekend with their wives. Hospitality was lavish – too lavish in the event – as all the guests drank too much and Aspinall, who came over for dinner, became extremely combative and made a great deal of noise. No scope for statesman-like discussions.

Buck refused to go to bed at 2am when everyone else had dispersed and steered me back to the study 'for a last whisky'. He repeated several times the concept of an ideal arrangement whereby he was Secretary of State for Defence and I was Minister, '... or perhaps the other way round'.

'No, no,' I said, 'don't be ridiculous.'

Actually, there is not the slightest chance of his being promoted. Like little Winston, whose sexual athletics are being luridly recounted in two rival tabloid papers at this moment, he is a 'has-been'. In his cups Buck mumbled resentfully about Winston having three weeks off from the Whip to go to Cambodia, but I see that W. had to get Minnie[2] out of the way when all this dirt was being made public and the trip was really a kind of leaving present from the Whips Office.

I drank ginger ale (which, in the glass, looks like a medium strength whisky). Buck said 'goodnight' from time to time and made one or two efforts to rise to his feet, but slumped back (he was sitting in the corner of Bonny mama's red sofa). Finally he made it and *reeled* off upstairs.

The long-term purpose of the weekend was to create a 'good impression' to John Wells of the set-up; of my suitability to succeed

---

[1] Antony Buck, MP for Colchester since 1961, chairman of the Conservative Defence Committee since 1979 and thus AC's 'boss', AC being co-secretary with Robert Atkins, MP for Preston North since 1979. AC was convinced that he specialised in defence as the British Aerospace factory manufacturing the Panavia Tornado was situated in his constituency (his majority of 27 was the smallest in the House).

[2] Winston Churchill, MP for Stretford since 1970, married Mary Caroline d'Erlanger in 1964; the marriage was dissolved in 1997.

him when he retires etc., probably less certain. JW did not drink as much as the others and was somewhat inscrutable.

Cloisters   *Tuesday, 5 February*

I asked a supplementary of Mark Carlisle[1] today on the assisted places scheme and the subject simmered on for the rest of Question Time. It must be crazy to tamper with this at the same time as they are presiding over the dismemberment of British heavy industry. If he condemns the bright child to the drudgery of the state system without hope or escape there will be no one to take advantage of the new slim-line economy if we finally bring it off. I took ten minutes off and strolled out into the Members' Lobby where Ian Gow was prowling. He asked me if I had a question in mind (the Prime Minister was due to start answering in ten minutes time).

'Nothing special,' I said. 'Anything I can do for you?'

Out of the corner of his mouth he said, 'Ask when they are going to put some teeth into the Employment Act.'

I know that Ian loathes Prior and never ceases to complain about him, but what I found worrying was that the Prime Minister is so isolated in Cabinet that she has to send her PPS out into the Lobby to try and raise support at random from backbenchers at Question Time. I warned him that I might not get in as the Speaker had already called me once on a supplementary and my name was not on the Order Paper. Sure enough there was an enormous crowd and although I got to my feet repeatedly I was not called. However, Bill Clark, so recently and deservedly knighted,[2] got in with a similar question and I assume this had also been planted.

---

[1] Mark Carlisle, MP for Runcorn since 1964, Secretary for State for Education since 1979.
[2] Sir William Clark, MP for Croydon South since 1974 (E Surrey 1970–74), and former vice-chairman of the Conservative Party, knighted in New Year's honours list.

E Cloisters   *Early morning, Wednesday, 20 February*

I said something to Jamie on the lines of 'I wish I were you ... I'd know what I'd do all right ...' etc. 'So would I', half to himself, very much implying – if you were dead I'd get going etc ...

Actually, little does he know, we're still highly strapped. Interest charges – I can barely think about them. Oh how I pine for the open air, nature, return of vitality, happy times with Jane; some days the heat here is so oppressive, the air stale, and only triangles of blue sky are perceptible through the leaded panes. I can't do anything after lunch, virtually for the rest of the day, I'm so drowsy.

Albany (later)
Dined with Tony Buck. The occasional flash of wit. Towards the end of the evening he confided in me that Rhodes James disapproved very strongly of my 'reputation', how badly I treated my wife, mumbled something about Valeri. All total balls, and I am extremely annoyed considering RJ has been to Saltwood and never reciprocated in any way. Also slightly disconcerting is that RJ has obviously been spreading this around for years.

Afterwards, decided on spur of moment, although frightfully tired – kept looking at myself in mirror and thought somewhat pale and bigheaded, with thick neck and domed effect as hair continues to recede – to go to a late party given by Peter Tapsell[1] in his chambers at Albany 'for' Dr Savimbi.[2] When I arrived (an hour late) the doctor was on his feet, on the window sill in fact, addressing the multitude. And most effectively he did it. These Africans are extremely formidable. There is something very impressive about the powerful orator, immaculately dressed, who has only lately arrived from the Bush and who that very evening was flying back to Luanda and the Kalashnikovs. I said all this when I shook his hand.

---

[1] Peter Tapsell, MP for Horncastle since 1966 (Nottingham West, 1959–64).
[2] Leader of the anti-communist FNLA guerrilla movement in Angola.

Saltwood   *Saturday, 23 February*

A glorious sunny spring day after much rain.

Absurdly frantic with *pressure on time*. Whole night/morning thrown
out by James doing (even for him) exceptional young-person night
disturbances finally going to bed at twenty minutes to five – *GROAN!*
Jane and I had heart-rending discussion about it in the small hours.

This morning, staggering with fatigue, I went out to the Barbican.
Wouldn't I have about 1,000 *days* left before I was a buffer? 1,000
days to put affairs in order, finances in shape, car collection disciplined,
châlet paid off – everything – plus a *HOLIDAY* with dear Jane.

Albany   *Tuesday, 26 February*

Yesterday evening, feeling very tetchy and harassed with so many
pressures, correspondence in arrears, tax statements behind, children
wayward and *désoeuvré*, though lovable, walking up the deserted
Smoking Corridor I saw Rhodes James in the distance approaching
me from the dining-room end. I stopped and looked at the ticker
tape. Donnishly acid, he said, 'I saw you featured in the *Sunday Times*
yesterday . . .'[1]

'Featured means fornicate, Robert,' I said.

He affected not to hear, muttered something about, '. . . had visions
of you picking coal with your little pick.'

'Like Candy,' I said. I don't think he got the allusion.[2]

I had been a little apprehensive about my reception this morning
as colleagues do hate one getting publicity unless it is overly scandalous
and retarding But most people quite jolly. Those who disapprove as,
eg Costain, just twinklingly, or icily, as their mood may be, 'very good
photograph of you in yesterday's paper.'

---

[1] Headlined 'The "civilised" Tory Tribunite', the profile drew attention to the similarity
of AC's views to those of the Labour left wing: favouring 'import controls, complete
withdrawal from the EEC,' although his expressed 'guarded admiration' for Bismarck
and Hitler, the profile suggested, was 'to tease his unlikely new friends in the Tribune
Group.'

[2] Candy was the nubile, blond *demi-vierge* in Terry Southern's 1964 novel of the same
name, who at one stage found herself at a coal face alongside the lecherous Grindle.
Candy whiled away the hours picking at the face with an ice pick, laying minuscule
fragments on her silk head-square which she had spread on the ground.

Not having any appetite I decided to go and listen to the Prime Minister being interviewed by Robin Day. She was wonderful and very glamorous looking, though slightly spoilt the effect with over-much ocular grimacing.

To such an extent that I worried that she might have got a blob of mascara into her eye and was alarmed, at some camera angles, to see a tell-tale red glow therein. As always she let out a few impromptus, notably the revelation that Jim Prior was 'very, very sorry' for his indiscretion.[1]

There was still three-quarters of an hour left before the vote and I thought I ought to eat something. I couldn't face the dining room, so went down to the cafeteria. I was chatting to Tony Buck and David Madel[2] at their table when I saw Ian Gow come in, almost immediately followed by the Prime Minister who stood alone at the counter waiting to be served. I rushed up and congratulated her on the programme and Ian invited me to join them. I told the Prime Minister that a guffaw had gone round the television room when she said that she had found Ian Gilmour's speeches 'scintillating'.

Almost coquettishly she reminded me of her other comment ... 'something in there for everyone.' Peter Hordern[3] joined us during the meal and was grave, thoughtful and 'correct' about financial matters. But I could see the Prime Minister preferred gossip. Ian grinned benignly as I joked about Prior's reproof and her breaching for the first time the notion that she might 'think about considering whether to withhold our EEC budget contributions'.

But goodness, she is so beautiful; made up to the nines of course, for the television programme, but still quite bewitching, as Eva Peron must have been. I could not take my eyes off her and after a bit she, quite properly, would not look me in the face and I detached myself from the group with the excuse that I was going up to heckle Michael Foot[4] who was doing the winding-up for Labour.

---

[1] Some days before Prior, Secretary of State for Employment, had 'leaked' to the lobby that the chairman of British Steel 'would have to be replaced ... as soon as the strike was over.'

[2] David Madel, MP for South Bedfordshire since 1970.

[3] Peter Hordern, MP for Horsham and Crawley since 1974 (Horsham 1964–74), a member of the Public Accounts Committee and the Executive of the 1922 Committee, and before entering politics a member of the Stock Exchange.

[4] Michael Foot, MP for Ebbw Vale since 1960 (Devonport 1945–55); the successor to James Callaghan as Leader of the Labour Party later in the year.

After the 10 o'clock vote I walked back to Albany and at the lower crossing place in St James's Street I saw two shadowy forms, elderly, decrepit even; but with a strange Episcopal authority, in their great black cloaks. The traffic – as always at that hour – made up of drunks and car thieves, was travelling at a colossal speed, so I helped them make it to the first island. I saw to my delight that one of them was Harold Macmillan, wearing his long-range multi-focals that look like sections of a glass rolling pin.[1]

'Are you going, sir, to Pratt's or Brooks's,' I asked him. 'The Carlton,' he replied tersely and shuffled off. But then paused, turned and called after me, 'It's too late for Pratt's anyway,' and waved an enormous half-hunter watch. 'They will be shut.'

A pleasant evening. Two Prime Ministers in the space of an hour and a half. Odd, how I keep meeting Uncle Harold when I least expect it.

Saltwood   *Sunday, 2 March*

If I don't make it by the next reshuffle it's withdrawal, but as the reshuffle now looks to be deferred until Christmas I get a nasty feeling that this is going to be one of the fullest summers.

Back shows no sign of healing – haven't been able to touch my toes for nearly two months.

Cloisters   *Tuesday, 18 March*

I was munching my buns at a table in the Tea Room when Jim Lester[2] came and sat down holding a lot of papers. I used to think he was rather objectionable, but I will say that he has been very effective from the box at Question Time – one of the successes among the junior 'wetter' appointments.

---

[1] Macmillan had celebrated his eighty-sixth birthday a fortnight before.
[2] James (Jim) Lester, MP for Beeston since February 1974; Parliamentary Under-Secretary of State for Employment since 1979.

I touched on the subject of import controls with Lester and asked him what his 'boss' thought. Somewhat to my surprise he answered that, '... he (Jim Prior) is in such hot water at the moment that I would not think he would want to put his head above the parapet on anything else.' The reference to hot water quite surprised me. Some correspondents give the impression that Prior is virtually autonomous, with so much backing in the Cabinet that the Lady hardly dares to approach him. But Lester's timidity was quite genuine.

Saltwood   *Wednesday, 19 March*

Oooh – the pressures! A frightfully depressing day yesterday. *Missed* through sheer spontaneity (ie overloaded memory bank with appointments and obligations) the joint meeting of Industry and Trade with Nott and Joseph. Nearly missed, too, the little conspiratorial meeting chaired by Dick Body[1] – but after my arrival I was clearly the most authoritative person there – to organise the anti-EEC EDM at Ian Gow's behest.

Swallow Room totally collapsed – roof not draining at all. Such filthy weather, combination of freezing fog *and* high wind (how can that be?) day after day of wet pavement. My shoulder/arm quite objectionable – doesn't like slumping in chairs or turning. Perhaps too many rail journeys.

Albany   *Thursday, 20 March*

Joei now gone mad; rings only making threats – it's a highly innocuous, run-of-the-mill heterosexual tale, but I suppose it could 'sell' – eg scandal about MPs is news and would certainly screw any career prospects. Just think of formula: 'I do not under any circumstances discuss my relations with the ladies. I am a gentleman, not a hairdresser.'

---

[1] Richard Body, MP for Holland with Boston since 1966, member of the Commons Select Committee on Agriculture since 1979.

Also medium-term worries, like what about Broomhayes? What is beloved 'Boy' going to do next? Do I/can I sell the Moore bust to pay off the chalet etc?

Saltwood   *Friday, 28 March*

Back for the weekend – we had cancelled Zermatt, I hope not disappointing 'Boy' so as to get to grips with the Estate and papers. Although somewhat tired and crotchety (Ali totally withdrawn, sod it, paid that £·5 for nothing) did steel myself to Osprey the Bailey. Saltwood just starting to 'smile', but so much to do, so many small deteriorations: why is the moat still losing water? Did a last walk in failing light, thinking about Andrew coming back from the geography field trip and going straight on out to Zermatt We, in spite of being rascally 'young' and non-bufferish, bore them. I stood at the yard gates and looked across at the dark mass of the Great Hall and Courtenays, the moon almost full. Are we to be driven for the next five years, slaving away to keep the place going – for what? Will our grandchildren want it anyway? Quite suddenly and unexpectedly my daily horoscope said that the next two years are going to be 'unsettled'.

Zermatt   *Saturday, 12 April*

Julian Amery dined last night. A little heavier than formerly; said he skied better in the afternoons and drank a litre (!) of wine at lunch. We spoke non-stop about political matters until midnight. He is well *versé* in foreign affairs. He doesn't acknowledge flattery. He sees things somewhat apocalyptically especially in the mid-East. Wants to get an expeditionary force (still), to south Iran to offer as 'alternative' Iranian government. Sounds a bit cloudy to me, shades of South Vietnam etc.
But interesting, as always, historically. Threw light, at first hand, on

the celebrated 'Cipriani' incident.[1] Confided that Willie Whitelaw[2] had told him how he intended to 'smash' the Unionist Party when he was Secretary of State for NI. At breakfast, Andrew cunningly said 'was there much talk about the reshuffle?' Not really, but Julian too agreed that everyone in the Cabinet loathes the PM, is out to do her down. Sole exceptions Biffen (too distracted) and possibly (my addition) John Nott; himself somewhat constrained by his own leadership expectations long-term. Howe now a contender, has advanced massively since the budget – though God knows why.

Cloisters   *Monday, 14 April*

In the lobby for a 3-line vote I was joking with George Gardiner and Tony Marlow (bad company in establishment terms).[3] Marlow was trying to get me to sign an E.D.M. and I declined jokingly, asserting that I only signed them '... on Europe and animal welfare'. General laughter and as I turned away I saw the Prime Minister approaching in conversation with Raison.[4] Raison's expression, as always, was grave and humourless, but as hers was relatively amiable and her distance away from me less than three feet, I quickly composed my features and framed a deferential smile. To my great alarm she looked straight through me, her own expression altering to one of icy disdain. I am worried about this. What have I done wrong? We enjoyed very good relations immediately after Christmas and I was optimistic. I suppose I was too brown; being brown indicates idleness and (at this time of the year) foreign holidays. Albeit in our case an exceedingly

[1] Elsewhere AC records as follows, circa late 1979: Anthony Royle 'told an interesting story of Heath's loathing of Julian Amery and, through his personification, the old Whites', that 'magic circle' strain in the Tory Party. In the early 1950s Julian and friends were having drinks on the terrace of the Cipriani in Venice when Heath appeared in gym shoes and made some gauche remark which Amery, slightly tight, tore to pieces and then held up the fragments for his cronies to laugh at. Heath never forgave him and still suspects that every Member of the Parliamentary Party from that ambience is waiting to do the same thing.'

[2] William Whitelaw, after four years as Opposition home affairs spokesman, had been Home Secretary since 1979.

[3] George Gardiner, MP for Reigate and Banstead since February 1974; Antony (Tony) Marlow, MP for Northampton North since 1979.

[4] Timothy Raison, MP for Aylesbury since 1970, Minister of State, Home Office since 1979.

short one.[1] Also my laughter may have been too loud. There was something in the Prime Minister's manner that reminded me of my mother, who also hated loud laughter, and it put her in a bad mood.

Cloisters   *Friday, 18 April*

On Wednesday night I was feeling ghastly and was dropping a 1 mg tablet of Redoxon into a glass of mineral water at the Smoking Room bar when Peter Morrison *volunteered* that he could 'help' with a pair the following day, Thursday. An unprecedented suggestion – was I really looking that ill? But on Friday morning I realised why: there had been a revolt of 37 back-benchers against a provision of the Employment Bill and he had wanted to get me out of the way, or save me embarrassment? Nothing in this place is what it seems. The Machiavellian undercurrents, the need to be permanently on one's guard, to know how to read the codes and smoke signals; how to assess people's real motives, and discount their superficial courtesies and protestations – is what makes the game here so fascinating.

Headland Park, Plymouth   *Saturday, 19 April*

Sitting in this mouldy little 'headquarters' – conveniently walking distance from the station though – just a year since the middle of the election campaign when all was whiz and fizz and I used to shut myself in here and lech at Veronica opposite. There, facing me on the table is one of the election car stickers – did I really look like that only a year ago?

Now time for a last *reflectif* to close the 'black book'. I don't want to make it sound too melodramatic, God is so good to me in waves. But it must be sadder, this note, than the close of earlier volumes.

Even the Katoomba 'red book' which saw the dizzy spiral down from 1972 'too good to be true' to 1974, 'a bailiff at the door'. The testosterone was higher. In the train coming down this afternoon I sat most of the time in that special melancholy that comes from separation,

---

[1] The Clarks had been in Zermatt for five days.

parting almost with a loved one. Realised it was not the 'blondes' –
partly because I can't believe it has really happened (had a 'click'
call only last week) and half of me looks forward to the rows and
reconciliations, the other half is heedless enough (now) to quite enjoy
the 'siege'. No, the loved one who has gone is 'Boy'. Have lately (as
last night) been waking and worrying about him; (a) that he is
destroying his substance; (b) that he finds us so boring – he didn't
have a single meal with us the whole time he was in Zermatt and the
last two nights he couldn't even face sleeping under the same roof –
(c) what the hell is he going to do?

Then I can't deny the physical decline that has occurred in the last
five years. It's partly the passing of time – the weekends are so precious;
partly the sheer fatigue accumulated by back pain, rheumatics etc that
cut down on – and virtually eliminated – exercises. I can't run and I
doubt if I could really do Summerhouse Hill without feeling awful. I
have had the ticket for the Berkeley swimming pool now for two
years and have never used it.

Financially these have been appalling times. I don't really miss the
Moore bust, only a showing-off colour, but haven't yet told Jane who
didn't want it to be sold (not realising the extent to which one was
still in hock on Zermatt). The half Cézanne deal is a mystery – where
the hell did it all go? On doing the rooms (although the Great Hall
still leaks and drips ominously) and the kitchen and wood system,
school fees and heavy expenditure on 'Boy'. Had to sell the Bira –
and this with the windfall of Dennis Wright's[1] could get us nominally
'straight'. Even so, as darling Jane who so nobly struggles now with
the VAT books laments, output still rages ahead of input, or 'coin'.
We can only last a certain amount of time longer and I would say my
father is good for at least another four years.

Politically, one might say I have advanced, or at least consolidated.
I would have said that I have made *considerable* progress in this new
parliament – with my confident interventions, better relationship with
the whips, distinct and lucid and insistent advocacy of protectionism –
being 'noted' by even John Biffen and 'The Lady' – but all of a sudden
'The Lady' has gone cold, freezing cold on me. Ian Gow, too, seems
to be avoiding me in the lobby.

I've catalogued these random impressions, not all by any means.
But it's maudlin really, isn't it? The full, full life. One is never content,

---

[1] Cottage in Saltwood village.

but think of poor Nanny, nothing to do but walk slowly in Hythe and listen to what people say. I thank God for the incredible variety and privilege he has bestowed on me, also for strength to take advantage of it. God? I hardly ever speak to him now, except for the ritual 'touch wood' of thanks on my knees before getting into bed.

One last epic memory of the period the great dice against the two super bikes in the green Porsche turbo. Cin was with me and I'm glad of that, as so many of my hopes are now with him.

Thank God for keeping us all so fine, for saving Jamie in his aeroplane and virtually curing Tip of asthma, for still giving me 'highs' and inspiring dear Bonny mama to leave me her fortune.

Cloisters   *Monday, 21 April*

At a loose end I went to the European Affairs Committee. I am due on Welsh Radio the following morning to talk about Carter and United States 'sanctions' against Iran and as Europe is plainly feeble and divided on this subject I thought I might pick up some tips. Ian Gow came in and sat at the far side of the room. On impulse I went over to him and asked him if he was free for dinner.

'Sadly not,' he replied. 'What are you doing after this?'

This was good, but unfortunately I had the Home Affairs Committee at 6 p.m. and as we were due to discuss the Bristol riots I could hardly shirk it.

'Come to my room at 5.30,' he said.

We sat in the leather chairs of the PPS's room. As always he was serious, attentive and conveyed that special sense of urgency and concern of which he is a master. I plunged straight in.

'I say, am I in the Prime Minister's bad books at the moment?'

'No, no, not at all . . .'

'I just seem to detect a certain *frisson* . . .'

'Oh no, she has a very high opinion of you, you are one of her . . .'

'Say no more, no, no, please say no more', I held up my hand in the time honoured Trevor-Roper gesture.[1]

---

[1] Hugh Trevor-Roper, now Lord Dacre, had been AC's tutor at Christ Church and had a special characteristic wave of the hand which he used indiscriminately to halt praise or criticism, or to dismiss argument.

I went straight into the topic of the 'rebel' votes against various aspects of the Employment Bill. It was immediately plain that Gow was anxious to encourage them, 'I can assure you that if you should vote in that lobby it would not make the slightest difference to your standing or reputation' (he only just stopped himself from saying 'career prospects'). He speaks quite openly about hostility between Prior and the Prime Minister. I said that Prior was probably more frightened of dismissal than might appear to those who see him in day to day action in the Cabinet Room and told the story of my conversation with Jim Lester in the Tea Room last month. Gow said that if he were to be sacked he would be more dangerous as a focus of old Heathites and progressives on the backbenches. I said that I hoped the Prime Minister realised the full extent of the armory of weapons at her disposal and how she had nothing to fear provided she realised that whatever happened – short of a defeat on a vote of confidence – she was in power, personally, for another $3\frac{1}{2}$ years. 'It is very difficult to promulgate any policy without the agreement of the Cabinet,' said Gow. 'Well the obvious answer to that is to change the Cabinet,' I replied, 'but I agree there are strategic considerations.'

I told the story that Ray Whitney[1] had recounted to me about how he was so offended by Prior's jokes and criticism of the Prime Minister, with Hayhoe acting as feedman, that he had walked out of a dinner party. Hayhoe is a classic example of a wet and a fifth columnist in a job to which he is totally ill-suited without status of any kind that might make his sacking difficult – and anyway I know I could do the job (Minister of Defence for the Army) better than he does.

'We have never had this conversation,' said Ian. 'Of course not,' I said. Somebody tried the door, we both looked round guilty and I got up to go. Ian unlocked the door and Tony Royle walked in.

'Six of the best,' I said, 'I hope you have got your telephone directory in place.'

The door closed behind him with the key turned.

---

[1] Raymond (Ray) Whitney, MP for Wycombe since 1978.

Cloisters   *Thursday, 24 April*

I was lunching in the Members' Dining Room with two nonentities (I cannot remember their names) when the Chief Whip[1] came and sat at our table.

Conversation strayed round to the events of the previous evenings.[2]

'Don't you think,' I said, foolishly (why did I say this?) '. . . that the list of rebels last night was qualitatively superior to that of the night before?'

'I never consider there is any quality among those who vote against their own government,' he said icily.

Unhappily I tried to be flippant, but it was no good. He was not friendly. I fear I have lost much ground. The Chief Whip fulminated about others (I know Gerry Neale[3] was among them from what he told me) who had voted against on a three-liner the previous week without any warning or apology afterwards. I left the table early and bolted to the Members' Post Office where I scribbled out a full, but I fear largely illegible, letter of apology which I then rushed through to the Chief Whip's office in the hope that it would greet him on his desk on his return from his meal.

House of Commons   *Monday/Tuesday, 28/29 April*

Horrible 'austerity' book[4] opens with gloom.

Woken last night by the Albany blackbird, so glad he is still around, he went off quite quietly, almost as soon as the chorus started.

I thought through the various 'last times'. This thing I have. There is, is bound logically to be, a 'last time' you do everything before you die. The first times you know about; they may be good or they may be bad. Sometimes they mirror first times, sometimes they overlap. I mean the first time you are impotent does not immediately follow the last time you have sexual intercourse (in my own case 1955 and . . .

---

[1] Michael Jopling, MP for Westmorland since 1964, Chief Whip since 1979.
[2] The 'rebellions' on the Employment Bill. The number of back benchers voting against the Government had increased from 37 the previous Thursday, to 45 on Tuesday and to 48 the following evening.
[3] Gerrard (Gerry) Neale, MP for North Cornwall since 1979.
[4] New journal, as described in Introduction.

open). But the last time you don't know, not really know because there is always hope, until much later.

When the boys were tiny I used to go up to their room and kiss them goodnight, always with Jane, and this was lovely, the very best part of the whole day. Then Jane dropped out and I used to tell a story (the 'Badgers', the 'Tidy Pig' etc), and this was even better. Then that stopped (to much protestation, some of it slightly formalised) as a punishment for 'tinkling' behind the cupboard on the top floor at the Manor. I think I still did occasionally tell a story, as a treat only for a bit, although often urged to I never wrote them down and can remember very few, only the theft of the cartridges for Guy Fawkes day in full – but a little, dimly, of the kidnapping on the *Hesperides*. Anyway, the next stage was just saying 'goodnight' and perhaps a little chat with them in bed; then with them standing, and dressed in their room; then often downstairs or in the corridor; finally (in James's case) *they* had to check in with *us*.

I composed the letter, which I still have to put on paper, to Tip, both explaining how much I love him and how I agonised when he was tiny. James always outshone him. He wants a black GTI. I can't refuse, because he never asks (until now) for anything. But of course it's even more like OLA – much more – and much faster (because OLA, being as it were 'vintage' imposes its own discipline). I hope to pose certain restrictions – no dicing? – not over 70 etc.

Later

It was the second day of the Defence White Paper debate, for which I had put in a special plea to the Speaker stating my reasons. Although I had asked him to help I suspect that Carol Mather[1] deliberately spoilt my chances. Chris Patten[2] a bumptious but intelligent little careerist was called in my place. I am in bad odour with the whips. And their memory is long. A great nuisance as I thought I had been 'mending my fences'.

---

[1] Carol Mather, MP for Esher since 1970, Defence Whip since 1979.
[2] Chris Patten, MP for Bath since 1979.

Saltwood   *Monday, 5 May*

Jane stays lovely, always bright, happy and has lovely grey eyes and
magic powers of observation. She 'found' a Miro in the drawer in the
library table yesterday looking through old Christmas cards.

As I closed the Bailey this evening I couldn't help thinking – I
really am getting quite a bit older. My physique didn't change at all
from 20–30, very, very little from 30–40, and tiny bit faster from 40–
45. But the last seven years have been devastating. Is it my life-style?
The Commons? It is certainly coinciding with it. I am using up my
reserves so that when I am 60 I will actually be like someone of 60.

Saltwood   *Thursday, 8 May*

The Iranian Sanctions Bill is being rushed through the House. Total
balls of course from beginning to end, and can only do harm. Tam
Dalyell[1] did an incredible job filibustering, speaking for up to two
hours at a time without ever being irrelevant or out of order.

I was in a dilemma – and not one of conscience. There was a
running two-line whip with the likelihood of votes every three hours
or so to get 'closures'. I have no pair and the last thing I wanted was
another rumpled night on the back seat of the Chev. I hung around
in the early stages and made interjections, also a short speech in which,
interalia, I consolidated my position on the US Embassy black list by
referring to the President [Carter] as, 'the worst incumbent of the
White House since President Harding'. Ioan Evans, the amiable, but
presumably lecherous and corrupt, Tribune M.P. for Aberdare,[2] was
also taking part in the early stages of the debate. I sensed he would
probably want to go about eleven and asked him for a pair. But he
would not break his arrangement with Michael Hamilton. 'I will give
you a name though boyoo', he then said, 'I will give you a name'.

'Yes, yes', I was over eager.

'Donald Coleman',[3] he said.

I went straight to the Whips' Office and gave some cock and bull

---

[1] Tam Dalyell, Labour MP for West Lothian since 1962.
[2] Ioan Evans, MP for Aberdare since February 1974.
[3] Donald Coleman, MP for Neath since 1964.

story about having arranged a pair yesterday and forgot to register it. They were firm that it had to be registered with Peter Morrison (the implacable pairing whip who, if he had his way, would never register *any* pairs). I knew better than this, so I sought out dear Bob Boscawen[1] and told him that although I had voted with the Government the previous evening I was speaking in favour of a number of amendments and to save embarrassment I thought it would be better if I was paired at this Committee Stage and could he tell Peter.

Later that night at the 'Business' vote (exempt from pairing arrangements) Peter Morrison actually told me to shut up and desist from taking part in the debate. He tried to claim that although I was paired on the amendments I should still attend to vote in the 'closures'. But I was not going to have any of that and went home to bed.

It is hellish not having a pair, I am going to run out of tricks like this in the end. I *must* write to the next Labour candidate for a safe seat at a by-election.

H o C, Committee Room   *Tuesday, 13 May*

Almost fell asleep at Brooks's dinner, solitary on Perrier water. We had to be back in the committee room by 9 'on the dot'. As I blew the two-pressure horn on the little 'Mickey' I was reminded, suddenly, of driving back from the Lavingtons, having been, in all probability with the beagles on Salisbury Plain. Fifteen years ago! What a decline in one's physique, sexuality, appearance. Could I recover? Or rather *how far* could I recover?

Albany   *Monday, 19 May*

I awoke this morning and decided to pick a fight with Willie Whitelaw. I am sick of him. I am pretty sure he does not like me and I suspect that he has a big influence in the higher counsels of the Party. I have long admired his intuition and political skills, but I read over the weekend that the Home Office was actually increasing the grant to

---

[1] Robert (Bob) Boscawen, MP for Wells since 1970, a whip since 1979.

the Voluntary Services Unit, an outfit devoted exclusively, it seems, to funding subversive activities and concerning which I had asked a number of pretty taut questions when we were in Opposition. I thought this was really too much.

However, in politics we are all in the kaleidoscope; give the thing a kick, or even a light tap and it may change out of all recognition. And later that day when I was in the Tea Room eating a rock bun and preparing myself to raise the VSU question aggressively at the Home Affairs Committee in five minutes time, up came Ted Gardner[1] and asked if I would chair the new sub-committee which Willie had asked to be set up to look at the question of Civil Defence. I realised at once that this could be a very useful rung on the ladder. In Committee Ted approaches these things in a very circumlocutory way. I do not know whether he had second thoughts or doubts of any kind, but he almost failed to manage to announce it to the Committee, who nonetheless applauded loudly, led by Hugh Fraser.

Mary Whitehouse[2] had been invited to address us that day and everyone had forgotten. After waiting in the corridor for half an hour she somewhat deferentially tried to get in and had to be shown out and kept waiting for a further fifteen minutes.

So far so good. After the Committee had dispersed little Jim Pawsey, a real cheeky-chappie complete with glasses and bustling papers, stayed behind and we discussed what we were to do. Ted had suggested that I invite Pawsey[3] to be secretary as he had made a lot of mileage on this subject, asked an enormous number of P.A.s etc. He believes it will make his career, and let him go on believing this as he will gladly shoulder the leg work. However, there were hurdles to be leapt.

That evening we were invited to attend a joint meeting with officers of the Defence Committee in Willie's room behind the Speaker's Chair at 10.30 p.m. It was immediately apparent that Willie, dressed in a 'slub' silk dinner jacket, had had too much to drink. I know of old that when his skin is livid, and he carries his head in that special one-sided gait he is fighting hard to beat off the depressant effects of many, many millilitres per centilitre; and sure enough he very quickly got 'on the bellow', recounted an exchange between himself and

---

[1] Edward (Ted) Gardner, MP for South Fylde since 1970.
[2] Mary Whitehouse, President of the National Viewers' and Listeners' Association since 1980. Articulate upholder of conservatism and decency in the media.
[3] James (Jim) Pawsey, MP for Rugby since 1979.

General Creasey[1] in which they appeared to have both been completely uninhibited. Creasey had called Willie a wet and a shit. Willie
had apparently shouted 'fuck you' in public and followed up with, 'I
hated you when you were in Northern Ireland, I have always hated
you and I hate you now.'

By the time we came to actually discuss the arrangements for the
Civil Defence enquiry he had become totally lost. All he had done
was to repeat at great length twice or three times over his reasons for
deferring the Review (our numbers were constantly being swelled by
the arrival of various delegates who had been sent for at thirty minutes
staggered intervals). When Ted finally got round to the subject of
the sub-committee having been promulgated and that I had been
appointed to chair it the news went down like a lead balloon. The
whole room was furious and Willie was put out – blustered that we
would not have time to report before he published his own Review
(not half we won't, I will take care of that). Poor little Jimmy Pawsey
foolishly and youthfully suggested that I should make a statement.
Willie affected not to hear and shouted this down. I was sly because I
knew that I had already released the news to the Press Association and
the London heavies and that I was going on radio the following
morning so they could not get rid of me or change the plan.

Afterwards in the Members' Lobby the odious Atkins came up to
me and said, 'It looks as if your committee is going to have only one
member.'

I had already had to put off at least half a dozen applicants since it
was promulgated that afternoon and said as much. He switched
immediately and asked if he could join. But I made a non-committal
reply.

Got to bed at 1.20 a.m. and will be woken by an alarm call from
the BBC at 6.15 a.m.

---

[1] General Sir Timothy Creasey, Commander-in-Chief, UK Land Forces, had been GOC,
Northern Ireland, 1977–79.

Albany   *Tuesday, 20 May*

In the Lobby, Ian Gow, in a dinner jacket, gave me a slightly beady
look. I was meant to be at a Reception at No. 10, but had felt so tired
that I could not be bothered to change and had spent most of the
previous hour dozing in a chair in the Library. However, I abandoned
RJ and pelted after Ian, 'to whom do I address my apologies, I don't
think I have a dinner jacket in London, don't wish to be discourteous
by attending improperly dressed'.

He pressed me to come, insisted, said he would take me in his own
car. 'The Prime Minister would be absolutely furious if you don't
come,' he said. He is such a dear. I ran down and put on a white shirt
and joined him in the Mini which was parked (as he often amusingly
does) on the space 'reserved for the disabled' in Star Court. Charles
Fletcher-Cooke[1] – always good company – was already in the car
though, naturally, wearing a dinner jacket.

The moment we got to No. 10 Ian abandoned us, whizzing into
his own office on the ground floor.

There were *very* few people at the Reception who were not in
dinner jackets. I have a high confidence level, but it was not too good.
However, the Prime Minister did not express disapproval and when she
introduced me to Dr Kurt Waldheim[2], she actually said, 'Something –
something, something' ('specialises in', was it? the noise in the room
was deafening) 'defence'. This I suppose was encouraging. Stum-
blingly I muttered about my new committee.

Dr Waldheim inclined his head. I do not know what he thought
of things. The 'Reception' seemed to me rather inchoate not to say
disorderly. The Prime Minister herself was rather *waxen*-faced and
disconcertingly broad in the beam as she sometimes can be. She must
not 'go dowager'. That would detract a lot. But how does she sustain
her interest on those occasions? My God, when I am Prime Minister
I will never go to receptions.

---

[1] Charles Fletcher-Cooke, MP for Darwen since 1951.
[2] Dr Kurt Waldheim, Secretary-General of the United Nations since 1972.

Saltwood   *Saturday, 31 May*

We have had some wonderful summer days. Unfortunately the filling
of the pool delayed by the wait for the (new) plastic bubble cover that
was meant to keep the heat in and the leaves out. Pool only just
reaching the top and no swimming yet.

Last night I worried about James (what else??) who had walked off
after dinner. Tip-toed down about midnight and found him in the
Green Room. We looked at the atlas of the British Empire in 1935 –
all gone, in 40 years, all of it. And he told me that his friends said
the Sea-Harrier was still not fitted with HUD [Head Up Display].
Depressing.

Albany   *Tuesday, 17 June*

I've been in vile mood all day. A new List has been published. Michael
McNair-Wilson,[1] as always, was languid and mocking. 'The "K's" are
really flying around, aren't they?'

Michael went on to suggest that Freddy Burden's was 'post-
humous'.[2]

Now we are stuck on some long, rambling, useless 2-liner. So
drained by the horrible fetid air, tight shoes, suits rumpling. I had a
full day here, getting in before 9 a.m., then realised at 7 p.m., when
'the world' was slacking off and putting on its slippers that I still had
another five hours – minimum – to go.

Was feeling randily expectant as Nanny had told me the previous
day that someone 'well-spoken and cheeky' had rung and said that (as
it were) 'Mimi Schluckleberger will dine with you on Wednesday
night.'

The phone rang as I was making cocoa; Ali; I knew Valeri was
there. Suddenly *she* snatched the phone and said, all Lausanne-station-
voice, 'you stupid little bastard' twice and rang off. I was scared and

---

[1] Michael McNair-Wilson, MP for Newbury since February 1974 (Walthamstow East,
   1969–74), PPS to the Ministry of Agriculture.
[2] Frederick Burden finally retired from the House in 1983 after 43 years representing
   Gillingham. He died in 1987.

thought of bolting; went down and told 'Shea'[1] not to let anyone in. Was somehow randily expectant, in spite of it. However, Ali rang and said (late, about 10.30) that 'she' was livid, got it in for me, was going to get Bodoni to work me over etc.

Ugh. Totally dry mouthed.

I rang Janey. She had had *two* tours, bless her. And that morning had mowed the Bailey herself, because if Cradduck had seen Eddie on the new (sit-down) Atco [mower] he'd have been hysterical with rage. But what's the point of employing two gardeners if the *chatelaine* has to do the work herself? I wish I was at Saltwood.

Earlier, the mood in the Cloisters was light-headed. The talk strayed to by-elections, and I invited wagers for my betting book.

Gerry Neale pretended to be shocked. So, camply, did Michael although it was he who started the whole thing off by saying that he had a 'horror' of going up to the main gents for a quiet crap, opening the cubicle door and finding Alan Glyn[2] sprawled across the 'pedestal', jaw hanging open, eyes rolled round in their sockets. I am offering 11 to 4 on Freddy Burden (must be favourite), 5 to 4 against Graham Page,[3] 2 to 1 Glyn, 3 to 1 Costain and 4 to 1 (an interesting outsider) Hugh Rossi.[4] It's the shortish, fattish, tense-ish ones who go first.[5]

Saltwood   *Tuesday, 24 June*

First day of a lovely long weekend, full of promise. I was on Gossie most of the morning. Burning hot sunshine, and chasing Tom almost as hard work as beagling. The soil on the bank is very sandy. Not pure sand, which would be dangerous of course, and put the Jack Russell in peril when, as he does most often, he goes underground. He was out of sight for almost an hour, though occasionally I could hear him

---

[1] A porter at Albany.

[2] Dr Alan Glyn, MP for Windsor since 1970.

[3] Sir Graham Page, MP for Crosby since 1953. Died 1981.

[4] Hugh Rossi, MP for Hornsey since 1966, Minister of State for Social Security and the Disabled since 1981. Not a good bet. Rossi out-lived them all.

[5] In fact Glyn (d. 1997) was to outlive Sir Michael McNair-Wilson by more than six years. As previous entries have shown, AC had a vested interest in the future of Albert Costain whose constituency included Saltwood. Costain died in 1987.

barking. Tom 'makes free' with the warrens, going in at one hole and coming out at another. Which must be a bore for any resident rabbits. Watership Down with a difference.

When I got back there was no sign of Jane. Nanny was disapproving. Apparently a young, unidentified, female had been on the telephone. 'Is Al there?' Nanny doesn't think people outside the family should call me 'Al'. When offered Jane instead the caller hung up.

Nanny drawing on fifty years of experience both Up-, and Down-, stairs, said that she was *well-spoken, but cheeky*.

'Was she in a call-box?' Didn't know.

Could something tiresome be about to happen? Damn, damn, blast, etc.

Saltwood   *Sunday, 6 July*

Have been, for the last week, extremely *apprehensive*; heavy depression, alternating with fear both short and long-term.

Started on Monday night; foolishly stripped off at Brooks's, played a little b'gammon losing £100 to Villiers and Burnett (but if I can't play with them, then I really have given up).

Dined at Julian Amery's house in Eaton Square. The most *beautiful* library, L-shaped, using the whole depth of the house (which is virtually next door to Henry Wilson, shot on his doorstep by the IRA in 1920) and abutting on a particularly marvellous conservatory just filled with old bushes and plastic bowls. Meant to be for the Crown Prince of Jordan, who didn't show up. Offered champagne, I asked if it could be mixed with orange juice. Julian demurred, said it was 'rather good'. My God it was. Greedily I drank as many glasses as I could. Of the guests I can only remember one, recently beknighted captain of industry. Odious, bullying and livid to be faced with a pipsqueak back-bencher. I didn't give a fuck. During dinner (good wine served by intoxicated, English, man-servant) I heard him asking Julian who I was, and instantly . . . being given . . . 'Lord Clark'.

However, to return to main theme. Had quite a longish session with Desmond Corcoran who was very reluctant to stump up £5,000 on security of Miro (looking rather grand in its bright gold frame, but apparently unsaleable). However he did so, repayment deferred until 30 September.

Cloisters   *Monday, 7 July*

Fortunately nothing in any of the Dailies today 'following up' yesterday's horror item in the *News of the World*.

Willie Hamilton caught me in the Lobby just after the afternoon
vote.[1] Somewhat pale and put out, he tried to assert that he had not
given my name to anybody, claimed that he had written to the *News
of the World* and insisted that they apologise, etc. 'It will be interesting
to see if they print my letter,' he said. (You bet it will.) He is rattled
about the affair and, indeed, may well have been trapped into giving
my name either by an adroit reporter or by Winston or Nick Winterton. I do not put much value to what he says, but at least it is
something to have him nominally on my side and not out to cause
more trouble.

Later in the evening I was walking down the Smoking Room
Corridor to go towards the dining room and have some dinner when
St John Stevas, purple shirted as always, hailed me; 'What is all this
about you and Princess Margaret? ...' I told him the story. It is
amazing how many people read *News of the World*. I never see it from
one quarter to the next. Stevas tried to get me to say who it was who
had originally expressed disapproval and did not like it when I would
not. I wandered on into the Dining Room. Most of the tables were
either full or with people obviously finishing a meal over their coffee.
Hal Miller, who was sitting at that long table by the window which
is notorious for its dreadful service, hailed me almost with a note of
desperation in his voice. He was alone with a huge, but unidentified
female companion, presumably a peeress. It was apparent that she was
exceedingly the worse for drink. A cross between Bonny mama and
Christabel Aberconway on a bad day. She ground away at us and
naturally neither of the two bad-tempered waitresses came anywhere
near. Then Ian Gow came in, beaming as always, and suggested joining
us at which prospect naturally we first brightened then, as he turned
away and announced that he was going to bring the Prime Minister,
blenched.

The Prime Minister duly arrived and was immediately pinned by
the giant washerwoman (who turned out from a *sotto voce* enquiry to

---

[1] Under the heading 'Willie and his Palace mole' AC was implicated in being the
alleged intermediary between a royal equerry and the anti-monarchist Hamilton, who
suggested he lay off the Queen Mother (approaching her eightieth birthday) and
concentrate on Princess Margaret instead.

Ian, who was on my left, to be Dame Hornsby-Smith[1]). On and on she huskily rambled consuming no fewer than four chain-lit Philip Morris filters during her soliloquy, and all the time the Prime Minister looked at her with an expression of rapt fascination and sympathy, occasionally nodding her head in agreement or making a polite interjection to show how closely she was following the story (itself a long untidy affair about precedence of Privy Councillors at a dinner and how Hornsby-Smith ended up going into the room on the arm of the Duke of Edinburgh).

At intervals Gow suggested, far from inaudibly, that there was a division in the Lords. Then, smoothly, Hornsby-Smith shifted across from anecdote to current affairs. She described the present state of play in the Lords regarding the passage of Clause 7 the following day.[2] It is quite clear that due to Labour abstentions and other bungling it is, to use Hornsby-Smith's phrase, 'going to be a very dicy affair'. As she said this some sixth sense made me look up from the tablecloth at the Prime Minister who simultaneously did the same thing and we exchanged a conspiratorial look. Not a wink, but a look into the iris of the eye – very exciting.

Earlier the Prime Minister had seemed to be going out of her way to be friendly and said how she had told Ian, 'that is Alan's voice ...' when I had been showing encouragement in the hurly burly that surrounded the announcement of our restricted pay increase and in particular how I had barracked Edward du Cann's pompous and unpopular short speech.[3]

In the fullness of time, there *was* a division in the Lords and Hornsby-Smith heaved herself to her feet and disappeared. I told the Prime Minister that there was not another Premier in history who would have shown so much attention and good nature and adroitly she semi-rebuked me, said what a wonderful person Pat Hornsby-Smith was and how tragic it was to see her like this, how she had had cancer of the throat, etc. I must say that if she has had cancer of the throat she has certainly adopted a very curious kind of homoeopathy to eradicate it.

The Prime Minister lingered at our table for nearly an hour and there was much anecdote and good natured gossip. She was completely

---

[1] Patricia Hornsby-Smith, MP for Chislehurst 1950–66 (1970–February 74), DBE 1961, Life Peer 1974. She died in 1985.

[2] In the Employment Bill, a clause relating to trade union membership.

[3] Edward du Cann, MP for Taunton since 1956; chairman 1922 Committee since 1972.

relaxed and delightful – buoyed, I don't doubt, by the MORI poll which shows her in the lead for the very first time ever.

At the end, Ian, also in high good humour, dated me for dinner for the following evening and I rushed away to ring up Jane in the highest of spirits. During the phone conversation the division bell rang and coming up from the Lobby I again saw the Prime Minister, but this time talking most intimately tête-à-tête to Geoffrey Pattie, who always makes me jealous, although I recognise his concept of defence for the UK is probably the soundest in the Government.

Saltwood   *Wednesday, 9 July*

More girl trouble.

Someone rang at the House and asked for an appointment. Alison told me that she was calling back which she did on the dot of 4.15. Clearly going to put the bite on. I icily shook. Went and dug out a senior police officer – useless. Gave mouldy advice, wouldn't get me bugging kit; said Yard 'would only supply it if I preferred charges ...' etc. Dived about the place in a state of high anxiety and found myself sitting next to Nick Budgen[1] and confided in him. He wasn't much use, but did give one name – Jonathan Aitken.[2] Caught Jonathan in the lobby at the 10 o'clock vote. He said he was at a dinner, but pressed me to come along; I demurred; it turned out he was with a bird at some flat ... He was calming, gave good advice. Trysted me for next morning at his (incredibly) sumptuous Saudi Arabian offices. We discussed tactics, then round to 'counter-spy' shop for a 'recorder brief-case'. Tried to settle for smaller (lapel-type) recorder, but trial showed defective workmanship. Walked out as couldn't get discount, then, with just 20 minutes to spare back and bought it. (Amexing it.)

Briefly experimented, centred it on my desk and up to lobby (no sign of the police, I may say). She was waiting, *very* pale ... out to the Harcourt Room. Oh she was so silly, wasn't she ... eased gently into the subject – no hint of pressure, almost as if she had been warned against being recorded. Strictly according to schedule good old Jon-athan A turned up to testify that he had seen us together. Finally she

---

[1] Nicholas Budgen, MP for Wolverhampton South-West since February 1974.
[2] Jonathan Aitken, MP for Thanet East since February 1974.

came out with it – wanted £5,000. 'Certainly,' I said – 'you can have £5,000.' I don't think she thought her victory would be so easy; she mellowed and allowed the occasional sparkle to shine through – so much so that at the end, and feeling generous ... I invited her to come 'round the block' in the Cadillac. This, however, she declined. I was greatly relieved. Put me in the clear, a 'good omen', acted as a signing off gesture.

Later that afternoon, in the lobby, I told Jonathan I had agreed to pay her £5,000. Amusingly he said, 'I should have offered her £4,000 and the briefcase.'

Cloisters							*Thursday, 10 July*

Met her (less good mood this time) and 'handed over'. She a bit waspish – 'it's only gnat's piss to you' etc.

Bratton-Clovelly						*Saturday, 12 July*

Out here very late after a 'meet-the-Member' party. Dear Jane came down and I met her train in the hired, colourless, Vauxhall Cavalier. I said, 'we'll have to stay till ten.' She said, 'nine.' I didn't make my piccolo speech until 9.20. Left as soon as one decently could after that. Eileen clearly disappointed. This morning I said, 'perhaps we should have stayed for the washing up.' 'No, the Heseltines always left after half an hour,' she replied.

Meeting of the Executive on 25 July – 'West MP on the carpet ...'. Have rehearsed my little, 'I have nothing to say' speech in which I end by saying '... and I bid you goodnight', and pick up the Aitken briefcase and walk out.

Saltwood   *Thursday, 14 August*

Broke off to help Jane move the new broody, then, impromptu, to
clear out the 'junior' hen house; then spray Winifred's radiator grill
(very effective); then go back to clean out 'senior' or matrix hen
house. Very hot and muggy. Decided, while struggling on major sell-
off, for a 'tight ship' plan from now on.

Saltwood   *Monday, 1 September*

Apprehensive about James – 'not come in' yesterday, according to Mr
Thingummy of Turner Aviation. Was there something 'strange' about
his voice? At least he's not 'missing' on a flight, but worried about
him being terrified in a bar. This gave me a bad night, as did the
knowledge that I have exactly one day left to complete my Petty
Expense form and my desk just is a total mess and shambles, floor
hasn't been hoovered for twelve months.

Zermatt   *Saturday, 6 September*

Went up on the Wednesday before we left to dine with Ian Gow. He
was late, and I drank two 'Bucks fizz' at the Cavalry Club. Gave me
the impression, somehow, that he was not quite at the centre as much.
Gloomily said, 'I won't be doing this next year . . .' or something to
that effect. Then later, when I returned to the subject, he said how I
would be a 'perfect' successor, in so many ways but 'too senior'. What
does that mean? (Other than for 'senior' read 'unsuitable'). Awful
already to be in a position when that oblique, but damning compliment
can be paid – not forgetting that 'senior' is the Latin for 'older'. Have
I, in my concentration on the House, undermined some of my other
positions – most noticeably, of course, the virtual, tacit, 'writing-off'
of the constituency. Looks at present as if I won't be able to 'open the
season' with Stan Radford's 'at home' on the twentieth as I will be at
the Rhine Army manoeuvres.

Saltwood   *Tuesday, 14 October*

We did two days at conference – struck standard Brighton typhoon weather, wind sucking with extractor force down those little side streets that lead off at right angles on to 'Royal Parade' (or whatever it's called). Was being 'done' by Thames TV as one of the subjects in *Westminster Man* and so followed around by cameramen. Invited on to platform for Civil Defence debate and 'mentioned' by Leon Brittan (unusual). *Naturally* no Plymouthians in the hall at the time. Still, this gave me enough confidence to ride through them at the dreaded 'W. Area cocktail party' that evening.

We came back after tea on Wednesday and have had a lovely 'free', or shirking week. Jamie returned the next day with lots of lovely presents and quite unchanged, though slightly on a down on his looks. Andrew and I got the Locomobile going and it was incredible, the most exciting thing I have driven since the Lago-Talbot and Andrew is very enthused and helpful.

Cloisters   *Monday, 27 October*

A series of coincidences started to build up today into quite an interesting 'situation'.

Getting to the Palace too late for lunch but feeling rather flu-ey I turned into the Smoking Room for a glass of Malvern water into which I plopped my massive 1 mg tablet of effervescent Redoxon. John Langford-Holt[1] was sitting reading the paper in an otherwise almost deserted room. I sat down beside him and tried to steer the subject to the question of the cuts. He was not especially communicative and kept raising his newspaper as a protective screen. I was really getting nowhere when the Chief Whip [Michael Jopling] came in. He hovered, and then sat down with us.

'We were talking about various subjects appertaining to defence matters,' I said.

'It did just cross my mind that you might have been doing that.'

---

[1] Sir John Langford-Holt, Chairman of the all-party Select Committee for Defence since 1979.

He was clearly in a very anxious condition about the whole thing. I told him that I believed the Party would probably accept the cuts provided they were attached to sweeping and equivalent reductions in other departments, but they would not be acceptable if defence was singled out in isolation on account of its previous (so-called) immunity. He seemed especially interested in all this and very anxious to please. I had to take my place for Prayers because it had suddenly struck me that I ought to ask Heseltine a Plymouth–Plymouth–Plymouth question about the housing moratorium when he made his statement about the ban on council house building, and you have a better chance of being called on such an occasion if you are there to bow to the Speaker when he comes in for Prayers. I duly put the question, which was mildly critical and related to penalising under-spending councils along with the massive over-spenders in the Labour heartlands.

For some reason Ted was in the Chamber, sitting in his usual place, which is three away from me, but with no one between us. To my amazement, as I sat down he swivelled massively in his seat (though retaining two fingers in the famous 'V' position against his right cheek) and said, 'At last you're beginning to learn something', then swivelled ponderously back and stared ahead. I simpered acknow-ledgement (a mistake) but said nothing. What on earth can he have meant? At first sight it seemed to be a compliment, but on reflection I suppose it wasn't. What I suppose he meant was: 'all of you idiots who voted for The Lady are now beginning to realise the mess you are getting yourselves into'.

As I left the Chamber Bob Boscawen buttonholed me and said in a *very* conspiratorial way that he wanted to see me privately. Heavens! Thoughts of having been caught in some frightful misdemeanour flashed through my mind. In the past when whips have said this it has been to issue a reprimand for such offences as smashing a telephone or having more than the correct quota of cars in the underground car park. I suggested the Tea Room, but he demurred, it was too public (!). I *had* to eat, having missed lunch, so insisted that we go to the Pugin Room where I know that the patisserie are rather good. He, too, wanted to question me about the Party's attitude to the defence cuts and I repeated what I had said earlier to Michael. I got the feeling that Boscawen was trying to lead me on to various light indiscretions which might have helped to form an opinion about my attitudes to general issues prevailing.

'That is one of the people giving us the most trouble,' he muttered to himself as someone got up and left the Pugin Room. Too short-sighted to see who it was I said 'Who?'

'Peter Walker' he muttered, *very* inaudibly. I was interested in this because it is unusual for whips to criticise individual members of the Cabinet;[1] they always pretend we are one big happy family.

Cloisters   *Tuesday, 28 October*

There was an urgent message this morning to meet in Francis Pym's[2] room at 2 p.m. (i.e. before Questions). But the discussion was very light, being confined simply to tactics and a quick survey of the Order Paper. Certainly not as orderly or effective as those pre-question meetings which we always used to have with Willie on Home Office days, when we were in Opposition. However, Francis did express his wish for someone to ask a question about the moratorium, which I duly did, thus getting another opportunity to plug Plymouth on two successive days. Perchance I had received only that morning a letter from a firm of metal painters, a long rambling complaint, itself virtually unanswerable, but to which, by coincidence one could give the semblance of instant action.

That evening at 6 p.m. we again met, this time at Francis' room in the Ministry of Defence. The MoD building always reminds me of a large rather run-down teaching hospital with miles of beaten-up lino, smelling of Dettol, institutional beige paint, strip-lighting etc. The impression is heightened by the shambolic arrangements at the main door where a few 'security' guards, either in their late 50s and, plainly, suffering from a variety of degenerative diseases, or younger versions, pasty and overweight with hair over their collars, lolled about. Our arrival coincided with an outward collection of mail. Trolleys of loaded mail bags were being pushed, with much forced bonhomie (but not always very effectively) through the special 'secure' swing doors. It reminded me of those endless loads of hospital laundry that used to be run out through the basement doors at St Thomas' when I, inevitably arriving late, used to try and take a short cut from the

---

[1] Peter Walker, Minister of Agriculture since 1979.
[2] Francis Pym had been Secretary of State for Defence since 1979.

governors' car park to whichever distant committee room where, as Chairman-designate, I was being awaited by a group of peevish consultants.

It did not take long for me to realise that the substance of *this* meeting was in fact very significant. What in effect Francis was saying was that he was going to resign if any further cuts were forced on him. In his declamation he managed to include a number of coded asides about his doubts on existing Government or, as he called it, 'Treasury' policy. As I listened to this I realised exactly how significant Francis' resignation could be, as he is the only person who can take such a step without splitting the Party. If it were done by Prior or Walker then they would accumulate a coterie of 'wets' – but still be in a substantial minority for the Parliamentary Party. If by John Biffen or Geoffrey Howe, the same would be true except that their personal following would consist of discredited and resentful monetarists. Only Francis could combine the old Heathite gang, those who are resentful of cuts in public spending, *plus* the Union Jack Right who will go to the stake on defence and law-and-order issues.

It was not only that he was candid about his own intentions, he was also indiscreet about who supported him in Cabinet – Carrington, Gilmour and Soames.[1] There was a good deal of diffuse talk – the meeting went on for $1\frac{1}{2}$ hours – and certain tentative suggestions that articles should be written to the *Daily Telegraph* etc.

So blinding was my vision of what Francis ought to do and the possibilities that were open to him, that I resolved to stay behind after the meeting and have a quick word. Unfortunately, though, this was not practicable as two of his Ministers (Geoffrey Pattie and Barney Hayhoe) hung back. Accordingly, I walked back to the House with the other members of the Committee. All seemed perplexed, and certainly did not fully appreciate the significance, in Party terms, of what we had been told.

---

[1] Lord Carrington, Foreign Secretary since 1979 and Lord Soames, Lord President of the Council and Leader of the House of Lords since 1979, were the two most influential Conservatives in the Lords. Ian Gilmour had been Lord Privy Seal since 1979.

Cloisters   *Wednesday, 29 October*

I had told Hal Miller[1] that I would quite like to have a private word with Francis today if possible. He said that he thought that the Secretary of State would not be in the Commons at all that day as he was still entertaining the Italian Defence Minister.

Just before dinner I had a drink with Ian Gow in the Smoking Room and warned him of the very grave possible consequences, as I believed, of Francis' resignation. He looked glum. 'Are you telling me that the Secretary of State is seriously considering a threat of this kind if he fails to get his way?'

'Yes, I am,' I replied.

Ian made some routine noises in defence of the Treasury. His monetarism runs very deep, and of course his commitment to the defence field is not particularly strong, certainly does not compare with his obsessive identification with the Treasury heartland. Still, I feel that I had to do my duty as one of his part-time informers.

Just before the ten o'clock vote Hal Miller caught me in the Members' Lobby and said that Francis would, after all, be able to see me for a couple of minutes afterwards if I waited outside the 'Aye' lobby. I duly hung around until it was almost empty. Still no Francis. The trouble when one is waiting to catch a colleague is that others – most people are a bit tight by that time of the evening – try and get into conversation, tell one scraps of gossip, etc. I was simultaneously fending off dear John Wells who wanted to invite Andrew to go shooting with him on Saturday, and I was conscious of Ian Gow hovering (I did not want him to see me in conclave with Francis). Then the Secretary of State, round-shouldered as ever and wearing a dinner jacket, finally emerged through the division doors. Better leave it, I thought. I was getting cold feet. But Hal spotted me and waved at me to come over.

'Can I see you quite privately?' I asked. We turned right into the long corridor that cuts down towards the Speaker's Room. Even there it seemed a seething mass of people bellowing and eavesdropping. I made some variant of Oliver Lyttelton's joke about the trenches, '. . . too many people', with which he agreed. He seemed quite benevolent so, encouraged, I told him that speaking as a historian I felt obliged

---

[1] Hilary (Hal) Miller, MP for Bromsgrove and Redditch since February 1974, PPS to the Defence Secretary since 1979.

to put a case to him, but that I would neither invite nor even expect him to comment. He looked a little wary at this, but I pressed on.

'If you should finally get pushed into the position where you have to resign . . .'

'Which I certainly hope I do not have to,' he interjected.

'. . . you must realise that you are the only person who can take such a step without splitting the Party and that you would, in fact, have a broad franchise, spreading right across from those who are opposed to public spending to include those who, like myself, are sometimes depicted as being on the right. And the likelihood is that you would be Prime Minister in two years time.'

As I finished the concluding sentence the effect was electric. A huge slug of adrenalin visibly shot through his system. Far from dismissing me (as, e.g., Willie might have done) his manner became very intense. 'Come upstairs to my room,' he said, and we turned round and went to the stairs, pushing past three people who were all waiting to see him, including Hal and Keith Speed.[1] Once we got into his room I could see he was highly excited about what I had to say. I developed the theme; explaining that if The Lady were to crash within the next 18 months, there was no need to have a general election, but obviously the Party would have to find a new Leader and were he to resign now and on this issue he would be incomparably better placed than anyone else to unite it. I also pointed out that in the last 18 months of a Parliament it was far easier to alter course and frame election-winning policies if the personalities identified with the old and unpopular ones had disappeared. Francis was very attentive, claimed that his only feelings were for the Party and the Country, etc., etc. But plainly he was greatly encouraged, indeed fortified by the concept which I had put to him. I cannot believe it had not occurred to him; but he is so cautious he probably had not taken any *soundings* and was cheered to get some back-bench encouragement from a (probably) unexpected source. Hal is amiable but too bluff and 'straight' to see things long.

What a rich, endlessly varied and exciting world politics is for those who are addicted to it. And how inextricably woven are the different strands of greed, ambition, cowardice and idealism. No one's motives are pure; certainly not mine.

---

[1] Keith Speed, MP for Ashford since October 1974, and Minister for the Navy since 1979.

Albany, B5   *Tuesday, 4 November*

With a free evening I drifted into Pratt's, having taken the precaution
of dressing beautifully in a new Blade's suit, pale pink cotton shirt,
etc. Three incredibly boring buffers occupying the middle table,
dressed à la Macmillan in cardigans making desultory conversation,
and ill-informed comments on politics. The cooking remains exe-
crable, not that any of the members seem to have palates. The English
upper classes really are unspeakably awful. Were they always like this,
or is the country in its decline because they have changed character,
or have they changed character and become rebarbative and introverted (as well as stupid) because the country is in decline and they
can do nothing about it?

I went back to Brooks's and had quite an amusing dinner, although
too much claret, with James Vance-White, who told me how Euan's
aunt had recovered from her deathbed at the age of 96, revoked the
power of attorney which she had arrogated, and was now beadily
going through the cheque stubs.

Saltwood   *Sunday, 16 November*

John Erickson[1] says Russians are going into Yugoslavia soon, and
identified 'hit' units in SW order of battle, so that requires major
strategic think-out. I drove Jane back up to London in Winter Car
and asked her where she would like the shelter, Bratton or Saltwood.
She prefers Saltwood, I think rightly, although am apprehensive of
Dungeness explosion.[2]

Cloisters   *Tuesday, 25 November*

Yesterday the Chancellor made a 'statement on economic policy'
(generally hailed by the press as a 'package', with all the uncomfortable
evocation of that word). Very unsatisfactory. He gabbled through an

---

[1] John Erickson, military historian specialising on the Soviet military.
[2] Dungeness nuclear power station being south-west across the bay from Saltwood.

unintelligible Treasury brief, couched in their most obscure jargon, then came to the point. Only £1 billion further cuts in public expenditure – of which £200 million were to come from Defence – in other words £800 million was coming from all other sectors combined. So the shortfall had to come from revenue, in the form of increased 'contributions' under National Insurance. The net effect is that the workers are going to get less in the righthand column of their payslips, while the so-called Social Wage remains intact. This is precisely contrary to the theme in which our campaign was presented and a rejection of the endorsement we received from the electorate last year.

At the very end of his statement the Chancellor announced, with what for him was presumably meant to be a flourish, but which came out in Evelyn Waugh's phrase, '. . . more in the tones of a nanny than a Master-at-Arms',[1] that interest rates would be reduced by 2 per cent. This cut in interest rates is totally unjustified by the present state of the money supply or public sector borrowing and the measures that the Chancellor had described would not be becoming operative until next year anyway. It is perfectly plain that Government policy is now seriously off course – with consequences that can only be bad both for the Party and the country.

Later that evening I went to Willie's room on Ted Gardner's instructions in order to 'have a drink with' Leon Brittan and Tim Raison as Willie was allegedly absent. I duly turned up at 7 p.m. and found that not only had the time been changed, but that Willie was there in conclave with his two Ministers and that prick John Patten. What the hell was he doing there? I later found out that he had taken Esmond Bulmer's place as PPS.[2] He is so ambitious that he squeaks when he walks, and cannot manage to smile at any colleague inferior in rank in case he compromises himself in some way.

I see that George Morton[3] pleaded guilty today of an act of gross indecency in a gents in Manchester and was fined £25. Simultaneously his constituency chairman announced that he had complete con-fidence in him and that it was a 'private matter'. God alive, I would only have to be seen with a blonde on the front seat and the Plymouth

---

[1] Evelyn Waugh's *The Ordeal of Gilbert Pinfold*.
[2] John Patten, MP for Oxford since 1979, had been appointed a PPS to Brittan and Raison, succeeding Esmond Bulmer, MP for Kidderminster since February 1974.
[3] George Morton, Labour MP for Manchester Moss Side since July 1978.

Association would demand an instant vote of no confidence. Some people have all the luck.[1]

In low spirits I went to the Finance Committee meeting in Room 14 at 6 p.m. There were fewer colleagues present than I had expected. John Biffen sat at the end of the platform, radiating gloom, with his head in his hands. Up got the Chancellor and re-gabbled. He reconfirmed, also, the impression that he had really lost control of policy and events. It is the first time that I have ever been to a Party committee attended by a minister or shadow minister who has been more or less openly heckled *sotto voce*, sniggering asides, etc. I sat next to Esmond Bulmer (a good centrist fellow) and he asked a critical question. In front of me sat Tim Sainsbury who did likewise and periodically exchanged an incredulous and mocking commentary with William Waldegrave[2] who sat on my right. Every speaker was in one way or another critical, being led off by Terence Higgins[3] who, although utterly wet on racial matters, is extremely hard lined on monetary ones. The Chancellor was fielding the questions in batches of three which made it easier for him to dissimulate. But the general impression remained of an authority seriously diminished.

I left the meeting early as I had promised to get home and help Jane with the VAT and there was no whip.

Cloisters   *Wednesday, 26 November*

The *Daily Mail* ran a huge front page editorial about the manner in which the Government is falling down on all its policies and pledges and urged the Prime Minister, though not, in my view, strongly or prominently enough, to purge her Cabinet and return to the straight and narrow. At breakfast Jane reinforced this with her own pure common sense views laced with wisdom from working class people like Eddie and Peggy. What the hell *is* going on? I have had no fewer than five telephone messages from Plymouth Sound asking me to call

---

[1] Morton's career as an MP ended, however, at the 1983 general election.
[2] William Waldegrave, MP for Bristol West since 1979.
[3] Terence Higgins, chairman of several Commons committees and a member of the executive of the 1922 Committee.

them back. But I won't do so as there simply is not a comment that I can make on the present state of affairs that would not sound subversive or demoralised.

Later, walking across the Members' Lobby I saw Ian Gow, and asked him if I could have a moment. As always he was delightfully attentive and we went down to the Terrace, which was deserted. Up and down we paced in the biting East wind. What was dangerous, and almost unprecedented, I told him (as if he needed telling), was that the Prime Minister and the Treasury team in combination had been defeated in Cabinet. We all knew that she had made an error of judgement in weighting her Cabinet so heavily with passé Heathites when it was first formed under the scrutiny of Atkins, Thorneycroft and Whitelaw.[1] But was not the theory that by retaining all the Treasury posts for her own supporters she would in the last resort be able to get her way on economic policy? In fact, this did not last and she is now being defeated even on this selected battlefield. No wonder she looks so wan (though still beautiful) and sits with her head bowed at Question Time.

It is clear that The Lady is now well and truly beleaguered. I urged Ian to press her to stand alone, appeal to the country, stage a night of the long knives,[2] stressed that there was still time left for a ruthless policy to pay off. What I cannot make out is to what extent Ian's expressed views reflected his own prejudices, and what he believes to be mine; and to what extent they present a true picture of The Lady's own misgivings and anxieties. One must always remember that she is, must be, a more adroit politician than sometimes appears. Perhaps she, being plagued by inner feelings of insecurity, and being determined to hold on to her position, is consciously trimming now.

In the Tea Room Tony Newton and David Mellor[3] came and sat at the table. Tony asked me what I thought about 'the position'. But I would not answer. One can do too much public declamation, particularly at a table in the Tea Room where there are two whips present. I made various high sounding generalities about the import-

---

[1] Humphrey Atkins, since 1979, Secretary of State for Northern Ireland; Lord Thorneycroft, former Minister in Macmillan and Douglas-Home governments; chairman of the Conservative Party since 1975.

[2] As Harold Macmillan had done on 13 July 1963, when he dismissed six Cabinet Ministers. AC observed, 'butchery on this scale unprecedented in the annals of the party.' (*The Tories*)

[3] Tony Newton was Whip to the Finance Committee; David Mellor, MP for Putney since 1979.

ance of everyone keeping their heads down, and one not being indiscreet, etc.

After leaving the Tea Room I was caught again by Tony Newton in the corridor leading down to the telephone lobby and the Members' Staircase, and I was again asked what I thought. I told him that we were going through the sound barrier and there was a lot of buffeting; either we slow down and settle for a quiet life, or we accelerate it and hope to break through into serene, but supersonic, tranquillity. Then, I said (always tell people what you think they want to hear) that I was an old-fashioned Tory, that Geoffrey would have to go, but that on the whole my choice for the succession would be Francis. I said I hated saying this because of the implied disloyalty to The Lady and her policies, but these were being so badly mismanaged at the moment that they were doing more harm than good. As I anticipated he agreed, sounding both relieved and elated. 'I am sure that there are a very large number of people who agree with you but don't yet like to say so . . .'

I hope that by my two conversations today I have maintained confidential links with both camps in the Parliamentary Party. We shall see.

Saltwood   *Tuesday, 2 December*

And *still* we are ground down (though not yet, fortunately, in the lower millstones of God's foundry). Yesterday Barclays produced a most insulting letter giving (effectively) three weeks notice to put account in credit. Signed cheque on C. Hoare & Co. and sent down by hand. This means CH is 25+ and then the loan (now down to 20) and also the Clydesdale at 20. *But* Westminster is out of the way and now Barclays. How the hell do I raise the 65 to get completely clear? Had a bad night, early waking etc. Fictionalised with collapse of Italian front.

After five years of financial crisis and seven of intolerable interest charges, it is, I suppose, a miracle that I am still with the major structure intact. But in 1975, if you'd told me 'you've' got to hold on for five years . . . I'd have said (a) I can't and (b) 'it' can't be as along as that.

Cloisters   *Wednesday, 3 December*

Headache/dizzy this morning. Blood pressure? More likely combination hangover, stuffy night, but it remains manically cold.

Went to a 'grand' dinner party at the Royal Academy last night;
Jane came up for it, wore her blue dress and masses of pearls and
looked ravishing. Patrick Lindsay[1] was host, we had expected 150
people bellowing and filthy food – actually only 24, ultra posh, Jocelyn
Stevens[2] and Teddy Hall[3] only people without titles; Jane sat between
Cranborne (future Marquess[4]) and Dalkeith (ditto Duke[5]). The pretty,
and somewhat confident and *sly* Countess of Halifax sat on my right.
Looking at her ghastly red-face husband I thought she ought to be
ready for a bit of *interest*, but later on, as we engaged in private view
of the Chatsworth 'treasures' I noticed the young Duke of Roxburghe[6]
(who I had earlier taken to be a young Naylor-Leyland) with his arm
around her.

Bratton   *Saturday, 6 December*

Drove down yesterday in the K10, against a 40–50 mph headwind *the
whole way*. Petrol consumption slightly under 10 mpg – don't think
I've got any car to do this since the Bi-carb. Last bit in pouring rain.
On way back into Plymouth was stopped by police, just out of
nastiness really. I quickly pulled rank, but after opening the bazaar in
the Guildhall (where I put on a most good-tempered show) I had to
go back to Crownhill police station. The officer was probing with his
questions about how long the vehicle had been in the country etc.

This put me 'out of sorts' and I was only just getting back into
smooth waters (sic) by the fuel gauge not having moved, due to gentle
driving, when there was a message from Nanny to ring back (although,
all credit to her, she did say 'Boys all right').

---

[1] Director of Christie's.
[2] Jocelyn Stevens, former editor of *Queen*, had been deputy chairman and managing
director of Express Newspapers since 1977.
[3] Edward (Teddy) Hall, portrait painter.
[4] of Salisbury.
[5] of Buccleuch.
[6] Guy David Innes-Ker had succeeded to the title in 1974. He married Lady Jane Meriel
Grosvenor in 1977 (they would divorce in 1990).

'Now here's some bad news for you . . .' she stated with relish; then recounted how my father had come over with Mrs Sly and taken over 30 books from the library. V. depressing. He is such a shit, so sly and weak, without the *slightest* concept of succession and the boys. Also, with each fresh move, Nolwen increases her hold on him and spreads her tendrils through the Estate.

Both Jane and Nanny urge me to 'speak out'. It's not moral scruple, or cowardice, that prevents me doing so, God knows; simply a residual calculation that there is more to lose than to gain by so doing. Furthermore, his action does somewhat clear the decks for my right to the Cézanne still-life drawing with which I intend to obliterate indebtedness, and restart the 'calculus'.

Will see what happens, but I don't like the look of things (broke off for a minute to visualise kicking her down that last stone flight of steps at Saltwood . . . 'oh Nolwen, I *am* sorry, how awful etc . . .'). So I was again in a bad mood for a fete, this time the Bratton one.

Cloisters   *Wednesday, 10 December*

Won the election for vice-chairman of the Defence Cttee today. I was reasonably confident, as I know I get quite a little vote from the centre, now, Party venerables and others. It's no good just having the Left or Right 'whipped' vote behind you. You have to be able to pick up something from the uncommitted. Conversely, of course, it's no use *just* being one of the uncommitted because however well-liked you are, you are bound to get squeezed between the two – so many people delete every name on the slate except the one printed on their 'whip'. This was what happened to Nick Budgen in the Finance Cttee yesterday – now everybody regrets it, but that's no use to him – and to Ivan Lawrence[1] in Home Affairs on Monday. I think there was an element of this in the fact that I defeated poor, pleasant (but clever) Julian Critchley[2] instead of, as I had hoped and expected, little Winston. One doesn't like advancing to office over the corpses of one's friends, but that's show business.

---

[1] Ivan Lawrence, MP for Burton since February 1974.
[2] Julian Critchley, MP for Aldershot since 1974 (Aldershot and North Hants, 1970–74).

Afterwards, I caught sight of Adam Raphael[1] in the lobby and taxed him with his extraordinary theory that the likeliest 'candidates' in a reshuffle were Francis, Ian Gilmour and Norman St J Stevas.[2] But no, this was his assessment on the basis of a hard tip. He told me that all three, who were used to talking to him freely, had been bitterly offended. Raphael's theory is that Francis will be moved to Leader of the House, Norman dropped or, more likely, sent to Education in place of Mark Carlisle who will *definitely* be going (everyone seems agreed on that). But anyway what about this dam' reshuffle? The Lady appears to have got into a face-loss situation here, ie whatever she does will be an I-told-you-so, so she is just holding on. When there was an official briefing, printed in the *Sunday Telegraph* about three weeks ago that '. . . there will be no Ministerial changes for at least six (or was it twelve?) months . . .' I got a few laughs in the tea-room by saying that this meant they were imminent. Now I'm not so sure. Raphael thinks that it may be the Treasury team that goes, and not of their own volition.

Cloisters   *Thursday, 11 December*

Treasury questions. Peter Shore[3] up for the first time and not much use. Fumbled and almost lost the place in what were virtually mini-speeches. Geoffrey H much more confident than formerly (God knows why) and more mellifluous than the First Secretary who has presently a voice that is at the same time hoarse and low-volume (shades of Bonar Law?). Biffen still in his new *persona* more aggressive than formerly and used the word 'damned', as in damned sure, and was instantly rebuked by the Speaker.

At the start of Business Questions there was a scuffling noise and a massive thump at the bar of the House. The Chief Whip,[4] carrying papers, had fallen flat on his face. 'A slip', presumably (to quote one of Harry Carpenter's over-used phrases) as he doesn't drink. He was livid.

---

[1] Adam Raphael, political correspondent of *The Observer* since 1976.
[2] Norman St John-Stevas, MP for Chelmsford since 1964, Chancellor of the Duchy of Lancaster, Leader of the House of Commons and Minister for the Arts since 1979.
[3] Peter Shore, MP for Stepney and Poplar since 1974 (Stepney, 1964–74) had just moved from Foreign Affairs to become opposition spokesman on Treasury matters.
[4] Michael Jopling, MP for Westmorland since 1964, Chief Whip since 1979.

A little later, who should be called but 'Sir Harold Wilson'.[1] Amazing. He stood erect and slim (cancer-slim one could say) in a beautifully pressed blue suit, in contrast to his usual rumpled and hunted demeanour, and asked a question about his Report on the City's institutions. Down memory lane, with that curious flat nasal twang, that I used to hear so often and so maddeningly at PM's questions when we were in opposition. A certain sadismoid pleasure as I reflected on how the roles were reversed in more than one sense.

That evening we were on a running three liner from 7 p.m. I slipped out to Brooks's for a little backgammon after the first vote, and there in the bar was Roy Jenkins,[2] fat, puffy and unhappily ingratiating. I made some bantering remarks about the Big Push, threw a few scraps of Commons gossip around. He did *not* want to have intercourse.

Fifteen more votes that night. Horrible torture of the fabric and substance. Finally in bed for 2 hrs sleep at 6.45 a.m. I have to be up tomorrow for the Brandt Report debate.

Cloisters   *Friday, 12 December*

Sat right through the Brandt Report without getting called. Disappointment as I had a lovely debunking speech ready, quoting the late and great Ernie Bevin: '... I've been here all night and all I've 'eard is bloody clitches'. No breakfast, no lunch. I did the Christmas card list on my lap, periodically making objectionable interruptions.

At other times I brooded. This autumn there have been a lot of upsets in Committee elections, and *every* person who has lost their seat – Knox (employment), Hicks, Dykes (Europe), Bruce-Gardyne (Finance), Lawrence (Home Affairs), and Critchley and Atkins (Defence) have all taken it *very* badly.[3] Dear Nick Budgen is the only one who has shown any *tenu* at all.

---

[1] Harold Wilson, MP for Huyton since 1950 (Ormskirk 1945–50), Prime Minister 1964–70, 1974–76. Knight of the Garter 1976.

[2] Roy Jenkins, President of the European Commission since 1977, having been a Labour MP since 1948.

[3] David Knox, MP for Leek since 1970; Robert Hicks, MP for Bodmin since 1970; Hugh Dykes, MP for Harrow East since 1970; Jock Bruce-Gardyne, MP for Knutsford since 1979 (South Angus 1964–74).

Saltwood   *Saturday, 13 December*

Saltwood just not a haven at the moment. Untidyness as piled papers seems even worse (like indebtedness) than when one began.

My father *distrait* on the phone (this is tricky as he is going to get my Cézanne letter this week – ugh[1]). Also have a loose front tooth, obviously going to pack up over Christmas or in Zermatt.

Saltwood   *Sunday, 21 December*

Walked out on the steps and looked at the full moon behind the trees. Very cold, but clear. Had spoken to C, who had agreed to meet me at Albany tomorrow to discuss Cézanne still-life. Looked around, and up at the towers. Am I, at last, some £500,000 later, really going to own it all, unencumbered? Will have to do a *really* careful think through at the turn of the year.

---

[1] The incomplete draft of AC's letter begins: 'Dearest Papa, this is bad, I'm afraid...'

1981

Apprehensive as freedom from worry poor – only really brighten up when talking about my o/d being paid off – appearance *not* improving, and then this evening blow fell: RESHUFFLE.

And, monstrously, not announced what it was in detail, just that it will be announced later this evening! Took one totally by surprise. A sad blow for me. I had never really expected to get into government àt formation, but hoped and felt that I had made enough general ground in the interim; friendship with Ian Gow, giving notice of questions etc. Perhaps I had, then blew it just recently.

Recalled how I had prayed for George to come back and promised that if he did I would do my Defence Study. He did come, and I didn't. One's relationship with God shouldn't be like that. I should be grateful for everything that he has given me, accept that what–is–written–is–written. But I still have this residual hope, belief, that I can do something for my country. What must I do to deserve it and pave the way? Perhaps this year should be much more political.

Had a very bad night – compounded (of course) by rage at once again boys not coming in until 1 a.m. Thought we would just go back to England today. I felt so sad at losing the 'double', perhaps finally both my love and friendship with the boys – reduced to Bonny papa's state, i.e. more or less of a nuisance, but got to keep in with him for inheritance purposes – and any possibility of doing something for my country. Woke, dragged up from 4 hours sleep at about 6.15 in a kind of 'was-it-really-a-dream?' recollection, and its certain dreamlike qualities – Biffen to Trade, Nott to Defence, John Patten a minister (as a gesture to the new intake etc). No, it was not a dream.[1] I still feel *very* uneasy about 1981. 'Flagellation Year' its provisional title.

---

[1] In Mrs Thatcher's first reshuffle, appointments also included Francis Pym as Leader of the House (succeeding Norman St John-Stevas), thereby proving Adam Raphael's tip (see 10 December) correct. John Patten moved to Northern Ireland Office as Parliamentary Under-Secretary of State.

Saltwood   *Saturday, 10 January*

Got back today. Tip-book had forgotten to phone Nanny and so we
were driven up from the docks by a dear-old-boy ('old coach man')
who remembered bringing my father up – 'your old [sic] father', he
called him – for 8/6d. I gave him £4. Actually, I suppose that is about
right, a ×8 depreciation since 1952?

The dogs gave us a lovely welcome. Children substitute really, the
illusion complete with Nanny in charge. Looked through the mail,
incredibly dull, only pleasurable indication of new regime, just fucking
boring all round. Last a/c of Hoare's still being kept in credit by
income. Looked at the Whip, and got really quite angry as I think of
these bloody people just bossing us around. *Waddington*[1] a minister;
that self-same little tick who blocked me from going to Europe or
whatever it was. Goodlad a whip, Goodlad of all people![2] The stock
example of an MP who looks like a pig and did NOTHING. Much
of the flavour will be diminished from the House I suspect.

Cloisters   *Monday, 12 January*

I saw Patrick Mayhew and congratulated him on his promotion; he
has been moved from Employment back to the Home Office.

'Aren't you glad I stopped you from resigning?' I asked. 'Well it is
not over yet,' he said. More or less conveying that the appointment
of John Nott (or John 'Nit' as poor Norman so injudiciously called
him) was an indication that still further and more savage cuts were in
store. Patrick cheered me by grinding his teeth at the quality of the
junior promotions – 'all whips and wets'.

Ivor Stanbrook[3] quite predictably had also agreed, said it was an
insult to people like himself who had been in the House for so long
that someone like John Patten should be made a Minister after two
years. But he was defeatist. Said, 'You cannot do anything, it will look
like sour grapes.'

---

[1] David Waddington, MP for Clitheroe since 1979; now a Parliamentary Under-Secretary
of State, Department of Employment.
[2] Alastair Goodlad, MP for Northwich since February 1974.
[3] Ivor Stanbrook, MP for Orpington since 1970.

I spent the morning dictating my vitriolic analysis of the reshuffle which I sent to Paul Johnson with a copy to Bill Deedes. I have some doubts and pensées d'escalier, perhaps it was too aggressively expressed – a fault of mine – perhaps it was unwise to quote that small, but I believe significant, experience as an example.

I delivered letters of commiseration to poor Norman and Jim Lester[1] who although very left, always performs well at the Despatch Box. Tony Buck came up to me and suggested a drink(!). 'Tea,' I replied formally, at which his face fell. Conversation was somewhat stilted as neither wanted to be the first to admit how disappointed he was at being left out of the reshuffle. It was quite clear that he deliberately arranged a meeting with the Prime Minister for the previous week, but later cancelled at her request, at a time when he knew I would be away and which would allow him to 'impress' her without being overshadowed. (Hal Miller later told me that AB and Victor Goodhew[2] were the only two able to go to that meeting.) AB made a specific point of asking me to give him 'an hour or so' briefing about weapons systems and so forth before we see The Lady on Wednesday week. The only interesting thing was that Ian Gow had been absolutely furious at my article in the *Telegraph* (as expected) although whether that had anything to do with subsequent events I do not know.

On my way back through the Lobby I was talking to David Hunt[3] who said that John Nott was very anxious to meet the officers of the Defence Committee at the earliest opportunity, he didn't want it thought that he was coming in with 'a pair of scissors', he would take some time before coming to decisions, and so forth. Hunt also said, 'You are a very odd lot, aren't you?' 'What do you mean?' I said. 'Well, I mean, you represent all shades of the Party.' (Silly ass) All these wets think only in terms of 'shades', whether people are right or left, or whatever the case may be.

While we were talking poor Jim Lester came up to us and blow me if he didn't burst into tears (presumably for the eighteenth time). He was very brown, but looking awful. Fancy being told of your dismissal over the telephone while on holiday in Switzerland.

---

[1] Lester had been a junior minister at Department of Employment.
[2] Victor Goodhew, MP for St Albans since 1959; vice-chairman of the Conservative Defence Committee since 1974.
[3] David Hunt had followed John Nott from Trade to Defence as his PPS.

Cloisters   *Tuesday, 13 January*

I had been dictating letters until ten past three, but had foresight to put in a Prayer Card as I knew my place would be kept free for Prime Minister's PQ's.

Incidentally, I noticed that for the first time Ian Lloyd had 'shown respect' by leaving a space for me to put my card in, even though he had got to the bench earlier that morning. In the past he has always squabbled with Emery[1] for the place one up from me and if Emery got there before him he would always put one on my seat. I was gratified to see that although Emery had got there before him he had for the first time left my place vacant and put his card on the seat below mine. It will be interesting to see if, when he is pre-empted by Lloyd, Emery does the same.

Just before going in I had soaked myself with Vetiver, even so this did not attract the attention of the former Leader of the House who I noticed was standing at the bar when I entered. (Nick Winterton was putting a long rambling question and because of his position at the end of the front bench it would have been out of order to have walked past him to our places.) When Nick sat down Norman 'made his entry' with that curious mincing step of his. I was glad to see that he got massive applause – not all of it ironic by any means – from the Opposition.

Later, in the course of Questions he was sorely tried by the Prime Minister who said how glad she was that the Arts were no longer an independent ministry, etc. But he did not rise.

I then went into the Tea Room, hopeful of getting some gossip. Maddeningly one large table was already completely full of the young and eager, all of them in an animated condition. However, Hal Miller came up and indicated that he would like a word. We moved over to the armchairs on the other side of the screen and I started to eat the Ryvita sandwiches – I had not lunched – which Jane had sent with me in the train. Hal is still very concerned about Defence matters. Said that they were all relying on me as being the only person of real quality on the Defence Committee – 'Winston is a non-starter; Victor is, err, inscrutable (I admire the neutral adjective) and Buck is bone idle.'

It turned out that one reason why Hal was irritated with Buck was

---

[1] Peter Emery, MP for Honiton since 1967 (Reading 1959–66).

because Buck had asked him for a brief before the meeting with the Prime Minister (just as yesterday he had asked me for one).

I was much cheered talking to Hal (one always likes compliments anyway) and particularly by the fact that Francis was still taking a general interest in things and watching from afar. Later that afternoon I had a brief chat with Tony Royle who told me that he had heard in Pratt's the previous night that Francis was very dejected at his transfer. I talked Tony up about Francis as much as I could, hoping that it would get back to him as Tony, he told me, was meeting Francis that very evening. Hal stressed that the situation was very grave, that it was complete nonsense to say that John Nott was going to take his time before coming to any decision. Hal Miller also said that the decision was so close that, by the time we saw the Prime Minister, it would already have been taken, and much of our meeting would be lost. However, he told me that one element of the decision had been to reinforce the Army at the expense of the Navy and indeed, the original title of the White Paper had been to lay emphasis on the need to reinforce the Central Front (i.e. the one place where it is very unlikely that the Russians will ever attack).

I am meeting Buck this evening and undertook to force him to send a letter by hand to the Prime Minister asking that no final decision should be made until after her meeting with the officers of the Defence Committee.

Went round to Norman Shaw North for the meeting in AB's Room to discuss our tactics for the Prime Minister and Nott. A dear little secretary with very short hair and enormous ovoid glasses – rather like Dora in the Library, but less flat and intellectual. I had not seen her before, but she giggled amiably. Buck, I thought, rather hunted and *chétif*. It was almost as if he had overheard the conversation between Hal Miller and myself a couple of hours earlier in which Hal had more or less said how much Francis would have preferred me to be Chairman of the Committee. Neither of the Committee secretaries were present and Winston was rather more subdued than usual. I let them do the talking, then suggested that Tony should write immediately to the Prime Minister expressing the hope and assumption that nothing would be decided before our meeting with her. He agreed that this was a good idea. We spent some time discussing tactics, but none of the other three seemed to realise that a simple rigid defence of existing spending targets is not enough. What we have to do is steer the Department into a general scrutiny of our defence commitments and make sure that they come up with the right conclusions. Winston, for example, wanted to take £2 billion off the Social Security budget and bang it straight into the RAF. Lovely, but in terms of political *realismus* so impracticable as to put everything else that we argue into disrepute. I also raised with them the question of a possible 'demonstration' (i.e. abstaining in the lobbies). This had not really occurred to them either, but the more they thought about it the more they liked it. I emphasised the need for complete secrecy at this stage. Abstention on the defence estimates – which is what we are talking about, in effect, will only be significant if practised by at least forty colleagues. Easier to drum this up after the reshuffle than before, but still an up-hill task when it comes to the point.

I returned to the House and went into the Smoking Room. Julian Amery was holding court in the corner table between the bar and the fireplace. He was in good form. I noticed George Brown[1] and one or two Labour MPs in the outer circle.

'Now Alan, we are just agreeing that we are all hand-to-heart behind the Prime Minister in her economic policies, but the trouble is we don't know what these are, can you tell us?'

This is not a good sign, this kind of irreverence from senior and respected Privy Counsellors on the Right of the Party, and later that evening in the Lobby poor Nick Budgen told me how terribly depressed he was. He told me that the Prime Minister was an *au fond* popularist and that she was trimming. We agreed that both Geoffrey Howe and Leon Brittan had not a political principle between them and that they would soon get the ship round on its new course.

I started to get steamed up about the junior appointments in the reshuffle, but Nick did not take as extreme a view as I did.

'All bland,' he said, 'they are all bland men without identifiable personalities, this is to be the keynote of the Government from now on.'

When I got back to the Library I saw bright, intelligent, able little Robin Cook from Edinburgh North, who was always a very keen and very well informed interrogator of Ministers in the defence field, but has been promoted by Mr Foot to a shadow Treasury job. I

---

[1] George Brown, former Labour MP and Minister in Harold Wilson's 1964–70 government, took the title Lord George-Brown on being made a life peer in 1970.

congratulated him. I remarked ruefully that talent was being better used in the Labour Party than in our own. He said that this was due to Michael's innovations. He cited the example of Tam Dalyell[1], saying that he was absolutely brilliant, then adding somewhat to my surprise, '. . . but he is unreliable'.

'Unreliable? What do you mean?'

'Well, he sometimes goes his own way, you cannot rely on him always to speak to the ministerial brief. Which is a good thing of course,' he said hurriedly, but unconvincingly.

Cloisters   *Wednesday, 14 January*

I went into the Smoking Room to get some Malvern water for my fizzy Redoxon and George Brown was there alone drinking a double whisky (it was 11.10 a.m.) and smoking a large cigar. While we were in Zermatt Nanny had told us that she had heard him on the radio saying that The Lady would be dumped by the Conservative Party this year, and having noticed him on the periphery of Julian's group last night (perhaps he had never left the Smoking Room and been there all night), I asked him about this.

GB said that she had got things hopelessly wrong, was still doing trivial things that made her unpopular, but in fact turning her primary policies round so that the basic objectives such as reducing inflation etc. would not be met. He told me that he had written an article saying something to this effect for last Sunday's *Express*, but John Junor had turned it down. Apparently, the Prime Minister had had a special meeting of about six editors to try and subdue criticism, but, of course, as George Brown said, this is highly unpopular with all the other editors who have not been invited along.

I suggested that it was apparent that The Lady was already trying to slither out of her difficulties and he agreed. The telephone went and he was summoned back to one of the bars in the Lords(!). I walked down the corridor with him and mentioned the junior promotions – of which he was fully aware and agreed with my judgement. 'She is making exactly the same mistake as Wilson, trying to please everybody and particularly those who distrust her.'

---

[1] Tam Dalyell, opposition spokesman on science since 1980.

'She has included all her own bully boys,' I said.

'Yes, a great mistake.'

I asked him who he thought the next Leader would be and he said Francis or Jim, '. . . but if I was a Conservative I would prefer Francis.'

Cloisters   *Monday, 19 January*

I received a very friendly reply from Ian Gow, totally disclaiming any disapproval of my celebrated article in the *Daily Telegraph*[1] before Christmas.

Am I paranoid about this? I don't think so. There was no doubt that The Lady cut me dead on the night of Monday 15 December and that for some weeks I G was extremely chilly. However, in politics one can never admit these things and it is easier to turn, or pretend to have turned, the blind eye. This evening, just as I was dictating letters at my desk the telephone rang and it was IG's secretary suggesting dinner. We agreed to meet at 7 p.m., but, in fact, there was a vote then and afterwards I had to go to the Home Secretary's room along with other officers of the Committee. Willie, as always bellowing and small-eyed, lost his temper briefly and alarmingly when Ted Gardner repeated my having raised the question of 'No Go' Reggae areas for black people, police timidity in breaking up parties and so on. Willie thundered and blundered about his Ministry being loaded with so many responsibilities he would find himself 'at breaking point' etc.

However, I held my ground saying, 'This is not a question of Ministerial responsibility for all-night parties.'

This got a bit of a laugh and lightened the atmosphere, just as well because I went on to say that if the police had acted on the complaints that neighbours made a number of lives could have been saved. Willie undertook to talk to the Commissioner about this – but I rather doubt if he will.

I found Ian in the Smoking Room and he took me to the Savoy. Really, his driving in his little blue Mini is now completely berserk. He delights in it, and it makes one's hair stand on end – particularly as he is not a specially skilful driver. At one point as we screamed along

---

[1] On defence policy.

the Embankment (it was pouring with rain) I envisaged a terrible accident with the tiny Mini somersaulting across the dual carriageway, an incandescent fireball. He told me that he sometimes drove the Prime Minister in the car with a detective sitting in the back.

We indulged in small-talk in the new, or rather revealed, foyer with its delightful art-nouveau décor and onyx columns, practically deserted. Over the food he returned to the question of the letter and then almost immediately we got to discussing the junior appointments. He defended these as best he could. I grumbled though that so many appointments had come from the Whips' Office, '... we would all like to be Whips'.

'Would you like to be a Whip?' he said sharply.

'I would rather be a Whip than nothing,' I replied.

He muttered something about how hard they worked and I agreed. Then he said, 'Who do you think should succeed me as the Prime Minister's secretary?'

'Very difficult,' I replied. 'I very much hope that you are not going to stand down.' (On looking back I see that this was rather tactless as he would not stand down but be promoted and given a department of his own).

'Would you do it?'

'Nothing I would like more outside the Cabinet itself.'

'But how would Jane take it?' he said.

We talked a bit about wives living in the country etc. I tried hard to steer the subject away from this as (perhaps wrongly) I did not want to appear to be too keen. I do not know how much power he has to recommend his successor or – same thing – how much attention the Leader would pay to what he says. But of course the more I thought about it the more excited I became. He told me that there would definitely be another reshuffle in September and I inferred that it would be then that he would get a department of his own and other changes would be made.

So there it is, one is quickly forced back by a combination of bribes and compulsion into towing the line, being a good boy, etc. I do not quite know what I should do to make myself, or perhaps confirm myself, as being the most suitable over the next six months. I did write him a short note afterwards thanking him for the dinner and saying that what appealed to me most about being a Whip was the intelligence-gathering, rather than the disciplinary function. One lives in hope, but this one seems almost too good to be true.

Cloisters   *Thursday, 22 January*

I wrote to Bill Deedes today explaining why I thought that the time was not quite right for another article on Defence issues until John Nott had had time to settle himself in as I did not wish to seem to be harrying him. I thought it might be an idea to enclose a personal note telling him that Ian had intimated to me that I might succeed him and enlist his help. I wrote the letter and was just about to put it in with the other text (but in a separate envelope) when something made me telephone Jane. She was doubtful about the wisdom of the idea, reminded me that someone (I honestly cannot remember who) said that you could not completely trust Bill Deedes and rightly pointed out that you could not trust *anyone* in politics. Anyway, never put anything in writing she said. If you must, go and see him.

I rang the *Telegraph*, fearing that he would not come in on a Friday, or that he had already left for the country. However, he was somewhere in the building and I drove round in the 2CV and weaved my way round through various corridors (they appear to be involved in some kind of redecoration). He received me, as he always does, with great warmth. The moment we were alone I told him of the conversation, asking, if he possibly had an opportunity, if he could be of any help. Bill was very enthusiastic, said she badly needed somebody, I would do the job excellently and so on.

I was buoyed up by this, but when I told Jane later she was rather dismissive, said he was far too experienced not to say that, whatever his private feelings might have been.

On the way from the *Telegraph* building to Brooks's, where I was going to meet Euan, and driving somewhat *Frenchly* I just failed to slip inside a red Hillman as he accelerated away from a pedestrian crossing. The occupants immediately put on police caps and flagged me down. They insisted I take a breath test. 'If this bag changes colour one iota I will give you £100,' I said. Of course, looking back I now see that might have been constituted as an overture for a bribe. However, fortunately the celebrated 'crystals' did not alter colour at all. It is somewhat alarming though as one puffs down the plastic tube to see them darkening. This is simply the moisture in one's breath and not the alcohol content, which in my case was nil. All the same, I noted that the division of the colour beyond which a positive reading is indicated and a blood or urine test follows seemed very high up the

Saltwood Castle
in the mid-1970s.

AC and his father walk in front of the moat with Jane, Andrew and James.

Plymouth, February 1974. At a function during AC's first election campaign: Derek Priston, the agent, is on AC's left, and Tom Bridges, the chairman, next to him.

AC beat off the challenge of the Labour candidate, Brian Fletcher (here seen with AC at the Guildhall after the count), to win the Sutton division by 8,104 votes.

A photo call with Jane for AC's election address.

Before the October 1974 election, with his fellow Plymouth Conservative candidates, Dame Joan Vickers (left), who was endeavouring to win back Devonport from Labour's David Owen, and Janet Fookes, who was defending a slender majority at Drake. On the day, Labour emerged 20 seats ahead of the Conservatives. David Owen increased his majority; Janet Fookes only just scraped back by 34 votes. AC's majority fell to 5,188.

AC disliked microphones having had a nasty experience with one many years before when trying to gain the Conservative nomination at Havant.

In August 1974, AC, Jane and their younger son Andrew traversed all eighteen miles of Sutton's constituency boundary in a sponsored walk, picking up supporters for stretches along the way.

Very different vintages of cars at Saltwood: AC drives 'the Antique'. In 1974 the family pose for a pre-autumn election shot with the Citroen Mehari, recently acquired.

The 'prophet's visit' – in December 1972, Enoch Powell and his wife Pam lunched at Saltwood after AC had been selected as prospective Conservative candidate for Sutton.

George, the jackdaw, takes a painful peck at AC's ear.

At Zermatt: AC's father on his only visit in 1977 – it was not a success, and there is no mention of it in the diary. Andrew (above), like James, was a keen skier.

Above 'Yet again trying the Zapata moustache, which adds to haggardness. What's the point?' It was shaved off at Zermatt. (September 1972)

Above right AC with Bonny mama outside the newly-built Garden House at Saltwood in 1972.

Above At Benalmadena in Spain in April 1973, the home of Jane's parents, Bertie and Pam Beuttler (centre): James and Andrew are in the foreground (left and right). 'Spain revolting,' wrote AC, 'though individual Spaniards reasonably anxious to please. Architecture, pollution, simply awful.'

Above On skimming duties at Saltwood's pool, built in 1973.

Right The Clark family at Saltwood in early 1980: Andrew holds Tom the Jack Russell, AC's stepmother Nolwen sits between Jane and his father.

AC has his arm around the shoulders of Mrs R.M. (Betty) Easton, a formidable figure in the affairs of the Sutton constituency. She later went on to be Lord Mayor of Plymouth.

The 1979 election saw AC returned with his largest majority yet in Sutton: 11,287. The Conservatives, under Margaret Thatcher, won 339 seats, Labour, 269 and the Liberals, 11.

His Westminster secretary, Veronica – seen here at the constituency headquarters – joined the campaign.

Among party workers in Sutton. The Clarks at a Plympton St Mary buffet dance, with Lawrence Speare, often a thorn in AC's side, on his right.

CITY OF PLYMOUTH

PARLIAMENTARY ELECTION

PLYMOUTH (SUTTON) Constituency
Date of Election 3rd May, 1979.

I hereby give notice that the TOTAL NUMBER OF VOTES GIVEN for each Candidate at the election was as follows, viz.:

Name of Candidate	Number of Votes given for the Candidate
ALAN CLARK	29892
JULIAN GORDON PRIESTLEY	17605
JOHN SCANNELL	6226

And that the under-mentioned Person has been DULY ELECTED to serve as Member for the said Constituency.

ALAN CLARK

The number of Ballot Papers rejected and not counted by me at this election was as follows :–
1. Want of official mark ...
2. Voting for more than one candidate ...
3. Writing or mark by which voter could be identified ...
4. Unmarked or void for uncertainty ...

Total ...

William E. Evans
Returning Officer.

Dated 4th May, 1979.

Printed and Published in Devon by © Underhill (Plymouth) Ltd.

The all-party delegation to
the Falklands in October
1982 included Antony Buck
(on AC's right) and Roy
Mason (foreground).

AC meets the Falklands
Governor, Rex Hunt.

No signs that a few months
earlier a war had been
fought here.

AC in the Falklands
in front of a crashed
Argentinian Pucara.

tube; I got the impression that not much of a drink would get one into trouble.

A little later that evening I went downstairs into Pratt's, which was empty except for, sitting heavily and gloomily in one of those upright circular leather chairs, holding a whisky and soda dark as a piece of mahogany veneer, the Home Secretary.

'Ah, Alan', he said, not greeting me with any great warmth.

'I have just been breathalysed,' I said mischievously (breathalysed invariably means '. . . and produced a positive reading').

But the Home Secretary was very splendid, thundered and sputtered, said it was monstrous, where did it happen, on what grounds did they stop me . . . To my delight I realised that he was angry with the police at breathalysing me, not the other way round. I told him that the test had been completely negative and he was almost disappointed. I think that he might well have done something about it if it had been positive. The Drinker's Union.

Saltwood   *Saturday, 24 January*

Things *consistently calmer* with 'indebtedness eliminated'. But real thriller at the moment is IG's mention of the possibility of my taking his place (!!!). Jane and I think of nothing, talk of little else. Of course it must, I suppose, still be reckoned an ambition. But like getting reported in the *Eton Chronicle* as having got my House Colours (in 1944) even though I hadn't (though deserving it) it is a most timely and magical compensation.

What a coup to overtake, with the most sensational of all ladders, everyone else! The third or fourth most powerful person in the parliamentary party! How they will all cringe and creep! And how well will I do it. A 'posting' – darling little Jane said.

I think of my clothes – a series of dark grey suits and waistcoats with the gold watch chain, grandpapa's, in morning, and BHLH in evening with dark blue. Blue shirts in morning, white in evening. Always Eau de Cologne and Turkish cigarettes in the offices. Also a terrace party in May, constituents from Plymouth and Folkestone (!), colleagues and carefully chosen people. Oh, bliss! But also has more serious possibilities. It would still leave all doors open. On to the FO (with a knighthood), then back to Lord Privy Seal (general duties), then Defence, the Home Office and the leadership election. Truly in politics, as in backgammon, anything is possible.

Jane has some muddled idea (but naturally could not find the paper in which she had seen it, although the whole house is choked with old daily papers) that, in fact, Ian's departure was fairly imminent, as she had read something about some impending honours. The more I think about it the more I realise he would not have been taking 'soundings' if the decision was as far away as I had first thought it was when he mentioned it more or less in the same breath as a September reshuffle.

I spent a lot of time jogging backwards over various tactical mistakes I had made, notably writing to him that handwritten letter in which I qualified my reasons for wanting to be a whip. This must have been a tactical mistake. I was *far* too lukewarm at the time that he mentioned the PPS possibility and then I suppose, in the abstruse code in which one uses to communicate on such matters, my letter about the whip's job will have been interpreted as an oblique way of saying that it was that which I had my eye on rather than the PPSship.

After some torment I decided to write, yet again, to Ian, affirming both my total readiness to serve and making a general request of advice on how to conduct myself. Jane agreed with this course of action. Then I changed my mind and decided to write a formal letter expressing my readiness to serve and an informal letter with a request for advice and enclose the two in the same envelope. However, partly because time was pressing (due to the last collection from Saltwood Post Office), I decided to confine myself to the formal letter of readiness to serve. I wrote it on Saltwood writing paper, did not use a House of Commons envelope, but paid for the stamp (!), marked it 'strictly private' and sealed it using the big James II silver seal of the lion on to which my grandfather had grafted the family crest. I sent the letter to Downing Street as I know that is his first port of call in the mornings.

Cloisters   *Monday, 26 January*

Made an intervention today, though not as intemperate as I had originally intended, criticising Keith Joseph personally, and the principle, for meekly paying up another £1bn. to British Leyland. The

Lady was sitting in the Chamber, and I do not know whether such an intervention increased or diminished my chances of favour, but at least I had warned her about it the previous week. I used the word 'insouciance' which may have been a mistake as some of the Opposition laughed and as it was a serious moment one did not want it to be devalued.

At the Home Affairs Committee Nick Budgen coolly and clearly criticised the Home Office failure to apply objective standards in determining nationality in the new Bill which is to start tomorrow – 'presumably because they are fearful of offending fashionable opinion'. What a splendid, fearless and thoroughly valuable chap he is; no wonder Willie loathes him so much.

Cloisters   *Tuesday, 27 January*

To my gratification I find that my criticism of Keith Joseph got very wide coverage – twice on the radio and reported in full in every paper. Far from diminishing its effectiveness the use of the word insouciance seems to have pleased people. These tiny trivialities which seem to determine whether something is effective or not are very hard to predict.

There was a strange messenger on the Letter Board who did not recognise me and so the internal mail may have been accumulating there for some time. Just after tea I saw my light was on and with considerable alarm noticed that one of the letters on the Board was marked 'First Lord of the Treasury' in the top right-hand corner, which always means Downing Street. I took it away to a quiet corner of the passage which leads down to the Telephone Lobby and, conscious of an accelerating heart rate, tore it open. Inside was *another* envelope, also marked '10 Downing Street' and endorsed 'Private and Confidential' (shades of Ruth Lee and Arthur's communication with Ll G!).[1] I opened the second envelope and inside was a very short note:

'My dear Alan, Thank you so much for your letter of 24 January. You were not dreaming and I am glad to have your note for my file. We will have a further word. Yours ever.'

---

[1] AC had edited the memoirs of Arthur Lee, *A Good Innings* (Murray, 1975).

This very tiny little note at least confirmed that I have not been fantasising as there is documental evidence on both sides of the exchange. Indeed, just looking at Ian's text one can see no possible reason as to why it should be marked 'Strictly Private' and put into two envelopes unless the idea remains a real possibility.

Later, at the Burke Club Dinner, dull and poorly attended and conversation *exclusively* devoted to the Social Democratic Centre Party, Shirley Williams ad nauseam.[1] I did not please people by asserting that the whole thing was balls, no one would vote for them, they would blow themselves out, quarrel, sub-divide, etc. long before the general election. At the very end we went round the table discussing what were the Government's 'achievements' to date. The only one I could think of was, as I put it, that we really have succeeded in putting a lot of people out of work. (Unhappy, indeed Japanese, laughter all round the room, particularly from Lord St Oswald who I suspect to be an old school centrist.) Wedgwood Benn is absolutely right, the Trade Union Movement is disciplined by the fear of being put on the dole and this is a considerable, though brutal, achievement.

Saltwood   *Friday, 20 February*

Reading *Ancestral Voices*, Jim Lees-Milne's[2] volume I, for which I have been searching for two years since first hooked on *Prophesying Peace*. That in itself makes one experience all those beautiful gifted or interesting people – either dead (Nancy Mitford, Cecil Beaton, Eddy [Sackville-West] etc) or just tired old husks. I recollect 'bumping' into poor J L-M coming out of Brooks's the other day. That generation *can't* really communicate. I used to think, naively, that I would always be able to do so with our boys, but I really know better now.

---

[1] Roy Jenkins, David Owen, William Rodgers and Shirley Williams had just announced the formation of the SDP, a new force in left-of-centre politics.

[2] James Lees-Milne published a series of his diaries that began during the Second World War when he travelled the country on behalf of the National Trust.

Cloisters *Wednesday, 25 February*

A letter in *The Times* today signed by the four 'Wiltshire Wets', Morrison, Hamilton, Walters and Needham,[1] 'calling' for the Government to change course, insisting on 'moderating' (you have to get that word in) the strength of sterling etc. As Jane rightly observed, the letter will have been written by Sara Morrison, Heath's scrawny *éminence noire* at Central Office in the old days, and she will have got poor old Charlie to sign it and rope in the others.

Who are they? Well, Dennis is the least objectionable of the quartet. Said to have an overpowering attraction for the ladies – such powers are very seldom apparent to those of the same sex as the person alleged to have them, and Walters is no exception to this rule.

Then Needham, absolutely odious. He is really the Earl of Kilmorey, but so anxious to appear proletarian that he affects not to use his title and I actually heard him in the Tea Room boasting of having shot 'eighteen pheasant', when even the most parvenu stockbroker is, or should be, taught at his first shoot to score the birds in brace.

Michael Hamilton I have always disliked, but he is much *réclamé* among the wets. He dresses old-school with a stiff collar and blue shirt, usually a brigade tie, never has a hair out of place and invariably smoking Virginia cigarettes through a long black holder ('Winchester Cathedral', etc). We had a narrower escape than I like to contemplate from his being made Chief Whip instead of Michael Jopling, and indeed it might even happen if the regime changes. He is an extremely malicious man and in conversation with me, which I avoid as much as possible, he usually makes a guardedly offensive reference to my father. I suppose he assumes that this causes me pain. Those who know me better could enlighten him.

Nonetheless, there is no doubt that the Party is in poor shape. Much divided among itself. The wets want to go back to full Heathism, the dries are livid at all these extravagant grants to the nationalised industries; others, like myself, are deeply gloomy about the absence of an industrial, or indeed any other kind of, strategy, and the way we seem to be reacting *ad hoc* and in panic to instant crises.

Just after 12.30 p.m. I set off to the Savoy, sharing a taxi with Mark

---

[1] Charles Morrison, MP for Devizes since 1964, Michael Hamilton (Salisbury), Dennis Walters, MP for Westbury since 1964 and Richard Needham, MP for Chippenham since 1979.

Lennox-Boyd, Jack Page and poor old dried-up Paddy Wall,[1] rattled, disappointed and unfriendly in his now rather obvious hair-piece. Jack Page told us how his secretary, Daphne Hickson, elderly and prudish, had been rung up by an irate woman who had asked her who she was, how old she was etc. and told her that she suspected her husband of having affairs with other women and had found her name, Daphne Hickson and the House of Commons extension, written on a piece of paper. Flushing (one suspects), Miss Hickson explained that she worked for a senior backbencher and can only assume that the person in question had a problem and had this number given him for referring. There was a long silence and the aggrieved wife said 'thank you' in a most sinister way. Presumably yet another piece had fallen into place in her jig-saw.

At the door we were greeted by little George Jellicoe.[2] He was just as rubbery as I remembered him in 1965 when he called in at the Chalet and tried to push Sue[3] into a cupboard. He indicated having remembered the incident by asking me if I had 'been skiing' lately. I seem to remember he had to resign a government position about two years ago for some other sexual misdemeanour, but has again bounced back, which helps to prove the generally accepted rule that constant sexual activity has a rejuvenating effect.

The Prime Minister delivered, in her beautiful melodious tones, a rather trite message about the importance of technology, innovation, etc. I suspect that it will not be reported in the papers at all. [It wasn't.] She is off to see President Reagan and I hope will be well received as she needs a bit of relaxation and a boost to her morale.

While I was signing my letters in the Cloisters Michael McNair-W. engaged me in conversation. He said that the morale of the Party had never been lower, that David Howell should have resigned immediately, and that this view was widely felt.[4] I must say that on reflection I agree with this, and indeed think it would have been tactically prudent for The Lady to insist that he do so. Unusually for him, Michael went down the list of Cabinet ministers arguing that

---

[1] Mark Lennox-Boyd, MP for Morecambe and Lonsdale since 1979; John (Jack) Page, MP for Harrow West since 1960; Sir Patrick Wall (Haltemprice).
[2] Earl Jellicoe, a Minister in the Macmillan, Douglas-Home and Heath governments, now President of the Parliamentary and Scientific Committee, whose lunch it was.
[3] Sue Davis was an au pair girl looking after AC's children.
[4] David Howell, MP for Guildford since 1966, and Secretary of State for Energy since 1979, had been seen by Tory backbenchers as giving way to striking coal miners.

Joseph, useless; Biffen complacent, suffering from male men-
opause; Howe 'had had it'. Gently he worked it round to the thesis
that only Walker, Prior, Pym and Jopling still had their credibility
intact.

H'mm. Not wishing either to put him off or encourage him at this
stage, I made some complimentary remarks about Patrick Jenkin[1] for
whom I have a considerable regard as a bland and highly competent
fixer. Michael agreed, said that Patrick could always be relied on to
do as he was told. But who would tell him what? Michael went on
to say (and I judge it came from Peter Walker himself from the very
low tone and anxious guilty looks round the room that accompanied
it) that the Prime Minister was now governing on a purely day-to-
day basis, making decisions on impulse and without forethought. 'Just
like Eden during the Suez Crisis' he said. I simply nodded. 'Margaret's
credibility has gone you know,' he said, 'and once her credibility has
gone she is a pushover.'

I did not like the sound of this. Playing the *agent provocateur* I
suggested, 'Once she becomes a pushover, perhaps she ought to *be*
pushed over?' He became very excited, shifted about in his seat, etc.
This is the first time that I have actually heard it said, in relatively
neutral and centrist quarters, that it might be advisable to rid ourselves
of The Lady, although I do not doubt that it has often been discussed
in the privy counsels of the extreme left of the Party and I did myself
mention it as a possibility when I had my talk with Francis Pym.

Cloisters   *Tuesday, 3 March*

I sat throughout the Trident Debate today and made my long deferred
speech recommending the withdrawal of the Rhine Army. The House
was thinly attended, but not as empty as it usually is at that hour (7.50
p.m.) and I was gratified to note that quite a few people from both
sides came in and stood at the bar while I was talking. Enoch 'hear-
hear'ed' energetically throughout, which is always encouraging and it
was extremely 'well received' by everybody present. Unless one dis-
poses of power (which I do not) congratulations from colleagues are

---

[1] Patrick Jenkin, MP for Wanstead and Woodford since 1964, and Secretary of State for
Industry since January (Social Services, 1979–81).

rare and so all the more welcome. I even got a note from the Chair, delivered immediately by one of the badge messengers, expressing appreciation and ending 'well done indeed.'

Cloisters   *Wednesday, 4 March*

Balls-aching news. The constituency have suddenly decided to hold a 'really important' Wine and Cheese and have booked the tennis court at Saltram for Saturday 6 June. Betty [Easton] rang and asked if I would arrange for a 'really important speaker' to come down and attend ('Alan Clark to invite a personality ...'). I have been caught like that before. You simply cannot win; if the 'really important speaker' dazzles everybody then they ask themselves why they are lumbered with a nonentity as their own Member of Parliament; if he disappoints, they blame you for having invited a dreary guest. Rather stuffily I said that all speaking engagements had to be made through the Central Office network.

In addition, this and 11 July are the only two Saturdays that we are absolutely committed to Saltwood, as Jane has invited the whole regional hierarchy of the St John's Ambulance Brigade to have their AGM and a fete at the Castle. She will have to be there and she told me that Peggy had expressed a wish that I could also be in attendance, '... so that people could see his other side (!).'

However, as I ground my teeth thinking about this, I realised that the only way out was in fact to short-circuit the Central Office procedure, personally invite a 'really important speaker' and simultaneously explain that neither she nor I could manage 6 June. Francis was the obvious choice and much later on that evening I found Hal in the Speaker's Corridor and fell into conversation with him. H. seemed to think that the invitation would be welcome and also reminded me that I had invited F. to dine with the Defence Committee at some point before Easter. I said I would still be delighted to do this, but rather thought that all his responsibilities in his new field had crowded this out. We fell to talking about general matters.

H. started a little restrained, said that Francis was playing his cards close to the chest and so on. But he soon loosened up. Very slowly we walked down the deserted corridor towards the Speaker's office, our voices sinking lower and lower. We were both talking out of the corners of our mouths, like convicts in the exercise yard. In the Library Corridor we finally came to a halt, leaning against the serried ranks of calf-bound reports of the East India Company.

It is clear that Francis is still on the rampage. Hal told me that there was another 'blockbuster' on the way (for blockbuster I read keynote speech criticising present trends in policy). He also told me that F. had blocked the new provisions for sickness benefit payment in the Legislation Committee of the Cabinet, even though, as Chairman, he was out-voted in that Committee. It is not so long ago that I remembered Ian at dinner delivering a brilliant defence of these provisions when he asked the assembled company why it was right that *they* should have to pay sickness benefit for one of *his* employees when that person fell ill.

Cautiously, I brought the subject round to changes in personalities as well as policies. Hal said that these had to be radical and the need for them was urgent. F.'s great objection (one of them) to The Lady is that she is such a bad butcher, and the dismissal of Normie [St John-Stevas] was held up to ridicule. I forbore to mention that the people *she* wanted to butcher were very different from his own list and might in all probability include himself. Hal quoted to me Francis saying 'it is easy to be a good butcher. All you need is a sharp knife and a thick apron.'

Systematically H. ran through the names of those to be purged – Geoffrey – to go to the Woolsack as soon as possible; it was agreed he could not be demeaned, had performed excellent services for the Party etc, etc. Willie – time expired, too unpredictable and blubbery. I warned Hal that there was very serious trouble brewing if W. tried to impose any sort of bill, in whatever form, to shorten prison sentences or let people out of jail early, and he agreed completely. And if it should be the occasion of W.'s resigning – so be it. Keith – now totally bonkers and a liability. Biffen – as I have remarked earlier in this journal, has suffered[1] a change of life and was now useless. Lawson – universally loathed. Everybody wants *his* head. Hal agreed that David Howell should have resigned. But, hey, just a minute, aren't these all the names that are meant to be supporting The Lady in Cabinet?

Naturally, I didn't say this. Then followed the discussion of who was to take their place. Somewhat disconcertingly Hal suggested

---

[1] AC's comment: For 'suffered' possibly read 'enjoyed', as he had just got married.

Terence Higgins as Chancellor.[1] I mumbled something about the Party might be restive if so senior a job was filled from the back benches, even by someone with previous experience. But then who the hell should it be. Nott? Too scatty, we both agreed and this tallies with Ian's verdict when we walked on the Terrace last summer. It had to be Francis. And then Home Secretary, he suggested Peter Walker. I said no, too grand and would lend weight to his claims for the succession, 'you must always put your rivals in places where circumstances and the passage of time will be discrediting them by the time any possible leadership contest could come up'. Hal gave me a very quizzical look indeed when I said this, but I think he liked it, and I hoped it would be repeated.

A better solution was to make Peter Walker Minister of Labour and have Jim Prior at the Home Office, then the leadership contest would be a 'natural choice'. We both of us agreed that given such a choice the Party would be bound to choose Francis – which made it easy to be generous.

With the question of junior appointments we were moving closer to home and I judged it tactful to tail the conversation off. But we are very short of senior talent. H. did not like the idea of promoting Patrick Jenkin, agreed that Michael Jopling might be brought into the Cabinet with a Department, but *his* successor presented difficulties. Tony Kershaw[2] possibly. I mentioned Michael Hamilton and got the reaction that I hoped, namely, one of total rejection.

Cloisters   *Thursday, 5 March*

I asked a supplementary of the Home Secretary today. A lot of anti-NF stuff was being bandied about apropos of Willie's decision to ban their march next week. That lazy, greasy slob, John Hunt,[3] stuck in a question about right-wing publications. 'What about the black ones,' I interjected. The Speaker very splendidly and exceptionally called me *after* the Opposition Front Bench had sat down when, by rights,

---

[1] Terence Higgins, although a Minister in Edward Heath's government, had only briefly served Margaret Thatcher, as Opposition spokesman for Trade until 1976.

[2] Anthony Kershaw, MP for Stroud since 1955; chairman of the Commons Select Committee on Foreign Affairs since 1979.

[3] John Hunt, MP for Ravensbourne since 1974 (Bromley 1964–74).

he should have moved on to the next question. This is what I said:

'Can my right hon. Friend think of anything more overtly racist and criminal, or a clearer demonstration of a breakdown in public order, than the behaviour of the young blacks in the march through Southwark on Monday, when they broke into and damaged shops, terrorised the white population and shouted objectionable slogans about the monarchy to try to provoke the police? . . .'

This was quite a dodgy opening and the fun lay in seeing if one could stand up for the whole passage.

'. . . Will he not recognise that he has to be seen as being completely even-handed or else he will simply add to the very discontent that gives rise to the organisations that Labour Members find so objectionable?'

The House held its breath for a second and then applauded, almost with relief, when I emphasised the necessity for being 'even-handed' etc. Amazingly the other side were silent and half-way through I saw The Lady settling into her place. I hope she enjoyed it. I am completely bomb-happy with Willie now. He has done enormous damage to the Tory Party over the years with his obsessional regard for the *Guardian* vote. Sunningdale[1] was the most outrageous example. But he is at it the whole time, chipping away at our traditional values. After the way he shouted at me and Ivor Stanbrook I realised I could never mend my fences with him. From my conversation with others I feel that he is unlikely to stay the course and I am now enjoying my new recklessness.

I had a quick talk with Adam Raphael, who was so very well informed about our last reshuffle, and trailed the idea of the changes which Hal had discussed with me last night (though without of course attributing). He took a more realistic line, said that The Lady was far tougher than we realised, could not possibly tolerate the wholesale massacre of all her old court, etc. No, I don't think she could. But, of course, the unspoken corollary in my conversation with Hal was that she too was expendable.

---

[1] Unofficial meeting with IRA in country house surroundings when WW was N. Ireland Secretary in the Heath Government.

Cloisters   *Monday, 9 March*

Tim Raison is even more of a leftie on racial matters than Willie. I remember him being put up to make the anti-Enoch speech at the Blackpool Conference in 1971. And also the way he behaved on immigration 'hardship' cases before the Home Affairs Committee clipped his wings. This evening he was talking to us about the Nationality Bill. I suddenly got sick of the sneering way in which he was referring to people of 'British stock' who would be made ineligible to transmit their nationality by descent because of their living or working abroad. (He is constantly sticking in little weasel amendments that elevate the status of the coloured 'citizens' and, by exclusion, penalise our own good people.)

I said all the convolutions attaching to the Nationality Bill sprang from the basic fact of political cowardice in tackling the question of colour head-on. Afterwards Nick Budgen gave quite a funny imitation of me, '. . . and honestly I can not be bothered to conceal either my Etonian drawl or my intention to offend and insult . . . so you can just take it or leave it.' This will certainly be passed on to Willie with relish both by the whips, the PPS and the Minister. On thinking it over I am not sure that this self-indulgence was wise, although I have very little respect for him or desire to please. We shall see.

Cloisters   *Tuesday, 10 March – Budget Day*

I walked into the Chamber at five minutes past ten and found the benches submerged in a positive snowstorm of place cards; nowhere at all left on the front bench and very few on the one behind. A quick scan of the cards showed that they were all heavies and entitled to sit there, except for Anthony Beaumont-Dark.[1] I put my card in his usual place on the second row and telephoned him. Tactfully, I explained that one sat on the Baronet's Bench by invitation; that splendid man though he was he did not quite qualify for a day as important as Budget Day. I suggested that he and I swapped cards. I must say that he took it very well and agreed to do so. He claimed that he was simply doing it out of friendship. This does not fool me for a minute

---

[1] Anthony Beaumont-Dark, MP for Selly Oak since 1979.

of course, but I am gratified that he should think that I am sufficiently important to make it desirable for him to accede to my request.

I lunched in the Dining Room and there was a certain amount of what is known as good-natured chaff. I was at the corner table by the cold buffet, Jean's table (goodness Jean really is getting *so* old and shaky, though still massively dyed, powdered and trussed. I feel the moment is very near when she will be called to her father's 'in harness' hopefully upsetting a dish of scalding soup over Michael Heseltine). I was at a rather dull table, Alex Fletcher[1] and a couple of new Scots MPs – and I inferred from their conversation that they were none of them particularly enamoured of The Lady's policies. Next door sat a more interesting trio, Robert R.J., Jim Prior, and Kenneth Baker.[2] On their way out they stopped and chatted to us. I said I hoped that the intimations of gloom were a double bluff and in fact there might be some 'good news' in the Budget. Jim Prior leant over my chair and said, 'Has it not occurred to you that the rumours of badness are simply to soften you up for something even worse?'

And sure enough the Chancellor was quite uncompromisingly 'firm'. His figures were pretty horrific where they related to the old targets which, of course, had all been wildly overshot, but as soon as he said that tax allowances were not being raised I realised that it was all hard line. That ass Winterton shouted, 'you must be joking' when the Chancellor announced an extra 20p on a gallon of petrol. Although the Gallery described him as wearing a 'sober' grey suit, it seemed rather louche to me. Like his old boss, Ted Heath, Geoffrey Howe affects a curiously opaque café-au-lait complexion. A combination, presumably, of sun lamp and TV studio foundation cream.

Afterwards there was a brief scuffle with the local lobby correspondents. What the hell could I say to them? I 'deplored' the rise in petrol prices, made some anodyne remark about the small business fund and the cut in MLR, then shot up to the Finance Committee.

Here the Chancellor was getting quite a tough time. Cormack,[3] ever an assiduous band-waggoneer, claimed that this measure would ensure that we lost the next election unless corrected. Terence Higgins had led off, perhaps carrying at the back of his mind my flattering suggestion to him (following my conversation with Hal Miller) that

---

[1] Alexander Fletcher, MP for Edinburgh North since 1973.
[2] Kenneth Baker, MP for St Marylebone since 1970, a Junior Minister at Department of Industry since January.
[3] Patrick Cormack, MP for Staffordshire SW since 1974 (Cannock 1970–74).

he was a preferred candidate to take GH's place. Maxwell-Hyslop[1] was crotchety in the extreme about the petrol price rise, '. . . if I could have the Chancellor's attention for a moment . . .' when G.H. bent briefly over to pick up an aside from Lawson.

I really felt I had had enough of the Budget and politics for one day and wanted to get home and see Andrew, who has just returned from Zermatt. But on the telephone Jane was so insistent that I simply could not walk out on the '92' Dinner scheduled for that evening without leaving a formal apology with somebody, that I got the feeling that I really ought to stay up for it. And sure enough in the Tea Room corridor, Jill Knight[2] told me that there was a 'whip' out on attendance at the dinner.

Edward du Cann spoke only briefly and said little of interest. Throughout the meal I had been in conversation with George Gardiner who was talking of forming a Conservative 'Manifesto' group. I asked him if he spoke often to the Prime Minister. He said very seldom, although some weeks ago he had spent three hours with her at Downing Street and she had cooked him and Ian Gow supper. Rather disconcertingly he said: 'Now that you and I no longer have any hopes of office . . .' (Oy, just a minute!) and used this as justification for our taking a more positively critical role. One lesson I *have* learned, and I learned it very early on, is do not go high profile in 'positively critical' roles of *anyone*. As if by thought-reading (our conversation took place before E. du C's speech) Edward du Cann made scornful reference to the idea of a Conservative Manifesto Group, said one must communicate with one's whips.

Bob Dunn, who is a decent chap, that attractive combination of a quiet but intelligent Catholic,[3] said that there was not a single whip who could be trusted and he would not dream of talking to his whip about anything concerning his real anxieties. Little John Townend[4] remade a point about the closed shop and encouraged by Ian's presence – he was scribbling away – I switched from my original intention to warn the group about WW's plan to legislate for shorter prison sentences and made a pungent attack on Jim Prior, saying that his remarks (apropos the young girl who was sacked forcibly for not

[1] Robert (Robin) Maxwell-Hyslop, MP for Tiverton since 1960.
[2] Jill Knight, MP for Edgbaston since 1966.
[3] Robert Dunn, MP for Dartford since 1979, and Parliamentary Under-Secretary of State for Education and Science since January.
[4] John Townend, MP for Bridlington since 1979.

joining a union[1]) that, 'in the last resort you cannot force anybody to employ someone if you do not want to' were, in my opinion, the most dishonest ever made by any politician in my hearing – and that is saying quite a lot. Of course, the wretched local authority sacked her not because they did not want her, but because they were obliged to by NALGO.

I left early because I wanted to get the last train down from Waterloo. But I heard later that Patrick Wall, who always cocks up everything, had forced a resolution through at the last minute to send a deputation to see the Chief Whip and 'express our views'. This seemed to me extremely illjudged and the following day I sent MJ a letter disassociating myself from it.

Cloisters   *Thursday, 12 March*

Sitting at my desk this morning Bob Boscawen came over looking very solemn and leaned across in that special whip's conspiratorial way and said it was time to steady the banks and not rock the boat, etc; it would be good if I said something to that effect at the '22. All the evidence of a Whip's panic.

I had a question down to the Prime Minister and thought of saying something about the closed shop, asking her if she agreed how unfortunate it would be that a representative of her Government should be defending the closed shop before the European Court of Human Rights at that very moment. As is my practice, I slipped a note in to Ian's office saying that I had this in mind. Just before Question Time an answer was delivered saying that this was not the moment to do so.

So naturally I felt very complacent when Michael McNair-Wilson, who does not adopt this practice of early warning, launched into a great ramble on the same subject and got a lot of his facts wrong. The Lady let him down very gently, but I could not resist showing him Ian's letter afterwards, particularly as I had said to him before lunch that I was number 4 on the list for the Prime Minister and had he any suggestions.

The '22, as so often happens, when everybody anticipates harsh

---

[1] Joanna Harris, a poultry inspector employed by the Metropolitan Borough of Sandwell.

words and many declamations, was a damp squib. Peter Tapsell sat prominently, with his watering eyes and negroid hair, exuding a desire for martyrdom. But no one even glanced at him.[1]

The level of debate was personified by poor old John Stokes[2] who, relishing his big moment, got up and announced – and only someone of his ineffable complacency could have combined membership of one regiment (The Royal Fusiliers) with enunciating the motto of another – 'Steady the Buffs'. 'Buffers', I whispered to Esmond Bulmer, who was sitting beside me.

Cloisters   *Friday, 13 March*

Last night we went to dinner with Jock Bruce-Gardyne at his little house in Kelso Place. Talk about impoverished dons! The diners were separated at simple tables and overflowed into what was apparently a ground floor bedroom, as I had a wash basin with chromium taps next to me and bumped my elbow on it from time to time. Paper table cloths and napkins and cheap steel cutlery. I have this terrible handicap of a very low boredom threshold and compensated later in the evening by being rude to a soldier called Ramsbotham,[3] who I believe, has some sort of senior command in Northern Ireland. But like all soldiers he regards the Rhine Army as his raison d'être and wants to sink the navy in order to save money.

We left early (but not early enough) to drive to Exeter where I was meant to be lunching with the Chief Constable and his colleagues. Blinding rain and a headwind, I had to stop and phone a message of apology for being late via a startled emergency officer from one of the M5 telephone posts. John Alderson, as always, almost too good to be true, like a very distinguished and expensive General Practitioner with his white hair, dark eyebrows and soothing bed-side manner. He desperately wants to be the next-in-command of the 'Met.' and I

---

[1] Tapsell had called, on the evening of the Budget announcement, for the Chancellor's dismissal as having lost the confidence of the City of London.

[2] John Stokes, MP for Halesowen and Stourbridge since 1974 (Oldbury and Halesowen, 1970–74).

[3] General David Ramsbotham, Commander, 39 Infantry Brigade since 1978.

talked to him at length about his plans.[1] He makes a point of talking to me because of my position on the Home Affairs Committee. He must have been sad that I was late as I noticed from the place cards that he had originally put me opposite him at table, later substituted by Peter Mills.

Saltwood   *Saturday, 14 March*

Last night we had the dreaded AGM. Following my instructions there were, once again, no questions. Knowing how their minds work, there is always a danger that a lunatic may strike at such an event, as that stupid prick Jack Courtney did and catching me completely by surprise some three years ago at Frank and Rhianon's CPC Supper. In fact, it was very poorly attended and everybody was as friendly as could be expected. (In Betty's case that means not much.) I gave a 'rallying' speech, although forgot to read out a long list of subject headings which Alison had carefully prepared for me.

Saltwood   *Sunday, 15 March*

All the Sunday papers carried reference to the fact that after the Budget The Lady had gone into the Tea Room on what was variously described as a 'search and destroy mission'. I know from direct personal experience that this is total nonsense. She and Ian came in, separated and The Lady sat down next to me at one of the large tables at which were also present Michael Shersby, John Stokes and two others who I cannot remember.[2] Conversation was totally banal, as it usually is on such occasions and the habitual standard of sycophancy was not moderated in the least. After about twenty minutes, they both got up from their respective seats and sauntered out.

---

[1]John Alderson, Chief Constable of Devon and Cornwall since 1973, had been in the 'Met' in the 1960s. He did not return.
[2]Michael Shersby, MP for Uxbridge since 1972.

Cloisters   *Monday, 16 March*

Brocklebank-Fowler staged his defection today.[1] The air was already heavy with rumour about the number of colleagues who were going to abstain or vote against the petrol tax. Michael Spicer[2] told me before lunch that it was going to be a 'surprisingly close thing'. I thought, but kept it to myself, that the only time I had ever known it a surprisingly close thing was the celebrated no-confidence vote that brought down Callaghan's Government in 1979. Usually when it comes to the point the Government of the day always wins more comfortably than people in their excitement estimate for.

J. Prior opened the debate adopting that well-known technique of the moderates of bellowing any point concerning which his con-science made him uneasy. He was followed by Eric Varley,[3] who, although a very nice man with a lot of sound instincts, cannot speak or even read particularly well and did a lot of mispronunciation, gasping (presumably from nervousness), losing his place, etc. Then we had Norman St John-Stevas, mellifluous, reasonable and without any bitterness. Then Enoch, who was perfectly brilliant – what a superb Chancellor he would make – totally demolishing Peter Shore's speech the previous day when he had argued for reflation. Rhodes-James ostentatiously groaned and left the Chamber the moment Enoch rose to speak, but a large number of others came in while he was speaking and by the end the Chamber was almost completely full.

Then up spoke Brocklebank, pretty objectionable stuff it was, much laced with reference to electoral reform, third world and so on, then in a rather stilted little display he walked down the gangway from his own place and over to the front bench right opposite me, where, mysteriously, all the Tribunites had disappeared except Russell Kerr,[4] who was still asleep, and the Social Democrats were sitting on one another's laps. Poor nice Roddy Maclennan got up to make way for Brocklebank. The whole House roared with laughter, which was not the reaction intended by the Social Democrats. Various members leant

[1] Christopher Brocklebank-Fowler, MP for Norfolk NW since 1974 (King's Lynn 1970–74), crossed the floor and joined the Social Democrats.
[2] Michael Spicer, MP for South Worcestershire since February 1974.
[3] Eric Varley, MP for Chesterfield since 1964, and a Minister in the Wilson and Callaghan governments.
[4] Russell Kerr, MP for Feltham and Heston since 1974 (Feltham 1966–74).

across to try and shake his hand, one of them, John Roper,[1] actually missed three times.

Afterwards, Jim Prior came into the Tea Room and said that he thought Brocklebank had made a 'very good speech'. I have reported this to Ian Gow.

Cloisters   *Thursday, 19 March*

Just as I was going into Prime Minister's Questions Jonathan Aitken caught me in the Lobby and told me that he had been talking to Chapman Pincher, who was now going to 'blow' the whole story of Roger Hollis[2] and the penetration of MI5 by the KGB. As I sat in my place waiting for the Prime Minister I chatted intermittently about it to Peter Hordern, who confirmed my view that it could have the most damaging effect on the Government.

At 3.14 p.m. on the digital clock (i.e. with less than a minute to go) I scuttled up the aisle in the stooping position, turned left up the gangway and push-stumbled my way along the bench behind Ian's place. I whispered to him that the whole Hollis affair was going to blow at the weekend and did he know, should I have a quiet word with him afterwards? He indicated assent and I went back to my place.

When we met in his room it was clear that he did not have any idea of who Hollis was. ('Where is Hollis at the moment . . .' etc.) I sketched in the background briefly, said that I felt the Prime Minister ought to be forewarned in case she did not know. Security scandals always seem to bounce up and hit governments when they start to get a little shaky. Although, of course, I did not say this.

On my way back from the Prime Minister's room I was caught by Adam Raphael in the Members' Lobby. He told me that he felt conspiracies to displace the Prime Minister were now becoming quite flagrant; that she has made so many powerful enemies (the Governor of the Bank of England, Chairman of the CBI, etc.) and that he regarded her as being highly vulnerable if the policies did not start to show results

---

[1] Robert (Roddy) Maclennan (Caithness and Sutherland since 1966) and John Roper (Farnworth since 1970) had both crossed the floor from the Labour benches to join the SDP.
[2] Sir Roger Hollis, Director-General of MI5, 1956–65, was alleged to be the 'Fifth Man' among the Cambridge spies. Subsequent historians disagreed.

during the summer. But we both agreed that the 'wets' were useless –
not called 'wet' for nothing. Raphael said that the unanimity of speeches
last weekend arose simply because each in turn had been 'screamed' at
by the Prime Minister and told to go out and do something.

AR went on to say that this was going to be the theme of his article
this Sunday, coupled with the implication that Francis Pym was the
obvious choice of successor. I suggested that he kept Francis Pym's
name out of the article as it would be dangerous to draw attention to
him at this stage, his own reputation being so high, that people would
pay special credence to what he was saying and so on. AR mumbled
something about flattery did not make any difference, he must stick
to his theme, but he would do it very carefully.

So, I had to go back to IG and warn him of this also. I felt that the
Prime Minister should be forewarned of a text which might come as a
disagreeable shock to her. Ian nodded gloomily, but made no comment.

Later, when I got home, I thought it would also be appropriate to
telephone Francis and let him know as he, too, might appreciate a
word of warning, as there was always the risk that The Lady might
read the piece first, ring him up and scream at him without his
knowing what it was all about. 'But what can I do,' he said plaintively.
Nothing, I agreed, but it was just as well to be forewarned.

Saltwood   *Sunday 22 March*

I see that George Gardiner[1] has got a lead item on the front page of the
Sunday Express 'denouncing' members of the Cabinet who intend to
stage a coup against the Prime Minister. I assume that he was tipped off
by IG immediately after I had left him on Thursday and they agreed
that a pre-emptive attack of this kind was probably the best defence. In
actual fact AR's article did have the Francis Pym reference toned down
so low as to be almost unrecognisable (so hereto I can take, I believe,
personal credit for influencing the course of events). But Michael Jones
in the *Sunday Times* also bandied the question of a coup around on the
front page; so it is clearly a lobby discussion point at the moment.

---

[1] George Gardiner, MP for Reigate and Banstead since February 1974, previously a
political journalist.

Saltwood *Monday, 23 March*

A rejuvenating experience today. Sitting in my place for (boring) Employment questions, I allowed my eye to range along the gallery opposite. Lots of birds and birdettes. On the far edge of the front bench, where it joins the Members' Gallery, sat a blonde. I looked up at her, wearing my glasses, she briefly returned my gaze; haughty, composed. I took off my glasses, chatted on with the boys (JB-D[1] and Tony Fell). My thoughts became obsessive. I contemplated going upstairs and sitting beside her – clearly impossible and ludicrous. Well, anyway, let's have a good old stare ... put on my glasses again and stared. Same routine. She *was* strangely attractive in the true sense. Went back to talking and joking with the lads. Then thought, well, sod it, let's go up to the gallery, 'have a look round'.

To reach it you have to go through various colleagues' offices, the door opening *in* towards you as you step out (to an incredible view and acoustics, incidentally). I went over and sat beside her noticing with a faint pang of anxiety that she seemed rather young, not to say child-like, and under-nourished. And yet in that subtle, secret way that one's animal senses tell one, not *rebarbatif*.

After a few seconds in which I gained my confidence by waving and grimacing at B-D and Fell below, I said 'How're you enjoying it? Is it frightfully boring?'

'Oh ... not yet' she answered (!). With each step surmounted, as in all seductions, retreat by either party becomes more difficult than advance. We chatted, I joked. To my delight I noticed she was very, very pretty. Mouth and eyes terrific; skin a little puppy-spotted. She did not mind, indeed *initiated* remarks and questions. Also she leaned towards me at intervals when not quite 'catching' what I had said. Finally emboldened, I said, 'Come and have some tea'. (Willie had been taking PM's questions and Heseltine had got up. She said she was quite keen on him, but having seen him close to was disappointed.)

'Yes, I'd love to' (with some disclaimer about having to be back). A marvellous, ecstatic moment, comparable almost to getting into bed for the first time – indeed more perfect as less fraught – as I unhooked the ropes and she skipped through into our gallery and off we went!

---

[1] John Biggs-Davison, MP for Epping Forest since 1974 (Chigwell, 1955–74).

Tea in the members' cafeteria. Gosh she was pretty! On the way back she said, 'I like this place'.

'I hope you'll come again', I said.

We exchanged phone numbers in the gallery (as Division Bell was ringing) and I kissed her hand. Super.

That great big booby Geoffrey Dickens[1] rose at Question Time and put a classic 'own goal' point to Francis Pym, aggressively asking about seating accommodation for the public, or something of that kind. The Speaker called him with that special weary inflection that his voice carries when he does not at all wish the Member concerned to speak, but he sees no way to avoid it (in this case because no other Member of the House of Commons was on his feet at the time). Actually, I am getting rather a taste for Geoffrey Dickens. He is a big fellow, with a red face and tiny eyes and mouth. He dyes his hair a dark reddish brown, sweats profusely and his suits are rumpled. (The 'familiar' pinstripe suit, in journalists' code.) But he boxed heavy-weight in the Army and put Don Cockell on the floor – no mean feat and explains why he is such a good dancer – verily, he is the personification of the 'Sapper' cliché, 'the big man moved with amazing speed'.

Cloisters   *Wednesday, 1 April*

I did not make an entry for the Monday, when I rang the bird from the gallery, Jessica by name, and she gave 'blanket' refusal – '... I'm terribly busy' etc, and how low this made me.

Went to Sotheby's this morning to tie up the deal for my introductory commission on the Clark Collection Sale. There was David Westmorland[2] looking a little less confidently polished than in former years; I noticed that his hand shook when he was folding the documents. But of course the great advantage of Sothebys is that they have discarded all pretence – unlike Christie's – of being *gentlemanly*. We construct a deal and do not waste time on the veneers. Col pronounced a sound dictum about the upper classes in such circs: 'When you do a deal with a New York Jew, or even an Italian, there is a kind of

---

[1] Geoffrey Dickens, MP for Huddersfield West since 1979.
[2] The Earl of Westmorland, chairman of Sotheby's since 1980.

residual acceptance that although they are trying to get the better of you, they hope to leave you with just enough satisfaction and self-esteem to come back for a bit more of the same later on. But with the English aristocracy they simply want to take you for as much as they possibly can and hope you drop dead the next day.' However, in our case it was Greek meets Greek. I am getting £12,500 down on an introductory commission for the whole sale of £180,000. To avoid tricky questions about special interest, breach of equity etc., it is being presented (quite legitimately) on a purchase of the copyright to the tapes which I am cutting with my father in which he describes the items in the collection and how he acquired them.

Then to the curry lunch at India House. A good, but not outstanding array of dishes – not in the class of the Kundon for example. I sat between Roddy Maclennan and some dear old Labour war-horse whose name I do not know, who stuffed himself in silence and drank his free wine. *Not* an active Member, but whereas I despise such people in our own Party, in Labour I understand and sympathise. These are dear old boys, living in terraced houses in God knows what heavy-industrial conurbation, bruised and battered by monotonous years on the shop floor and low-key conspiracies in the smoke-filled rooms of the lower reaches of the Trade Union Movement. They have earned their – quite literally – 'free lunch'. RM was interesting about the Social Democrats, thoroughly agreed that the Liberals were poison and should be avoided. A nice intelligent man, but *wet*.

Around the huge 'U' shaped table there were at least 60 acceptances. That fat slob John Hunt appeared to be chairing the proceedings and sitting on the right of the High Commissioner, himself a poor-person's Onassis with silvery hair and immensely thick thorn-rimmed spectacles. On the other side sat Julius Silverman, always said to be the King Street paymaster of the Labour Party CP sleepers,[1] but of late rather somnolent and grey-complexioned. He frequently disturbs me in the non-smoking end of the Commons Library with his exceptionally heavy snoring. Other characters stood out, including a very stylish Guru with white hair and beard at the top table and an unpleasant bearded communist, who sat opposite me, who appeared to be something to do with the Foreign Office.

---

[1] 14 King Street, London, WC2, headquarters of the British Communist Party. Julius Silverman, MP for Birmingham Erdington 1945–55 and since 1974 (Aston, 1955–74).

The High Commissioner was spectacularly incomprehensible in his speech of welcome, except when he suddenly slipped into overdrive and began to denounce – most tactlessly it seemed to me – the Prime Minister's attitudes to foreign aid, arming Afghan rebels, and the Redeployment Force. Then, after he sat down, up got little John Hunt again and announced that an Indian 'pop singer' had been asked along at the last moment and would entertain us. Immediately, up bobbed the Guru and made a longish, jabbering speech explaining the virtues of a plain, middle-aged lady, quite acceptable in appearance, but no beauty, who also rose and plucked meditatively at an enormous guitar, while the Guru was jabbering. She then walked down to the end of the room where a king-size microphone was located and alternately spoke and sang clearly and attractively. A curious and unexpected end to a rather jolly lunch.

Cloisters   *Monday, 13 April*

Dined at Downing Street after a really frightful day of trivial but insistent pressures – compounded by that special sense of angst and frailty that affects one on one's birthday. No cards or tributes (fortunately I am not on *The Times* list. I say 'fortunately' because I do not like people knowing how old I am).

I was exhausted, as there was a tube strike and no cabs so earlier I had to *walk*, carrying a full two gallon can of petrol, from the House of Commons to Albemarle Street where I finally got a taxi by *force majeure* and then on to Sussex Gardens where the faithful Citroen had puttered to a halt on Friday while I rushed to catch the Plymouth train. The only bonus was that she had stood unharmed and unticketed on a resident's parking space throughout the weekend. She started instantly, as always, and I drove her back to the Albany so that Jane could use her to pick me up at the Commons. Then I walked *again* from Albany to the House of Commons. I got back just in time for the Home Affairs Committee which was briefly, and bellowingly (invariably a sign of guilt and apprehension), addressed by Willie on the subject of the Brixton Riots. The Party's reaction is not as strong on this as I would have hoped.

Earlier I had asked a question, following the Statement, regarding police equipment and police considerations of reinforcement. This, as the *Guardian* rightly spotted, Willie deliberately chose to mis-understand. But the police understood it very well and were pleased. Two of them on the Westminster staff congratulated me immediately afterwards. I have really come to the conclusion that Willie is the most subversive member of the entire Cabinet and practically the worst Home Secretary we have had this century with the possible exception of Roy Jenkins. He is an arch appeaser and lives only for crumbs of praise swept from the table of the National Council for Civil Liberties.

We arrived at Number 10 a little late, after the Rumanians had made their entry. Filing up the stairs I noticed a few stars, like Michael Foot, Keith Joseph, John Biffen, Michael Havers[1] etc., so was glad to realise that it was not a 2nd or 3rd XI affair. Not having done this before I did not know how good the drink would be at dinner, so hastily and greedily downed three dry sherries off the itinerant salvers while talking and joking with Biffen. His wife, Sarah, is surprisingly young and pretty to wed someone so staid and avuncular.

Julian Amery, now the complete senior statesman, heavy in girth and ludicrously empurpled, introduced me to the Rumanian Ambas-sador as (his excellency spoke only the language of the Corps Diplomatic) 'Un de que brillants de nos jeunes députés'. The Ambas-sador was tall, handsome and corrupt looking, very much the old, Mdme Lupescu[2] school. No ascetic nonsense about people's courts etc.

On the way into dinner each person was handed a map of the *placement* with a little red hand indicating their own name. The table was an inverted 'U' and I sat down at the end between a blonde in a red dress and a rather matronly lady in a blue chiffon blouse who turned out to be Jane Parsons, one of the original Number 10 boiler-room girls (to use Harold Evans' expression).[3] She told me that she had been there for 35 years and had served under nine Prime Ministers, starting with Attlee. Naturally, Macmillan was easily her favourite and as he is also mine we got on top hole. This was just as well, as at the

---

[1] Michael Havers, MP for Wimbledon since 1970, Attorney-General since 1979.

[2] Madame Lupescu, mistress of King Carol of Rumania in the 1940s, was always a favourite character of AC and in *Barbarossa* he told how, in 1945, a convoy of fourteen motorcars was needed to move her luggage out of Bucharest when the Russians invaded.

[3] At the time AC was reading *Downing Street Diary*, Sir Harold Evans' book on life at Number 10 under Harold Macmillan, 1957–63, when he was the Prime Minister's official spokesman.

halfway stage I had foolishly and mischievously 'got on the wrong side of' the blonde in the red dress.

It happened like this. She turned out to be a German and I, having reluctantly and timorously consumed the sea-food cocktail, had turned away the second course which was a minute and delicious looking poussin stuffed with grapes. (After all 85 per cent of all chicken is supposed to contain salmonella bacteria isn't it?) I told the waitress I would just have vegetables. The waitress was sympathetic, but the blonde said rather haughtily,

'Are you a vegetarian?'

'Yes, like the Führer.'

She affected not to know that Hitler had been a vegetarian and I elaborated on Frau Maziali and the delightful vegetarian dishes she would prepare for him. I could see that this was not going down very well and so, partly to provoke, I said, 'He was ahead of his time in that as in so many other things.'

'What other things?'

Well here I am afraid my precise memory fades, but I did construct some sentence, clear in syntax but ambivalent in meaning, about the genetic need for racial purity. Then, seeing how shocked she was, developed it. I had not anticipated the intensity of her reaction. Her eyes filled with tears, she kept looking at me in horror and saying, 'You are appalling, I think you are appalling, how can you represent people and say these things,' etc.

I gave as good as I got, said that was she really condemning me for my opinions – because she certainly could not condemn me for my actions. Was it not as wrong to condemn people for their opinions as it was for their race or the colour of their skin?

I switched my attention to the young lady opposite, a kind of demi-cutie called (as I was to discover later) Clara Hauser. She was engaged in conversation with John Bayley. This was dear dotty John Bayley who is married to Iris Murdoch and who I remember meeting at the Stones at Long Bredy in those carefree distant days of the sixties when Jane and I used to drive about in the Jaguar and spend long weekends with our friends in Dorset. John Bayley said something about late nights and I said how much I loathed them.

'You look very tired,' said the girl.

'Oh, do I?', I answered (I never like this).

'Yes,' she answered, 'absolutely devastated.' Not -ing, but -ed. This was really too much.

I turned my attention to Jane Parsons and kept it there for the rest of the meal. Actually, it may have been an ill-wind as the following day Jane suggested that I might have been put next to Jane Parsons as part of a scrutiny process for Ian's succession. However, this has faded so dim that I hardly think about it any longer, although as he is still there the vacancy presumably remains.

Ian and I, and Michael Havers left together for the vote, Ian complaining bitterly about Hauser (the demi-cutie's father) who had been sitting near him during dinner and apparently propounding a stream of Marxist and subversive sentiments. After the Division we went to Ian's room and watched The Lady do a TV interview with Alastair Burnet. Ian had been apprehensive about this, but I did not think it such a disaster, although she was very strained and intense in her expression – quite different from her demeanour at the dinner.

Afterwards we returned to Downing Street. Ian had told me to wait behind until the other guests had left, but I did not do so and we took our leave at the same time as our own Ambassador in Bucharest who wanted a lift to Grosvenor House. I swished him round there in the S2 (always be nice to Ambassadors as they can be so helpful when one is travelling), but the effect may have been somewhat spoiled if the trade plates, that were lying on the back seat, were noticed.

Cloisters   *Tuesday, 5 May*

I dined with little Winston and Julian Amery at White's. The old school. Julian is very clever, with a nice command of language and an attractive and deep rooted cynicism. If he were Prime Minister (which he was expected to be, and should have been – if the whole Macmillan succession had not been warped by the intrusion of the Heath/Walker syndrome and the 'new' Conservative Party) he would certainly have had me in his Cabinet. But I was alarmed to note that he seemed to be getting a tiny bit ga-ga and, as I recorded at the Downing Street dinner, he is putting on weight alarmingly fast. He is also obsessively, dottily, anti-Soviet and pro-Zionist.

Little Winston has mellowed, perhaps on Julian's advice.

White's is not as nice as Pratt's. Conversation is more inhibited. We were joined by a piggish and I suspect a slightly infradig member who the wine waiter referred to as 'commander', and later by Lord

Cowdray[1] to whom the years have lent a superficial benevolence. But below the surface he remains just as nasty as ever. I was not 'respectful' to him, which to my pleasure I could sense him resenting. He spoke with pride and affection about his dreadful, hirsute, smelly son and how he had rented a helicopter to bring his wife's hairdresser from London to Bordeaux.

Cloisters   *Monday, 11 May*

Willie is quite changed. He has lost over two stone. But it is not a cancer loss, it arises out of a regime, a purging. His skin is clear where formerly it was blotchy and his eyes water less. Ostentatiously he refuses drink. Like the Reichs Marshall (though of course not on that scale), he has made a tremendous effort of will and kicked the habit.

But why? He should be amiably, but sozzledly tottering towards an Indian summer in the Lords. Instead he is slim, vigorous, attentive and, most unexpected of all, amiable.

What is he preparing himself for? 'Crossbencher', who has also noted this, wrote some idiotic piece in the *Sunday Express* to the effect that Willie's sole purpose was to defend the Prime Minister at every possible moment. Total balls of course. I find the whole thing rather disconcerting.

Saltwood   *Thursday, 14 May*

I am drinking *far too much*.

Yesterday	1 bloody mary	} lunch
	1 glass wine	
	2 glasses red wine	} dinner
	2 glasses white wine	
	1 vintage port	

---

[1] Lord Cowdray, former chairman of S. Pearson & Son, owner of, among other things, the *Financial Times*.

| Day before | 3 glasses wine | dinner |
| Before that | wine and port | |

Cloisters   *Monday, 18 May*

The *Daily Telegraph* carried the most appalling scare headlines about 'slashing' the Navy, getting rid of the three-deck cruisers and the marines etc. Jane quite rightly worked me up into a rage about this and I left early for the Commons where I suspected that there would be plenty of action.

The phone had been ringing all weekend with journalists asking for my comments on Keith Speed's speech to his 'constituents' about running down the Navy.[1] To my mingled gratification and alarm, I saw myself described in two of the Sunday newspapers as *Chairman* of the Defence Committee. I suppose it is a tribute to my personality that most people in and out of the Party think I am the Chairman, but this annoys Tony [Buck].

Poor little Speed, whom I used to hold in some contempt, dating back I think, to the time when, as a junior minister for the Environment, he addressed the Conservative College at Swinton and was so muddled and inarticulate that at the back of the room I started giving a running imitation of him, to the delectation of various YCs who were grouped there. We were all candidates at that time, but since then he has what is known as 'come on' and I know that he has been in despair over the options for some weeks. It was only last Thursday that Tony and I saw him in New Palace Yard as he got out of his official car (almost for the last time, as it turned out). He implied that he was on the point of resignation, then, and looked grey and distraught.

Actually, if I had really had my head screwed on I would have understood the significance of what he was saying at that chance meeting and deliberately gone low-profile on the 'storm' that had inevitably to follow his speech. I would then have been in a strong position as one of his potential successors.

---

[1] Keith Speed had served in the Royal Navy and was appointed Minister for the Navy in 1979.

As soon as I got to the Commons it was clear that Keith's number was up. The whips were spreading it around that he had been 'disloyal' and senior backbenchers were echoing this with the view that he had 'mismanaged' things – should have resigned simultaneously etc.

Almost immediately after I got in I had to do a broadcast on the *World at One* programme and that evening I went on television twice. It is so easy, even for someone relatively experienced like myself, to allow the journalists to lead one on into rather extreme, or at least excessive, comments. As the whole thing was rumour anyway, I suppose I may have overdone it, but colleagues who had heard the broadcast were enthusiastic. Although, in some cases, of course, this could have been tinged with satisfaction at my so obviously putting the kyebosh on my own chances.

In the evening we had the celebrated and long-postponed dinner for Francis Pym and the old officers of the Defence Committee. The postponement had been due to my own spasticity in not getting the original invitations confirmed. But as it happened, it was almost theatrically timely. Someone, presumably Buck himself, had told the press, and the *Evening Standard* featured it as a major item, putting the word 'coincidence' in double quotes.

I made sure that the food would be good and the wine excellent (on the previous Thursday I had won £70 playing backgammon with Lord Armstrong[1] and this led to my credit in the restaurant). We had two bottles of white burgundy and three of excellent claret and Francis became mellow and benevolent – except towards little Winston, with whom he was sharp; 'you are obsessed by your grandfather and comparisons with his period' etc. Winston is *so* thick skinned, is he simple? Francis was not particularly 'loyal' and I exploited my host's prerogative to enunciate one or two personal aversions, Keith Joseph, Nigel Lawson – which I knew he would share. But I would not say that anything very spectacular came out of the meeting except 'goodwill' and we all know what a soft currency that is.

I had kept a place at the table for Hal Miller[2] but he did not turn up as he was making his resignation speech on the floor of the House at that time. Just in case Francis asked me to take Hal's place I rang

---

[1] William Henry Cecil John Robin Watson-Armstrong, 3rd Baron, an underwriting member of Lloyd's.
[2] Hal Miller resigned from his position as PPS to the Chancellor of the Duchy of Lancaster in protest at the Government's attitude to the private steel sector.

Jane to clear it with her that I would, as tactfully as I could, say no. It is the second or third most important PPS in the House, but although I like Francis and hold him in high regard, the drudgery of mucking around with the business of the House does not appeal to me. The right answer, but I am not sure if I would have the courage to give it, is 'ask me again when you are Prime Minister'.

Cloisters   *Tuesday, 19 May*

Yesterday I had written to Tony with copies to all the other officers and the Defence Whip apologising for constantly being referred to as 'Chairman' of our Committee.

So I really was alarmed this morning to see that *The Times* carried in its lead item on the front page not only a report of our having dined with Francis, but a full quote of my combative question, saying that we cannot indefinitely support British Leyland while being asked to make brutal economies in the defence sector, 'as *Chairman* of the Defence Committee'.

There was a phone message from Buck asking me to meet him and Victor Goodhew in the Smoking Room at 12.45 p.m. We should have co-ordinated our line in this afternoon's debate, but in fact the Smoking Room is such a bad place for meetings of this kind that very little was decided except that the officers should ask for an audience with the Prime Minister immediately. I thought this was ill-judged as well as being rather offensive. Clearly protocol demands that we wait until the debate has run its course and all the openings and wind-ups have been heard. Winston of course is so crazy that he wants to charge in immediately with imputations of bad faith, etc. To my surprise Buck, who should be somewhat warier, was also in favour of an immediate meeting *and* telling the press that we were asking for this. Not a good idea.

I listened to Nott and Keith Speed, then the debate seemed to run out of steam somewhat and I went up to the Deputy Speaker and took my name off the list. Perhaps this was a tactical error as I was in fact quite high up on it and it might have been helpful, in more than one sense, if I had made a temperate and constructive speech.

Cloisters   *Wednesday, 20 May*

I have lost count of the number of people who have come up to me and asked me if I am going to be the next Navy Minister. There was a rumour going round the Press Gallery yesterday afternoon and Elinor Goodman (*Financial Times*) said that she had heard it. The Lady can hardly appoint someone who publicly congratulated the speech of the person she has just dismissed, but the rumour did momentarily get some substance when Sir Raymond Gower[1] approached me in the Tea Room queue this morning and said, in that special senior backbencher's undertone, that he understood I was the new Minister. He is one of those people, like Marcus Kimball and Timothy Kitson,[2] who have an extraordinarily efficient bush telegraph. Also when I told Spencer [Le Marchant] that I was going to speak this afternoon he looked rather uneasy, more or less said 'I would not if I were you.' Perhaps he too knows something?

There are cruel disappointments in the House of Commons at every turn and their piquancy is aggravated by the hot-house atmosphere in which one's hopes can soar.

Cloisters   *Thursday, 21 May*

I left the House about 6.00 p.m. and ran into Nick St Germans[3] at Brooks's and we played backgammon until half past eight. He used to be a very dangerous international player, but he must be in his late sixties now and although he knows all the old prize fighter's tricks he occasionally makes a soft move. However, he had amazingly good dice and to my great irritation I lost a lot of money. The same syndrome as when playing Harold Lever – who is not nearly as good as he thinks either.

We had dinner late and at the corner table sat Norman St John-Stevas and friends. About halfway through the meal Nick started complaining that he had seen Heseltine in Pratt's one evening and who the hell had brought him in? For some reason he had got it into

---

[1] Sir Raymond Gower, MP for Barry since 1951.
[2] Sir Timothy Kitson, MP for Richmond, Yorks since 1959.
[3] Nicholas Elliot, 9th Earl of St Germans.

his head that it might be Norman. I thought this very unlikely and so popped over to interrupt their meal and ask him.

'Lord St Germans is very concerned because he thinks you brought Michael into Pratt's. I have told him this is highly unlikely, will you confirm?'

'Michael who?'

'Michael Heseltine.'

'Michael *Heseltine?* Good God, I would never take him anywhere.'

Norman, who was clearly a bit bored, moved over to our table and dazzled with his bright tales, quips and anecdotes. He is one of those people whose brain is that much faster than my own and can have a slightly stilting effect. Maurice and John[1] both used to do it.

Norman told me that he thought Buck would be the choice for Navy Minister; also that there was no sign of a let up in The Lady's hard-line policies, that the opposition in the Cabinet was ineffectual – 'they are not called wets for nothing'. I had forgotten that he was the origin of this very shrewd judgement which, naturally, did not please anybody. He told me how terrifying The Lady could be, and of one spectacular row that they had had, with her pacing up and down the room screaming at him. Were they alone, I asked? Only Willie, he had replied, but he was slumped in a sofa and said nothing from start to finish.

Later, we moved on to Pratt's where Nick generated an atmosphere congenial to Norman by recounting how his father was something-or-other in the Household to six monarchs in succession. The boys took the brunt of Nick's reminiscences and Norman continued to confide in me out of the corner of his mouth. He said he was determined to remain in politics; that the Queen had been perfectly charming to him when he surrendered the seals of office and said what a horrific business politics was; that the Queen Mother had made a point of inviting him to dinner a few days later and then not letting him leave after the meal and so on.

I was impressed by him. He is delightful company. But I am afraid the Tory Party will only tolerate someone as eccentric and witty as he is if they (a) dispose of real personal power and (b) offer the prospect

---

[1] Maurice Bowra, Warden of Wadham College, Oxford, 1932–71; John Sparrow, Warden of All Souls College, Oxford, 1950–78.

of patronage. And I fear that in his heart Norman realises that this is true.

Saltwood   *Wednesday, 27 May*

At this moment I have got what darling Jane called 'reshuffle chum-blies'. Still no Navy Minister appointed . . . Buck still tipped. Wouldn't mind this as the Party wouldn't specially like it and I should then be able to be Chairman [of Defence Committee]. A flat election, anyway. But of course even better if I could get the Ministry myself. Really impose reform, impress the House and The Lady and be moved to Secretary of State when Nott becomes Chancellor.

The great thing about politics is that at any time one can throw double 4's. I am unlucky at backgammon and psychic. I have this capacity to psyche my opponent into throwing the shots I've thought of. Alas, it has got to stop. I've said this a great many times. Now I have decided on it.

Finally there is the 'question' of *The Gems of Brazil*. It started a year ago when I saw a Mallets ad – presumably for the 'Two Humming Birds' – identified the artist and forget his name . . . 'An American'. Then last year, after his good job on the Fantin [Latour] I got Valentine[1] to get them cleaned. He brought them back – very satisfactory; they really looked nice, rich, decorators' items and with a certain 'something'. I was glad to have them. Then on his second visit, at the end of the evening, he produced a colour ad from (as it were) the *American Connoisseur* showing the 'Two Humming Birds' – possibly the same picture that I had seen earlier at Mallets – and identifying the artist as Martin Johnson Heade. I lost the reference and Valentine left the next day.

Then, coming back on the train from Paris, after changing out of the sleeper, with *The Times* bought at the Gare du Nord, I saw Geraldine Norman quip that 'American artists of the XIXc are now worth more per square inch of canvas than any other except Cézanne and Rembrandt'; she gave a few artists and prices, among them 'Martin Johnson Heade'. I *still* didn't twig. Not for some days until I rang Valentine and asked for a copy of the ad. Yes it was. Then it

---

[1] Valentine Gould, conservation adviser and old friend of the Clarks.

moved quite fast. I contacted the shop by phone, and they told me
… sold at $40,000, would now ask 50 or even 75. Contacted West
Central reference library and looked up Theodore Stebbings Junior's
book and found out that these were the 16 missing paintings done in
Brazil for the 'Chrome Lithographs' and later sold to Sir Morton Peto
(Valentine had told me that on the back, when cleaning them, he had
discerned the word 'Peto').

Took them round to Desmond – exaggerating the story of Martin
Johnson Heade and a provisional 'price' was 'agreed' of $1.2m.

I could hardly, can hardly, don't really, believe that this is actually
happening. And now Desmond seems to have gone cold (total radio
silence). Am so tired, depressed and martyred, but hourly remind
oneself that one has got 16 highly important and interesting missing
items by a very valuable XIXc American artist. In the slides they look
incredible, so skilful and touching, the 'Luminist' school. Jane rightly
said they were a present from George and the birds, and that we ought
to keep two.[1]

Continued Saturday

We go to bed *so* late, and Angus got us up so early that I am *averaging*
6–6$\frac{1}{4}$ hrs sleep a night! The Estate endlessly demanding. It is only
because it is steadily, insistently summer raining that I have been able
to spare the evening in the Gt Hall writing this text. So, am ash eating.
The motto is 'can't afford it'. Not drinking (!) now 2$\frac{1}{2}$ days. No
b'gammon. Sod the cars '… not interested, old boy.' Will try to get
Alison to keep the blondes at bay. The Philosopher Prince – *reflectif*.
But thanking God, none-the-less. I said on the 'w': 'I'm certainly not
going to Zermatt this September.'

'At the present rate,' said Jane, 'one probably won't be alive by
September.'

'Probably alive, but in hospital and on drip-feed.'

She rebuked me, and rightly. We are enormously, colossally lucky.
Such a glorious place, such possessions, fulfilment and security. I am
enjoying my martyrdom – St Gregory; and may God continue to
protect us in the future.

---

[1] Heade (1819–1904) visited South America in the early 1860s to paint the humming
birds for *The Gems of Brazil*. It is thought that he did twenty paintings in all. In the
end the Clarks sold their sixteen.

Cloisters   *Tuesday, 2 June*

I went to the House to try out the new breakfast arrangements which have been set up by Charles Irving[1] for those of us too lazy or incompetent to make our own. 'I am just an unhappy bachelor', I had said to Charles before the Recess and, to do him credit, he quite enjoyed the joke. He, of course, being a 'confirmed' one.

On the way across the Lobby I ran into Hal Miller and we indulged in our routine grumble about how time was slipping past and how things were not really coming right etc. We agreed that it was impossible to get rid of The Lady and, indeed, would be politically highly dangerous. But it was equally difficult to get *through* to her or to suggest/impose the necessary changes in personnel. Hal told me that he still saw Francis and spoke intimately with him. But I got the impression that the Cabinet is a muddled, leaderless and unhappy lot. There are shadows of the closing years of the Heath administration, though painted in starker colours. The principal difference being that Ted was a rude and arrogant flobbo without an ounce of patriotism in his body; whereas The Lady is the most wonderful person and could still work miracles.

Saltwood   *Thursday, 11 June*

Idly thinking of taking a sabbatical next year. 'Castle closed for repairs.' Selling the *Gems* does induce a certain feeling of tranquillity. I don't think so much about Bonny papa dying. In fact quite the reverse, I want him to live on and annoy Nolwen.

Cloisters   *Friday, 12 June*

I believe that these last few days have been the ones when I finally (or is it first?) realised that I was not going to get any office or preferment whatever.

---

[1] Charles Irving, MP for Cheltenham since October 1974; Chairman of Select Committee on Catering since 1979.

Spurred on by Jane, I had felt it my duty to caution the Prime Minister against putting in Heseltine as Chairman of the Party. This is a perennial threat, much bandied about by the media from time to time and had been trailed on the front page of the *Sunday Telegraph* last weekend. Also, interestingly, with Norman Tebbit's name. T, too, is completely ruthless and ambitious, but in some way not quite so odious as Heseltine, not so totally synthetic and opportunist. I remember first warning dear Airey about Heseltine and explaining that once installed as Chairman he would try and change, or covertly encourage the changing, of the rules governing election of the Party leader. Because of course the Parliamentary Party would never give him a majority. But if we widened our franchise as have the Labour Party and the Liberals, he would have a chance.

It seemed to me that I should repeat this to the PM. All the more so as the Government is, remains, an 'Unhappy Ship'. It is impossible to predict the outcome in politics. The scene can change with nightmare speed in a matter of weeks, and at any time.

Anyhow, I rang Ian on Thursday morning and asked if I could have five minutes with the Prime Minister, '... in your presence of course', as what I had to say might have been embarrassing if relayed at second-hand. To his great credit he asked no questions, and after a split-second interval, looking at the engagement book, said 'Come to my room at ten to four, she will see you as soon as she comes out'.

Earlier that afternoon I had been asked to a 'discussion' on Defence at Central Office (!) with two visiting Americans, stereotype hawk heavies from the military-industrial lobby who were touring Europe on a promotion trip for their new glossy magazine, *Military Science*. We sat down in the 'international Conference Room', myself at the head of the table and the two Americans, much encumbered by recording equipment of various kinds on either side, and two willowy, but unsympathetic, middle-rank twits from Central Office in attendance.

The session was quite fun as I was able to dazzle with my specialised knowledge of weaponry – something they would certainly not have got from any other member of the Committee – and hard-boiled attitude to 'relationships' etc.

When they produced an enormous tape-recorder, one of the CO twits left the room in a panic, presumably to ring up MOD. I became more and more reckless in my answers. The remaining CO twit/spy finally interjected feebly, 'Why don't you ask us about the Labour

Party's attitude to Defence?' Typically spastic reaction by an unthink-
ing little toad. If they wanted to know about the Labour Party's
Defence policy there was nothing to stop them having a meeting with
my counterpart on the Labour side, I said. They agreed. As well as
recording the whole interview, one of them constantly clicked and
clucked with an expensive looking Pentax. Presumably it will all be
published in a forthcoming issue.

I had to cut it short, with the pompous – but perfectly genuine
excuse – that I was going to see the Prime Minister. Full of adrenalin
I pranced across the pavements from Smith Square. Then followed a
long wait in Ian's office. Vast numbers of whisky bottles covered his
desk, awaiting the Prime Minister's signature on the label, and outside
in the hallway a few backbenchers hung around. I saw Michael Brown
and Colin Shepherd[1] waiting to carry away their trophies which would
presumably be auctioned or raffled at constituency bazaars.

After 4 p.m. numbers of those identikit 'private secretaries' in grey
suits, horn-rimmed spectacles and supercilious manner – are they civil
servants, party officials, research assistants or what? – piss off I wanted
to shout at them. Finally, The Lady emerged. I could tell from her
special rustling, clucking movements that she was not going to stop.
'I have got an ambassador waiting,' she said, 'put it off until next week
when we have got *longer*.' Coquettish, debby almost.

She disappeared with the identikit and Ian called me into the long
room. *He* seemed in a bit of a hurry too. I explained my misgivings
about the prospective choice for the Party Chairman. Ian told me that
he had warned The Lady about eighteen months ago that he believed
Heseltine was a threat to her, but now he thought that this was less
true. I agreed that Heseltine had lost ground in the last year, but
warned him of how quickly things could turn around again. IG made
the perfectly valid point that the Party would be still less likely to
accept changes in the election system when they could see what a
mess Labour had got themselves into in experimenting with it.

I followed him out into the Central Lobby where he shook me off.
My relations with IG seem a little more distant at the present time.
This was a distinct impression and it depressed me for the rest of the
day.

That evening Michael McNair-Wilson twitted me endlessly (he

---

[1] Michael Brown, MP for Brigg and Scunthorpe since 1979; Colin Shepherd, MP for
Hereford since October 1974.

knows how vulnerable I am on this) with the fact that I had been making a good impression and 'yet again' had 'said something' that had spoilt it all. What *can* he be referring to? I have only spoken once in the last fortnight – on MPs pay. Was it that? It may have been. Sadistic teasing. Perhaps he is a closet queen; it is always slightly suspicious when men get married late in life to women with teenage children and then have none of their own, isn't it? 'One thing I can tell you, Alan', he said, smiling gloatingly, 'with absolute certainty, and that is that you will never be Navy Minister.' I went to bed exceedingly depressed.

Cloisters *Monday, 15 June*

The weekend papers are full of forecasts that the Government are contemplating major 'strategic' changes in policy. But what did it all boil down to? Building the Channel Tunnel. I ask you. One is moved to despair. They have cocked the thing up solidly for two years and are now proposing to win the election on an inflationary programme of public works. Depression both personal and general drags at one.

At 6 p.m. there was a combined meeting of the Defence and Foreign Affairs Committees at No. 10. I left ample time (too ample as it turned out) as I decided to go along Birdcage Walk and up Clive Steps. A young, plump, personable, but unco-operative policewoman refused to let me through the gate so I had to go all the way round again, breaking at intervals into apprehensive and flustered pounding (which is the best verb I can describe jogging fully dressed). As I came into the hall of Number 10 the major domo took pleasure in telling me that they had already gone up. Panic! Am I in an accident-prone phase?

However, although the backbenchers were assembled in the White Drawing Room, the Ministers had not yet appeared. Little (and he is little) Carrington came in first, very bronzed and la-di-dah. I do not think it is paranoia, I think he really does loathe me. The majority of people rose to their feet as he came in. I did not, nor did Peter Bottomley[1], and at the far end of the room I was glad to see that

[1] Peter Bottomley, MP for Greenwich, Woolwich West since 1975.

Victor Goodhew had also remained seated, although he has a heart condition of course, which gives him an excuse. Notters was next in, as always slightly rattled and gangling. He is the embodiment of high rank *without* gravitas.

The Lady came in and sat down on the yellow silk sofa on which Carrington had perched himself. There took place one of those curious, almost petty, but completely feminine, scenes which remind me of my mother. We all had drinks in our hands. Carrington had put his on a minute coffee table beside the right arm of the yellow silk sofa. The Lady had nowhere to put hers but an empty chair immediately on her left. Just as we were about to begin she called to Ian, who was at the far end of the room, and asked him to bring her a table for her glass. Ian was fussed by this, there was no table in sight or accessible. As he looked round Carrington got the message and got up. Against a background of 'no, no Peter', etc. he removed his glass, put it on the mantelpiece, picked up the small table and stooping carried it round the sofa and put it down by the Prime Minister's left hand. I enjoyed this, not least because I could see that he did not. *What* a bore for all those men in the Cabinet to have as their leader not only a woman, but a woman who, whether subtly or overtly, insists on being treated as such.

Tony Buck led off, rambling, incoherent almost. I could see members of the Cabinet getting fidgety. The contributions were exceedingly disparate and, perhaps deliberately, the red herring of the Israeli raid trailed repeatedly across our proceedings. Winston hogged the floor, as always, and spoke again and again. Twice he actually tried to shout down The Lady, holding on so that they were speaking simultaneously for quite a long time before her voice actually won through. She made no commitments, told us nothing we did not know already. The standard, somewhat banal lecture. A purely cosmetic exercise.

This evening the small, but select black tie dinner in Dining Room 'C' for Hinch[1]. A disparate lot, some distinguished, some less so. Quintin[2], Julian Amery and John Peyton among the heavies, Hal Miller and myself representing those of lighter weight. Many had

---

[1] Victor Montagu, formerly Viscount Hinchinbrooke and MP for S. Dorset 1941–62, when he succeeded his father as 10th Earl of Sandwich, but disclaimed his peerage. He celebrated his seventy-fifth birthday on 24 July.

[2] Quintin Hogg, Lord Hailsham of St Marylebone and Lord Chancellor since 1979.

heard of the dinner and (apparently) been offended by not having been invited. Peter Thorneycroft had excused himself on thinnish grounds. Cranborne,[1] who had accepted, never turned up and his shrivelled grapefruit stood reproachfully in front of his *placement* card throughout the meal. Speeches were made, and reciprocated. Hinch sat looking pink and benevolent, but stooped. The leading personal example – of which there are always plenty – of someone who needlessly and pointlessly sodded up his political career out of sheer bad judgement. I could not help reflecting that many of the tributes were all the more heartfelt by an unspoken vein of at-least-I-did-not get-it-that-wrong-ery in the speaker's mind.

Saltwood   *Saturday, 4 July*

Sitting in the Great Hall – always lovely in here on summer evenings. The only remaining place in the estate where one can reach a truly contemplative state. I prefer it to my father's study. I love the high, high hammerbeam roof, the swallows darting excitedly in and out, the looming presence of so many books that I will never, could never, read.

Cloisters   *Monday, 6 July*

Today's papers are full of accounts of the rioting. Simultaneous out-breaks in different parts of London, Liverpool, Manchester, etc. Apparently, the police have taken very heavy casualties in Liverpool. All this was totally predictable once it was apparent that the people who rioted in St Pauls, Bristol had been handled with kid-gloves at the time and those few who had been arrested were discharged without penalty by the courts. Indeed, I am surprised that it has taken so long for the practice to spread. The Scarman Enquiry into the Brixton Riots has not helped of course, with his constant sniping at the police and dreary toleration of endless monologues about social deprivation, etc.

---

[1] Lord Cranborne, MP for S. Dorset since 1979; heir to 6th Marquess of Salisbury.

Willie is down to make a Statement and will then be attending the Home Affairs Committee to elaborate. I am deeply gloomy; that man will sell out anything. He is an arch-appeaser, but cunning with it – a combination of Horace Wilson and Horatio Bottomley.

Cloisters   *Tuesday, 7 July*

Today is the debate on the Defence White Paper. I would quite like to speak, but I gather the list is enormous. However, I will sit it out and, hopefully, get on the record with a few interventions.

Later, as I was walking back from the Tea Room, I thought I should just check with the Speaker if I had any chance, and my steps took me through the deserted 'Aye' lobby. I heard my name called and I G sidled up beside me. 'Ted is going to speak,' he said.

'Oh really, is he going to be objectionable?'

'I should think inevitably,' he said. 'Can you do anything about it?'

'Yes,' I answered. 'He only sits a couple of places from me. I will find a good time to interrupt him, leave it to me.'

Having an official assignment and sense of importance I went back to my seat.

In the fullness of time Ted got up and started off. When he came to the bit about renewing our presence East of Suez I forced him to give way. Everyone listens to Ted's speeches in the expectation of, and more or less exclusively for, some critical reference veiled or otherwise to The Lady and her Government. But this speech seemed to be perfectly clean.

'I have been listening with great attention to my Honourable Friend,' I said, 'and most of us would agree that what he has said *so far* ...' (lip curling); I went on to point out that the withdrawal East of Suez had been carried out by his Government. It was a carelessly-phrased intervention and it allowed him to slap me down, as in fact it was *implemented* by the Labour Government. I should have said, 'was *decided* upon by ...' etc.

Anyway, I sat down, conscious of the fact that I had not covered myself with glory, and listened to the rest of his speech. It was extremely good, slightly isolationist and with a number of ingenious suggestions for arms control negotiations. Sometimes I think that Ted is really rather marvellous. After he had finished, I popped out and wrote a little handwritten note of appreciation. In it I more or less admitted that I had been put up to it, 'you know how these things are arranged'. At the time some great grey cloud exuded warning as it hung over the desk. This was pure sneaking and trouble-making. I lightened it with a benign reference to that charming little piece that he wrote about his childhood at Bexhill and popped it straight on to the Board.

Much later I was still in my place when Ted, still in his pale, pale grey suit, returned for the winding up. With a thrill of horror I saw that he was holding my note in his hand. He opened it, read it and very slowly and deliberately put it back into the envelope. As usual his face was totally expressionless. Was he offended? I had a sudden nightmare that he would take it straight to the Chief Whip and complain.[1]

This has been a very bad day in which the Government, and The Lady in particular, have taken a lot of punishment. Yesterday Willie blundered and bellowed his way through the Statement about the riots in Toxteth and Southall and then came and talked to the Committee. As Nick Budgen so percipiently remarked to me afterwards, Willie, to whom the concept of strategic thinking or the national advantage are completely alien, was preoccupied with the narrow political point as to how the House would accept the fact that CS Gas had been used for the first time in Britain (very effectively as it turned out in Toxteth). He was plagued too by a minor worry, namely that the quality of the 'protective headgear' to be issued to the police might prove to be sub-standard and (although of course he did not articulate any of this) the Public Accounts Committee might ask questions later. 'The best is the enemy of the good', he kept repeating.

At Question Time today it was apparent that the Labour Party had pulled themselves together and decided to make the most of this unexpected bonus. It could have gone either way. Law and order situations usually rebound to the credit of the Tory Party in electoral terms, but in this case, either by accident or design, they hit on the notion of attributing the civil disturbance to unemployment. Totally

---

[1] In fact some days later AC received a very polite and appreciative note from Edward Heath, thanking him for his letter and saying that he 'quite understood'. However, sequels with a wider impact were to follow later.

spurious of course – 'There are no riots in Consett, are there?' I shouted from my seat, but as it was repeated from all quarters on the opposite side of the Chamber they came to realise that they had hit on something. They bashed away at Willie all through Home Office questions and by the time The Lady rose to do her bit they were in fine fettle.

The principal danger of this is a political one, and I find it menacing in the extreme. Most of the press, and indeed, most of the Cabinet, have been waiting for 'rioting' to follow The Lady's economic policies. Now that they have got rioting – though for different reasons – they are delighted to be able to link the two and use it to proselytise their own arguments. That toad Prior has apparently already said that unemployment '... has something to do with it' in order to raise money for his maniac ego-boosting Youth Employment schemes. *The Times* has published Peter Walker's Open Letter to the Prime Minister about young unemployed in Brixton. Of course this was originally printed in 1976, and I well remember the rubbery little shit making that very speech on the subject from that place next to me on the Front Bench below the gangway at that time. But bringing it up to date was another flagrant expression of the treachery in which he specialises.

This really is the Tory Party at its worst; a few senior politicians, who feel themselves thwarted, are combining to use a disastrous national crisis to advance their own personal ambitions. It is also desperately dangerous, as if we lose even our identification with law and order, we have no electoral cards left to play whatever. The high point of our prestige came at the time when the SAS broke the siege at Princes Gate. Yet all the majority of the Cabinet want to do now is buy their way out of the trouble in compensation, grants to the inner cities, etc. etc.

I do not think it is exaggerating to say that if this continues the Government, or at any rate The Lady, could very easily fall on the issue. If the disturbances maintain their present pitch she could be forced into consultations with leaders of other parties, followed rapidly by a coalition.

Saltwood   *Saturday, 11 July*

We gave a grand dinner party for Aspinall's Ball at Port Lympne. Edward and Fiona Montagu, Jonathan Aitken and his wife, Lolicia (or Lutz as, disconcertingly, appears to be her nickname),[1] also Jonathan Guinness[2] with his wife and two of his sons, Valentine and Sebastian. One of these latter never combed his hair or took off his overcoat, as far as I could see, throughout the weekend, but was quite sympathetic nevertheless.

The food was delicious and the table almost overloaded with Meissen, solid silver, Venetian glass, etc. I gave them two magnums of Batailley '61, as well as much other good stuff. They polished off a full bottle of Cockburn '55.

Aspinall promised that his Ball would be the most expensive since Charlie Bestigui in Venice in 1951. He had boy scouts holding torches of pitch the whole way down the drive and girl guides doing the same thing on the walk up from the car park. The floodlighting was spectacular and the flower arrangements quite incredible. Everything had been done on a kind of nothing-but-the-best principle, and there were literally vats of caviare, surrounding polar bears carved out of ice etc. I noticed faces from the past: Vivian Naylor-Leyland, still consorting with the young, I saw. His face seemed curiously swollen and stricken and his speech impaired. Surely, he is still too young to have had a tiny occlusion?

Unfortunately, the weather was a touch too cold and although we wandered in the grounds and climbed Philip's Great Steps behind the Tea Garden, we were driven back into the marquee in the early hours. Frank Williams[3] joined us at our table. I must say that I liked him better this time. I thought he was a phoney patriot and simply beating the drum because he was making money out of the rôle, but his indignation at the rioting and the softness of our responses was totally genuine, as was his simple incomprehension of the difficulties of operating inside the Tory Party, if you are a 'reactionary'. His presence was a great coup for the boys, whom he promised tickets for the British

---

[1] 'Lutz' was the name of the SS Commandant at the Colditz Camp where AC's son, James, had worked the previous summer.
[2] Lord Montagu of Beaulieu and his second wife; Jonathan Guinness, former chairman of the Monday Club, and his second wife.
[3] Frank Williams, founded Frank Williams Racing Cars in 1975. His number one driver, Carlos Reutemann, was at that time leading the World Championship.

Grand Prix. Befuddled by drink I muddled up Carlos Reutemann and Ronnie Patterson which, I could see, embarrassed Andrew, although he was very sweet about it and helped me correct my mistake.

Jane and I spent most of the time sitting on stone seats in the garden or walking in the more secluded regions (naturally most of the guests simply turned left and went straight down to the marquee where they stuffed themselves with as much free food and drink as they could for four hours).

We wondered how Port Lympne was taking it. I know, because I went there as a child and because Sybil[1] showed me the visitors book, just how much of a centre it was on every summer weekend for twenty years, and of course tonight's party was not really grand in the full sense. The boys, who stayed until the bitter end, told me that there was one person there being referred to as 'Your Royal Highness', who was 'covered in rocks' and Jane told me that she spotted quite a lot of good jewellery. But au fond it was an unselective 20 per cent of café society, a leavening of aristocratic gamblers, from whom Aspinall had won large sums twenty years earlier, and an unfortunately high number of more shadowy figures, presumably Mafia, or 'multinational', who have access to enormous bank accounts.

Yet the presentation was tasteful, no vulgarity whatever, except in the sheer abundance. It was sad too, Gatsby-like in its transience, because poor old Aspers has no money at all, not in the real sense; he could go broke overnight. The great house with all its memories and evocations, that had slept for so long, then drowsed uncomfortably in the last two years while the public trampled about its gardens and ground floor, had been put into a time machine – but a synthetic one: it had not really been awakened, simply put on a life support system that was turned off again at 5 a.m.

---

[1] Marchioness of Cholmondeley, sister of Philip Sassoon, who built Port Lympne.

Cloisters   *Monday, 13 July*

Willie is coming again to the Home Affairs Committee. He must not be allowed to get away with it this time. As I was crossing the Lobby, David Rose of ITN came up to me and said, 'On Lobby terms, what would you most like to get from Mr Whitelaw at the Home Affairs Committee meeting this evening?'

'On Lobby terms,' I replied, 'what *I* would most like is for him to announce that he had put his office at the Prime Minister's disposal.'

Cloisters   *Thursday, 16 July*

I suppose today was the high point of my social life to date – in so far as that depends upon my status as a politician. As I boasted to Charles Howard, 'I have got the Queen at four, the Prime Minister at six, and a private dinner with the American Ambassador at eight . . .' 'Watch out it is not God at midnight,' he answered, quite wittily.

It was my first time in the Buck House garden, although to get to it we walked through that courtyard where I remember dismounting for the great Armstrong-Jones wedding ball in 1959, when Dukey tried to pick up Jane. Vast numbers of people, most of them in ill-fitting and low quality morning dress, with stained and dog-eared grey toppers. The garden is rather featureless, although the beds and borders are most densely planted and the edges crazily clipped. The south side of the Palace is undistinguished in yellow sandstone and a bit of a muddle, rather like the northern aspect of Ston Easton.[1] The tea was delicious, a sort of Indian Hukwa, and so was the fruit cake. Other items, like the drop scones and most of the patisserie were less good.

We joined the line to catch a glimpse of the Royals and seeing Tony Buck I mischievously asked him if he was going to dinner with the Americans that night (they had marked the invitation 'in honour of Mr and Mrs John Nott'). He was startled and angry to hear about it, almost more so than I had anticipated. Said he would complain, etc.

---

[1] Ston Easton Park, near Bristol, which the Clarks nearly bought in 1964 and which was subsequently sold to William Rees-Mogg, Editor of *The Times*.

We sheered off to another part of the line. The Queen slowly made her way along, preceded by a posse of buffers in slightly better-fitting morning dress than the majority of the guests, and made conversation with certain selected invitees – the statutory person in a wheel chair with bearded mentor etc. When you see the Queen in the flesh she is always smaller and more beautifully made up than one remembers. She was wearing a white silk coat (like Jane) and a navy blue straw hat. We had to leave early as I had been warned that there might be trouble at the '22 Committee concerning the press releases from the Home Affairs meetings which Willie had addressed. But in fact nothing was raised and we went on to Downing Street, arriving with the first guests.

The Lady, although as always enthusiastic in her greeting, struck me as being a little bit triste and blotchy, which I recognise as being one of her stress symptoms. The room was full of MPs and their wives and really rather dull, although in the yellow drawing room I was glad to be able to point out to Jane the actual coffee table which had been a prop in the events of Monday, 15 June. Notters was already in his black tie and so we shot back to the Albany in order to dress up for the Americans.

It always takes longer to get to Regents Park than one anticipates. I was using the old green Bentley as my faithful 2CV is presently immobilised with a puncture. The custodian at the gate said, 'The name must be Clark', from which we inferred (rightly) that we were the last to arrive.

The Ambassadress greeted us, tall and distinguished looking, but not as tall and distinguished as her husband, whom I liked immediately. He has that special quiet authority which very, very rich Americans carry, and I was amused to note that he did not specially respond to my ritual diplomatic praises of the President. He perked up a bit, however, when I talked to him about the Bond Market and where it was going.

The food was quite good, but the drink egregious in the extreme. The gins and tonics were long, but weak. The white wine thin, the claret restricted. This did not matter to me, but I do recognise it as being a potential handicap in some company. A number of speeches were exchanged and I was delighted to hear the Ambassador say that 'We have the whole defence department here this evening ...' (!) How *did* I get on to that invitation list? All the Ministers were there and the PPS, but I was the only officer of the Committee. Perhaps it was Frank Cooper or Arthur Hockaday[1] who fixed it, as I have got on well with them and – hopefully – impressed them at the Wehrkunde and Chatham House Conferences. Or was it one of those muddles which occur from time to time, as when *The Times* printed me as being 'Chairman' of the Committee? I told Geoffrey Pattie that Buck was going to complain. 'That will be a change,' he snorted.

Saltwood   *Saturday, 18 July*

A lovely family day. Both boys around, and divine.

The [*Gems of Brazil*] cash – 950 US is already on deposit in UBS Brig. Due to emerge at 960 (or 910 ex Desmond) on 3 August. It is agonising to dispense any of it, as it edges its way up so close to the big 'M' – I mean this in *cash*, that's really quite good at any time, and particularly now.

Cloisters   *Tuesday, 21 July*

Very surprisingly, England won the test match [against Australia] by 18 runs when Willis took 8 wickets for 43 in just over the hour. Charlie Morrison, deaf and gangling and ill-disposed, got up at PM's Questions and made a characteristically awful intervention. As he can neither compose nor articulate a perfectly normal English sentence, he was unable to get through even his opening words of congratulation to the English Test side without furtively glancing down at his notes. 'Reading,' everybody bellowed with ritual glee. Then he came to the tricky bit. 'Was not this a good example of change of tactics,' he asked, 'which we might emulate?' In fact it was very much less clear than this and brought in some muddled reference to change of *captains* also. So the lobby went abuzz with the news that he had recommended – as may well have been his intention – a change of captain. That is to say, by inference, of substituting Prior for The Lady.

---

[1] Sir Frank Cooper, Permanent Under-Secretary of State. Sir Arthur Hockaday, Second Permanent Under-Secretary of State, Ministry of Defence.

Charles M. is absolutely dreadful. The rotten *old* school, as opposed
to the poncey opportunist new wave. Many upper-class Conservative
MPs, like Gilmour and Whitelaw, allow their feelings of guilt to
intrude on their decisions – but at least Ian is highly intelligent and
Willie is cunning. C. Morrison has conned the majority into thinking
that he is 'nice'.

In the evening I had my end of term dinner with Ian Gow. I got
to Pratt's early and ordered half a bottle of champagne, which I
thought we could split. However, 'George' poured the whole bottle
into a large silver tankard and set it in front of me; very healthy and
reviving. Shortly afterwards, Jonathan Aitken came down the stairs,
followed a little later by Bill Benyon.[1] They enjoyed the fact that I
had sent William Pitt[2] (sic) a telegram yesterday telling him to 'hold
firm, . . . this is what Liberalism is all about,' etc. and signed it, 'Ten
gay Party workers in Datchet'.

Ian arrived a little late, having walked across the Park. I noticed
that he had lost weight and he seemed nervous. He is smoking a great
deal. He reproached Benyon, or 'Buckingham', as he calls him, for
advocating selective reflation. Jonathan and I also argued for this,
although I was more candid. 'You have got to bribe the electorate,
buy the votes,' I said, 'in order to get you through the next election.
It is far too early to start now, but it is something that you must carry
in your mind when you plan the '83 Budget.' IG was shocked by
this, genuinely shocked I think. 'You are an innocent', I told him, 'a
complete babe in arms.' How can someone who is so good at his
job and so very alert to political undercurrents and attitudes in the
Parliamentary Party have standards of integrity that make him so
dangerously vulnerable in policy matters? Fortunately, I think that
The Lady is more realistic.

We moved on from Pratt's and had a tête-à-tête meal at Brooks's.
IG mellowed with a good bottle of claret and became less edgy. He
told me that The Lady was completely unperturbed (personally I

---

[1] William Benyon, MP for Buckingham since 1970.
[2] The vacancy for the Croydon North West by-election was the subject of vicious behind
  the scenes in-fighting between the SDP and the Liberals. By an unwritten agreement
  it was the Liberals' 'turn' to field the candidate and they already had one in place,
  William Pitt. In political terms Pitt was a nonentity who had already lost his deposit
  twice contesting that seat. He was a member of the Lambeth Housing Committee and
  a supporter of Gay Rights. Shirley Williams, who was the SDP favourite to contest
  the seat, and had the backing of David Steel, the Liberal leader, was blocked by
  determined resistance from Liberals at local level.

doubt this) and determined to press on. He asked me who should be Chairman of the Party. I simply could not make a convincing suggestion. He mentioned the two leading contenders, Heseltine and Tebbit, and added a third, Tom King. A bit light on charisma and bell-ringing I told him. He looked gloomy. Was there anyone in the Lords? he asked. 'Here we are, knowing the Party as we do,' he said, 'and we cannot think of a single candidate of whom we could wholeheartedly approve.' I did not answer.

At some point I remember telling him that he must take a department soon. He liked my saying this, but I still have the feeling that he would like to stay where he is for the whole Parliament. And yet it was exactly a year ago, when we dined at the end of the 1980 term at the Cavalry Club, that he gave the impression of being fed up and on the point of departure. IG said there would be a major reshuffle in the autumn and that The Lady would be bringing in many of her friends. I laughed and said that I did not believe it. IG became very concerned. 'Oh no,' he said, 'you wait and see, you won't be disappointed, I guarantee that.' Whether he meant me personally, or objectively, I do not know. But I rather fear the latter as earlier he had been digressing on the Chief Whip's power of veto.

We had been talking about people who had been left out or disappointed and I had mentioned Iain Sproat[1] and how good he was and how I thought he was turning sour from having been so completely overlooked. IG was indiscreet about two other figures whom he has always defended in the past. Carrington, he said, was 'a bad influence'. I remember getting my head bitten off when I had trailed this particular idea on previous occasions. Then the subject of poor Tony Buck came up. I told Ian of how angry Tony had been at my being invited to the Ambassador's dinner, and he more or less said that Tony was self-evidently passé. 'You cannot be in his company for more than two minutes without him reminding you that he was at one point Minister for the Navy.' I am glad somebody else has noticed this. In contrast, I pointed out that dear Geoffrey Johnson-Smith, who does not drink, is completely on the ball, and never mentions his (much longer) period as Minister for the Army.[2] Ian agreed,

---

[1] Iain Sproat, MP for Aberdeen South since 1970.
[2] Geoffrey Johnson-Smith, MP for East Grinstead since 1965. He had spent nearly two years at the MoD in the early 1970s.

and it is possible that Geoffrey J-S. might get something in the reshuffle.

What I did not manage to break into was the manner in which the Cabinet split over the riot measures. Although I did notice that Ian was much less resolute in his defence of Willie than previously. Most of the meal we spent gossiping; for example, he told me that [Robert] Atkins' wife, whom one would expect to be a bright young trollop, was in fact extraordinarily plain and *common*.

I drove him back in the green Bentley, which he greatly liked, and we blew the siren going down Birdcage Walk (which he did not like).

Cloisters   *Wednesday, 22 July*

The Lady came to the 1922 Committee and to suit her convenience we sat one hour earlier than usual, at 5 p.m. It was not a happy occasion. The mood of the Committee was gloomy, sepulchral almost. The Lady was 'lackluster' (as the *Wall Street Journal* describes, every day, the bond market).

Edward du Cann, that master of the coded message, who conceals the dagger in his toga until the very last moment, ended by saying that '... although a week is a long time in politics, two years is a very short time until a general election ...'. And everyone got the message – although of course du Cann is nothing like as powerful or as influential as he was in 1974–75 when he was manoeuvring the '22 to overturn Ted.

Saltwood   *Thursday, 23 July*

July fatigue/gloom. Everything should be lovely, but there is, in some sense, too much of it. If I were to write down the *good* things they would be:

Total solvency for the first time ever, nil indebtedness and $\frac{3}{4}$m in US, giving 100 US per annum.

Both boys lovely and settled in what they want to do.

Reasonably high status in H of C.

Hobbies – cars, writing, restoring – all give pleasure.

'Active' and in good health.

Cloisters   *Friday, 24 July*

The House sat all night and those who were not on their feet had been told to return by 8 a.m. for a 'closure'. Needless to say, there was no vote, but I had a cup of coffee while waiting with Jim Lester, who told me that he thought the Prime Minister would announce her reshuffle immediately we rose as a tactical device to muffle the sounds of protest – many people being away on holiday, lobby correspondents in the South of France, etc. I do not believe it. I do not think there will be a radical reshuffle and such as there is will, I think, take place in September and be conformist in the extreme.

This view was confirmed to me by Michael McNair-W., who also said that Peter Walker had told him that Quintin (whom I have always suspected of being disloyal) said that The Lady was like Herbert Hoover and would lead us to such a defeat that we would be out of office for thirty years.

While McNair W. and I were gossiping, Boscawen went through the office and on through the cloister buttoning up his collar and told us we should be in our places for the Prime Minister who was going to present the Queen's response to the Loyal Address on the occasion of The Wedding. Apparently, this was the first time that a Prime Minister had done this since Attlee.

Just in time I got to my seat. The Lady looked rather small and nervous and, as always, very feminine. I hope she noticed me. She could hardly fail to as the bench was empty except for myself and Fell.

A note of farce was introduced because immediately afterwards that idiot Steen[1] got up and declaimed a petition about sex shops in general and in his constituency in particular. The preamble was detailed and explicit about what these shops do and purvey, unnecessarily so, and unfortunate at that time in the morning.

---

[1] Anthony Steen, MP for Liverpool, Wavertree since February 1974.

Saltwood   *Friday, 31 July*

The weather this summer has been appalling. Usually I swim every day once the pool has been filled – this year less than six times I should think. As I swam 'powerful strokes' the other day I said to Jane: 'The truth is I'm not a Renaissance Prince any longer.' I have a little spare tyre, which flaps over my belt when I'm sitting down. My canine tooth is very short and discoloured and can give the impression of a gap.

Saltwood   *Monday, 14 September*

It's ages since I made an entry. The House went down at the end of July, just petered out really with the last three days on running two-liners. But discipline had 'gone' and I gave Bunny a case of (cheapish) white burgundy and told him to 'carry' me.

August was consumed, as it always is, with openings. One thinks one has the mornings free, and I made grandiose programmes for fixed hours at my desk – which was an incredible shambles – Alison came down a couple of times a week and I did a minimum, or modicum, of constituency correspondence. We would sit on the front steps under the portcullis so as to catch the sun (the sun shone every day in August) and hear the telephone, and at intervals fierce little gusts or eddies of draught would whirl the papers around, sometimes carrying them out onto the gravel, to my irritation.

The sun has shone every day since the wedding of the Prince of Wales on the 29 July, and the pool temperature is still over 70°, but this last fortnight I don't seem to have had nearly as much time to myself, and 'on the land' as I would have wished. On the day after Bank Holiday I had to be in Plymouth at 10 a.m. for a day's voyage on *Valiant*. These jaunts are always clogged by members of the Peerage *with nothing to do*. Usual quota of dear (and not so dear, the Welsh ones are the worst) old boys, plus Earl Fortescue. I've never seen him before. We didn't take to each other, as he was obviously uncomfortable about 'placing' me. This is a factor which always affects my relations with the huntin' & shootin' upper classes. Jane even mentioned it this morning when, discussing the reshuffle (of which more, much more, below), I said that I had no protector, and how much Willie disliked and distrusted me.

My God, it's nasty in a submarine. They submerge as soon as they leave port and may stay at sea for *months*, not surfacing again until they return to their home port. The viruses and bacteria go round and round in the ventilation (sic) system which recycles the stale air through some acidifier that 'purifies' it. The heat in the engine room (115°), the lurking menace of the reactor, which needs four people constantly monitoring its evil dials, the claustrophobia, not just of being submerged in the deep, but of sheer confinement, of having nowhere to which one could retreat for any level of privacy at all. The only area, curiously, with any sense of space is the torpedo room in the bows, and firing the torpedoes or 'fish' as they call them (we staged a mock attack) is exhilarating.

Most of the time it was painfully boring – like going round the laundry at St Thomas's (which is, of course, in the basement), and it was all I could do to stop myself nodding off here, there and every-where that our stooping, shuffling tour came to a halt. Once we had surfaced again for our return into the Sound, I insisted on going up into the 'Fin' as the Conning Tower is now called. And that was marvellous. One climbed up this narrow, wet – the whole fin is flooded while the boat is submerged – iron ladder, some 30 feet up and there one is, in this iron balcony, with the black hull below, foam pouring off her as she cleaves the waters at seventeen knots.

The only other MPs on board were David Hunt: still putting on weight, but reasonably amiable; and poor Neville Trotter[1] who works so hard and has so much defence expertise and is always being passed over. On the platform of Plymouth Station I said something about the reshuffle. I can't remember his exact reply, but it was very much to the effect that all junior appointments were made by the Chief Whip and so (implied) I didn't have a chance, a view which had been most unwelcomely also propagated by Peter Hennessy,[2] one of my August visitors who had let it go almost as an aside.

I reflected on this gloomily last night and throughout this morning as the reshuffle, or reconstruction as it has been in some quarters predicted, gets (apparently) under way. Long-heralded, like some ponderous offensive by the Russian Army, and preceded by much

[1] Neville Trotter, MP for Tynemouth since February 1974.
[2] Peter Hennessy, Whitehall correspondent of *The Times* since 1976.

leaking and counter-leaking chiefly by the protagonists of Prior and Tebbit, it has of recent days appeared that The Lady is going to get her way, and purge the wets, as Ian promised me she would when we dined at Brooks's just before the House rose. But I am afraid, I kind of *know* that I am going to be left out. As Jane percipiently observed, the Whips would have rung by now '. . . to check on your where-abouts'.

I had been looking forward to today as little Graham Turner, mole-like journalist famous for his in-depth articles for the *Sunday Telegraph*, was due to pay me a special visit to collect material for an article he is doing for pre-Conference Sunday on the state of the Party. I waited around all morning and the phone rang less and less frequently. Faint, very faint hopes with the earlier calls which turned out to be Col, muddled cashier at UBS and other dimnesses. After about noon was totally silent. I had put chairs out on lawn, but drizzle started. I got a bottle of Yquem '67 on the ice – the first this year – but it turned out he didn't drink. I was made slightly late fetching him at Folkestone station as I had to combine this with dropping dear, amiable but *slow* Mrs Dewsbury and at the last minute decided to change out of my ultra-casual denim shirt and kickers into more Hadleighfied kit.

We sat in the red library. The Yquem smoothly did its work on an empty stomach and I sparkled. But perhaps the interview went on a little too long and my tight rein relaxed (I am often, but on each occasion too late, reminded of Tim Rathbone's comment, 'Al should realise that there is more to politics than being amusing'). All the time I was unhappily aware that the phone was silent. Completely silent.

I took Graham Turner to Sandling at 4.30 and from the platform he telephoned, with much clicking and crashing of 10p pieces, to Ian Gilmour of all people! Confirmation that he (Ian), Soames and Carlisle had all been sacked.[1] Other changes '. . . still going on'.

With a heavy heart I drove back to Saltwood. By now I must have had it. We listened to the hourly bulletins on the news, but little else came across. That evening I re-watched *Cabaret*,[2] which kept me diverted. After that wonderful, uplifting scene in the beer garden, when the young SA boy leads the singing of 'Tomorrow Belongs to Me' I switched off and went to bed.

---

[1] Ian Gilmour, Lord Privy Seal since 1979; Lord Soames, Leader of the House of Lords since 1979; Mark Carlisle, Education Secretary since 1979.
[2] *Cabaret*, film with Liza Minelli, of the Kander and Ebb 1966 musical based on Christopher Isherwood's *Goodbye to Berlin* stories.

Albany   *Saturday, 19 September*

I see no prospect of a political breakthrough. One can enjoy the *spectacle*, and the intrigue – though with a little less confidence and authority than when a job was in prospect, but I will have 'to consider my position'. I will choose the appropriate moment when we are reassembled and ask IG why, say, I did not get Philip Goodhart's job.[1]

Saltwood   *Saturday, 3 October*

This morning a wonderful rainbow, a complete one from the Great Hall to Thorpes, perfect and defined. Both boys at home (James did a lot of exotic solo flying in his helicopter last week) and still safe. They have chosen their terribly dangerous callings. Is it this that gives me unhappy angst – and will I ever be free of it?

Blackpool   *Tuesday, 13 October*

Ted Heath has been making a number of fierce attacks on The Lady and her Government, clearly timed to provoke a crisis at the Conference which opens at Blackpool today. Last night he was appearing on *Panorama* with David Dimbleby and I put off my dinner in order to watch him, which I did in Charles Jerdein's bedroom, Charles very nobly agreeing to forgo the first episode of *Brideshead Revisited*[2] on to which he switched his video machine. To my great alarm – though a sixth sense warned me of this – Ted, when questioned about the Dirty Tricks, concerning which he had mentioned a number, cited a distinguished journalist, who admitted to having been fed misinformation, and a Member of Parliament, who quite recently had been put up to interrupt one of his speeches but later retracted and apologised [see entry for 7 July 1981].

---

[1] Philip Goodhart, MP for Beckenham since 1957; had lost his position as Parliamentary Under-Secretary in the Northern Ireland Office.
[2] Television adaptation of Evelyn Waugh's novel proved an enormous critical and commercial success.

I rang Jane later from Aspers and told her this and she giggled. But of course she does not know the whole story, namely that I *had* been put up to it and by no less a person than IG. I slept uneasily, conscious of the fact that all my skills of tact and improvisation could be severely taxed in the days to come.

Cloisters   *Monday, 19 October*

The House of Commons at its worst. Dull, fetid, everyone discontented and *chétif*. We prowled about morosely in our blue suits (many of them, my own included, rather shiny). The whips hadn't the face to publish a three-liner on the first day back, so they played their usual trick of calling a running two-line and then putting a footnote to say that the Opposition were 'believed to be' on three-line and that Members are asked to 'verify their pairing arrangements'.

As a result, most people were in attendance and all were ill-tempered. At tea Francis said gloomily, looking up at the annunciator screen as we waited for the third division of the day, that it seemed as if we had never been away, never had any holiday at all. One might have expected to find the place seething with intrigue and dissent. But no. As can sometimes happen with the Parliamentary Party, it is such an obvious subject that no one refers to it.

Bored, I resumed my sly and smearing tactics. The previous day's *Observer* had carried an article by Simon Hoggart in which he reported Ivor Stanbrook as, 'calling for' Willie's resignation at a public meeting. I composed a letter to Ted,[1] expressing the view that this was very bad manners and inappropriate for an officer of the Committee and that he send Willie a note protesting our loyalty. For my own purposes, in the hope that it would retain some residual favour with Willie, whom I expected to see after the Home Affairs Committee that evening, I lodged a copy of it with Roger Sims, his PPS. *Et tu Brute* – but what the hell.

This evening I thought of absenting myself for three hours and playing Backgammon at Brooks's. I got as far as the garage and – rarely for me – my conscience spoke. I felt I really *could not* take off

---

[1] Edward Gardner, Chairman of the Conservative Home Affairs Committee.

quite so early in the session. In any case, I have given up backgammon, haven't I?

Sadly, I trailed back upstairs and, as I was crossing the Members' Lobby, George Gardiner asked me if I was thinking of standing against Tony Buck for the Defence Chair. I hummed and hahed. It is always tricky opposing a friend – especially if you are not certain of the outcome. Then I had a brainwave. Why not ask David Hunt, that way I could both gauge the mood of the Whips Office and of the Secretary of State, whose PPS he was until recently.

Somewhat to my surprise Hunt said that the move would be very welcome, gave me the impression that the Whips Office would support it. 'It will be interesting to see how effective this support is,' I said. 'One reason I was asking you was that I had wanted Phil Goodhart's job and had been told by three people, including one in the Whips' Office [Nick Budgen], that John Nott had opposed the appointment as he thought that I would obstruct the renewed cuts that he is going to have to impose on the Services.'

Hunt denied this with real vigour, said that Nott did not know anything about the change until the last moment and was very upset to have lost Philip. He more or less said that the Whips had chopped Philip because he was inarticulate at Question Time.

I was uplifted by this, even though, as Jane astutely observed when I told her the following morning (I left early and went down to Saltwood for the day): 'You cannot trust any of them. It is just their little way of consoling for not getting a job.'

Cloisters   *Wednesday, 21 October*

I had dinner as the guest of General Dynamics, one of their little promotional meetings to 'sell', in the widest sense, the cruise missile. I do not go for leftist phrases, particularly their reckless use of the adjective 'obscene'. But I must say that I did find it highly unpalatable, the casual, sanitised manner in which all these thrusting young executives talk about this deadly, dangerous – but still profoundly unsatisfactory – weapons system. The top man, who was called Ray Jones, had put me on his right and I noticed that he smoked five cigarettes before I had finished my melon. I was glad to have to leave early.

I then walked up Horseferry Road to the St Stephen's Club where the '92' was in conclave to sort out the Committee appointments. No one was particularly enthusiastic about supporting me for the Defence Chair and I was mildly amused to note Winston (who I suppose, nominally, is the rightful claimant) huffing and puffing and proposing Phil Goodhart and Victor Goodhew in turn. The trouble is that there were at least five people in the room who felt that the Chair was rightfully theirs. By tradition, Defence appointments carry a great deal of prestige on the backbenches and there is a feeling, which may very well do me considerable damage in the election, that they should be reserved for Party elders or ex-Ministers.

Cloisters   *Thursday, 22 October*

Today I am meant to be in Taunton, or more accurately, Bishop's Lydeard at 7.30 p.m. How in hell am I meant to get to Bishop's Lydeard, and more particularly, how to get back to London?

I cannot bear staying with people, unless it is Scottish baronial, or Philip Sassoon baroque. Why did I accept in the first place? These dates seem so distant and innocuous, particularly when they are separated by the sunlit plains of the summer recess. I tried to get out of it a fortnight ago, told Alison to send my apologies, excuse the whipping system, etc. But no, Edward du Cann [Taunton's MP] cornered me on Monday, insisting.

I had told John Cope, the pairing Whip, that I really 'did not mind' if I was confined to the Palace of Westminster all day and all night on Thursday. He was surprised, but affected to understand. I just hope that he did not let on to E. du C. because in the fullness of time I heard from the Whips' Office that I could not leave.

And so here I am working at my desk, instead of training the substance of a 350-mile round trip to talk on a subject which, to us in Government, is at present slightly embarrassing. I suppose this means that I am not a professional politician, but at least it allows me to hear Weinberger[1] (who is coming to attend a Lord's Committee and the 1922 Committee) and, hopefully, to go to the BRM sale which Christie's are staging at Motorfair.

[1] Caspar Weinberger, US Secretary of State for Defense.

Later

I was sitting next to Charles Morrison in Pratt's when his brother, Peter,[1] came and sat down beside me. We avoided politics during the meal, but he invited me back to his house to watch the Croydon by-election result.[2] I said I wanted to go to bed early, but he muttered something about 'wanting a gossip' as well and I always fall for this.

Peter lives in a narrow terraced house just off Warwick Way, where I remember some tortured nights prior to my wedding in 1958, staying in a back room. It was drearily, but not particularly cheaply decorated, the walls hung with old dealers' dredge-ups, little oils of XVII century maritime scenes, etc. Bookshelves one degree lower – 'runs' of Walter Scott and Dickens bound in plastic imitation leather and (presumably) photo-printed pages. Peter chatted away about the state of the Party, name-dropped, referred to his father's great wisdom, etc. etc.

I have never been specially keen on Lord Margadale as I attribute – perhaps wrongly – the very heavy sentence I received at Steeple Ashton Magistrates Court, for driving without lights in 1971, to the fact that he took an instant dislike to me. (He was attending the court in his capacity as High Sheriff that day.) Later, he suffered the curse of the Gnome for his actions, when a policeman, quite properly, apprehended him for being slumped over his own steering wheel smelling copiously of drink etc. He was disqualified for a year and moved, more or less permanently, to Scotland.

Peter is unrepentantly pro-Lady and I noted the various light smears with which he daubed her possible successors, including Francis Pym and Peter Carrington – never been in the House, did not know how to conduct himself at Question Time, etc. At intervals I murmured that he was bound to be Chief Whip very soon – he did not dissimulate.

Peter also spoke a great deal about his relations with his Civil Servants, how friendly and attentive he was to them, and yet how firm. Once we were tuned into the television commentaries he produced his red despatch box and rustled papers, but this was plainly for show only.

---

[1] Peter Morrison, younger son of Lord Margadale, promoted to Junior Minister at the Department of Employment, in the September reshuffle.
[2] Won by the SDP/Liberal Alliance candidate William Pitt.

If it was all meant to make me jealous I suppose it succeeded. It would be nice to be a Minister and I am grumpy – sometimes very cross – at not being one.

Saltwood   *Sunday, 25 October*

It was a week ago yesterday that Albert Costain publicly announced that he was not going to stand again for Folkestone. I do not know why, but I get the impression that my position is very much weaker than it was two years ago. I do not seem to know anyone in the Association, and it seems ages since I had a speaking engagement down there. In the past I could never go anywhere without somebody asking why I wasn't the MP yet.

Yesterday we saw Beth[1] in the street. 'Are you putting up?' she said. I said I was and asked her round for drinks today to talk about it.

However, when she arrived she avoided the subject until the very last minute. Then, more or less said that I was too much disliked locally by people I had been rude to, thrown off the grounds, etc. I am not sure if I think this is all that important, or indeed incorrectable by personal contact, but it was lowering nonetheless. It must be said, too, that Beth is nowhere near the centre of the Association (not, for example, the way Graham Butland was in the Plymouth Association in 1972).

She did not even know the name of the new chairman or any of the officers. She said everyone loathed Bunting[2] and wanted to get rid of him and I agreed that Bunting's enmity is not as disastrous as it might be if he was widely liked and respected. But he could still be obstructive in an administrative way, losing particulars, delaying applications, etc.

I had already decided to give a posh weekend, have Anthony Royle down and precede the dinner the previous evening with a drinks party for all the local big wigs. Beth agreed that this would be a good idea. A bit obvious I feel. But there is no harm in that.

---

[1] Mrs Evans-Smith, the physiotherapist who treated AC for his back trouble, was an officer of the Saltwood and Newington Ward of the Folkestone Conservative Association.
[2] George Bunting, local constituency agent.

Cloisters   *Monday, 26 October*

I am worried about poor old Tony Buck as it is already getting back to me that he is 'taking it badly' that I should be opposing him for the Chair of the Defence Committee. There was a message from him this morning via Alison that he would like to 'have a talk about it'. And this afternoon, Victor Goodhew told me that Tony had already been ringing round complaining, saying that I was a chum. We agreed on policy, he couldn't understand it, etc. etc.

Later that evening I heard the door open half way through the Home Affairs Committee and, turning round a few seconds later, who should be there but Tony. I sent him a placatory note and suggested that we had a drink afterwards. He was simultaneously nervous and unfriendly, although superficial courtesies were maintained. I said that there was nothing personal in it, it was no more significant than a game of billiards. He rambled on, '... always recommended that you should be a Minister, seem to agree about everything, regarded you as a chum, etc. etc.'. All very awkward. I was saved prolonged embarrassment by the Division Bell, after which the officers of the Home Affairs Committee had to go and see Willie.

Willie was slimmer (still!) and younger looking. His hair was cut and brilliantined down. Despite his ordeal at the Conference he looked fifteen years younger. He made a point of greeting me, so presumably Roger Sims did show him the copy of my note about Ivor Stanbrook, which I had taken the precaution of letting him see but which he had not acknowledged.

At the seven o'clock division John Nott came up to me in the Lobby and said: 'I hear you are putting up.'

'Yes, I am,' I said. 'Can I see you privately about it for a minute?'

I told him that Tony was very upset, put me in a difficult position, what did he think?

'I could not possibly comment, you must understand I could not, it would be quite wrong for me to say anything.'

'In that case, why did you raise the subject?' I said.

'Well, if you will not repeat this to anyone, I must not really, should not say anything...'

'No, of course I won't.'

'Well, I think you should put up.'

'Thanks. In that case I will.'

An encouraging little exchange, I suppose, but like the pledged support from Hunt in the Whips Office, I don't know how much use it will be. Tony is a dear old thing and very popular and has already started spreading the word round, that I-always-knew-he-was-a-shit syndrome. I thought I might get Julian Critchley to put up as well, and split the nice-person-vote, but he would not do this because he was a friend of Tony and because Tony had already complained to him about my disloyalty. There is reference in this diary to Hal Miller when he was PPS to Francis, implying that I should be Chairman, and so I do not think JN was just trying to console me for not getting a junior defence position in the reshuffle. But the hard arithmetic of the ballot box may tell a different story.

That evening I dined at Pratt's. John Colville[1] was there. Every time I meet him (which is not often) I think he is (a) over-rated, (b) snobbish and (c) not specially bright or nice. He name-dropped massively (surely not necessary at Pratt's?), but did tell one little story illustrating his poor judgement. After the general election in 1959 Harold Macmillan asked him at a private dinner whether it would be a good idea if he (H.M.) 'gave up', having set the Party and the country on the road to peace and prosperity, etc. etc. Foolishly and tactlessly Colville said that he thought he should, said that it would be a seignorial gesture, that the whole country would rise to the nobility of it, his place in history assured, etc. etc. Naturally, Macmillan was furious and did not speak to him again for five years.

Cloisters   *Thursday, 29 October*

Halfway through Prime Minister's Questions Tony Royle came and sat beside me. He had already refused our weekend invitation and, as is the way in politics, did not reveal his principal motive until we had been talking for some time. He said that he had heard rumours that I had put my name in for Folkestone. 'Not true,' I replied. Nor is it, although Vivienne Hepworth, the *Western Evening Herald* correspondent, had been fussing me all day yesterday about how the rumour was 'all over Plymouth'.

Like everybody else, including John Lacy (area agent, S.E. Area),

[1] Sir John Colville, private secretary to Churchill during the Second World War and again 1951–55; also to the Queen when Princess Elizabeth.

Tony tried to talk me out of it, said I would get into frightful difficulties with Plymouth etc.

'I know, I know,' I replied, grinning. As indeed I do. I know all these things, but still think that I will do it, just for the thrills and spills. Afterwards, I suspected that he probably had felt it more tactful not to accept my invitation for the weekend for the very reason that he suspected he might be being set up as a tacit sponsor of my candidature. In fact, this was not my principal intention. I simply wanted him to see Saltwood, and to see how appropriate its setting was for the future MP.

As a matter of fact today I feel so flat, dejected, tired, and stuffy that I hardly want to continue at Westminster at all, and have not even got the energy to campaign properly for the Defence Chair, which is essential for my political plans in 1982.

Plymouth train   *Friday, 30 October*

I must admit I like the Plymouth express. The 3 hour journey is almost too short as one comfortably rolls along suspended from communication or pressure, travelling *free* and closeted with one's papers. I must look at my career prospects. How bad will they be when the dream goes – for good I mean, and people push past?

Incidentally, what is perfectly clear is that my 'intimate' with IG and The Lady has blown. They know the truth about the Dirty Tricks letter!

Trouble is, have lost zing and no adrenalin. A back number. The lobby correspondents no longer approach me as I walk across the lobby.

Bratton   *Saturday, 7 November*

Beleaguered at Bratton, I watched the birds, tits and blackbirds from the first floor window. A blackbird worked his way right along the path, getting at the leaves and poking at wormholes. Afterwards I went out and looked at his handiwork and a very good job he has done. How much better one understands birds after George and how

I feel for them with the giant benefits they bring us.

Couldn't make the fire light; only place and time in the year when it is always earlier than you expect when you look at your watch. 'En Garçon' as Jane has to lay the wreath at Saltwood tomorrow, while I had constituency engagements on Friday, Saturday, Sunday and Monday. Armistice weekend (as I call it) is always loaded.

On the Friday I had undertaken to 'talk to' the F&GP of the Association about 'my intentions' regarding Folkestone and Hythe, and they were summoned to Headland Park, the dingy, peeling, and dry-and-wet-rot smelling, terrace headquarters off North Hill, at 6 p.m.

Mrs Ayres, the secretary, who Jane maintains is well disposed, but is unquestionably slightly mad, specialises in the jarring phrase, almost Nanny-like in its wince-making property. One of her favourites is: 'People are asking when is your next surgery . . .' – invariably uttered within twenty-four hours of the last one – and she had fixed up an 'emergency' surgery for me that evening at 5 p.m.

The Paddington train was late and the traffic frightful. It is not only in London that everyone stops work on a Friday at 3.45 p.m. My first call was on dear nice loyal, but slightly dotty Kay (should be spelt with an 'F') Hamlyn, who was having trouble with access over Railway Property behind her house. Glumly we examined the site, accompanied by a minute and choleric man in a tweed jacket whom she introduced as 'Colonel Hamlyn, my former husband . . .'. He boomed and bellowed and claimed to have three thousand acres at Bridestowe. He repeated the boast several times over tea, but he certainly didn't *look* like a millionaire, not even one of the Q-ship class, and poor Kay's house was dreadfully humble; mouldy and faded to a degree, with the Embankment road traffic thundering past, making the windows shake.

I had to stay for tea – 'We blend our own, you know, we learned how to do this when we were stationed in India . . . such happy times', etc. The 'Colonel' stayed demi-petulant – 'Kay, will you let me speak?' he kept saying, even when she was perfectly silent.

Anyway, the upshot of all this was that I did not get back to Headland Park until 5.30 p.m. Mendicants everywhere. Worse than an ordinary surgery: a little old lady who wanted to sue the Housing Association because she had fallen over a lump of concrete; a 'Bikey' who wanted to argue the case against crash helmets – these were not emergencies! I ground my teeth. Soon, down below, I could hear the

F&GP assembling. They had no 'other business' to discuss and would not wish to be kept waiting.

My problem was, how to finesse the hand. Of course I would prefer to sit for Folkestone. Bigger majority (even), less travelling, easier to socialise, new faces, honeymoon period, etc. As I left London, on one of those lovely dry sunny November mornings when you can kick the leaves, I thought I really am fed up with this. I go on getting older and my precious time is being used up doing bugger all, just moving or waiting or deferring to the egos of others.

The night before I had come across Tony Royle and Albert Costain talking in the Lobby – 'We were just speaking about you.' Ugh. Tony and I went to a private corner and he gave me a 'fatherly' talking to. Albert had said I hadn't a chance, they would never choose the laird, wanted someone he just stopped himself saying 'younger', substituted 'more in touch with ordinary people'. Utter balls of course. Why should it be legitimate to 'discriminate' against the rich and well-educated, when heavy penalties are attached to doing so against the black, the fat, the homosexual, the handicapped, the female, etc. etc.

I was quite prepared, I said, to answer the charge of carpet bagging. Wasn't I deliberately making the sacrifice of throwing up a safe seat, putting everything at risk, simply for the honour of representing my home division, the place where I had spent my childhood, my own children had been brought up? He mellowed slightly. Perhaps if I did it *cleanly*, notified my own people of my intention not to stand ... As he said this I thought of that draft letter of resignation, first written in 1976, and a great weight seemed to lift. How wonderful, and yet how sad! But how tempting!

But then Tony's brow furrowed again. What if I *was* adopted in spite of everything, and then Albert died suddenly and there had to be a by-election? 'Two by-elections', I said. He looked unhappy. 'Your name will be mud in the Party.' But still he is a friend. The bond of the upper classes, pretty thin on the ground, even on the back benches of the Tory Party. He said he would have a word with the agent on Monday, make some enquiries. 'The Agent hates me.' Worse and worse. He'd speak to the chairman, ring him up.

But all this, and the fact that no one in Folkestone *has* been beating a path to my door, has lowered my estimate of my chances. And so, at the meeting of the Plymouth F&GP, I funked it. When Mr Boyette asked me which I would prefer, '... if both were in the hand', I paused reflectively for a long time (knowing full well which was my *real* preference) then said emphatically 'Plymouth'.

Several of them, real dears, clapped. John Arnaud led the testimonials, very splendidly saying that it didn't matter that I wasn't living there. Mike Gregory also came down on my side though with a few qualifications, and Wally Rowland, a well-known Vicar of Bray, also came out pro, though with the coded disclaimer that it might be better *for me* to change. Only that little gnomeprick Jack Courtney said that the matter ought to be 'referred back to the wards.' So we ended friends, with my position here greatly consolidated. Any sign of trouble in the future and I can always refer to that meeting as justifying (a) my fighting all the way, and (b) threatening to stand in any case as Independent-Conservative – against-the-Common-Market or whatever.

All the same I felt a somewhat heavy heart after they had all dispersed. *It might have been.* I am not really *of* Plymouth, and I don't know how much longer I can keep up the pretence.

Cloisters   *Wednesday, 11 November*

Oh dear! A decision, followed by an indecision, followed by a contradiction, followed by a referral.

This afternoon I was scheduled to present the British Safety Standards Award to one of my constituents in the Cholmondeley Room of the Lords. Alison booked me to go down there at 12 noon, but I found that the actual presentation did not take place until 1.30 p.m. Apprehensive of my boredom threshold I went back upstairs and drifted along the Lords Corridor to Euan's room where we started opening my present from M. Goisot,[1] the Sauvignon, of which I had bought him a case. It was at room temperature, but we nonetheless drank copiously. Soon we were joined by some of his colleagues, Derek Rippengal,[2] who is always held up as being the cleverest man in the Palace of Westminster; and then by that grave, handsome bachelor, James Vance-White. Later still, in popped little John Webb,

---

[1] M. Goisot, proprietor of a vineyard at St. Brie from which the Clarks import their house wine.

[2] Derek Rippengal, Counsel to Chairman of Committees, House of Lords since 1977.

somewhat chubbier of countenance than formerly and still very fidgety.

What a jolly lot they are. We sparkled and scintillated. At intervals the popping sound of a cork could be heard, and reheard. These little lunch-time parties are a more or less regular feature of those comfortable bay-windowed offices that look out on to Parliament Square and I, perhaps fortunately, do not go to them as often as I should like. And, indeed, my thoughts strayed from time to time to the mass of Safety Council activists waiting in the Cholmondeley Room.

Finally, a little unsteady of gait, I detached myself from the committee of Established drinkers in the Lords and went and sought out my constituent.

He was a splendid man, a Mr Robins, who had served thirty-three years in the Air Force, including three as a POW after being shot down in a Halifax over Berlin in 1943. I questioned him closely about his experiences and he enjoyed 'shooting a line', as he called it. In the fullness of time I presented him with the award, but made the mistake (as I now see) of speaking to him quietly, as person to person, as we held up the diploma (which was huge) while the photographers clicked and flashed. I should, of course, have bellowed my words of praise so that all and sundry could hear. I noticed that all the other MPs that followed me also spoke *sotto voce*, but it was Mr Robins' big day and I think he would have appreciated it.

Later that afternoon, and still somewhat 'irresponsible', I ran into David Owen. He, too, seemed to be tight – or was this my imagination? He spoke very freely and indiscreetly about political arrangements in Plymouth. He had not seen my statement about standing and believed, or affected to believe, that I had said I was not standing. David launched into a great speech about how I was bound to lose Sutton, how strong the SDP were in Plymouth and how he would really quite like it if I did move, strongly suggesting that I did, etc.

It surprised me that he should be leaving Devonport and if he was, that he should not fight Drake, which looked a better bet. But no, he warned me in the most good-natured terms that I would be 'taken to the cleaners' in Sutton. I was jaunty and blithe. But after he had gone I stole into the Library and looked up the relative percentages of the two seats (Sutton and Folkestone). There is really very little to choose, as in both cases the Conservatives polled approximately 50 per cent in 1979 and approximately 45 per cent in 1974. The percentage points are in every case slightly in favour of Folkestone, where the Labour and Liberal vote is identical in size. But these figures are very much 'at the margin'. David had promised that he would send me a copy of the analysis which his department are doing on the different seats and this may be interesting.

However, it did make me more uneasy than I showed. I suppose it *is* conceivable that one might lose Plymouth Sutton, though God knows what that means for the size and fate of the Tory Party in the country. I cannot think of anything more boring than having to slave away there being nice to everyone for another two years and then lose – that is not part of the bargain at all.

But then *immediately* after this little episode I walked into the Members' Lobby, where I was hailed by Tony Royle. He told me that, as he had promised, he had spoken to the Chairman at Folkestone and that, in fact, he (the Chairman) was not ill-disposed to my candidature and that although no guarantees could be made, I would certainly have a 'good run' if I put in. This is too vexing. Particularly as Tony said that both he and the Chairman and Albert all agreed that it was essential that I should write to my own constituency and 'completely clear the decks' with them.

Now what the hell am I going to do? I suppose that I must proceed with Folkestone. But of course it is more difficult in one sense because of last week's 'statement' in Plymouth. Fortunately though they are not selecting until January. This means that the 'statement' will have bought a little time, quietened the thing down and allow me to write the letter of resignation over the Christmas holiday.

In the meantime I have got to look more closely at the situation in Folkestone and revert to the plan of having a great baronial party before Christmas, somewhat on Astor lines, more official, that is to say, than social. I telephoned Jane to ask her to book the bell ringers for the first Saturday evening in December.[1] Jane, bless her, gave a kind of spluttering giggle at this volte-face. She asked me very pertinently whether I was not making the same mistake, in political terms, that I had already made in the bond market. Namely of switching out of one great lump into another, just as the first one was about to fructify. I am afraid there may be something in this.

---

[1] A group of locals in the Saltwood area who play a (limited) repertoire of musical tunes on handbells.

Cloisters   *Tuesday, 17 November*

I am pretty sure that I have got the Defence Chair in the bag. Both Ian Gilmour and Nigel Fisher said that they would be voting for me and this must be a good augury. With friends and supporters on the Left and in the Centre, coupled with a good single 'word of mouth' (earlier I had seen Patrick Mayhew at tea and he said unequivocally: 'You'll get it'), plus the deployed strength of the '92, I should be invincible.

I stayed on late at my desk and checked through my personal canvass list. I am sending reminders to about twenty-five people who have given me a verbal assurance, and another twenty whom I have been unable to contact, but whom I regard as certain supporters, have received a different type of letter which went on their board this morning. Out of this I should trawl a vote of about 60 and the '92, getting 100 plus out of a total available franchise of approximately 200. It is inconceivable that 200 colleagues will actually vote in the election and so even with 'wastage' I should be home and dry.

Dick Body's secretary came in and said that Buck was in a frightful state, cursing and shouting in his office, always at the gin bottle etc. Poor old Tony, I feel kind of awful about it, but that's Show Business.

Cloisters   *Wednesday, 18 November*

We assembled in Room 10. Little David Trippier[1] started to say something in his flat northern tones about how he thought I was probably doing the right thing ... etc. Knowing that he would vote against me I said, 'No, no, no, all the officers must vote for Tony (grand seigneur!).' As I looked round the room I noted complacently that my supporters predominated. A whip (I cannot remember which one) handed me a pile of ballot papers. I marked one and distributed a few others while holding on to the pile. Unfortunately, Tony was sitting next to me, otherwise I might have succumbed to a reckless impulse to 'vote often.' As it was when I went up with my ballot paper to the return pile I did manage, surreptitiously, to vote once more. I am sure Buck didn't see, but little Neil Thorne was watching

---

[1] David Trippier, MP for Rossendale since 1979.

me closely.[1] At the table I made a joking remark to Tristan Garel-Jones, who takes the 'wet' whip, but had assured me that he would vote for me. He was actually in the process of marking his ballot paper, but doing it so heavily masked by other papers which he was pressing over the names, that it was impossible to see what he was doing. Buck was also leaning over his shoulder and I don't doubt that he had given him assurances too. Now he found himself in difficulties.

These committee elections are a shambles. Perhaps just as well, I thought, although I was rather alarmed when Buck said: 'You have voted three times.' Supposing Neil Thorne had seen me cheat? Was Buck going to make a scene? He seemed good natured, though on edge. I thought my majority would be so huge that I could, if he insisted, readily submit to a recount, excluding my own ballot paper. But the thing died down. Bob Boscawen handed over the ballot papers to Tony Berry who took them outside and we listened, not very attentively, to some boring Group Captain from the RUSI, who was telling us how to 'combat' CND. Then Bob Boscawen came back. He had the result. I didn't catch his eye, although he was only a few feet away from me. Relaxedly I stretched my legs out below the desk; a sidelong glance at Buck showed that he was both sweating *and* smoking.

Then, in between the end of the talk by the Group Captain and the taking of questions, Boscawen announced, in an extremely flat tone, the result – Antony Buck has been elected.

I felt like one of those characters in melodrama who scream 'No, No!' or 'I can't *believe* it.' Little Winston, returned unopposed in his post as Vice-Chairman, and sitting on the top table, grinned wolfishly and sought most blatantly and gloatingly to catch my eye, which, naturally, I did not let him do. I had, of course, made instant and ritual obeisance to Tony and congratulated him. What the hell had happened? Perhaps Berry, who loathes me and had, I believe, black-mailed me for the Whips' Office, had subtracted the necessary number of ballot papers on the way back to the Chief's office where the count took place? This would have been divine punishment for my shiftily voting twice, just as God always punishes one, instantly, for cheating in a backgammon game. Perhaps some of the '92 had in fact voted anti? Little Winston certainly. Very probably Patrick Wall, who has been jealous of my expertise in defence matters ever since I entered

---

[1] Neil Thorne, MP for Ilford South since 1979.

the House; Nick Bonsor,[1] who thinks I snubbed him when he was trying to make the running on the Civil Defence Committee last year. Dear old 'Tone', has, of course, no enemies. He is the personification of '... always has a cheery word for everyone around him'.

Oh dear, though, how very flat making. I slipped away and telephoned Jane who, as always, was sweet, loyal and indignant.

Cloisters   *Thursday, 19 November*

I was sitting in the Committee Room Corridor dictating an introduction to the *Time* and *Life* World War II series, when I noticed Ian Gow walking towards us at the far end. Alison and I always go up to this corridor when we have to dictate anything that is not simply constituency material as there is so much eavesdropping and mischief-making in the Cloister office.

My relations with IG have been cool in the extreme since we returned. Cool on my side from a combination of resentment of being passed over in the reshuffle and guilt at my role in the Ted Heath/'Dirty Tricks' scandal that broke during the Party Conference. On his side, I had assumed that guilt and resentment were also present, though for symmetrically opposite reasons, namely guilt for not having pushed my case at the time of the reshuffle and resentment at my having spilt the beans to Ted. Privately I had written off our relationship and resigned myself to a purely Party role – another reason why I was feeling so depressed about my defeat for the Defence Chair.

I continued dictating and assumed that he would walk past with no more than a courteous acknowledgement. He is an exceedingly courteous man and I am sorry that our friendship has been spoiled. We have had two incidents in the past, but this time things were different. However, he stopped, put his hand on my shoulder and asked me if I would dine that evening. For a moment I feared that it might be one of those terrible strained affairs, when The Lady and one or two other backbenchers are also present and conversation is artificial, but, as it were, competitively banal. No, he suggested the Cavalry Club, so I knew that it would be 'intimate'. After he had

---

[1] Sir Nicholas Bonsor (4th Bt), MP for Nantwich since 1979.

gone I went to telephone Jane. What was I to say to him? I was glad to have overtures made to me so soon after my recent setback, but simple words of consolation would not be enough. Jane took a very strong line, spoke most articulately about the injustice of promoting so many duds; said that The Lady, for all her qualities, was a prisoner of circumstance, of communist civil servants, fudging and cowardly ministers, establishment and, for all her fine words, 'consensus' pressures. Jane said she had only realised the extent of this and started to lose heart after that dinner at Downing Street when that little prick Graham ... was still in position in her Questions Office, even though he was unashamedly (and against all regulations) a committed Labour supporter and had inspired many of the sneers and smears in the 1979 campaign.

IG drove me to the Cavalry Club in his blue Mini – now definitely showing the effects of the almost continuous traffic thrashing it has suffered in the last four years. If anything this made the ride, on wet roads, even more alarming than usual.

On the way he asked various routine questions about morale in Plymouth, spoke unhappily about Crosby (he had been the previous day),[1] described how our candidate was now completely shell-shocked, would not meet the press, could not bring himself to talk to strangers etc. etc. Ian said that the candidate, when asked hostile or even faintly awkward questions, would only answer, 'no comment'. This is particularly unfortunate as politicians are meant to 'comment' on everything, and to say 'no comment' invariably means that personal dirty linen is being washed, or threatens to be washed.

I had hoped to avoid drinking too much, as I knew myself to be in a gloomy, critical and self-pitying condition. I did not want to warm up too soon under Ian's hospitality. While we were in the bar we talked in a melancholy way about the opportunities that had been lost in the first two years. Ian agreed that the Chancellor's difficulties were never so acute, that our old objectives of controlling the money supply and public spending were virtually unattainable. It required a Herculean effort, even to control their rate of growth – which was already far higher than it had been in 1979. We agreed that indexing was the real obstruction to wiping out inflation. If we had de-indexed immediately, at the outset, everything – public servants' pensions,

---

[1] Crosby by-election, caused by the death of Sir Graham Page, where one of the SDP's 'Gang of Four', Shirley Williams, was standing.

benefits, the whole lot, there would have been a tremendous outcry
and eighteen months of hardship, but the prospects now would be
very good. But now . . .

We were made late in getting to our table by three incredible
boozers who were the only other occupants of the bar. One of them
cornered Ian and said: 'I always used to see photographs of you
standing near the Prime Minister and now I do not see them any
more. Are you in disgrace?' We kept them at bay for a bit, Ian being
more polite and attentive than I. But this man (I thought and assumed
he was a high-ranking Cavalry officer, but actually it turned out that
he was a salesman 'in' tubular steel scaffolding) kept saying, 'I never
see you photographed next to the Prime Minister now, why not?' and
pushing his face aggressively forward. Finally, Ian said to him: 'It is a
matter of complete indifference to me whether you see photographs
of me next to the Prime Minister or not,' and we went up to take
our table.

He asked me about the Defence Committee elections. I explained
the background (even though he probably knew it), and that I had
been encouraged by the Whips' Office, the existing Secretary of State
and the former Secretary of State. Buck had complained to Ian,
possibly even hoping that Ian would restrain me. However, I was
interested to hear that, according to Ian, he had made reference to a
'nice' note that I had written to him, although Ian is so skilful and
subtle in his approach that he could well have been mentioning this
in order to heal any possible bad feelings between Buck and myself.
From what I hear of Buck's remarks and comments in other quarters
in the run-up to the election, I rather doubt if these were particularly
friendly to me.

Gow said: 'The thing about Tony is that he is someone who simply
cannot resign himself to the fact that he will (lowering his voice) never
hold office again.' I said to Ian that this was as good a moment as any
for me to ask him, in all candour, if he could tell me, confirm my
suspicions, that the same was true of myself, only I left out, of course,
'again'.

This, clearly, was the point which he had been working round to.
Immediately, he started to talk very fast, avoiding a direct 'yes' or 'no'
answer. He first drew the analogy with his own experience. Said that
John Stanley,[1] on the two occasions when the Shadow Ministers had

---

[1] John Stanley, MP for Tonbridge and Malling, was the Prime Minister's PPS, 1976–79,

been shuffled, had sought him out and said that he was sorry that he (Gow) had not been included, that the Prime Minister had great things in store for him, etc. Ian said, as I knew, that he had nothing to do with the first administration, he had only been called in at a late stage. He *had* sat in on both the January and September reshuffles where the junior posts were effectively apportioned by a quartet consisting of the Prime Minister, the Chief Whip, Willie, and himself in a simple advisory role. He said that it was so difficult as so many factors had to be reconciled. So and so would make too much trouble if kicked out, so and so had to remain for reasons of balance, so and so had to be treated mercifully because he was getting divorced, so and so had to be brought forward to encourage the 1979 intake. So and so, etc . . .

He said, somewhat to my surprise, that Michael [Jopling] had 'had a good opinion' of me, that in September he had talked of my possibly being a Whip, that on both occasions my name had been discussed favourably. He repeated his assurance that if he were 'sacked', he would, without hesitation, recommend me to the Prime Minister as his successor (this was something of a relief because I had feared that the Dirty Tricks episode had ruined that possibility once and for all, although I am now as certain as can be that Ian himself will go the full term of the Parliament in the Prime Minister's service).

Who then was blocking me? It must be Willie? Ian did not give a very clear answer. Ominously he said that some things I had done had irritated Willie. Willie had 'told' him (I think this is balls and that, in fact, Willie had objected, or at least demurred, when my name came up at both these meetings). Willie cannot bear being criticised.

I asked if I had been blackballed in the Whips' Office, as there are only two people there who would do it. Berry would do it in any case. Gummer, if he could, but he is such an oily little creep, he might not have done.[1] Ian mumbled and gave the impression that there had not been a blackballing in the Whips Office, but that other conditions supervened. I suppose it was at this point that they had decided to put in Nick Budgen and this may well have been Willie's doing as the appointment of Budgen has effectively silenced one of Willie's most tiresome critics.

---

while the Conservatives were in Opposition. When the Government was formed he became a Junior Minister at Environment and remained in obscurity.

[1] John Selwyn Gummer, MP for Eye since 1979, and recently made a junior government whip.

Nevertheless, it was a consummate performance. Ian managed to convey to me that my chances of promotion still remained very strong – and certainly it was a relief to hear that Michael, if not an ally, then at least was not an opponent. And yet . . . if one looks at the thing objectively it is simply not good enough being told that one's name was actively *considered* twice. It is, irritatingly, just enough to keep one in line for a little longer (which was obviously the intention).

When I told Jane that evening she said that at least it was a kind of compliment that he had to search me out so soon after the Defence Committee defeat and give me three hours on my own. At least it means that they are still afraid of me, she said. But in some ways I felt like a sucker who had called a meeting to try and get his money back and then being conned into investing a further £15,000.

It was only much later when the significance of a peculiar category in Ian's list of factors-that-had-to-be-taken-into-account suddenly dawned on me, 'so and so was going through a divorce'. Of course. That was Jerry Wiggin,[1] who had got Phil Goodhart's job which everybody recognised was rightfully mine. Perhaps it is as well that I had not picked it up at the time, but now I realise why he included it.

Cloisters   *Tuesday, 24 November*

Today had another ghastly experience. November is a horrible month, it always brings me disasters. Losses on the Stock Exchange and at the backgammon tables, personal setbacks, snubs, reminders of advancing years, material deterioration and other horrors. Early, at 8.15 a.m. I rang Ian Gow, in obedience to his letter of the previous evening in which he had asked me to 'talk' to him about Prime Minister's Questions where I was number two on the list, and first Conservative. Mindful of our improved relations and the encouragement he had given me last Friday, I said that I would do whatever I was told. He said he would call me back at my desk before 10.00 a.m.

I remained at my desk until five past one and he finally came through and gave me a verbative question about small businesses. Ugh. I loathe small businesses – and big ones if it comes to that – and would

---

[1] Jerry Wiggin, MP for Weston-super-Mare since 1969, the new Parliamentary Under-Secretary of State for the Armed Forces.

greatly have preferred something in my own field. However, I learned it by heart (as I thought) and prepared to do my duty. Michael White wrote a perfect account [in the *Guardian*] of what happened, which I can embellish by saying, first, that at the cries of 'oh' I was not in the least put out, indeed I toyed with the House, relishing that the impact of what I was going to say would be even greater; second, that The Lady did really grit her teeth as she straightened me out.

This is appalling. I have lost my key-elective position in the Party and now I have firmly embedded myself in The Lady's long memory as an incompetent.

'*Not* your finest hour, Alan,' sneered that creep McNair-Wilson in the Tea Room queue just afterwards. What is left for me! A lingering death? Or should I blaze away regardless?

Perhaps, now, I would do better if The Lady were evicted.

Cloisters   *Thursday, 26 November*

Everything is dreadfully depressing. Clearly the SDP are going to win Crosby. How fickle and spastic the electorate are. How gullible, to be duped by someone as scatty and shallow as Shirley Williams. And in today's papers there is the Scarman Report, with its ritual 'we are all guilty' and its call for positive discrimination (i.e., discrimination on the grounds of *colour* against white people and in favour of black). In other words, where a white person is better qualified and more suitable they should nonetheless be rejected in favour of a black person – 'in the interests of racial harmony', as the DPP put it when he withdrew the prosecution from the fourteen defendants in the Bristol Riot Trial.

On Tuesday in the Tea Room, when I was still smarting from my rout at Prime Minister's Questions, Ted Gardner approached me *sotto voce* and said that Willie was determined to include the executive power of release in the new Criminal Justice Act. He personally was doubtful about it, etc. etc, but Willie had already warned the officers at the Home Affairs Committee meeting on Monday (this had been put off from 7 p.m. to 10 p.m. and I had not been told about it).

Willie is obsessed, to the exclusion of practically everything else, by the dangers of a prison riot due to over-crowding, having to come to the House and make a Statement, etc. He thinks, rightly or wrongly, that by reducing the prison population he will make this less likely.

And also, of course, he secretly likes the idea of earning some plaudits from the *Guardian*, and other makers of received opinion, for a 'progressive' penal measure. Willie, for some reason, is very jittery about Kilroy-Silk,[1] perhaps because he usually occupies the corner seat below the gangway and is only a short distance away from him, perhaps because Kilroy-Silk articulates views and feelings which Willie sometimes secretly shares. At any rate, Willie accords him far more respect than he does any other members of the Opposition.

I simply cannot let this go through unchecked. It is a great nuisance as we know that it is Willie who is actually obstructing my promotion – not that *that* has not gone down the drain anyway now – but I still feel that I must articulate rightish opinion on this issue to him.

I contemplated having a word with Michael Jopling, prefacing it with the disclaimer that I knew Willie objected to me personally, but of course I had a great respect for him, etc. etc. and still nonetheless felt that this view should be expressed, etc. etc. Then thought it would probably be better if I went and saw Willie himself, although by chance I did briefly see Michael in the Tea Room and managed to score both by saying this and that I intended to go and see Willie immediately.

I went back into the Chamber and listened in a desultory way to the Law and Order debate on a Liberal motion. The wets on our side were prominent, although there was one very good speech by Dudley Smith.[2] After a bit I slid along the benches and asked Roger Sims if he could arrange a short meeting with Willie, and this was duly effected for 7 p.m.

Willie, of course, is a terrific operator. He was effusive when he greeted me: 'So good of you ... so glad you were re-elected ... I really mean that,' etc. etc. He led off and gabbled massively about his plans for prison building, raged at the Governor of Wormwood Scrubs for spilling the beans in the press and so forth. Whenever I tried to speak Willie said: 'Yes' gravely and fixed me with his oyster eyes. The substance of our agreement I set out in a letter, ostensibly for Roger Sims, but really for Willie's eyes, the following morning. Fortunately, Willie is more amenable to persuasion on this since his painful experiences at Party Conference than formerly. I do not know that the

---

[1] Robert Kilroy-Silk, Member of Parliament for Ormskirk, considered by AC to be extremely left-wing, member of the Select Committee on Home Affairs.
[2] Dudley Smith, MP for Warwick and Leamington since 1968 (Brentford and Chiswick 1959–66).

assurances that he gave me will amount to much, but I did my best.

Plymouth train   *Friday, 27 November*

Filled with 'set-backs' – my failure to get the Defence chair (which seemed to me to be 'in the bag', my cocking-up of the 'set' PM's questions and now today, devastatingly dear, beloved Tip-book's rejection by RCB.[1]

I just don't understand this; like Jane I am *shitted* by it, shitted *for him*, who so genuinely and unbelievably against all the odds triumphed at Pirbright and 'swotted up' for his lecturette. I was so proud, with all his new friends, and circle and prospects. What a blow it must be for him. What now? I somehow feel that whatever job he gets he will always think wistfully of the Guards. As will I. I will hardly be able to look at a Guards detachment, just as soon, it seems, I will never be able to cross Westminster Bridge again or drive round Parliament Square.

I will telephone Jerry Wiggin and see if he can get the papers from RCB – which could give us some help perhaps.

Saltwood   *Sunday, 29 November*

Still very depressed. I specially left Lilian a note last night to make sure he came up and said 'goodnight'. Excuse being that I wanted the copy of the *Motor* with the year's road tests in it. He didn't although James did. I lay awake for ages hoping he might and thought of my old age when it will be not hours, but days that I will wait sadly for a visit from the boys.

The Winter Office is so nice, but like everything and everywhere, it needs tidying, attention, TIME. A fine day, but cold, cold, and with a keen wind. Before breakfast darling Jane had 'hysterics' because the kitchen fire wouldn't light. I wish, I really do wish, I could find some way of saving her some of the drudgery. A minute ago I

---

[1] Andrew retook his RCB (Regular Commissions Board) the following year and passed. He would join the Life Guards, rise to the rank of Major and retire in 1994.

went into the kitchen and she was brillo-scrubbing the bottom of a saucepan.

At breakfast I grumbled something about the Deeds not being in the Deed-box.[1] She pointed out that she had not got the time to clear out the safe – with VAT two weeks behind, Christmas shopping to do, all the food for the party *and* the dinner to prepare, plus Christmas in prospect – and anyway from the bedroom window she could see ten vehicles 'standing out'. Perfectly true.

Cloisters   *Thursday, 3 December*

In some strange way I continue to warm to Ted Heath, who these days sits only one place away from me. David Howell had made a singularly inept and colourless presentation of the case for allowing heavy, or hea*vier*, juggernauts to free range over the roads of the Kingdom and the House was restive. Criticisms came from every side, although after about a half hour they had retained a repetitive quality. In an effort to produce something new Richard Mitchell[2], now of the SDP, raised the question of the dangers presented by static juggernauts at night – 'particularly as they are usually parked outside houses belonging to persons other than the driver.'

It was a case of the big-man-move-with-surprising-speed. Although he inclined his head very slightly, and his smile was arched and lethargic. Ted's reaction was instantaneous, faster than anyone else on our bench. 'That is a very insulting thing to say about lorry drivers,' he said to us, 'that they are always parked outside other people's houses at night.' Genuinely funny and unexpected.

---

[1] Although, surprisingly, AC makes no mention in his journal, all indebtedness to C. Hoare & Co. had finally been cleared a year before. The deeds arrived back at Saltwood on 23 December 1980.

[2] Richard Mitchell, Labour MP for Southampton, Itchen from 1971 (Southampton Test 1966–71) until joining the SDP earlier in the year.

Cloisters   *Tuesday, 8 December*

Lunched with Frank Johnson.[1] He is so quick and alert and youthfully intelligent; delightful company.

'There is an incredibly beautiful waitress who sometimes serves this table,' he said, nervously apprehensive. And our luck was in and she materialised, an absolutely devastating honey-blonde of about twenty-two; incredible, faultless in appearance, but when she spoke, utterly anaphrodisiac, ridiculous hockey-girl voice, 'Righty-ho,' Betje-manesque.

Frank pretended he wanted to talk about the Tory Party, but he really prefers to talk about the Nazis, concerning whom he is curious, but not, of course, sympathetic. Yes, I told him, I was a Nazi, I really believed it to be the ideal system, and that it was a disaster for the Anglo-Saxon races and for the world that it was extinguished. He both gulped and grinned, 'But surely, er, you mean . . . (behaving like an unhappy interviewer in *Not the Nine O'Clock News* after, e.g., Pamela Stevenson had said something frightfully shocking) . . . ideally in terms of administrative and economic policy . . . you cannot really, er . . .' Oh yes, I told him, I was completely committed to the whole philosophy. The blood and the violence was an essential ingredient of its strength, the heroic tradition of cruelty every bit as powerful and a thousand times more ancient than the Judaeo-Christian ethic.

Even he, I think, was slightly shocked. How can you say such a thing? he kept repeating. Meaning, not how can you say such a thing, but how do you dare put it into words. 'You might be quoted in Atticus.' I said I didn't care and, anyway, I had already been quoted as saying this very thing in Atticus.[2] He agreed, he and Hitchens had talked about it at the time and just like everyone here they took refuge in the convention that Alan-doesn't-really-mean-it. He-only-says-it-to-shock, etc. Frank said that people simply will not allow the reality that a 'toff' could be serious about these views, whereas if they were being expressed by someone like Tony Marlow or Nicholas Winterton, he would be ostracised.

The only time we talked about the Tory Party was when we both spontaneously at the same moment expressed our growing admiration

---

[1] Frank Johnson, Parliamentary sketch writer on *The Times*.
[2] AC was profiled in the *Sunday Times* Atticus column by Christopher Hitchens in February, 1980.

for Ted. I said that it was not necessarily his policies – although these were being expressed in a much more sensible and original style than of old – but his whole personal demeanour was creditable. He had been through the furnace, of rejection and contempt, and emerged unalloyed. Frank agreed. As ardent Heath-haters of old we felt that such a change was a credit to our objectivity.

Later that afternoon in the Economics Debate Ted spoke very brilliantly, ranging far and wide, a relaxed demolition job. He even managed to turn Enoch on the ropes when The Prophet, his own features contorted with fury, told Ted to 'take that grin off your face.' 'The Rt. Hon. gentleman can ask me to do many things, but that is not one of them,' said Ted, and the House roared with laughter in support.

Cloisters   *Wednesday, 9 December*

The Chef had sent a message, as I require him to do, that there was fresh lobster and so I left Brooks's early and went back to the House Dining Room at 9 p.m. Ian Gow was at the other end of the table I joined at which were also seated two Whips (John Stradling Thomas and John Cope), and two Ministers (Lynda Chalker[1] and Tom King[2]). Very ostentatiously and splendidly he passed me across the text of a Question that he wanted me to table for the Prime Minister on a 'set' subject – the accession of Portugal to the EEC. This was particularly loyal and kind of him so soon after my appalling gaffe over the *Morning/Daily Star*. He is *very* good at healing wounds, however slight and even when self-inflicted. When he got up to pay his bill I followed him into the corridor and gave him the amusing news, which I had discovered on Monday evening when I took Andrew to Pratt's, that both Peter Walker and Michael Heseltine had been black-balled. As Jane had said when I told her, this was practically the only encouraging bit of news in the last six months. What a splendid bastion of ancient squirearchical values that place is, that it should even these days feel

---

[1] Lynda Chalker, MP for Wallasey since February 1974, a junior Minister at Health and Social Security since 1979.
[2] Tom King, MP for Bridgwater since 1970, Local Government Minister since 1979.

strong enough to black-ball two up-and-coming Privy Councillors and members of the Cabinet!

However, things then turned nasty for, as we paced along the corridor, Ian told me that little Albert Costain had been making trouble about my intentions regarding Folkestone. Ian said it would be a 'snub' to people who 'had worked so long and loyally for me at election time, also the fact that I had abandoned them would "weigh very heavily" with the Selection Committee.' Sod, sod, sod, sod. Not only was this a tiresome thing to hear from such a source, but it also illuminated Ian's deviousness. Quite feline he is, or rather like some Russian Grandmaster, seeing always many moves ahead. Just as the reason he had taken me out to dinner the night after my defeat for the Defence Chair was not primarily to console me, but just as much (I suspect) because he already perceived my somewhat tetchy manner when I had questioned the Prime Minister about referenda the previous week and, knowing that I was number two on her list the following week, felt obliged to ensure that I didn't use that position to make trouble. And similarly his open impression of friendship and trust at the dinner table was designed to put me in a good mood before he warned off my overtures to the Folkestone constituency.

Cloisters   *Thursday, 10 December*

I had a mini-triumph today, and quite unexpected. The fascination of the House of Commons is that one can never be certain in one's prediction of the outcome of events, even from hour to hour.

I had been placed at very short notice on the Committee of the Local Government (Miscellaneous Provisions) Bill and went in neither having read the Bill, nor attended any stage of the debates on the floor. To my alarm and amazement I noticed that the very first amendment was being put by the likeable, but low-key, Shirley Summerskill,[1] requiring the Government to license pop festivals — and Raison, dutifully reading his Home Office brief, was actually resisting this! I rose in my seat and made a totally impromptu speech, referring to the closet trendiness in the Conservative Party and the absurdity of

---

[1] Dr Shirley Summerskill, MP for Halifax since 1964, and Opposition front bench shadow spokesman on Home Affairs.

resisting such a reasonable amendment. Colleagues pricked up their ears, abandoned their correspondence and it soon became plain to the Front Bench and the Whip that there was not the slightest chance of saving the clause after it was put to a vote. So now pop festivals will have to be licensed. One of those tiny little episodes for which one can claim credit – like me blocking the Local Government (again!) Ethnic Groups Grants Bill in 1979.

Saltwood   *Saturday, 12 December*

London has been snowbound all week. Lovely by the logfire – but not as relaxed as could be, hidden stress. I've totally lost interest in Plymouth, that's the fact. Don't bother with press releases any more, or any kind of self-promotion. I don't know anyone in Plymouth other than a few narrow Conservatives. I suppose it might be recoverable with 18 months dedication in the run-up; but can I afford the time? Have I the inclination? I must leave some record, and it should really be my big philosophico-historical treatise – can only do this with the Commons research facilities available. But everyone warns me against trying for Folkestone including, most recently and most disconcertingly, Ian Gow.

Drawing directly on from that there is our party next Saturday – the celebrated local benefit, now coming off in a rather different atmosphere to that which one had planned; people definitely wary, more suspicious. So much so that I said to Jane, only half in jest, that one should not put in for Folkestone at all, *but* announce an (sic) intention not to stand again in Plymouth. This would leave one free to apply for some of the other local seats (Rye, Maidstone etc). Much depends on the answers – in deeds as well as words – to my letter last week to IG. I would, though, be very sorry to miss the wheeling-and-dealing of the opening days of the new Parliament.

Saltwood   *Saturday, 19 December*

Our party for the local nobs. Much anxiety about who would or would not come, how the hell we identify them anyway, etc. Masses of flowers and greenery everywhere, log fires blazing in every fireplace and – for the first time in fifty years – upper and lower halls properly *lit*, as I had raided the Great Library and brought back a number of lamp standards. Jane valiantly changed plugs throughout the morning from three-pin to two-pin so that we could use all Mr Paine's old sockets put in in the early '50s. No fuses blew and the place looked wonderful.

First to arrive (and, incidentally, the last to leave) was the editor of the *Folkestone Herald* and his *very* young and pretty wife. He, a little Welshman with dark curly hair, not as unfriendly as I had feared. Soon they were pouring in. To get over the identification problem we had posted William[1] at the door in order to take guests' names and announce them. Jane and I stood in the lower hall and directed guests to the upper hall where Sarah and James handed them champagne. Thereafter they drifted about, most of them finding their way into the Library where soon a comforting roaring noise built up.

We had two set-pieces. First was the arrival of my father and Nolwen. He, very ga-ga and tottery (deliberately so, I suspect, like Harold Macmillan often is), was kind of wheeled across the Library by William who kept saying: 'Make way for his Lordship; his Lordship here wants to get to his chair,' etc. This went well and my father's eccentricities were much appreciated. Examples, when Sarah, who looked very glamorous, came near them with a plate of canapés, Nölwen introduced her, 'This is James' girlfriend . . .' A look of great pain spread over my father's features. All he said was, 'Oh dear.' I singled out and introduced a number of big-wigs. As each one approached, my father writhed and groaned. Sometimes he seemed almost to be holding up his hands with an expression of defensive panic, like those celebrated pictures of the Hungarian secret policemen being ushered out of their barracks before being mown down in the uprising of 1956. Curiously, though, this went quite well.

Everybody seemed contented and appreciative and, at just the right moment, the ringers of hand bells arrived (one of them, I noticed,

---

[1] 'William' had served Mrs Brown, a neighbour of the Clarks, as butler for many years and after her death he used to help at Saltwood on social occasions.

being that attractive blonde from whom I had bought crab apple jelly at the St John's fête the previous Saturday). They rang their bells, to the tune of a number of familiar Christmas carols, very prettily. It was a happy and nostalgic sound as it echoed off the gothic tracery of the lower hall and I saw poor Peggy,[1] looking drawn and beautiful in a black dress, put her head round the pillar of the top corridor leading from the dining room. Was she thinking of her dear dead Robert? I fear she must have been.

The chairman of the Association arrived very late. He drank a great deal and gabbled. He is a shameless 'wet' ... Why didn't MPs speak out? It was time to turn the tide, etc. I have seldom heard these arguments put so badly. He stayed until the very end, leaving simultaneously with the editor of the local paper. Indeed, in all but the narrowly medical sense, he was a complete spastic. I cannot make out whether this is a good or bad thing from the point of view of my own interests.

Saltwood   *Wednesday, 23 December*

Today we went to Jock Massereene's party (black tie) for not local – as ours – but county nobs.[2] Icy cold, the Hall of Chilham, standard medieval conditions as Jock had broken the central heating that morning and a huge oak tree blazed in the eight-foot fireplace, scorching those who stood near it, while those guests who stood at receding radii from twenty to sixty feet shivered and could see the steam from their breath as they spoke.

Guests, mainly worthy and rich rather than smart in the Chips sense. I saw Etonian chums like Robin Leigh-Pemberton[3] and Adrian Swire[4]. But Billy Rees-Davies[5] struck a raffish note and in some manner admirably contrived to have the three prettiest women in the

---

[1] Peggy Wilson, wife of the Head Gardener at Saltwood, who worked for the Clarks. Her younger son, Robert, worked as a keeper at John Aspinall's zoo at Canterbury and had been killed by a rogue tiger the previous year.

[2] Viscount Massereene and Ferrard, a friend of AC's with whom he shared an interest in animal welfare.

[3] Robin Leigh-Pemberton, chairman of the National Westminster Bank and Lord Lieutenant-elect of Kent.

[4] Adrian Swire, chairman of John Swire & Son since 1966.

[5] William Rees-Davies, MP for Thanet West since 1974 (Isle of Thanet 1953–74).

room around him and hanging on his words. Perhaps he enjoys that mysterious gift of being able to compel female attendance which William Orpen described so vividly in *Onlooker in France*.

We carried plates of food, which was delicious, '... all come in from mee estates in Scotland,' said Jock, into one of the ante-chambers and I found myself in conversation with a well-ish preserved blonde lady in her 50s who (something-something) living at Leeds.

'Did you know Olive Bailey?' I said to her.

'I am her daughter.'

Unabashed I immediately asked her about David Margesson,[1] who is the subject of fascination by me as he was Chief Whip at the time that the Tory Party had all the right decisions available to it as options and made all the wrong ones. But she clammed up and wouldn't say anything wider than that 'David-was-so-sweet-to-everyone ...' etc.

Bill Deedes and I had a long chat. We agreed that the miners strike was the key battle ground on which a spectacular victory could turn the tide of public opinion in favour of the Government. The Lady must *not* give in on this. Unpopular though she is at the moment, she could not be loathed as much as Arthur Scargill. All at once we could redeem our pledges 'to do something' about the unions.

Cloisters   *Thursday, 24 December*

Number two for the Prime Minister and, inspired by my conversation with Bill Deedes the previous evening, I had composed a form of supplementary that invited her to stand firm against the miners. There were frantic messages from Ian all over the boards asking me to get in touch with him. But in the light of the earlier débâcle I did not consult but simply sent him a note setting out in general terms the sort of question I intended to ask about the miners. Still greater panic, messages everywhere, whips and runners on the look-out for me all over the Palace. A scribbled note arrived. '*Don't* say anything about the miners. Ask a question about Poland.'

Hastily I improvised. It seemed that everyone had been requested

---

[1]David Margesson (1st Viscount). Legendary Tory Chief Whip from 1931; appointed Secretary of State for War by Churchill in December 1940, but made the scapegoat after the fall of Singapore in 1942.

to ask about Poland and by the time I rose there was very little left to say except the rather obvious point that suspension of aid would harm the Polish people who seemed more deserving of sympathy than retribution. This whole Polish business is a balls-up. Those cretinous hard-liners baying for blood. Their advice is the precise mirror obverse of Jeremy Thorpe's celebrated suggestion that the 'V' Bombers should be used to devastate the Rhodesian railway system.

Saltwood   *Boxing Sunday, 1981*

Lowered by the decline in the quality of my looks. My face now fat – I can feel it in the neck and cheeks when I wash in cold water, and all those double chins and neck creases. On Christmas Eve I went down and tried to contact the Rev Woods about times of services.[1] Just as I arrived an enormous congregation of worthies started leaving, filed out and down the steps of St Leonards Church, not *one*, or rather only one, a foxy-faced blonde, looked at one, even out of curiosity.

God, yes. How moving the *Brideshead* film was, because of course Lady Marchmain won, in the end. And the drama of that moment when C went in to 'talk' to him, and tried to persuade him to see the priest! I would convert, I would love to convert, if there was someone sympathetic I could talk to.

I wondered what's happened to 'Desmond'?[2]

---

[1] The Reverend Canon Norman Woods officiated at AC's funeral, with the Reverend Canon Reg Humphriss of Saltwood.

[2] Desmond Hazelhurst, friend of the Beuttlers, who left the army to become a priest.

1982

Saltwood   *Friday, 1 January 1982*

First day of the New Year – ORDER AND SECURITY. Not especially inspiring objectives but if we set certain relatively moderate resolutions, to be adhered to, improvements may occur within the frame (sic).

A little more care of fitness, figure and appearance. New Lesley & Roberts suits and San Marco shirting shall help here, plus shampooing, brilliantine, 'smell' etc. (I wonder if the Shadow will materialise from Michael Walker.)[1]

A general 'watching brief' in politics. The die is not yet cast with Folkestone, but looking unlikely. This will impose extra loading in Plymouth for a 'resurgence', but not impossible.

Total financial security now, but must hope in the finish to throw 4x4.

Saltwood   *Sunday, 17 January*

We were reading the papers at breakfast when I suddenly looked up to find a very curious strained expression on Jane's face. As she looked at 'Crossbencher' she started reading '... tea at Saltwood Castle ... don't come round,' as I moved panically across to read over her shoulder. I sat down. There was an item, not especially hostile, and certainly not inaccurate, about my designs on the Folkestone Constituency. H'm.

Cloisters   *Monday, 18 January*

First day back. The House lovely and welcoming in its embrace. A number of invitations to go on radio and television in pursuance of my dispute with Alderson about Special Branch files. (He has done me a good turn by threatening me with a two-year prison sentence, which gives the exchanges extra piquancy.) Jane amusingly said this

---

[1] AC had fantasised over Christmas buying this Rolls Royce 'just to keep in London for suits, scents and cigars.'

morning: 'You must face the fact that there are quite a lot of people dotted about who would be quite glad to see you put away for two years.'

At the Home Affairs Committee I made a long and withering attack on Willie for his pusillanimous attitude to the demands of law and order hardliners. Ian Gow, who had come in just in time to hear this in its entirety, came round and sat on the platform beside me at the end and asked me to go to the Smoking Room. 'I cannot, I have to go to Willie's room at 6.45 p.m. and if I don't go he will swing something at the Officers and be able to say "I didn't warn you because you weren't there," as he invariably does.' We agreed to postpone it, but it was a good sign.

Willie was thinnish, pale and slightly rattled. Ted Gardner very loyally did not 'shop' me, stated my views as broadly being those of the Committee 'as a whole'. And, luckily for me, Roger Sims had not been in attendance – although I assume that toad John Major[1] will report my attack. And, of course, Donald Thompson[2] will report it to the Chief Whip. In spite of having lost weight Willie has gone off a bit. Indeed, he gave the impression of not knowing, on occasion, his arse from his elbow. Said mugging was not a crime of violence (even his own Ministers were startled at this), that the dismissed Chief Constable had a right of appeal. 'Who to?' I asked. 'Oh no, not a right of appeal exactly, but could make a lot of trouble,' and so on.

That evening I dined at Pratt's. Michael Ancram[3] had brought in Robert Atkins and so we could have a laugh together about the 'Crossbencher' item. Of course, we dislike each other quite strongly – a true example of 'incompatibility'. He has an unpleasant, cruel face, and I am certain that he is by inclination and instinct a subversive. But I must admit that he does have a very fast wit. The Earl of Cathcart, as always, was at the dining room table. Told who he was, Atkins made some instant witticism about his being patron of Teddy Taylor.[4] We discussed the question of office, and both Ancram and Atkins paid

---

[1] John Major, MP for Huntingdonshire since 1979, recently appointed PPS to Ministers of State at the Home Office.

[2] Donald Thompson, MP for Sowerby since 1979, Whip to the Home Affairs Committee.

[3] Michael Ancram, the Earl of Ancram, MP for Edinburgh South since 1979 (Berwickshire and E. Lothian February–October 1974).

[4] Edward (Teddy) Taylor, an effective and uncompromising right-winger, much disliked by a section of the Party, including Robert Atkins. MP for Southend East since 1980 (Glasgow Cathcart, 1964–79). The Earl of Cathcart, a professional senior soldier (retired) and now a deputy speaker, House of Lords.

me compliments, said I should be in the Government – why wasn't I? etc. 'How the hell should I know?' I could say, though, with absolute conviction that I would never take anything in Education, the DHSS, or any PPSship, except the Prime Minister or Leader of the House.

Cloisters   *Tuesday, 19 January*

A message from a young girl reporter on the *Folkestone Herald* about the Crossbencher item. I had to give a good deal of thought to this. I said it would be a great honour, etc. etc., but my own Association had decided that they wanted me to stay in Plymouth and (key phrase, which required a lot of brain-racking), *unless they changed their mind,* there was nothing further that I could do or say.

She also asked me various questions about my row with Alderson, and on the whole seemed well disposed. But we will have to wait and see what the papers say on Saturday.

Saltwood   *Sunday, 31 January*

Decisions, hmm. Can no longer avoid the 'crunch' (sic) of *going for* Folkestone (which means abandoning Plymouth) or standing aside. Beth and Wilf came round and talked. All right as far as it goes, but of course they have *no* idea of how politics operate, very little idea about how a constituency association works. When I recall the skill and care which Graham put into fixing the result at Plymouth my heart sank at the scale of the task which was in prospect. We talked each other up into a state of mutual confidence. Of course I would really be far and away the best candidate for the division, but I always remember Jane's dry comment when I triumphantly read out that letter from some woman who had been arranging a flower show, or whatever it was, '... many would like you to be Folkestone's next MP.'

All Jane said was: 'Many wouldn't.'

The only point of any substance that emerged was how influential the Margarys were. It was suggested that I go and see them.

I telephoned Lympne Castle. An elderly but not particularly accommodating voice answered and said in somewhat peremptory tones that they were out to lunch. I rang again at 5 p.m. and they had still not returned. I finally caught Harry Margary at 7 p.m. and without any preamble asked him if I could come over and have a chat. He hesitated fractionally, then assented.

I have not been inside the private quarters of Lympne Castle since Murray Payne's[1] day and the quality of the furnishings had deteriorated considerably: worn, but not tasteful, chintzes, Benares brass warming pans, etc. I had forgotten how unpleasant the Margarys are. Exactly the sort of people with whom a mutual antipathy develops instantly. Harry motioned me to sit between them. They had a faintly conspiratorial look as of two people going to enjoy themselves at their victim's expense. I opened the bowling by asking if either of them (note the use of the word 'either') were proposing to apply for the vacancy caused by Albert's retirement. Fluttering disclaimers. 'But we have a problem ...' said Deirdre Margary, echoed by her nasty husband. They explained that their son (I didn't even know there was such a person) was going to stand. Subsequent enquiries showed that he was a watery stockbroker who seldom came to Kent and who had in the distant past been Chairman of the local Young Conservatives. 'Well clearly you must support him,' etc. etc., I could not get out fast enough. No point in wasting any more time.

Harry Margary didn't want to let me off so lightly, rambled a bit about his massive work at Shepway Council. Dutifully I paid appropriate tribute. They warned me off to some extent but there was no intimacy of any kind, indeed only the bare minimum of good manners.

Cloisters   *Monday, 1 February*

At some point last week in the queue in the Tea Room (I cannot remember which day) I fell into conversation with the Whip to the Home Affairs Committee, Donald Thompson. I repeated to him Paddy Mayhew's complaint to me about the proceedings of the Committee. Later I said that it is my personal opinion that in his

[1] Air Commodore Murray Payne, DFC, who was married to Hilma Howard de Walden and lived at Lympne Castle in the early fifties.

present position Willie is an 'electoral liability'. I thought Thompson looked a bit unhappy at this; and this is unusual for a Whip, who has been trained to hide his feelings and look alert and expectant at all expressions of opinion, however deviant. But I thought no more of it. I am now absolutely certain that Willie has been told – whether direct by Donald Thompson or (more likely) by John Major, who has always loathed me.

I had a quick word after Questions with Michael Jopling, told him the position, how embarrassing it was and suggested that he tick off Donald Thompson to make sure it doesn't happen again. My real motive was that he would bear this in mind and, hopefully, discount it when Willie next expressed his antipathy and disapproval. Michael was very grave and sympathetic, said that Willie had been getting a lot of flak lately; we must build up his confidence; that he was absolutely indispensable to the Prime Minister, always supported her etc. etc. Said: 'Anything you can do to help in this respect . . .' More or less said, in other words, that it was for me to try and repair the damage.

Later that evening I went into the Smoking Room with Tony Buck and was frozen out of Willie's circle with that technique at which he is such a master. Buck and I sat adjoining but were pointedly excluded, even with the tacit connivance of Ian Gow, who was also in the group, from the jollity and conversation. A little later we were joined by Billy Rees-Davies, making it a real duds table. Tony, who is a genuine habituated social and political climber, became increasingly uneasy and kept looking over to their table. It got worse when we rose to leave. With split-second timing (i.e. just as I had my hand on the door but Tony was a couple of paces behind) Willie hailed Tony with that great roar of greeting and hauled him over into the group.

I worried quite a lot about this, but curiously it had the effect of making me feel I ought to stay on at Plymouth and not take any risks. If Willie and I are going to be openly at war it means he can always block my advancement but, equally, with no longer any restraints on my being *really* objectionable towards him. As there was no vote that evening I journeyed thoughtfully homeward.

When I got back I told Jane both about my interview with the Chief and about Willie's behaviour in the Smoking Room. She got the point at once, said that it was the 'sign' we had been waiting for. 'You must stay on just so as to deprive him of the satisfaction of knowing, until the last possible moment, that you won't be coming back.' I agreed, said it was just like my determination not to give my father the pleasure of my dying before he did. She got the point completely, even before I had finished expostulating it. Though Willie didn't give a bugger about what happened to the economy, or even indeed the fate of The Lady. He is far more Machiavellian than he is given credit for (and he knows that I am one of the few people in the Party who has rumbled him) and the reason he gives The Lady so much 'invaluable support' is because he feels she is bound to crash and he will have a significant part to play in the Government of All the Talents that will embellish the Great Hung Parliament. The one sector where he *cannot* make any concession is in the Home Office field as there the changes might not be so easily reversible. So, he has made himself indispensable on the broad canvas, and is allowed a free hand to implement by stealth or otherwise the progressive policies of the Home Office.

Whether or not he has a veto on junior appointments and has twice vetoed mine (Ian has more or less told me), I will make a speech praising Willie and try and get it issued by Central Office and, hopefully, published in some of the national papers. I will then be able to show this to Jopling – and to Willie himself – as evidence that I am doing my best. This won't of course convince Willie, but it will satisfy Jopling and make it more difficult for Willie to veto me in the future.

Cloisters   *Thursday, 4 February*

I heard today an account of the two meetings which the Officers of the Defence Committee have 'enjoyed'.

On Monday they went to Downing Street. Julian Critchley told me how, for weeks beforehand, Tony Buck had been getting himself into a lather, asking him to prepare a paper, text of possible questions, etc. etc., just as he used to do to me when I was his vice-chairman. Julian had produced some material but, as it turned out, Buck appeared totally unprepared. The Officers sat (as usual) in the yellow drawing room with Blaker[1] and Pattie standing deferentially in the wings.

---

[1] Peter Blaker, MP for Blackpool South since 1964; Armed Forces Minister since 1981. Geoffrey Pattie had been Parliamentary Under-Secretary for Defence Procurement since 1981 also.

Everyone was waiting for Buck to say something but he was tongue-tied. After about 35 seconds of complete silence The Lady gimletted Julian with her icy blue eyes and said, in her most hectoring tone, 'Julian, why are you looking around the room like that?' Julian, as he said, simultaneously flushing but with a *faux-rire*, 'I was looking at that gilt mirror over your mantelshelf.' Winston then laid in, threw leather rather than punches.

Of course The Lady ran rings round them, picking off each one in turn and giving them a real rasping, or basting. So demoralised were they that they 'forgot' (unbelievably) to raise their principal bone of contention which was why the Chiefs of Staff had been forbidden to address the Committee. A breathless shambles, they were evicted from Number 10 after about forty minutes.

The next day they went to see the Secretary of State. He, if you please, had the effrontery to tell them that the reason the Chiefs of Staff 'could not' come was because if they did they would have to be prepared to talk also to Labour and SDP Committees – not that there are such things anyway. Amazingly some officers went along with this. Victor Goodhew with his old Whips training nodded sagely. Little Trippier, rubberily ambitious, said nothing. For some reason even Winston (perhaps chastened by his experiences the previous day) sold up. Tony Buck, however, as an ex-Minister, likes having the Chiefs of Staff and he, Critchley and Atkins put up a heavy counter-attack. Tempers flared and, by several accounts, glass was broken.

I saw John Nott at lunch today and made some jocular reference to the meeting, at which he grinned ruefully and rolled his eyes. I think I might leak details of it to Nick Comfort of the *Telegraph* as a quid pro quo for his carrying my laudatory speech about Willie in Monday's paper.

Cloisters   *Friday, 5 February*

I put the finishing touches to the Willie speech, slavishly adulatory. In my present mood it really sticks in the throat. I rang Paddy Mayhew from my desk, pretending to ask for advice as to what to include, but in reality in order to get the word spread that I was making a 'helpful' contribution. Then I approved the text and Alison took it round to Central Office and handed it to Leslie Way. I spoke to Leslie on the phone – it was lucky for me that he was duty officer this weekend because I could explain the background.[1] This is the first time I have ever released a speech through Central Office, and we will see what happens.

The Crownhill AGM was endless. Poor old Frank Harding and Wallie Rowland, a real geriatric pair, yur-yurred their way through the agenda, halting, stammering and stuttering. The only moment of interest came when a Mrs MacDonald, who had been sitting in the front row with that special demeanour of someone who is spoiling for a fight, suddenly felt herself to be insulted by a remark, an aside almost, made by the treasurer and stomped out with a great flurry of head tossing, apparel, rustling of papers, etc. At last my moment came and I had to snap out of my 'brown study'. (All too apparent to the audience, I was told later.) I plodded my way through the text. It was the only time I have ever made a speech to my own supporters and been heckled. John Dobell was the first to interrupt, and others followed him. Never mind, it is now 'on record'.

Saltwood   *Sunday, 7 February*

To my gratification, Michael Jones of the *Sunday Times* reported my speech in depth and quite got – indeed even embellished – the point about it being coded, about Willie being in jeopardy and so on. Things are working out exactly as I had intended.

Cloisters   *Monday, 8 February*

The first thing to appear in my box was a special handwritten note from Willie, sent over by despatch rider with a purple sticker on the envelope, thanking me for my support, saying how we must discuss these things more often, etc. etc. Probably penned, I suspect, before he read the Nick Comfort article on the same subject which went a stage further and carried the rather ominous 'Whitehall briefing' that

[1] L. K. Way, the former Political Correspondent of the *Western Morning News*, now worked at Conservative Central Office.

the Prime Minister was rallying support for the Home Secretary but if his performance still did not come up to her, or the Party's, expectations, she might be 'forced' to replace him.

At this evening's meeting in the Committee Robert Atkins, whose machinations as a subversive and mouth-piece of the left are almost, but not quite, as convoluted as my own in the opposite corner, made a statement saying how much he welcomed my speech on the weekend and how he would like to express his whole-hearted support of Willie Whitelaw, etc. etc. This did not go down especially well in the Committee, the Party's antennae are sensitive and people realise that my pro-Willie speech was a far more telling indication of my hostility to him than any form of public criticism. Within about twelve hours, and with my having said nothing further, it has changed in assessment from being supportive in character to being almost Judas-like. At the officers' meeting that followed the Committee Willie looked unhappy and would not catch my eye at all.

Cloisters   *Tuesday, 9 February*

Mark Schreiber [*The Economist*] rang me at the Albany, just as I was on my fourth cup of rust-coloured PG Tips.

'I want to talk to you about yourself and Willie.'

Well, I remember Mark Schreiber. I remember him when I was a candidate, or aspirant candidate, and he was one of the people, the new wave of humane classless (although he is in fact quite grand) Tories, whom Ted Heath was grooming for high office. His lip certainly curled at the sight and sound of me in those days. But successive Associations refused to adopt him and, disappointed, he became Lobby Correspondent for the *Economist*; from which position he continues to disseminate, though without much influence and his pieces are usually unsigned, his leftish sentiments.

So, after a longish pause, I said: 'I don't understand what you mean.'

'In the past you have attacked Willie, but over the weekend you made a speech in support of him.'

'I have never attacked him. I may have criticised him; but never in public.'

After a certain amount of preliminary jockeying, I did talk to him but it was clear that he was very sympathetic to Willie so I had to tread carefully. I could not resist saying though that although I was doing my best to defend Willie from public attack, I felt that there was a widespread realisation in the Party that he was an electoral liability and would have to go before we square up for the next general election.

Cloisters   *Monday, 22 February*

The night of our annual dinner with the Home Secretary in a private room at the Garrick. Things a little stilted to begin with; we drank champagne out of silver mugs. Mellowing set in. Willie is just a tiny bit uncomfortable with his officers, particularly as Michael Mates,[1] who will always do as Willie tells him, had not turned up. John Wheeler[2] has moved away from him a little, conscious, I suspect, that Willie Whitelaw's reign is to be of finite duration and he should start a little 'distancing'. Ivor Stanbrook he loathes – and I must say, both to Stanbrook's credit and in justification of Willie's feelings, Ivor never stops attacking him at every opportunity, both public and private. Ted Gardner he is suspicious of, told John Major that he was '... too much under Alan Clark's influence.' And Alan Clark, well there *is* a very tricky relationship. I think he is a little frightened of me; he seldom catches my eye, but when he does there is sometimes a watery, pleading look in his expression. The trouble is, each regards the other as a traitor to his class.

The Home Secretary soon became jolly. He told, with much bellowing and groaning, of his experiences last week at St Aldate's Church in Oxford where, booked over a year in advance, he turned up for one of those lay preaching, question-and-answer sessions in the pulpit. To his great alarm he found that the Church was filled to bursting and the atmosphere evangelical in the highest degree. He described how the entire congregation *mimed* the words of each hymn, raising both hands to heaven at such words as 'arise', etc. A man in the congregation had turned to him and said: 'I found God here on

---

[1] Michael Mates, MP for Petersfield since October 1978.
[2] John Wheeler, MP for Paddington since 1979.

Wednesday of last week, do you think you will, today?' 'I, er, don't know,' bellowed Willie, miserably looking round.

He went on to recount how half way through they had a break and he and other distinguished visitors, clerics, etc. went up to a room above the vestry with the preacher. They knelt and various dignitaries started to recite prayers in turn. 'I suddenly realised with horror that it was moving round the circle and *I* was going to have to say a prayer.' Very splendidly, when it came to him, Willie simply mumbled, 'For what we are about to receive may the Lord make us truly thankful.'

The dinner wore on. Willie 'peaked' quite early, was interesting and sympathetic during the *prosciutto è melone*; grave during the salmon; muck-sweat and combative with the cheese; martyred and somnolent over the port. He said, interestingly, that he always asked himself where a process would end, rather than what would be the reaction when he started. This arose, apropos, when I asked why he has not sacked Gregory, the Chief Constable of the Yorkshire police who had made such a balls-up of the Ripper Case. Willie had told us that he thought Gregory was 'going', but no one must say anything in case that caused him to change his mind and fight.

Willie also said he was terribly worried about being unpopular in the Party, claimed he did not care about the Parliamentary Party, but hated losing the affection of the Party in the country.

All these observations were undertaken against a background of almost continuous and, I thought, rather ill-mannered interrogatories from Stanbrook – you're not strong enough, you have got no back-bone, you're not giving a lead, you don't mean it, you are always looking for a compromise, etc. etc. At least twice I feebly said that we were assembled for a congenial and informative dinner, not as an annex to our usual post-committee meetings. Finally, and presumably inflamed by this, Willie launched into a great bellowing rampage against the *Daily Mail*. What triggered it off was that I warned him that there would be a row today when it was revealed that senior officers of the Commission for Racial Equality had had their salaries doubled in the last three years and got a £50 a day attendance allowance. Willie alternately roared on about how David English's sole purpose was to bring down the Government – no, no, surely not, we all cried – or to force him personally to resign – more likely we all thought, but said nothing.

At intervals Willie yelled that he would 'resign his seat' (the wrong phrase, he cannot really have meant this, surely?) or lapsed into melancholia, chin slumped on his waistcoat, 'I did not allow this; I did not agree to this; *why* is it happening?' and so on (about the increase in salaries for the CRE).

Promptly, however, at two minutes to eleven, he snapped out of it, rose to his feet, literally in the middle of somebody else's sentence, delivered a short farewell homily and made his way out to his armoured black XJ6.

Cloisters   *Tuesday, 23 February*

At breakfast today Tristan Garel-Jones surprised me by saying that he thought Willie should be 'moved'. I think he may even have used the word 'sacked'. As a card-carrying wet and general softy on immigration etc. I would have thought he would be one of Willie's rearguard. These tides of opinion in the Party are mysterious. There is no doubt that uneasiness about Willie has spread right across all shades of opinion. I told him to speak to his Whip.

He then told me that the real dynamo of opposition to the present Government on the backbenches was not Ian Gilmour, still less Geoffrey Rippon, etc., but . . .

'Chris,' I said.

'Yes.'

He was rather crestfallen at my having spotted this. Apparently everyone shows Chris Patten their speeches, asks him what they ought to be doing at any given moment etc. Garel-Jones had the brilliant idea that Neil Marten[1] should be sacked and Chris Patten put in his place. He could not afford to refuse; he would be out of the country for half the year; and he would be saddled with a reputable 'wet' job, but in a sector where, officially, he has reservations. G-J told me that he would ask for a meeting with Jopling at which he would argue this. Actually, it is a very tidy solution and I will mention it to IG, with whom I am having dinner tonight. I told G-J that as he was meeting Jopling privately he might just as well state his reservations about Willie at the same time.

---

[1] Neil Marten, MP for Banbury since 1959; Minister for Overseas Development since 1979.

Lunched today with John Wells and Geoffrey Finsberg.[1] The meal started slowly; John Wells always poses as a buffoon – which he very emphatically is not. But after a bit of wine had flowed the conversation moved into that special level of confidentiality which one only enjoys in the Members' Dining Room (and which was very much in my mind when I posed yesterday's question).[2]

John Wells has always been aggrieved at his exclusion from the Deputy Speakership. The train of succession that leads to the Speaker's Chair is, as JW. said: 'a very stubby ladder' and there is little room for intruders. But the discussion between him and Geoffrey about possible developments was fascinating.

Apparently, the Peterborough leak that Mark Carlisle might be the next Speaker was a Whip's plant to break the news gently to Jack Weatherill that he would not succeed. Both agreed, however, that Carlisle could not do the job. Geoffrey – gloomy and ill-looking as always – produced the brilliancy that *Willie* should be made Speaker. 'He cannot stay where he is' (every evidence of how widespread is this view in the Party I find welcome). For a while, briefly, there would be Conservatives as both Speaker and Deputy Speaker. But after the next election Jack Weatherill would go to the Lords in the Dissolution Honours and Joel Barnett (another inspired suggestion of Geoffrey Finsberg) would become deputy.

We discussed the errors and omissions of the first, 1979, Cabinet. JW, who certainly does not stand on the right of the Party, said that the historic consequences of Airey's assassination could never be fully assessed. I told him that the original list was drawn up by the quartet, Atkins, Whitelaw, Thorneycroft and the PM. JW rightly said that if Airey had still been alive he would have corrected many of those original errors of judgement. I must say that he also said that if Iain Macleod had been alive in 1972 Ted would never have made such a cock-up of the Conservative Government of that period. But, of course, if he had been, then history would really have been totally different and that is now too distant from us to be hypothetical.

Now I am going to go in to hear the Chancellor make his Budget

---

[1] Geoffrey Finsberg, MP for Hampstead since 1970; Parliamentary Under-Secretary, Health and Social Security since 1981.
[2] AC asked about Members' wives being allowed into the Dining Room.

Statement which I don't doubt will be very dull as well as being crowded and smelly (the capacity of the air conditioning system is inadequate for a completely full chamber). I have drunk half a bottle of white burgundy in order to induce a benign doze.

Saltwood   *Wednesday, 10 March*

AGM in prospect – always a grisly affair, with its quota of pigging malcontents. A message from Anne: '. . . Mrs Easton wants to know if Mr Clark will take questions after his speech . . .' Ugh! No, of course not, if anyone wants to ask a question they can ask me personally. I am not going to stand up there and, in James's phrase, just let them throw things at me.

On the way back in the train I travelled with Joe Haines[1] (whom I had seen in a most interesting TV programme the previous night, on Whitehall briefings, though that, too, showed how much *out* of things one is really). JH was talking to a fat pompous man with a red face, very pleased with himself. I intruded on this conversation, relished letting out that I was an MP. But the whole incident brought home to me how *naked* one would be without those initials!

Would that I had opted for Folkestone! On the walks I confided to Jane, who said, more or less, even if one did make the wrong decision 'you're ten years too old, haven't got long to go' etc. This was particularly unfortunate as earlier in the walk I had been saying that I didn't feel old – apropos of my father who is very shifty and unpleasant though in perfect health. She didn't answer.

The one thing I dread, which I had visitations of this morning on waking is a *void* in which, purposeless and disappointed one becomes first pre, then actually cancerous.

---

[1] Joe Haines, chief leader writer of the *Daily Mirror* since 1978, had been Chief Press Secretary to Harold Wilson in opposition and as Prime Minister, 1969–76.

A bunch of Argentinians are horsing around in South Georgia. The thing started as an operation to retrieve 'scrap' (by what right do they go in there and remove 'scrap' anyway?) but they have now apparently hoisted the Argentine flag. I don't like this. If we don't throw them out, preferably shedding blood at the same time, they will try their hand in the Falklands.

Before dinner we had a kind of *ad hoc* meeting of the '92' at the far end of the Smoking Room. John Farr[1] has got a Question tomorrow, which is a Defence day. Quite narrowly drawn, on maritime air surveillance in the South Atlantic, but many of the boys are lining up to get in behind him. It's all down to that fucking idiot Nott, and his spastic 'Command Paper', which is effectively running down the entire Royal Navy so as to keep the soldiers in Rhine Army happy.

So let him answer the question. We know how easily he can get rattled. Quite good sport. Because it is as a result of his compliance that the Foreign Office can't 'negotiate' at all. There is no final contingency plan.

We are all of the same mind. We are the Henty boys – 'Deeds that Built the Empire', all that. But I am not sure how much support we can mobilise in the Party. 'Defence' to most colleagues only means The Cold War. They no longer think Imperially. I was saying, surely Margaret must sympathise? Nick Budgen sliced in – 'Don't bet on that, Alan. She is governed only by what the Americans want. At heart she is just a vulgar, middle-class Reaganite.'

We broke up ahead of the ten o'clock vote, but not before it was agreed that the strength of our feeling should be conveyed to the Chief [Michael Jopling]. Patrick Wall[2] and Julian Amery are to press for a statement tomorrow afternoon, from Atkins,[3] but the betting is that, remembering what we did to Nicky he will get one of his juniors to 'field' it.

---

[1] John Farr, MP for Harborough since 1959.
[2] Sir Patrick Wall, member of the Commons Select Committee on Defence since 1980.
[3] Humphrey Atkins, Lord Privy Seal since 1981.

Saltwood   *Wednesday, 24 March*

Yesterday went well. Notters funked the Question on air surveillance in the South Atlantic and delegated it to Jerry Wiggin, his most junior junior. And a little later we got our FCO Statement and, sure enough, Atkins dodged it and put up languid, amiable, and faintly Godwatch Richard Luce.[1] The annunciator screen conformed to the requisite minimalist note by signalling the Statement as *South Georgia (Incident)*.

Perhaps this wasn't as clever as they thought. When a Cabinet Minister is answering there are many who, conscious of the whip-on-the-bench taking notes, will not want to seem too 'unhelpful'. With a Junior, though, such deference is not expected. Indeed many of those questioning him will probably want (or may even have been ejected from) his job.

Both Jerry and Richard are Etonians. Jerry is piggy-eyed, a typical Library[2] bully; Richard is handsome and courteous. Typical *Pop*. Jerry gave the show away immediately, 'The South Atlantic is outside the NATO area'. In other words we (or at least the MoD) don't give a toss.

Half an hour later Richard was almost swamped. At least thirty people on their feet, bobbing up and down, including Jim Callaghan – a rare intruder – and Denis Healey. Richard stuck to his brief. A few slices of pure FCO-speak – 'I much regret that some of the action which has been taken has not created a helpful atmosphere ...', and he repeated the Argentine claim that the whole operation was 'commercial', although having to admit that the ship which carried the 'scrap-dealers' was a naval one!

I could see the whips fussing, leaning down the bench and whispering to Ministers. John Farr raised the usual Point of Order after an unsatisfactory answer and signalled his intention to raise the subject in an Adjournment Debate. We've got the whole thing opened now. Clearly the Labour Party are also indignant, and if she [Mrs Thatcher] doesn't get the Argentines out by next week there will be a major disturbance.

But no sign of Ian Gow. He should be trawling the corridors, 'taking the temperature'.

---

[1] Richard Luce, MP for Shoreham since 1974 (Arundel and Shoreham, 1971–74), Minister of State at the Foreign and Commonwealth Office since 1981.

[2] 'Library' is Etonian parlance for Prefect.

On this topic I am disillusioned, as I believe are many, with The Lady.

Cloisters   *Thursday, 25 March*

Today I went on *Question Time*. I was meant to sparkle. But, as I said to Jane when I drove her to Waterloo after we had lunched with Julian Amery and the Turkish Ambassador, I felt like King Harold who was forced to march south and fight the Battle of Hastings immediately after Stamford Bridge. Because Julian, as always, had supplied one with the most wonderful food and drink (Jane only just caught the 4.30 p.m. train) and by 5 p.m. I was feeling acid and sleepy. My original plan had been to 'bant' and then rest, taking a quick slug of vodka half-an-hour before going on the air.

As it was, by the time I arrived at the Greenwood Theatre Hospitality Room, I was sombre and withdrawn. I sat hunched in my place and ate nothing. A full glass of *appellation controlé* 'claret' sat in front of me. Robin Day radiated bonhomie; little Arthur Scargill, so soft spokenly amiable as to be almost feline; John Alderson, returning the clichés with a straight bat; and Patricia Rothwell, a handsome blonde in blue who shed at least fifteen years under transmission (unless you watched her neck). All shimmered and contributed in their different ways at the dinner. Poor Barbara and Liz[1] became increasingly concerned. Was I egg-bound with nerves, they must have been thinking. They had made a defective choice. The other panellists were going to have to 'carry' me.

As the hour approached people came back into the room at shorter and shorter intervals, announced that the audience was being suitably warmed up, etc. Eight minutes before we were due to go on my hand shot out and I drained the glass of *appellation controlé*. I looked round the room frantically like the Charles Addams boy.[2] 'Do you want

---

[1] Barbara Maxwell and Liz Elton, producers of *Question Time*.

[2] AC frequently refers to the famous strip cartoon by Charles Addams, which depicts an innocent little boy playing with his chemistry set. Accidentally he stumbles on some overpowering and magical potion that transforms him into a ravening and hirsute monster. By about the eighth frame, completely transformed, he is looking round desperately for the glass containing the remainder of the magic fluid. He finds it, drains it and has in some curious way exceeded the critical dose, reverting to being a polite and charming child. In the last frame the nursemaid, having heard a terrible commotion as he rampaged round the room, looks round the door and finds him sitting inoffensively, as she left him, with the chemistry set strewn on the floor.

something?' asked Liz. 'Yes, another glass of claret.' She rushed to the sideboard and opened a new bottle. Minutes later we were seated at the table and of course it really went quite all right, although the audience was a bit piggy. Within a few minutes I was completely at ease (although on seeing myself later I thought I was still too facially disturbed when emphasising a point; this is a fault of mine which I have noticed on previous occasions. I must somehow correct it).

Afterwards we walked through the audience and I was lionised by cuties who were very pretty and shy and done up to the nines (in case the camera should alight on them for an instant, of course). But I was glad that I was appreciated, as I had made one or two remarks to which ardent feminists might have taken exception. Barbara Maxwell made a special point of being nice and said how good I had been. It was nice to have a bit of Tory wit, she said. But she meant 'class' as Jane said when I repeated her comment.

Saltwood   *Friday, 26 March*

I was in the train to Plymouth when Neil Macfarlane[1] walked past. For some reason I did not recognise him instantly, but he patted me on the shoulder and said, though not with any sincerity: 'You were very good last night.' He then went on through to the buffet car. I don't (or didn't) especially like Neil Macfarlane and I was offensive to him on the floor of the House about two months ago when I questioned him about the subject of the World Cup team logo. On the way back he again tapped my shoulder and said: 'No, no, you were very good.' We exchanged a few pleasantries and he went back to his place.

Earlier, I had seen some reserved cards for four nearby, where I had left my luggage. When I returned after breakfast there sat Macfarlane, his rather common (but painted up) personal secretary and a bearded civil servant – who presumably keeps him straight, i.e. progressive, on such matters as apartheid in sport. Within a few minutes Macfarlane was again at my side and sat down. 'What do you make of Hillhead'

---

[1] Neil Macfarlane, MP for Sutton and Cheam since February 1974; Minister for Sport since 1981.

etc., etc. We soon got on to the subject of (what else?) the next reshuffle. He showed himself to have a much higher level of political intelligence than I had suspected and made some interesting suggestions.

Saltwood   *Saturday, 27 March*

It's blissful. Next week we have the Easter Adjournment Debates. Vote free, and the House is winding down for the short recess. I have been cutting the Bailey lawn and the greens are so yellowy-fresh. When the air is still, as all day it has been, every scent of spring claims ascendancy. The birds are busy, and fly low as they pop to their nest with building materials, or food for the sitting mate.

Cloisters   *Wednesday, 31 March*

Today I asked an offensive question about Jews. It is always thought to be rude to refer to 'Jews', isn't it? I remember that slightly triste occasion, watched from the gallery, of my father being inaugurated into the Lords and my rage at Sidney Bernstein, who was being ennobled on the same afternoon and would not take the Christian oath. As loudly as I could I muttered and mumbled about 'Jews' in order to discomfort his relations who were also clustered in the gallery. Unhappily, Col kept trying to correct me: 'No, no, old boy, you say Jew*ish*.'

I had hung it round the Foreign Secretary's visit to Israel and the issue of stamps depicting Irgun terrorists who shot Lord Moyne in 1948. The House took it quite well, a few guffaws. It is always fun to see just how far you can go with taboo subjects and titillate the House without actually shocking it.

I did some dictation with Alison and on our way upstairs I saw that the Prime Minister was giving a statement on the European Council Meeting. I wondered if I should go in and support her and, hearing a great deal of noise as I passed the doors into the Chamber, decided to do so. Again the Speaker called me, this time with an effective question, which I suspect pleased her, drawing attention to the effect of socialist policies in France, with the interest rate over 20 per cent, etc. etc. Perhaps my rage at not being called in the Trident Debate has somehow percolated back to the Speaker and he is trying to make amends before he gets my letter.

Roy Jenkins made his debut.[1] He speaks from the second row back and, of course, the moment he rose to his feet Dennis Skinner started firing abuse with the intention of disrupting him in the same way as he does with David Steel, as they share the same microphone. There was also a great deal of booing from our side, although quite a few toads were shushing because they wanted to listen to him.

'ORDER,' bellowed the Speaker. He then delivered a personal warning to the Member for Bolsover [Dennis Skinner], saying that he would not tolerate interruptions from his position.

Thereafter, Jenkins, with excessive and almost unbearable gravitas, asked three heavy statesman-like non-party-political questions of the PM. I suppose he is very formidable, but he was so portentous and long-winded that he started to lose the sympathy of the House about half way through and the barracking resumed. The Lady replied quite brightly and freshly, as if she did not particularly know who he was, or care.

Saltwood   *Friday, 2 April*

I was due to go down to Plymouth this morning. But when I looked in at Dean's Yard to collect correspondence for signing in the train the whole room seemed to know that the Falkland Islands had been invaded. Delighted to cancel, I made my way over to the Chamber; but somewhat apprehensive as Atkins was due to make a statement at 11 a.m.

No point in hanging about. I got back to Sandling at six o'clock. 'We've lost the Falklands,' I told Jane. 'It's all over. We're a Third World country, no good for anything.'

She is used to my suddenly taking the *apocalyptic* view. Didn't say much. I ate some brown toast and crab apple jelly and, it being such

---

[1] As Leader of the Social Democratic Party; he had just won the Glasgow Hillhead by-election, to return to the Commons after a break of six years.

a lovely evening, went for a meander down the valley. I am so depressed by what I heard today – the shuffling and fudging, the overpowering impression of timidity and incompetence. Can it have felt like this in the Thirties, from time to time, on those fine weekends when the dictators, Hitler and Musso, decided to help themselves to something – Durazzo, Memel, Prague – and all we could do was wring our hands and talk about 'bad faith'? I have a terrible feeling that this is a step change, down, for England. Humiliation for sure and, not impossible, military defeat. An apparition that must have been stalking us, since we were so dreadfully weakened at Passchendaele I suppose, for the last sixty-five years.

Cloisters   *Saturday, 3 April*

I had hardly got home last night when I realised that the House would be so crowded that I would have to be there to book my place before 8 a.m. So I rose early – it was another glorious day with a thick heat haze – and took the 6.17 a.m. train. By 8.30 a.m. the Chamber was a snow storm of cards, like Budget Day.

I had spent the previous evening trying to convene a joint meeting of the Defence and Foreign Affairs Committees to discuss the question. For reasons of protocol I had advised Bob Boscawen and he, predictably, tried to talk me out of it, said it would be better to have a meeting 'after Margaret had sat down.' I knew very well what this meant. It was an attempt to shift all the most pugnacious Tory MPs out of the Chamber up into Room 10.

I would have none of it. Buck was unobtainable, presumably out drinking somewhere. Little Winston, following his new appointment of what must be the tinkiest job in the whole Government – that of 'presenting' Government defence policy under the aegis of Central Office – was somewhat spaced out in his response. However, I managed to get hold of a few like-minded colleagues and we had agreed to assemble in Committee Room 10 at 10.15 a.m.

Later, Bob Boscawen had rung back and said that he had arranged for Victor Goodhew (an old whip and very 'reliable' in crises) to chair the meeting. In fact when I got up to Committee Room 10 this morning I was gratified to find it extremely full and the panic that my moves had set in train was reflected in the fact that no lesser than the Chief Whip had been brought in to 'listen'.

Jopling led off by making a soft-sell appeal for (need one say) loyalty, absence of recrimination and so forth. This did not go down very well. Speaker after speaker expressed their indignation at the way the Foreign Office had handled things. Many were critical of John Nott. Much the best speech, and the only one that elicited the banging of desks, was by Robert Cranborne. Expressionless, Michael Jopling took notes. Then, fortified by our mutual expressions of empathy, we trooped down to the Chamber for Prayers.

The place was absolutely packed. Julian Amery, who very seldom puts a card in, had to sit on the stairs in the gangway between the Government bench and the lower block.

First, Humphrey Atkins made a clear, short, but unsatisfactory statement explaining why he had misled (unintentionally, of course) the House about the timing of various announcements yesterday. This certainly did not make The Lady's task any easier as it set the tone, giving further corroboration, as it were, to the general impression of almost total Government incompetence which was to pervade the debate.

The Lady led off. At first she spoke very slowly but didactically, not really saying much. But then, when she got to a passage, 'we sent a telegram ...', the whole Opposition started laughing and sneering. She changed gear and gabbled. Far too fast she rattled off what was clearly a Foreign Office brief, without any reclamatory, or even punitive action.

This was depressing for the Conservative benches who were already in a grumpy and apprehensive mood. Michael Foot followed with an excellent performance. Fortunately, for those of us who wished to thump the Argentine, the fact that they are a fascist Junta makes it very much easier to get Labour support – and my God we are going to need this over the ensuing weeks as, apparently, it will take twenty-one days for the flotilla to arrive on station.

I was tense and had written an excellent speech, provocative and moving. But as the debate wore on I realised that it might, curiously, have been inappropriate and was glad not to have been called. Although I did intervene when provoked beyond endurance by Ray Whitney's toadying defence of the Foreign Office, the weasel words in which he still and most ill-judgedly plugged the sell-out argument which we used to hear all the time from Ridley.

The debate wore on with Bernard Braine[1] turning in a robustious performance. One of his great ham displays of indignation. So splutteringly bombastic that in a curious kind of way he makes the House, that most cynical of audiences, pay attention.

Poor old Notters on the other hand was a disaster. He stammered and stuttered and gabbled. He faltered and fluttered and fumbled. He refused to give way; he gave way; he changed his mind; he stood up again; he sat down again. All this against a constant roaring of disapproval and contempt. I have seen the House do this so often in the past. Like the pack that they are they always smell the blood of a wounded animal and turn on it. I saw them last do it to Nicky Fairbairn in January, and once this mood is abroad it requires a superhuman display of courage and fortitude to overcome it.

The coup de grâce was delivered by David Owen, who had spoken earlier. He forced Nott to give way and he told him that if he could not appreciate the need to back negotiations with force he did not deserve to remain one minute as Secretary of State.

After the debate we all trailed, yet again, up to Committee Room 10. This time Carrington and Nott were both present. Thirty-three Members asked questions and, with the exception of three heavy-weight duds (Patten, Kershaw and van Straubenzee), every single person was critical. I asked a long, sneering question about the failure of our intelligence.[2] I made a point of addressing it to Peter Carrington whom, with my very long memory, I had not forgiven for snubbing me at a meeting on Afghanistan in December 1980, in the Grand Committee Room. As my irony developed, people in the Committee Room started sniggering, but poor Notters was still so rattled and blubbery that he leant across and answered it, while Carrington sat staring at me in haughty silence.

---

[1] Sir Bernard Braine, MP for SE Essex since 1955 (Billericay, 1950–55).
[2] After saying that he was not alone in the Committee in feeling deep dissatisfaction with the answer given about our intelligence reports, AC went on: 'The questions I would like to put to the Foreign Secretary are these: First, do we maintain a diplomatic mission in Buenos Aires? Secondly, if we do maintain such a mission is there anyone charged with collating and verifying intelligence material? Third, if there is such a person does he not have a duty to transmit this material to London? Finally, if he could find no material that was, in his judgement, worth repeating, could he not at least operate a press clipping service and send us extracts from the Argentine newspapers?'

This meeting finally broke up just before 4 p.m. I still had had no early morning tea, no breakfast, no coffee and no lunch, but felt wonderful, full of adrenalin. What an exciting and historic day. I could not go home as I was booked to appear on *Newsnight* at 10 p.m. Ravenously hungry I went to the curry restaurant, but it was closed. I was lucky to find a plastic carton on the back seat of the Chevrolet in which there were some old sandwiches and an orange which Jane had given me for a train journey to Plymouth. I drove into St James's Park and ate them and fell asleep.

Cloisters   *Monday, 5 April*

I am certain that there has been collusion between the Foreign Office and the Argentine over this whole affair. Why were there no casualties among the Royal Marines? Seventy-five determined men, as the Battle of Arnhem demonstrated (to take but one example), can hold off greatly superior numbers just using small arms and bazookas from drains and cellars in territory that they know. I have started the rumour that last night I rang Enoch, Julian Amery, and the *Guardian* – that there were sealed orders to the Governor to be opened when the invasion started, and that these orders were for him to declare an immediate cease fire. I believe this to be true. I also believe that unofficial representations were made by the Foreign Office to the Argentine indicating that all would be well provided no British blood were shed. And what is more, I believe that these unofficial contacts may still be taking place.

Accordingly, when I arrived in the House this morning at 9.30 a.m. I tabled three priority written questions on these three issues and sent copies to *The Times*, the *Telegraph* and the P.A. I then went along to James Callaghan, who had asked to see me privately in his room. I have a rapport with Jim. Nick Budgen says that he is an intellectual admirer of mine and, quite by chance, he has been in the Chamber when I have made three of my best speeches – on Blunt, on Bobby Sands and on the NATO commitment. I also sent him a copy of my Fortress Britain lecture, to which he replied at length. He was, as always, compos, amiable and clear-headed (it is in one's 60s, isn't it, that one starts to draw dividends from not consuming alcohol in middle age). But there is a certain detachment, impersonality, behind those powerful spectacles. I suppose this may be something that comes with the recollection of absolute authority – although of course little Wislon does not possess this at all.

Callaghan talked interestingly about the Falklands. He said it was the most frightful situation and fraught with danger, that it was important to find a way out, short of a full scale amphibious assault with all the casualties that might accompany it. He was gloomy about the long-term prospects about defending the Islands.

I tried to correct him about this and said that the Labour Party would rapidly back away totally from its position of support on Saturday. But he did agree that it was essential to punish the Argentines, and to sink some of their ships before negotiations restarted. He was very critical of the way the Foreign Office had handled the whole affair, said the whole administration was riddled with incompetence; the MOD was a mess, nobody there could think creatively.

He said that when he was Prime Minister, every week he had a briefing at which, on a Mercator projection, every major ship in the Royal Navy was shown, and every tanker. Apparently, this was an old practice dating back from Victorian times so that the Government would know at any moment the level of naval flexibility that they commanded. But the Civil Service finally got rid of it with the 'European commitment'.

After a bit Callaghan asked me to advise him on what he should say in his speech in the debate on Wednesday. This could be very important as he will be making a speech on a subject of which he has clear knowledge and a proven record of success, but from a position of objectivity as a senior statesman. Plainly he has to counsel against too bellicose an attitude, but I have got to make sure that his nerve holds and he includes a strong recommendation for a punitive strike to establish a grounding of strength on which to base negotiations. I will give this some thought and draft a memorandum for him. I will see him on Wednesday.

When I got down to the Members' Lobby from Callaghan's room there was a rumour running wild that Carrington had been sacked and sure enough it was confirmed a couple of minutes later. Carrington *and* Atkins and Richard Luce! A clean sweep. God knows what the consequences of this will be, but they cannot be all bad as Carrington's influence was grossly appeasing and the collusive element in the Foreign Office (see above) has now been decapitated. Party feeling seems to indicate that Francis Pym will become Foreign Secretary, but there are thrills – and spills – in store.

Little Patrick Cormack is chubbily rolling around the place, very pleased with himself and thinking he has done it all single-handed. As a matter of fact, I think it was the leader in *The Times* that finally tipped the scales, or was that, in fact, prompted by an inspired leak? These days, when intrigue and treachery are positively Neronian in their dimension, it is not always easy to put events in causative sequence.

The wets, of course, are livid and discomforted, they are taking it out on poor old Notters, saying he should be sacked, that it was intolerable that he should have survived, etc. etc. But Notters, I fear, comes later. His turn will be after the failure, or abortion, of the naval strike.

After lunch I went to 'Rab's' memorial service. Stuffed with politicians. Guess who was down to read the lesson – Peter Carrington. Listed, of course, as Her Majesty's most honourable Secretary of State ... etc. To do him credit he read the text with great aplomb. He, too, has large and impenetrable spectacles that conceal the emotions of the soul.

Very much less sleek was poor Richard Luce, who sat immediately in front of me in the stalls, grey and dishevelled, with a glazed look and deep eye ditches. Cancroid indeed, like the wretched Notters on television yesterday and, as Jane rightly spotted, as having auto-activated an instantaneous malignant condition.

After Questions there was a Statement about commandeering vessels and the trade embargo. Already the first odours of appeasement began to waft round the Chamber. Members on both sides were muttering and shuffling about commercial contracts, deliveries, banks, etc. etc.

On the way up to the Committee Corridor I was caught by Norman St John-Stevas, who could hardly contain himself with glee. 'Have you ever seen such a Government? So many nonentities. It is really pathetic, it would be farcical if it were not tragic ...'

He, too, was heavily anti-Nott, said it was extremely dangerous to have a Secretary of State for Defence, someone whose whole career depended on a successful assertion of martial vigour. I said it was not only the Secretary of State whose career depended on such a showing, but the whole existence of the Government, and indeed of the Party. St J-S said not necessarily so.

Well, he would say that wouldn't he?

Cloisters *Tuesday, 6 April*

At the Foreign Affairs Committee today. Feeling in the Party is still very strong, but already one or two predictable weasels are poking their snouts out of the undergrowth. That sanctimonious creep, van Straubenzee, made a long and unctuous speech – I think he actually 'wrung' his hands as he regretted 'a certain jingoistic tendency.'

Cloisters *Wednesday, 7 April*

People who should know better are striding up and down the Smoking Room Corridor telling anyone whom they can apprehend that the *Invincible* is sailing without her radar operative; that many of her weapons systems have already been moved; that the Sea Harrier cannot land on deck in a rough sea; that many of the ships in the Task Force have defective power trains, etc. etc.

It is monstrous that senior Tories should be behaving in this way. It is only on occasions such as this that the implacable hatred in which certain established figures hold the Prime Minister can be detected. They oppose Government policy whatever it is – they would oppose free campari-sodas for the middle classes if they thought The Lady was in favour. They are within an ace, they think, of bringing her Government down. If by some miracle the expedition succeeds they know, and dread, that she will be established for ever as a national hero.

So, regardless of the country's interest they are determined that the expedition will not succeed. The greater the humiliation of its failure, the more certain will be the downfall of The Lady's Government, the greater the likelihood of a lash-up coalition, *without* a general election, to fudge things through for the last eighteen months of this Parliament.

At the moment the House of Commons is very determined. One angle from which that determination can be attacked is via the so-called 'expert' opinion, which is that we just do not have the equipment to launch and sustain an expedition of this magnitude.

Some others are openly going round making the comparison with the Sicilian Expedition that led to the downfall of the Athenian City State. Sometimes, I must admit, this analogy occurs to me also, although I keep my thoughts to myself. If we are going to go, I feel, let us go out in a blaze – then we can all sit back and comfortably become a nation of pimps and ponces, a sort of Macao to the European continent.

Saltwood   *Good Friday, 9 April*

Pleasantly tired after mowing the *whole* Inner Bailey in one swoop – four hours dead. Daffodils out, but cold – though Saltwood just starting to 'smile'.

As I said on the walks to Jane: 'It's even a fudge; two to one a disaster and The Lady resigning from the despatch box; three to one a naval victory and the bunting round Nelson column.'

Cloisters   *Wednesday, 14 April*

Yet another Falklands Debate today.

I took the 07.19 train from Sandling – how lovely it is in the early morning. *Why* don't we, in the spring and summer, follow the birds turning in at dusk and rise with the ever-recurring beauty of the dawn? Train late, taxi to House, and wrote out note of encouragement to The Lady (Jane's idea, and a very good one). I had to do a second draft as I spelt Britannia with two t's, spastically. I walked with the envelope up to Downing Street and handed it to the policeman outside Number 10. A few mangy photographers with heavy beards and leather bum-freezer jackets hung around the other side of the barriers, but very few members of the public.

Then back to St Stephen's Gate, where I met the TSW crew.

Slightly unsatisfactory, as they were making a programme about the 'impact' (standard W. Morning Gasp word) of the Falklands crisis on the defence cuts. But it was not going to be screened until 29th, so much of what one was going to say could be overtaken by the march of events.

I did not take to the pasty, weasel-eyed, cortisone-cheeked 'interviewer'. He had a clipboard under his arm with various hand-written notes on it. 'What are those?' I asked. 'They were my questions to David Owen.' But when I started reading them he went pouty, said: 'I never allow politicians to see my questions.' 'But you said these were questions for David Owen, not for me.' Stupid pompous little prick. Anyone who uses the word 'politician', not themselves being one, means it as an insult.

The interview was held in the Lords' Gardens. Passers-by peered curiously and some hung about. He was a very unskilful interrogator and kept clumsily trying to 'trap' me into making critical remarks about the Government's defence policy. Naturally, I was quite equal to this and I fear some of my answers may have been tinged with irony, or, worse, sarcasm. On and on it dragged. Plainly it was going to be cut to pieces before it was shown to the public and I am afraid my replies will appear mulish and inconsequential.

Immediately, on returning to St Stephen's I was picked up by the Swiss Television crew. A much nicer lot, although the bearded guru who conducted the interview did put a number of awkward questions, such as about The Lady's future if things go wrong, and so on, which are not easy to answer. He winced a bit when I asked about a fee, but said he would telephone Andrew at the Chalet so that our friends in Zermatt could watch it.

After this I dictated answers to letters about the crisis, with one exception *universally* supportive, and went up for an early lunch in the Members' Dining Room. Beaumont-Dark, Steen, John Spence[1] and Ian Laing, the trite Scottish Whip (whom Michael Ancram asked me to sign for at Pratt's and whom I subsequently saw had accumulated very few additional names).

Colleagues were kind about my performance on *Newsnight* on Monday. I mentioned in the most cautious way David Howell's appearance on *Question Time* the previous week, which had – rightly – annoyed Jane so much. The effect was instantaneous; 'absolutely

---

[1] John Spence, MP for Thirsk and Malton since 1974 (Sheffield Heeley 1970–74).

disgraceful,' 'monstrous,' 'that man is useless', 'ought to be sacked'.

Beaumont-Dark, who had finished his meal, rose with a flourish saying that Howell had made a mess of the pit closures, a balls-up of the heavy lorries, and was so ineffective as to be unfit to hold any official position in the Party.

Who should then soft-spokenly materialise, but instantly, and take the empty chair but David Howell! There was an uneasy silence. Poor David. What very thin wrists and stooping gait and pale – but not clear – skin he has. Suddenly he turned to me and said: 'I ran into a branch of the Alan Clark fan club the other night . . .'. He was talking, of course, about Barbara Maxwell and Liz Elton who had told him that I was the best Tory backbencher they had found for ages, etc.

I left the Dining Room early. Anglia Television want me to do an hour long debate with Tam Dalyell on Friday night. Every single day has been busted to pieces by 'appearances' on the media. But I have to do it. I feel passionately, really deeply, about this issue. And I am fortunate indeed that I am getting so much opportunity to express my feelings instead of just grinding my teeth in the dark.

In the Members' Cafeteria and there was Tam, gabbling and dribbling and in the most frightful state. He has actually gone slightly round the bend about the whole thing, most extraordinary. He said that the *Hermes* was suffering from mechanical trouble and her propellers were seizing. Wishful thinking, I suspect.

I could not stay very long as I had a Prayer Card in. Once again the place was a snow storm of Prayer Cards, worse than the Budget. The debate was a fairly placid business. The Lady had recovered her composure and there was a level of unanimity on all sides. This is a relief as I had feared from trends that I had perceived in last Wednesday's debate that the House might be weakening; good-boys all trying to get in on the act with their disparate compromise solutions. But, other than a dotty plea for passive resistance by poor old Anthony Meyer,[1] and a ritual vote loser by Judith Hart,[2] the House remained firm.

There was a moment towards the end of the debate when, as usual, many colleagues had not been able to get in. Ian Lloyd rose from his place next to me and delivered a 'set' speech, referring to copious notes; 'reading' in other words. He rambled on with a positive *plethora* of quotations, mostly from the classics, Aristotle, Scipio Africanus,

---

[1] Anthony Meyer, MP for West Flint since 1970.
[2] Judith Hart, MP for Lanark since 1959.

Ludicrous Sextus, etc. Frequently he both shouted and spoke at eleven times dictation speed; he stumbled over his words and, more entertainingly, transposed the authors and subjects of his learned allusions: '. . . as Lucius Tertius remarked when he was cornered in the Appian hills by Scipio – no, I mean as Scipio replied when Lucius Tertius confronted him . . .' etc.

Immediately on my other side sat Rhodes James. How Rhodes James has diminished in stature and esteem over the last eighteen months! I suppose it dates from that absurd moment when it came out over the PA tape that he was 'considering' resigning as a PPS. Anyway, RJ also wanted to speak and was getting crosser and crosser as Ian used up all the time. On each occasion, and they were many, that the House was treated to a quotation from the classics Rhodes James groaned very loudly, and rolled his eyes.

At first Ian had completely 'lost' the House, which chattered freely to itself, cracked jokes, 'where are you having dinner?', that kind of thing. But slowly the House realised that this was in a curious way a kind of Parliamentary occasion. It was so ludicrous. The poor Lady, who had sat in throughout the debate, looked attentively down at Ian the whole time he was speaking. What can have been going through her head?

At five o'clock I went across and did a piece for Anne Perkins for BBC West. She tried to catch me out with a trick question about what would happen to The Lady if the expedition failed but, in boxing parlance, I 'got on my bicycle' and avoided it. Then at six I met Bruce Anderson of *Weekend World* and we went down to Annie's. We were meant to be having an intimate chat, but we were hailed by Simon Hoggart and two other journalists, whose names I don't know, but I am sure very important (one I think works on the *Express*). There was a good deal of general chat, some of it quite funny. In the middle *The Guardian*'s Julia Langdon came over and up to me, and I mean *up* to me, and said: 'We were having an argument about how old you were.'

'Oh, really,' I am both pleased and disconcerted by this.

'Yes, Ian (Aitken) said you looked so *ravaged* for someone in his forties. I said you were in your fifties. How old are you?'

'Sixty,' I answered. Off she went. She and Elinor Goodman (*Financial Times*) are quite decorative but really no good as political correspondents. You have to have an intuitive feel for the subject, really to be a politician *manqué*, to be any good.

Later Bruce and I repaired to one of the sofas and he gave me a great spiel about how the Cabinet was full of nonentities, how important it was for her to bring in some people 'larger-than-life'.

'For instance it is disgraceful that you have not got a job . . .'

'I quite agree,' I answered.

'. . . and Chris Patten and Nick Budgen!'

On the whole his judgement was quite good. He really is a politician *manqué* and for all I know will become a politician *réussi*. He wants to have lunch with me next week. But what is the point? He really is further out of things than I am. There is no use in constructing castles in the sand.

After the debate I walked back, once again, to Anne Perkins' office. Fortunately, she, herself, had left but some little chappie from BBC Wales interviewed me, and Anthony Meyer.

Let us just hope that all this will have a cumulative effect of conditioning people's thoughts. I had hoped to get back to Saltwood tonight, but have been booked for the BBC World Service at 9.30 a.m. and even then I cannot get away because I am to do a CBS live broadcast at lunchtime to go by satellite all over the United States.

Cloisters   *Wednesday, 21 April*

At a meeting of the Defence Committee today Michael Mates dwelt at length on the prospects of very heavy casualties and how we ought to warn the public, etc. I notice that now it looks as if we really are going to recapture the Islands, mount a full-scale assault, the antis have shifted their ground from urging the wisdom of negotiation and are trying desperately to counter-attack increasingly enthusiastic public opinion polls, hoping that if they can get the public uneasy enough, someone, in the words of a ludicrous headline in today's *Times* filed from Washington, will cry 'stop'.

Francis Pym[1] made a very unsatisfactory Statement referring to 'arrangements' for the Argentine withdrawal; the 'interim' administration that would take its place and so forth. In answer to a question following the Statement he said that we would not shoot while negotiations were still going on. Immediately afterwards, groups of

---

[1] Appointed Foreign Secretary on 5 April.

MPs were standing about in the Lobby, grumbling and speculating about what all this meant.

I was talking to Anthony Bevins of *The Times* (who interpreted it very bearishly) when the annunciator screen announced: STATE-MENT FALKLAND ISLANDS FRANCIS PYM. We all pounded back into the Chamber, but it was already over. Apparently Francis had reappeared to make a 'correction', saying that he did *not* exclude the possibility of shooting while negotiations were still in train, and then disappeared again behind the Chair.

We dispersed again. The whole Party is very prickly and unsure of itself. I dread a sell out. I am sure we are being slowly set up for one.

There was an ad hoc meeting of the '92' in Committee Room 18 in the Upper Corridor. 'Slatted', as the Americans say (I intend going to Washington tomorrow), for 7.15 p.m. On the way up I fell into step with John Browne, the handsome, but somewhat indecisive, young right-wing MP for Winchester. He complained about Tony Kershaw, who has been weakening by the minute in his television exposures, talking about ultra-short, or nominal periods of joint administration, before sovereignty is handed over.

'Why is he a member of the "92" '? 'He is a Whip's heavy,' I said. 'A mole, reports everything.' John Browne was quite put out. The meeting was assiduous, our mutual suspicions and paranoia feeding on itself. Poor old Patrick Wall, deaf and scatty, lost control of the meeting early, as he always does, and people were arguing among themselves, cross-talking etc.

I gave my view that the old Foreign Office lobby were still live and kicking, that they had already suborned a number of Party heavies (such as Straubenzee and Mates) to state the appeasement case in its various forms and that the situation was being aggravated by a number of people who saw it as an opportunity to do down the Prime Minister. I know I said that I was not happy about the Whips' role in this, although I cannot remember the actual phrases I used.

Kershaw, who was sitting opposite me, looked expressionless. Bob Dunn, who is quite percipient and *acutely* paranoiac about the 'left' in the Party, the Whips' conspiracy to retard everyone on the right, etc., suggested that a delegation by-pass the Chief Whip and go direct to the Chairman of the Party (who is of course a member of the inner, or 'War', Cabinet).[1]

---

[1] Cecil Parkinson, MP for Hertfordshire South since 1974 (Enfield West 1970–74).

Bob is Cecil's PPS and said that he would organise it for immediately after the vote. John Browne and others suggested that I should go with the delegation, which it was eventually agreed would also include Bill Clark, Jill Knight, and, of course, poor old Paddy Wall.

We went up to Cecil's room after the vote. No one, including the PPS, could make the lights work so we sat in the gloaming illuminated only by the desk light with a heavy green shade, which added to the sense of conspiracy.

Eventually Cecil arrived, somewhat spoiling his clean-limbed specification with a velvet dinner jacket. I spoke third and, I hope, lucidly. Cecil, I am glad to say, was *extremely* reassuring and replied most hawkishly. He more or less said that we would be going into South Georgia within the next couple of days, as there was not the slightest chance of our agreeing to any arrangement that left an Argentinian presence on the Islands. But at the end he said, something, something, 'as an old Whip I cannot listen to criticism of the Whips . . . etc,' and I smelt trouble.

Cloisters   *Thursday, 22 April*

Having boasted a great deal to people, including Plymouth Sound, that I am off to Washington today, '. . . with Francis Pym,' I cannot get out of it, however much I dread the journey. It is the usual story. If anyone can guarantee safe arrival and return one would spend all one's money on air fares. But I don't just hate taking off and landing: I loathe *going along*. And 'going along' at twice the speed of sound must be more hazardous than 'going along' sub-sonically.

Just as I was getting into my car outside Brooks's I saw Algy Cluff,[1] still very foppish, with a *very* thin golden and platinum watch chain, although having seen his net worth reduced by about £18 million in the last year. I told him I was off to Washington. He said that there was plenty of oil around the Falklands and he had the technology to extract it, '. . . if other disputes could be settled.' Good may yet come out of this dispute, because if we can really assert our strength there we should be able to participate in the exploitation of resources without being threatened or disturbed.

---

[1] Algy Cluff, founder of Cluff Oil, proprietor of *The Spectator* since 1981.

I did a couple of radio shows. Unusually, Robin Day appeared to be hosting *World at One*, and then hitched a ride in a taxi to Heathrow. The Concorde lounge carried an agreeable aroma of riches, whether personal or corporate. Three little cheeky-chappies with Mediterranean accents and red coats dispensed unlimited refreshments. I drank a glass of champagne and orange juice and thought of dear dotty Alistair Londonderry, who always has this drink set down in front of him, without having to ask for it, wherever he goes.

Concorde on take-off is everything that has been claimed for it. The feeling of superabundant power is absolutely overwhelming, fields and houses became minuscule dots and patches in the space of a few minutes. The aircraft was full of pressmen and commentators.

Right up in the front, head bowed over his papers so that no one should try and 'lobby' him, sat John Louis.[1] He now looks really alarmingly like the hit-man in *Bullitt*, who furtively prowled through the hospital in his raincoat in search of a badly injured witness who had to be eliminated.

I chatted with Simon Glenarthur.[2] Although rather chinless and stereotyped in appearance, he must be quite tough as he flew in the Army Air Corps and is a helicopter pilot with British Airways. He sometimes comes to the Defence Committee and is very hard line. Due to a muddle by the PA some people, including Robin Day, had thought he was Lord Glen*amara* (poor, nasty old Ted Short, of my opposition days) and the Concorde lounge had been plastered with urgent messages asking him to get in touch with correspondents who did not bother to conceal their disappointment when they found they were talking to a Scottish aristocrat instead of a Labour life peer.

About half way through the flight I strolled down towards the tail and had a quick word with Francis. As I parted the curtains to go into his cabin I felt like Ernst Strobe, when, as Goldfinger, he bobbed out and surprised James Bond and his girl when they thought they had escaped in the last reels of the film. The Foreign Secretary must have thought that it was really *too* much that I, who had been endlessly plugging the hard line on this dispute since the day it started, should now be pursuing him across the Atlantic.

Simon Glenarthur had arranged with the captain that I should go

---

[1] John J. Louis, United States Ambassador at the Court of St James, since 1981, previously a leading American businessman (director Johnson Wax etc).
[2] Lord Glenarthur, Government Whip, House of Lords.

through and sit on the Concorde jump seat for our landing at Dulles
Airport. It was with some relief that I saw that Dulles lies in flat
scrubland. No special problems on over-run or, indeed, even on
engine failure at take-off. Surprisingly rapidly the white runway
changed in size from a laundry name tape, to a ruler, to a roller towel,
to the cloth at a long banqueting table; all the time holding steady
and dead centre in the 'V' shaped windscreen of the great airliner –
the supersonic nose had been 'drooped' at 18,000' as we started our
approach.

The captain, Massie by name, was incredibly bland and unflappable.
I suspect also highly competent, as he had been given the wrong glide
angle to lock into his computer and we came in 350' too high.
But he overrode it manually and still managed, by using one 'g' or
better on both brakes and reverse thrust, to turn the aircraft at the
first runway exit. The pasty and rather common co-pilot, on the
other hand, was demonstrably nervous and lip-licking throughout
descent.

We had been told to look out for a 'young man' who would be
holding up a notice for us. He seemed clueless, explained he was a
part-time journalist, just 'helping out' the Conference while working
in Washington on a project. There are as many illiterate students
hanging around Washington dabbling in journalism and hoping to
uncover the new Watergate as there are cuties in Hollywood seeking
to make the big-time show.

Our guide drove in excess of the speed limits in a battered Honda
with Kansas plates which, he said, belonged to a 'friend'. Something
told me that the 'friend' did not realise that his car was being used for
this purpose.

When we arrived at the Dirksen building, a sort of American
Norman Shaw, full of Senators' offices, where the Conference was
being held, it was twenty-past four London time and some strong
Indian tea and buttered toast would have been welcome. But in
Washington it was only twenty-past ten and a bright sun blazed down
on the blossoms. Our guide repeated his earlier suggestion that we
should go to a hotel room and relax a bit.

'I DO NOT want to "relax",' I snapped. 'I want to go to the
Conference.'

Our guide wanted to get shot of us. What did we do with our
cases? We humped them up the great sham marble steps and through
the double portals of the Dirksen. An armed security man examined

them. 'Who do you work for?' he asked suspiciously. 'The British Government,' I answered. Unexpectedly this induced respect rather than hostility.

On the sixth floor we found the Conference. Crawling with candidates, both English and American, a smattering of Senators. Two very big MPs, Mark Carlisle and Peter Emery, were booming away. Lady Emery had accompanied her husband, ludicrously airs-and-graces, looking like an ultra-tall cross between the Queen and Nanny's niece.

Saltwood   *Wednesday, 5 May*

Now nearly four weeks into the Falklands 'Crisis', and for the last three of them I have been almost ceaselessly occupied. *Every single day* I have done at least one TV or radio broadcast, sometimes as many as three. On two of the Sundays a Citroen Pallas has been sent down (*plus* a 'backup' car!) to take me up to the studio and back again, for the direct, grand, bit of Brian Walden's *Weekend World* – itself the grandest of all the current affairs programmes. Hailed as man-of-the-week in the *Daily Express*.

Westminster   *Tuesday, 11 May*

Still the Falklands crisis drags on, stimulating, but heavily demanding in time, now superimposed on the galloping pressures of openings and the unsettling, evocative, nostalgic yearnings that fine weather always induces.

Today woken very early by Angus – sun right round and low, still on the doorhandle of our bedroom. 6.05 a.m. Let him out, shuffled across in my pyjamas to pump and started it first pull; next through to Barbican walk to ensure that water was glog-gulping out into the moat. Made tea; we talked about the huge accumulating demands of openings.

Walked dogs. Grass now dry enough to walk under the railway bridge, rootling about in the shippen, and back along the railway hedgerow. Newspapers fairly non-committal – no developments though much disturbing 'informed' comment by Peter Jenkins [*The Guardian*] about pressure for a settlement being applied to The Lady.

Saltwood   *Monday, 17 May*

This is *the* crisis. I am lucky to be in the House for it. Lucky, too, to be 'recognised' and allowed to 'achieve'. When one has seen this through, *then* one will have discharged one's duty.

Saltwood   *Tuesday, 1 June*

Back in the Great Hall. How lovely, its appeal this time of year hasn't altered for me in the slightest. Today spent lounging, sploshing, swimming – pool 72°.

Last night I left Saltwood at 2 in the morning to be driven up to the ABC studios for a night chat show, coast-to-coast on the Falklands (the drive back leaving London at 4.40, getting back to Saltwood after 6 a.m.). I have long since lost count of the number of appearances I have made on the Falklands – three times on Brian Walden alone, since the 'crisis' started.

And *what* a crisis! When I think back to the state of utter depression when I got out of the train at Sandling on 2 April – on trial, complete and utter humiliation; I even contemplated emigrating. Now not only have we redeemed everything that was at stake then, but one has advanced immeasurably in self-esteem and in the status accorded to us by the whole world.

And I *did* play my part in this – whether greater or lesser than if I had been a junior minister I don't know – I suspect the former. I was almost immediately recognised by the media – the 'leader of the war party' (Alan Watkins).

Terry Coleman came down to interview me. I had been looking forward to it.[1] But the more I think of it the more of a disaster it was. Impossible to charm him. Totally humourless. Didn't ask any of the

---

[1] Coleman, whose interviews appeared in *The Guardian*, had some years before interviewed AC's father.

right questions. Kept trying to push me into a corner about 'National Socialism'. I tried to explain to him about patriotism. No good. He wasn't interested in politics. He was heavily-built, totally unforthcoming, didn't thank Jane for tea, or me for a silver mug of iced Pol Roger – or for my time, come to that.

Saltwood   *Saturday, 5 June*

Financial dream blighted by discovery that £1 is worth about 5d (or say 2p) on 1936 figures.

Saltwood   *Monday, 7 June*

I sat 'within the walls'. Tremendous burgeoning greenery, baby birds everywhere: we just failed (by what chance I don't know) to revive two baby thrushes from the nest in the crab apple tree by the openings desk – having got them through to the fifth day; there is a rather sulky successor to George (named 'Max') in a box in the kitchen, and a few minutes ago I hooked a young sparrow out of the pool.

Cloisters   *Thursday, 10 June*

I telephoned Edward Adeane[1] at Buckingham Palace and told him that there was some concern that the Recognition Committee at the MOD might be parsimonious with their awards. I urged that these be distributed in the most profligate manner – and particularly in the Parachute Regiment which has performed such prodigies. He reminded me that the Prince of Wales was Colonel-in-Chief, and I hope he took my points to heart. After a period of *froideur* following that curious leak by Willie Hamilton about my criticisms of fat, ugly, dwarflike, lecherous and revoltingly tastelessly behaved Princess Margaret, our relations have improved and are now quite good.

---

[1] Edward Adeane, Extra Equerry to the Queen since 1972.

Saltwood   *Friday, 11 June*

Oh! How loathsome and draining it is to turn my footsteps westward instead of to the south on a Friday. I work very hard at Westminster and I am always *en poste* there, unlike other colleagues who scrabble around the boardrooms and come in late (if at all) for Questions, with expense-account fumes on their breath. And so, when the week is over I like best to go home and 'unwind' with the cars and the animals. And it is ghastly having to go to Plymouth and, racked with fatigue, keep silently mouthing 'brush'[1] as one moves round the faithful, and not-so-faithful.

Actually my status in Plymouth is quite high at the moment, due to all the 'exposure' that I have been getting over the Falklands. Enemies, like Speare and other malcontents, have gone quiet, they never turn up at meetings.

Although the complacent and self-centred Roy Williams came in to see me yesterday – he gets a free pass on the trains because he is a postman(!) and so likes to pop in to the House – and told me that it was very important that I should be on the Barbican (although that is not in my constituency) to talk to the fishermen (very few of whom are my constituents) at 11.30 the following morning, as he had 'arranged' for the TV cameras to be there. And, moreover, *Janet Fookes would be there*. Perhaps I was a little bit more clipped than I should have been. I mean how the hell could I possibly get to Plymouth at 11.30 the following morning at less than twenty-four hours notice?

Fortunately, Jane decided that she would come with me and this usually restricts my grosser excesses of temper. But on this occasion, having listened to some grotesque and preposterous cliché-bound bellowing – styled a 'speech' – by Sir Henry Plumb,[2] and my stomach being empty, as is habitual, I found that I snapped at some grace-and-favour female, a Mrs Randall by name, who gave me the I'm-not-certain-I'm-going-to-be-voting-for-you routine because of my failure to do something about the glasshouse industry.

God alive! I said I could not care less; that I was not in the business

---

[1] The Clarks had, early in their political life, discovered that the word 'brush', in the act of expression, draws the features into a pleasing smile; neither chilly nor leering, but authoritative and benevolent – one degree less effusive than the word 'cheese'.

[2] Sir Henry Plumb, Member of the European Assembly, former President of the National Farmers Union.

of buying votes with taxpayers' money; that I despised people who
tried to exercise pressure to secure for themselves particular tranches
of the revenue in return for electoral favours; and that she could
exercise her remedy at the next election.

'There are some Members of Parliament who might be frightened
by the sort of threats you are making, but I am not one of them.' I
have a feeling she is a friend of Joan Erskine, one of the Dunstone
carpers, who always used to complain about my lack of publicity –
although she can hardly mount that particular charge over the last
three months.

Cloisters   *Monday, 14 June*

I dined with Norman St John-Stevas, and, as always, he was delightful
company, talked obsessively about politics and what a 'dreadful'
Cabinet we have at the moment.

'There cannot ever have been a Cabinet with such a dearth of
talent,' he kept saying. He recounted how Norman Tebbit – whom
he described in a number of scatological terms – had come down to
a Conservative Club in his constituency, 'not at *my* invitation I hasten
to say,' wearing a coloured evening shirt and how, '. . . my dear, they
were all over him.'

I said that The Lady's autocracy was complete. She could make any
policy or break any individual. At the moment, I said, she is completely
fire-proof. 'Yes,' he replied, 'and will be completely combustible
shortly thereafter.'

Cloisters   *Tuesday, 15 June*

I was woken at 4.15 a.m. by a beautiful song-thrush; she rivalled,
surpassed indeed, the famous Albany blackbird, to whom I used to
listen in the spring of '76 when I would wake early in torment with
the figures going round and round in my head of accelerating interest
charges on my different overdrafts, and how was I to get the deeds of
Saltwood back out of Hoare's clutches. But this thrush sang incredibly,

never once repeating herself and with variations of infinite quality and delight.

I could not go back to sleep, still over-excited by the events of last night. I had got back to the House about 9.30 p.m., after dining at Brooks's with Edward Adeane, and was reading the tape over Phil Goodhart's shoulder when I saw something about, '... individual British commanders at all levels have been authorised to negotiate ceasefires'. 'It means they have surrendered,' he said.

The cloakroom attendant told me that there was to be a Statement at 10 p.m., after the vote, and when I got up to the lobbies I found the whole House, policemen, badge messengers, etc., everybody bubbling with excitement. I rushed up to catch the news headlines before the Division Bell rang, but for once we seemed to know more than they did; the BBC was behind the times and fumbling.

Foolishly I lingered so, after going past the division clerk, I found that 'my' bench was completely crowded. However, among its magic powers, as is well known, is that of infinite expandability, and they allowed me in lowish down – next to Alan Glyn – Peter Emery very nobly making that ritual pivoting of the lap which actually permits the small statutory triangle of green leather.

Hastily I scribbled some notes on the back of a card in case there were questions – but the rumour was that it was to be on a Point of Order. (How? Monstrous collusion by the Speaker?) And then The Lady entered, radiant, and there was cheering – bellowing, indeed. She made a very brief statement, but it was important in that she used the phrase, '... negotiate a *surrender*' (not a ceasefire). Trust her. She has led from the front all the way.

Again we bellowed. Order Papers were waved and, not having one, I fluttered my little white postcard. Michael Foot fumbled gingerly round the subject, to some heckling, but finally and generously managed to get out his congratulations, '... in spite of our arguments in the past.' Little Steel was short, and inaudible. And even David [Owen], who has behaved so well and so enhanced his reputation, could not be heard properly and aroused grumpy heckling, I noticed, from the Opposition bench when he congratulated the Government.

For a few seconds we were stuck in our places by some procedural back-and-forth; Leader of the House accepting an Adjournment of Business, etc. I rose rapidly, pushed my way through the crowd at the bar of the House and shot round through the 'Aye' Lobby to catch the Prime Minister as she emerged at the back of the Speaker's Chair to get to her room. No one else had the idea and I had a completely clear run. Not even Ian was leading her, although Willie was shuffling benignly three places behind. (What must he have been thinking?) Ignoring Willie I rushed up and said to her: 'Prime Minister, only you could have done this; you did it alone, and your place in history is assured.' She looked a little startled. Had she heard properly? She was still a little bemused by the triumph. Willie looked grumpy (maddeningly, he is not at all deaf); an unseemly display of emotion. We do not do things like that in the Tory Party.

So ends the Falklands Affair – which began in such despair and humiliation. How well I remember that first emergency debate and looking down the bench at The Lady when Enoch was speaking, at how low she held her head, how *knotted* with pain and apprehension she seemed as he pronounced his famous judgement, '. . . in the next few weeks the world, the country and she, herself, will discover of what metal she is made.'

I only hope he is generous enough to recall that moment when he speaks today.

Cloisters   *Wednesday, 16 June*

It is a great relief to me how kind people have been and how many compliments I have received concerning that Terry Coleman article. Last night I was standing in the Lobby while Jonathan Aitken was telling me what a good man I seemed in it, when David Owen came up to us and said exactly the same thing. Only a few Tory wankers are critical, they feign horror – Michael McNair-Wilson was literally speaking in whispers about it when I came in on Monday – but I suspect it is tinged with jealousy. '. . . Combination of hot sun, and fizz, was it?' said silly little John Heddle,[1] obviously delighted by my discomforture. The only mistake I made, in my estimation, was to ask him to tone it down; although, as Andrew Roth[2] said, he should never have revealed that, as it was 'operational'.

I lunched today with my old friend John Aspinall. I had undertaken to give evidence in support of his application for a licence for his club.

---

[1] John Heddle, MP for Lichfield and Tamworth since 1979.
[2] Andrew Roth, editor of Parliamentary Profiles.

I can do this with a clear conscience as I am not a gambler and I enjoy the social amenities, the restaurant and the backgammon board which it provides.

Excellent food, during which Aspers declaimed much good sense about the strength of the ordinary people of the nation, how they had brushed aside the nervous and decadent caution of the establishment to assert their nationhood, etc.

After lunch we climbed five floors to his office, where a minute beady lawyer awaited to take my deposition. Young, clear-skinned, bald-pated, he was cast in the Eric Levene mould. While we talked, Aspers huffed and gasped. I thought he was meant to be fit – wrestling with bears and gorillas etc. – but my own breathing had not altered in the slightest from running up the stairs. I suppose people who puff and pant do not notice they are doing it, but it certainly makes a great deal of noise.

Back in the House I met Adam Raphael and we chatted about the political consequences of the Falklands. He told me that 'favourable mentions' about me had been coming out of Downing Street; this corroborates what Frank Johnson told me on the weekend – but what is the point? I went on up to the Defence Committee where there was much discussion about the advisability of postponing the White Paper.

I dined with Bruce-Gardyne – who really is rather awful. Too self-satisfied and assertive, and quite unrepentant about his letter to Freddy Fischer.[1] A little later we were joined, very reluctantly and having looked around the dining room for alternatives, by Michael Heseltine. On closer scrutiny I see that his face is slightly changing shape, he is becoming rather pop-eyed. Then, almost immediately afterwards, came Trevor Skeet,[2] who booms and bellows and is ineffably complacent.

I used to think he was a staunch right-winger of the old school, but he would not even sign my Motion praising the Special Patrol Group on the grounds that it might offend the ethnic minority in his constituency. And he does not even have a marginal seat as his majority is 12,413. I found it very difficult to say anything. Michael Heseltine, as

---

[1] In a private letter to the Editor of the *Financial Times* J.B–G. had said that the Falklands were not worth fighting for, that the whole enterprise was 'crazy' etc. This was much in tone with the editorial attitude of the *F.T.*, but the text of the letter, which was politically embarrassing, was leaked to the *New Statesman* by a member of the *F.T.*'s staff.

[2] Trevor Skeet, barrister, MP for Bedford since 1970.

a leading wet, made some pompous remarks about how the Northern Ireland Bill rebels were subjecting Jim Prior to a 'campaign of attrition,' and how he disapproved. Was he trying to get at me? Quite difficult, as I am not opposing the Bill, and am indeed voting for the closures. There was some long and disparate conversation about what the Argentine prisoners were going to eat. I suggested that they should eat each other.

After dinner Bob Boscawen said that John Nott wanted to see me in his room about the White Paper. Victor Goodhew and Winston Churchill had also been invited to go along, but I am glad to say that little Winston did not turn up.

While we were waiting for Victor I said to John that I was very worried about all the rumours that were circulating about his impending departure (John Connell had told me about this nearly ten days ago, accompanying it with the really awful prospect that Peter Walker would be appointed in John Nott's place. There was also an item heavily displayed in a box on page two of the *Daily Mail* this morning, and a full length editorial on the subject in tonight's *Evening Standard*). JN said that there was a conspiracy against him. About half-a-dozen Admirals, many of the naval correspondents – Desmond Wetter etc. – and a coterie of disaffected colleagues, notably Keith Speed, Michael Brotherton[1] and Freddie Burden. JN said he had no intention of resigning.

We discussed the question of the White Paper. He wants to publish it as it is, but with a loose-leaf disclaimer of intent. Crazy, I said. Bob Boscawen said we had to have five defence debates and there had to be something 'on the table' for the debates to revolve around. Why? We have not *got* to do anything, I said, except raise money for the defence estimates, and that had already been done. Far better to issue a single-side Statement reaffirming our commitment to Trident, to NATO etc. and asserting that the complex and deep-seated lessons of the Falklands Campaign will take some months to be digested.

John thrashed about on his seat, crossing and uncrossing his legs, taking his glasses on and off. Rattled, but attentive. He had started off asserting his intention to publish even though not to publish the obvious conclusion, and I had said that if he insisted I would not oppose the idea publicly, but I still thought it terribly risky. Victor

---

[1] Michael Brotherton, MP for Louth since October 1974.

Goodhew supported me and was sensible and wise. We left things that John would continue to think the matter over.

Later in the evening I saw Ian Gow, who walks about the place looking like the cat that has swallowed all the cream. In his presence I had some badinage with Jim Prior and was cheeky to him about the Northern Ireland Bill.

Ian could not get away as for formal reasons he is bound to support the Bill in the lobbies. But I had one quick word with him – 'the Prime Minister has complete freedom of action now,' I said, 'no other Leader has enjoyed such freedom since Churchill, and even with him it did not last very long.' I suppose he may have thought I was referring to freedom of choice in making appointments, but I was not, really, I meant freedom in imposing domestic, foreign and defence policies.

Cloisters   *Thursday, 17 June*

I was delighted to see that Julia Langdon had singled me out for mention in today's *Guardian* in an analysis of politicians who have emerged with credit from the Falklands affair. All the sweeter as Churchill and I were the only Tory backbenchers to be mentioned, and I was compared favourably to him. I wonder who she got this from? Perhaps Jim Lester, although I know she also talks to Norman StJS. It is useful as 'plugs' from that quarter are far more valuable than, say, the *Telegraph* (not that I have ever had one there).

The Times had an enormous centre page article, complete with caricature, stating why John Nott should resign, and the *Sun* also had an editorial, 'John Must Move On.' What a miserable business it must be to be unable to pick up the paper without reading some anonymous call for your resignation.

As for myself, it really seems as if that rather horrific business with Terry Coleman did no harm. People do not read things very closely and the majority do not appear to have realised just how awful it was. Sometimes one can be the beneficiary of inattention instead of the victim. But whatever happens, I have had an awful lot of luck in the last three months. If there is one single person to whom I owe it, I suppose it would be Barbara Maxwell, who put me on *Question Time*, and has been singing my praises to people in the media.

I went and spoke to the Monday Club at Lympne Castle today. I really cannot bear the Monday Club. They are all mad, quite different from its heyday, when it was a right-wing pressure group at the time of Ted Heath's Government. Now they are a prickly residue in the body politic, a nasty sort of gallstone. But I could not refuse as Deirdre Margary had been so noble (it turned out) in plugging my name for Folkestone.

We trailed over to Lympne Castle and there was what is known as a good attendance. First cheese and wine was consumed and, naturally, no one was particularly interested in me, or wanted to make my acquaintance.

Then I delivered a splendid speech about how the country's mood had changed, the Jubilee, the Royal Wedding, the Falklands, etc. etc. But they are so introverted they hardly noticed. 'Questions' concentrated almost exclusively on the BBC and immigration. Groanworthily at the close of my speech cheese and wine resumed as an occupation. We could not escape as we were committed, out of noseyness, to dine with the Margarys.

In the fullness of time, Deirdre separated Jane and I, Jock Massareene and Annabelle, the local chairman of the Monday Club (heavily built and *rebarbatif*), an unsympathetic woman in late middle age who appeared to be some relation, and a young couple, and took us through into the private part of the Castle.

Nightmarishly, instead of going into dinner, Harry Margary uttered the dreaded sentence, 'I suggest we all have a drink.' I was practically dead on my feet – it was about 9.30 p.m. – and I drank orange juice. I sat, half-dozing, on the window seat, looking out over Romney Marsh, and the female half of the 'young couple' told me how she had been a girlfriend of David Owen, also something-something of Peter Carrington's daughter, but I did not pay as much attention as perhaps I should have.

Finally, we got into dinner, and I was dismayed to see from the number of knives and forks at one's place that a long sequence of different courses was in prospect. On and on the evening dragged. Almost as long as the Heddles', almost as boring as the Mitchisons'. *Never* go out locally. My boredom threshold is far too low. I should have 'sparkled', but couldn't. Gloomily I sat, my face drained and sulky. The male half of the 'young couple', seated at the centre of the long table, made from time-to-time an idiotic joke at which people laughed. Perhaps fortunately, I could not catch Jane's eye as she was shielded by flowers and table ornaments. Jock Massereene, who sat opposite me, talked good sense about animal welfare, told horror stories about deer poaching on his Scottish estates. But in all other respects the evening was purgatorial.

Fortunately, the heavily-built Area chairman of the Monday Club suffered (I assume) from an enlarged prostate gland and had to get up before the coffee and search for the 'toilet'. I took advantage of this, autogalvanised and rose also, saying that we had kept Nanny waiting far longer than we had promised, wonderful evening, everything so delicious and glorious, cannot thank you enough, etc. etc., and off we went. Ooh!

Cloisters   *Monday, 21 June*

This evening I dined with the Commandant General of the Royal Marines. A number of other officers were present at the banquet, which took place in the Stationers Hall – very collegiate, with polished oak tables on stone flags. They are all delighted about the Falklands – of course – and lobbied us (several MPs were present) for replacements to be ordered immediately, both for the Round Table class and for *Intrepid* and *Fearless*.

The officer next to me, a Major Hooper, was highly intelligent and soon showed himself to be a closet nationalist. We were in absolute sympathy over the direction of British defence policy in the '80s. He told me that the Russian attaché in Germany had said to him after the Crusader Exercise how glad he was that the British Army was so small. Hooper said the only other decent army was the German one. The US Marine Corps? The 82nd Airborne? He said they were useless. On exercise in Corsica last year, the US Marines were stoned so far that the officers in the Fire Control Unit were actually falling about and giggling for hours on end.

Cloisters   *Tuesday, 22 June*

Atkins came up to me in the Lobby and made a few oblique remarks about my 'publicity campaign', getting 'attention in the media' etc.; did this mean I might make another attempt at the Defence Chair?

Assuming that he was making the enquiry on behalf of Tony, I said (quite truthfully) that the extent to which I got attention in the media was quite outside my control. In any case, the Party had decided that it preferred Tony and I would not challenge that decision a second time. Somewhat to my surprise, he moved on into saying that he thought it would be a 'good idea', '... dear old Tony has a heart of gold,' but that the officers were so weak, etc. etc. I replied that I could only consider it if the Left 'whip' allowed a free vote in the election in order to counter-balance the various people like Pat Wall and Winston who always vote against me, even though I am on the '92' slate. He said he would think this over. But of course he is not particularly influential, although it was interesting that he should make the approach. From what he said I inferred that Cranley Onslow[1] was also in favour of the idea.

I *might* try once more I suppose, but really and truly if I do not get Minister of State at Defence in the reshuffle, or take Ian's place if he is given a portfolio, I think I will go into 'retraite'. More time for travel. Might even not be bothered to stand again in Plymouth. But I must not forget that I was turning all these things over in my mind as long ago as 1976. One has these moments of depression and futility – and if I had succumbed to temptation then, I would not have been in my place (and played such part as I did) in what was the most exciting and significant episode in our history since 1945. *What* a time to be in Parliament that was! Last night, during the Division, I stopped and had a word with the Speaker as I passed his Chair, and he agreed, telling me how he had been in his place for every moment of every debate that we had had during the crisis. He, too, played his part, subtly and welshly, obstructing the pacifists; hardly ever calling Dalyell and Faulds.[2] The basic patriotism of the working classes; far stronger than the what's-in-it-for-me motivation of the managerial class, 'Industry' and 'The City'.

---

[1] Cranley Onslow, MP for Woking since 1964.
[2] Andrew Faulds, MP for Warley East since 1974 (Smethwick, 1966–74).

Saltwood   *Friday, 2 July*

Still hanging over one is the agony of the September reshuffle. I ought, of course, to get a job: Min of State at Defence. But I know, from the Chief Whip's face as I see him in the corridors, that I'm not going to.

Saltwood   *Saturday, 10 July*

Yesterday I was hanging around by the swimming pool at Saltwood when something made me go in and ring the Message Board as I had given Alison the day off. There was a message from Alan Grundy of Plymouth Sound that I was to stand by at 6.15 p.m. on Saturday evening to fly out with the Lord Mayor to the *Canberra*. God alive! Another weekend busted; and how the hell was I to get to Plymouth? No trains, school holidays just beginning, traffic solid at all M5 interchanges etc. etc. Gah! Sadly I went back out to the garden. There is no fun in a Friday evening if you know the rest of the weekend is blighted. However I had to go.

In actual fact it was a marvellous, uplifting experience. We piled into the little Sea Otter, a sturdy twin-engined high-wing cabin plane, which gave one great confidence. After flying for about ten minutes into a grey, very South Atlantic seascape, with the horizon completely blurred, we saw the white turbulence from the double wake of a big ship with twin screws. Then seconds later her escort, a little frigate, tiny and vulnerable it seemed, with its single 4.5" gun forward. I felt very moved when I saw that little frigate and thought how she and her sister ships had sailed the whole length of the world to uphold the honour of the country and of the Royal Navy. What a truly wonderful epic event in our history was that Falkland Islands war. I have said this so many times in so many places, and on each occasion I can still feel almost tearful. There will never again be anything like that.

Then, seconds later, we saw the great ship herself. Curiously muted and solemn she seemed, there was no one on deck at all. No soldiers to wave at, no crew members unoccupied. Her bow completely rusted along the line of the prow, and frightful rust streaks and scars along the side of the hull. The complete absence of human life made her seem like a ghost ship. There was something very solemn and forbidding about it. It conveyed to one more effectively than anything else could have done how nearly she *was* a ghost. She had indeed come back from the dead, but in substance as well as in spirit.

Our pilot made many passes and lost altitude until we were only a few feet off the water and on his last two approaches he passed so close that one could have read a newspaper headline on the deck. There was something tremendously confident, detached almost, about the way that great ship, which had led a charmed life in the mortal perils of San Carlos Water, steamed on through the flat calm, monotone waters of the English Channel. It was a perfect prelude to the glorious display of abandon and rejoicing that was to break out when she finally arrived at Southampton.

While we were waiting for the plane, poor David Owen came up to me, looking ghastly. His hair is now almost completely grey, as is his complexion. He looks as if he has lost a stone-and-a-half and is obviously deeply unhappy. I had sent him a nice note of commiseration, all the easier to write because it was heartfelt. I had told him Jane's comment after watching his brief appearance on television that came at the end of a long boozy hesitant waffling by Roy Jenkins, after his victory. 'How could they?' she asked. He liked this.

He was still in an agitated state and kept asking me if I thought it all right if he refused to serve in the Shadow Cabinet. Kept saying how awful the Liberals were and so on. I tried to get him to come back and have a pasty at Bratton, which he would like to have done I know. But he claimed that he was expected home and got back into his Volvo station wagon to drive to Wiltshire.

Cloisters   *Monday, 12 July*

Willie made the most deplorable, slovenly, casual Statement today about the intruder who got into the Queen's bedroom. He treated it with no more gravity, but on a higher level of obfuscation, than he would a second-class riot, with some police injuries and a few broken shop windows, in, say, Stoke Newington. Talk about 'not rising to the occasion.'

Tactically, he succeeded in that the whole House was so flabbergasted and bewildered by the enormity of what had happened and the inconclusive routine way in which he announced it that he did manage to 'keep the temperature down'. But the press were already in a highly indignant state and by the time the Home Affairs Committee assembled some Members, notably Jack Page, were puce with anger. Usually Jack Page is never at a loss for words, but he addressed the Committee, absurdly on a Point of Order (the only other person to do this since I have been an officer, was Geoffrey Dickens). I do not think this affair is over by any means.

A little later in the proceedings I managed to make Tim Raison – whom I have disliked since we were together at Eton and whom I recognise as a closet Liberal – lose his temper. Sarcastically, I had commended the Home Office for its high-minded disregard, which it communicated to its Ministers, for the garnering of votes, citing its failure in the law and order field and its bland assumption that we could simultaneously disregard our manifesto commitments in the fields of both immigration control and animal welfare.

Tim went completely crazy. He snarled, made a dotty point about soldiers' faces terribly burned in the Falklands fighting, '. . . which we assume must concern you,' and animal research. I looked out of the window, delighted. I assume it will be reported to Willie, but it was couched in a form that makes it rather hard to relay as being openly insulting which, say, Nick Budgen and Jack Page had done.

Cloisters   *Tuesday, 13 July*

It is July in the Commons. Ugh!

Hot and balmy outside, and the Albany bedroom window, now in its fifth straight year without a sashcord, has to be propped with a block of wood and ventilates inadequately.

Inevitably, it is the Finance Bill Report Stage. A three-line whip – '. . . until this business is concluded,' which last night was at 3.50 a.m., although, naturally, the wastage was colossal, and by the end we were down to about 120. This morning I woke up and thought that *I must not take any more speaking engagements anywhere.* Indeed, I am in the mood to cancel those that I have hanging over me at the moment. Nor do I, at all, want to go to Plymouth again until – and possibly not even then – the next general election. How the hell do I get down there? The rail strike will probably last until October and the

West Country roads are totally congested except (putatively) between 2–4 a.m.

Yesterday, a typically filthy Monday morning. A dentist appointment; and correspondence scattered and not to hand; many small things (in addition to massive ones) left undone. Little Jackie Felce, who is very amiable and pleasant, came up and wanted a mine detector to look for her watch; which she had mislaid in the straw. Where the hell was the mine detector? I looked in the garden entrance (where it is always kept, but needless to say was not), the garages, the outhouses, Andrew's bedroom, Andrew's old bedroom, James's bedroom, James's dark-room, sundry other rooms and localities. Time, time slipping past. The sand *rushing* through the hour glass. Jane found it in Winifred.[1]

'Winifred's in a terrible state,' Jane said. Inwardly screeching I ran down to the garage. 'Look at this.' She pressed on Winifred's front wing. Barking my shin on some old motorbike parts, I climbed over and did the same. 'Perfectly solid, what's the matter?'

'Oh she is in such a dreadful state.'

I reeled away clutching my head, then howling at the heavens and shaking my fists in the air. Oh for time to linger on the estate, to polish and buff and mend and improve, and *unwind*.

Later, when I got up to the House of Commons, Frank Haynes[2] twinklingly, congratulated me on being the next Secretary of State for Defence. Being very vain and having a high opinion of myself I only dissimulated slightly, thinking he was referring to recent exchanges in the Commons (he kept talking about Jim Callaghan). But it turned out that Callaghan had written an article in the previous day's *Sunday Pictorial* entitled, *Why I Won't Rest Until John Nott Goes*, and had recommended me as his successor!

I rushed to the Library and made Rosanne do photocopies. It must be a treasurable compliment to be recommended by the former Prime Minister. But unlike Julia Langdon's compliment, it would not make the slightest difference in the Party. It may even be adverse. Perhaps fortunately, no Conservative ever reads the *Sunday Pictorial*.

I had a message from Mark Schreiber to ring him. I thought he was

---

[1] Winifred was the Clarks' name for a little Morris 8 two-seater which, due to its extremely short wheel-base, fitted snugly into a far corner of the long garage.

[2] Frank Haynes, MP for Ashfield since 1979; Labour Whip.

going to talk to me about the revisionist defence school and my article in *The Times*. But he asked me about what I thought of Willie's Statement.

Well, I know that Mark is congenitally pro-Willie as we talked before about the sort of pressures he has to endure from the Right, so I opened a little guardedly,

'Well I really did think it was a little inadequate ...'

Finding that he agreed and was extremely indignant, I developed the theme, told him about the noisy meeting of the Home Affairs Committee last night, Jack Page being literally apoplectic.

Mark described to me in detail the police arrangements for protecting the Palace, which are a complete shambles. There are no fewer than three police departments involved: A1 (duties in connection with royalty, under the command of a Mr Trestrail, who also has overall responsibility); A7 (crime prevention, which has an advisory role, under a man called Ashton); and A11 (diplomatic protection) *not* the Special Branch, under a man called Duffy, which is concerned with protecting the Queen's person.

All these departments overlap and, as the police are themselves conducting the enquiry, will presumably shift and shunt the blame between each other.

Mark continued to develop the theme of Willie's culpability. He pointed out that Peter Carrington had honourably tendered his resignation following what he judged to be a 'national humiliation.' Was this not a humiliation of an even higher order? I agreed, egged him on, I said I was keen on rehabilitating Peter Carrington (a total lie) and that it would do no harm as part of this process to draw the contrast between their two ways of behaving. I even suggested that they put it on the cover of the *Economist*, out tomorrow night. I doubt if he will manage this, but Mark is definitely indignant. It is very satisfactory when one can get the Left to bite each other.

Later, as I discussed this with Alison while dictating, it occurred to me to give Ian Gow a fright by warning him that I might draw this contrast myself at *Question Time*. As indeed I might. I very nearly lost my temper yesterday but on the whole probably not. It would be a classic *torschlüss*, wouldn't it?

Only last night Michael McNair-Wilson was saying to me that I had 'done enough.' All I had to do now was sit still, get through the next three weeks, and either I got a ministerial appointment in September, or I never would. Of course there is no such word as 'never' in politics, but I know what he means. It is a rather nice restful thought to have in one's mind, an excuse for not doing things, like bellowing *j'accuse* and releasing the great torrent of loathing which I feel for Willie and which, I know, is reciprocated.

Anyway, I put a call through to Ian at Downing Street. He was in with the Prime Minister. I explained the 'delicacy' of the subject matter to his secretary and she took a note in to him and put it under his nose.

A few minutes later he rang me back. I told him that some on our side, possibly even myself, might call this afternoon for Willie's resignation and contrast his behaviour with that of Peter Carrington. 'Don't do it,' he said. 'Whatever you do *you* must not do this.'

'Well some people may do it,' I said.

'Let them, but whatever you do don't you do it yourself.'

He was very intense about this. It really was a very direct message. So (needless to say) I won't do it. But I feel we are probably very near a now-or-never situation. Although whether he said don't do it because the Prime Minister has already decided to promote me (as Adam Raphael said she had), and if I had attacked the Home Secretary it would make it very difficult for her, or whether it is that Ian is hoping that it may happen, but still anticipates difficulty with Willie's veto, I really do not know. One is a strong position, the other a weak one.

My own natural inclination for cavalry tactics made me want to charge Willie head-on and hopefully get rid of him completely so the question of veto would not arise. But even if he did go, it might still be difficult for her to promote the first person on our side to call for it. Jopling would probably stop her. Ah well, we shall see.

Saltwood Great Library   *Tuesday, 20 July*

My father has had a *coup-de-vieux* and is now in unhappy decline. There is scarcely any longer a point in going over [to the Garden House] to call on him. He just sits, on his low green velvet chair by the big window. Col was very aggrieved the other day because as he approached my father smiled simperingly and said 'Ah, now, who's this?'

'It's your younger son, Colin, Papa.'

'Aha' (Of course my father knew perfectly well who it was. He just gets irritated with Col blatantly sucking up to him and talking a lot of recycled balls about art). Aha.

Of course my father would never have spoken like that to Celly. She would just have cackled, said 'You're completely ga-ga' or something equally brutal. He is frightened of her, as he is of most women. But, as far as I can make out, is still resisting pressure to set up a Trust Fund for Sammy.

Most of the time my father does not speak, or read, or really show any vitality whatever, although at intervals his face may indicate a cross expression. What is he actually thinking?

Disappointment, I would surmise, more than apprehension. And principally with his marriage. At first he started off jolly. But Nolwen is so odious, and *false*. 'Sweetie' this and 'Sweetie' that (this is, I suppose, a literal translation of *Cherie*), but he is her third husband, after all. And Papa has twice suffered 'intrusive' surgery since their wedding five years ago, once on his gall bladder, once his prostate. 'No surprises,' as Nolwen over-brightly told everyone – by which I assumed her to mean no indications of malignancy. But the operations 'took it out of' him. He is going to die. It could happen at any moment; but equally he could last for another three years.[1]

I hardly notice. Will Andrew and Jamie, if God spares them, feel like this about me? I suppose that it is inevitable. The five stages of fatherhood. First, protective. Then, love. Then, an idolised elder brother, racing at Silverstone, 'parping' blondes. Then, an old friend, giving counsel and the occasional 'treat' (or cheque). Finally the *nonno*, selfishly in the way; holding on for far too long, obstructing the natural course of inheritance.

When I said all this to Jane she said yes, but his face still lights up when you come into the room. And at once I felt terrible. If my father goes back to France this week (which I think improbable) I will write to him affectionately and just hope that Nolwen does not intercept it. She, of course, dreads him dying at the *Vieux Manoir*, knowing full well that I would seize the Garden House immediately and forbid her on her return.

---

[1] Lord Clark died in May 1983 (see *Diaries*, 1993).

Cloisters   *Monday, 26 July*

The day of the Falkland Islands Service at St Paul's. I only just made
the 7.19 a.m. from Sandling as the horrible little Renault, which has
already broken its reverse gear, stuck in bottom and I had to transfer
to the Trelawney's car at the village green.

I walked from the Commons to Horseguards where the coaches
were waiting. We surged to St Paul's, crossing red lights with the
assistance of police motorcyclists, and arrived an hour before the
Queen was due. So I slyly dodged round the barriers and found a
coffee shop, entirely staffed by black people, where I had coffee and
a sticky bun.

In spite of this I was in my seat three-quarters-of-an-hour early.
Every minute was interesting as the congregation assembled. I had an
excellent place, under the dome, and there in front of me, still hunched
and grey, just as he had been on that Monday, 5th April, at 'Rab's'
memorial service, was Richard Luce.

'What's going through your mind?' I asked him. He answered
candidly: 'I am shattered, absolutely shattered.'

And sure enough, a little later, up came Peter Carrington, relegated
to a row behind me with some very dud peers. Lady Carrington was
bright, but Peter still looked a bit sulky I thought – and who can blame
him, having to sit between Lord Peart and Lord De L'Isle. The first
member of the Cabinet to arrive was Norman Fowler; how common
he always looks. A little later up came Heseltine and I was glad to see
he had been (obviously deliberately) put at the very end of the
Government row so that he was blocked by pillars.

I squirmed and turned in my seat, staring shamelessly. Soon I
realised that the block behind me was filling up with next of kin.
Many of them were Para families and, very touchingly, they all wore
something red – the red of the Red Beret – about their clothing. The
girls wore ribbons or cardigans, the fathers handkerchiefs, and so on.
Only two rows behind me sat three adorable winklers, two little boys
and a girl, who were dressed in red jerseys with metal parachute
badges, looking enormous, pinned on their chest. With the exception
of the very young children, who were excited and jolly, most of the
relatives looked deeply unhappy. Some of the wives, or Mums, were
old NAAFI comforts and painted up to the nines, but the majority
were beauties, many of them raging beauties, and none of the young

ones wearing any make-up, which was probably just as well as most of them cried all the way through the service.

Willie arrived, stooping and flushed and wearing some heavy red ribbon round his neck. It looked like the Bath, what was it? He is absolutely imperméable. He now says that not only is he not going to resign, but he is going to fight the next general election.

The Royal Family arrived two by two, all in uniform I am glad to say, although the Duchess of Kent now looks very spaced-out indeed. Princess Diana looked thin as a rake and out-paced her consort with her special lanky stride. The Queen, as always, surprised one with how tiny she is; Philip consistent and splendid towers above her.

The service itself could have been worse. The most objectionable of the peaceniks' plans having been thwarted largely, I believe, following my question to the Prime Minister on 13th July. The second lesson was read by David Cooper, chaplain of 2 Para, and it was most fitting to hear that flat northern accent reading out the verses of St Mark, having last heard it coming directly from the tin church in Port Stanley on the day of the victory. Little Dr Greet,[1] with whom I have had several clashes in the last ten days, turned out to have quite a good microphone voice and his prayers were not as awful as one might have expected. And we ended with Psalm 23, but sung to Irvine's music, and there cannot have been many dry eyes in the Cathedral.

Afterwards the crocodile moved its way out very slowly down the aisle, starting from the top. I was on the civilian side, passing row after row of next of kin. Anxiously I scanned their faces, but the only emotion I could see was anguish, sheer anguish.

Cloisters   *Tuesday, 27 July*

Lunched today with Norman St John-Stevas at 34 Montpelier Square, an expensive address. It is always a good (or is it a bad?) sign when you see a house some distance away, obviously the chic-est and most painted-up in the street and, as you close the range, this turns out to be your destination. Lightheartedly, as we ascended the steps, I said, ' ... something-something fucking', to Jane and Margaret Argyll materialised at the same moment. But she is used to that kind of thing

---

[1] The Reverend Dr Kenneth Greet, Moderator, Free Church Federal Council.

and did not object. She is *unbelievably* preserved – 'preserved' being the word; but gave the show away a bit by moving very stiffly and hesitantly, being uncertain about steps, etc.[1]

The interior was gay as can be; bandbox gay, with bright paint and clashing reds and greens, and everything discreetly, but ingeniously lit by interior decorators with hidden lamps and bulbs. A smart little group, the ladies better than the men (and better looking too). Mary Roxburghe;[2] Olga Maitland, gossip columnist of the *Sunday Express*, rather scrawny and combative I thought, we did not get on. Lady something-or-other, who spoke with a strong French accent, and a young blonde cutie who had broken her leg in three places after being dropped by her boyfriend in a car park at a hunt ball and walked with a stick. At my head of the table sat Victor Matthews, just as common and nasty as *Private Eye* made him out to be, but with a very distinct vitality of his own. The ambience of power, good company.[3] I tackled him several times about the *Atlantic Conveyor* replacement. I both fluffed and slapped him. Told him that it was a question of *noblesse oblige* and that as he was now of the *noblesse* he must do what was expected of him. I told him, too, that 'Downing Street' (I had mentioned the matter to Ian Gow this morning) had said he was 'all right'. He was less susceptible to flattery than some of his breeding.

The food was very good, although the silver could have been better. We had a salmon mousse, perfectly reasonable filet of beef and then a soufflé. Indifferent white wine, an excellent claret. Does Norman have private means? There was nothing really first class in the contents, but everything was very shiny and Asprey-looking.

Maddeningly I had a summons to Ian Gow's room at 2.45pm, to be briefed on a question about the South Atlantic Fund, so we had to leave early. Goodness knows what they said about us after we had gone out. I would like to have stayed longer. Jane rightly pointed out that Norman is really a very kind person. He has a coruscating wit, but he only uses it against the hubristic and the nasty. He is never

---

[1] Margaret Argyll, around whom sexual gossip had been rampant; the third wife of 11th Duke of Argyll they divorced amidst much acrimony in 1963. At the time of this entry she was 70.

[2] First wife of the 9th Duke of Roxburghe (they divorced in 1953).

[3] Victor Matthews, created life peer in 1980, had through the Trafalgar House company owned the Cunard shipping line which in turn owned the *Atlantic Conveyor*, one of the non-RN container ships commandeered for Falklands task force, and lost in the campaign.

cruel and never – which is so easy – pots shots off the weak or the backward.

Cloisters   *Thursday, 29 July*

Peter Hordern had asked me to lunch. A rather boring terraced house in Cadogan Street, burgled four times in the last two years he told me. The other guests were Julian Amery and Nicholas Baker.[1] Hordern, who is very senior in the Public Accounts Committee, was trying to pick our brains about defence costings, concerning which he is, quite rightly, apprehensive. A very nice man, highly intelligent, but almost too fastidious for politics. It has always mystified me why he has not been made a Minister as he is extremely able. We were an ill-assorted quartet and although what Julian says is good sense, he is now a little deaf and when he is speaking himself his pauses-for-effect are so protracted that one finds oneself either interrupting or starting on one's own thesis in the assumption that Julian has finished.

The Adjournment Debate finished on time with a splendid duet by Dennis Skinner and John Biffen and we made our way to the Cavalry Club. Also present were two Whips, Carol Mather and Peter Brooke. One of the most engaging (but vulnerable) things about Ian is how *naïf* he is. Almost at once he started to complain to Peter Brooke that at an Embassy dinner party last week the Chief Whip had found himself sitting only three places away from Marcia Falkender, how tactless that was of the Embassy Social Secretary. I said that Lady Falkender wanted to join the Conservative Party and they all thought I was joking. But of course she is interested in power, she loves its ambience and misses its absence dreadfully. She is studying the Conservative Party closely at the present time and hopes to infiltrate it and become privy to many of its secrets.[2]

Over the first course, and I cannot remember how the subject

[1] Nicholas Baker, MP for North Devon since 1979; Parliamentary Private Secretary to the Armed Forces Minister since 1981.

[2] Marcia Falkender, created a life peer in 1974, had been private and political secretary to Harold Wilson, 1956–83, including two spells at Downing Street when he was Prime Minister. Elsewhere in his journal AC notes that she had enjoyed 'a room next to the Prime Minister's study in the Palace of Westminster and being able directly to influence affairs of state.'

originated, I said what a dreadful and dangerous fellow Robert Armstrong[1] was. To my great surprise and delight, while Ian was getting his breath back, Carol Mather chimed in with support, said he too thought Armstrong was 'creepy'.

'It is my personal belief,' I said, 'that he is a full Colonel in the KGB.'

Nobody demurred.

Cloisters   *Friday, 30 July*

Both Government and Opposition backbenchers are longing to get away. In the Smoking Room corridor gutting my locker – the first time since 1977 – I found an enormous mass of 1977 correspondence, unsigned and neatly slotted into folded envelopes by Sue, together with a good deal of material formerly urgent, now obsolete.

Already the House has lost its vitality. Cleaners and char ladies swarmed all over the place with enormous sacks of wastepaper, empty bottles, etc. The Chamber was empty and the lights out. Those colleagues who remained were scuttling about collecting their briefcases. Nobody wanted to talk politics; the clock had struck, and we had all changed back from footmen in powdered wigs into rats.

So ends the most enjoyable, eventful and uplifting Parliamentary session that I have ever known, or, undoubtedly, will ever experience again. I have made much impact and played a far from negligible part in bringing about policies concerning which I feel passionately. But I am afraid it was a high point. That sort of thing can never be repeated and I feel jaded now. My present mood is, what-of-it? I am no longer frightened of my constituents, do not want to be a Whip, do not really want to be a junior minister and think to myself that I could not accept anything lower than Minister of State. As the likelihood of my being put straight into that position must be rated at fractions of zero, it is hard to see what the future holds.

---

[1] Sir Robert Armstrong, Secretary to the Cabinet since 1976, joint head of the Civil Service since 1981.

Saltwood   *Monday, August 16*

Jim Prior[1] giving trouble again today. Usual stuff about a 'disgrace' having 3,000,000 unemployed, preliminary sparring in advance of (a) reshuffle, (b) Treasury 'discussions' on public spending. As to (a) I don't think there'll be one, except a few little cosmetic dibs and dabs at the lower levels including, I would guess, a painful-to-me change of junior ministry at MoD. JP's own reputation somewhat tarnished by his tinky behaviour during reshuffles *last* year, but he may have thought it prudent to stage a pre-emptive strike. There are still three wet heavies left in the Cabinet – JP, Heseltine and Walker. But owing to this ludicrous convention that Ministers measure their virility by the esteem in which they are held by their Permanent Secretaries, and as those PSs' own esteem among their colleagues is assessed on the scale of their spending budgets, each SoS, instead of considering the National Interest – still less Government policy in the strategic sense – has to 'fight his corner'. So the three heavies get the support of ponces like Younger and Edwards[2] who need funds for their wanky little principalities.

The whole distribution of Cabinet and Government posts has become absurdly distorted by what are, in the last resort, PR considerations. Minister of 'Sport', but no one for the Royal Navy. And if there really have to be Secretaries of State for Wales and Scotland in the Cabinet then they should simply be selected by the Prime Minister (like Cecil Parkinson in the 'War' Cabinet).

Also being bandied about is the succession to George Thomas.[3] Since we rose I have been meaning to talk to Norman [St John-Stevas] about this. Yesterday I finally tracked him down to his cottage. He spoke guardedly, but warmed up. Of course he would love it. I suppose he might make the Lodgings a bit *too* pink-and-apricot, but I think that his basic kindness, seriousness and constitutional sense would make him ideally suited – while coming as a bonus would be the wit and cattiness under fire. Really, if I don't get a job this autumn I don't

---

[1] James Prior, Secretary of State for N. Ireland since 1981; previously Employment Secretary.

[2] George Younger, MP for Ayr since 1964, Secretary of State for Scotland since 1979; Nicholas Edwards, MP for Pembroke since 1970, Secretary of State for Wales since 1979.

[3] George Thomas, the Speaker of the Commons since 1976 (he had been MP for Cardiff Central, 1945–50; Cardiff West since 1950).

see much point in going back at all – just using up one's time and substance – but with Norman in the chair it would still be fun to go into the Chamber. I get the feeling his constituency isn't very large.

Cloisters   *Wednesday, 1 September*

The BBC, still smarting from the criticism they attracted during the Falklands Campaign (why is it the BBC is so extraordinarily sensitive to criticism?) have set up a panel of Aunt Sallies from the MoD and have invited all and sundry to come and throw coconuts at them. The audience has been filled out with a lot of rent-a-crowd students who hated the whole operation anyway.

The only good moment came when one nameless colonel was finally goaded into telling how all the correspondents had filed copy about the attack on Mt. Longdon, ' ... preceded by the heaviest artillery barrage since Korea ...' etc., etc., and then, when the assault had successfully taken place at night, without any artillery preparation whatever, they had all scrambled to try and get their copy back from the teleprinters. That whining oaf Brian Hanrahan ('I counted them all out ...') maundered on about how journalists never tried to get scoops, never had any thought of advancing their own careers at the expense of their colleagues etc. To my private shame, when it was my turn, I omitted to make sarcastic reference to this, although I did lash out quite a bit.

Saltwood   *Wednesday, 8 September*

Telephoned to Jonathan Aitken today, to see if he could help over Andrew's expedition to the Yemen.[1] As always, he was pleasant and obliging; his wife has just given birth to a son so he was in a good mood. Just as I was ringing off he said, 'By the way I do hear, which is very good news, that there is a strong likelihood of your joining the

---

[1] AC's younger son was going to North Yemen to work with the Catholic Church at Raymah, as part of a stint of Voluntary Service Overseas, before attending the Regular Commissions Board.

Government . . .' I laughed, delighted. 'But,' (I can't remember exactly how he went on) ' . . . Gow is arguing very strongly for your inclusion, and Madam is said not to be opposed, but apparently Jopling is against it . . .' My heart sank. Jopling and Willie combined would be unstoppable, or rather *insurmountable*, if they were to veto a junior appointment. *Why?* Jane said that some remark I had made about Gail [Jopling] must have got back. But I really don't think I have made one to anybody except her. Jane rightly reminded me that indiscretion of this kind is an endemic fault of mine.

Jonathan had gone on to say that Jopling was trying to get rid of Gow himself – 'rid' of course meaning shifted to some dud ministry outside the Cabinet. J said that Jopling felt himself to have been worsted by Gow on a number of occasions – the Employment Bill, the N. Ireland Bill and was even elevating this into a test case. If that is so I *have* had it. Also I get the faintest suspicion (not that I have not had it, wrongly, in the past) that IG's influence is waning. The new accent is on the managerial – hence this ghastly, planted rumour that Heseltine is to be the new S of S at Defence. Well, what is written is written. I know I am incredibly well off and blessed, and worry far too much – about Andrew in the Yemen, about James in helicopters, about falling interest rates,[1] about my crowded desk and my (non-existent) sex-life, even about Tom crossing the road[2] – but I have got a tension-headache. Monstrous, as I said to Jane, in the middle of the recess. Also a strange weakness, muscular dystrophy in the arms, particularly the left arm. Anxiety induces hypochondria, but I have had problems with my left arm for some months. Strange.

Saltwood   *Thursday, 9 September*

This evening little Nigel Forman[3] rang. Soft-spoken in the extreme. He told me that he was having 'difficulty' with his Association and that Michael Jopling had suggested that he ask me to go down and

---

[1] AC now eschewed the stock market and kept his wealth in cash, on 28-day deposits.
[2] Tom, the Clarks' Jack Russell terrier, had no road sense, and had the habit of wandering off to the farm – which meant traversing Sandy Lane, a route frequented by heavy lorries and vans.
[3] Nigel Forman, MP for Carshalton since 1976; Parliamentary Private Secretary to the Minister of State at the Foreign Office since 1979.

make a law-and-order speech (apparently one of the accusations they are using to upset Nigel is that he is opposed to capital punishment) in which I said what a good fellow he is. I am quite ready to do this, because I quite like Nigel and he has in fact been useful in the Home Affairs Committee, stating a point of view which would normally be regarded as right wing, on such questions as the 'Supervised Release' scheme. Also I loathe constituency associations and with very few exceptions, will always back a colleague against them. I was both puzzled and encouraged that Michael Jopling had suggested I do this. I have always been at great pains to please MJ and do what he wants, and here I am doing it again. How can he possibly object to my promotion?

Bratton   *Friday, 10 September*

I arrived on the Hoe slightly late. Lots of smart Marines standing about, and the public arranged in a quadrangle with the nobs on tiered seats around a stand on which the clergy and senior commanders were located.

I had been put next to David Owen. We were surrounded by Conservative Councillors and dignatories who greeted me. No sign of Janet. The service itself was quite acceptable, heavily slanted towards 'triumphalism' with a quite flagrantly political harangue by John Watson, the Vicar of St Andrew's Church, at the end. The Royal Marines Band played a number of patriotic tunes as a mist closed in and beside me David Owen bellowed out the words, ' . . . God who made thee mighty, make thee mightier yet,' etc. When the music stopped there was a moment's hesitation before the crowds dispersed and we could see the navigation lights of a Nimrod coming towards us through the sea mist at a very low altitude. Just over the stands he lit all four after-burners and went into a steep bank. The noise was absolutely deafening, twice as loud as the fiercest peal of thunder you could hear and very dramatic. How they got the timing so split second, I don't know, but it was a fitting end to an appropriately militaristic service.

We had all been invited to partake of refreshment in the Major's Parlour, but I did not see much point in this as I had already established my presence by arriving late in full view of most of the people who would have criticised me if I had not attended. (Not that I would have missed it for anything.) And I had designs on David, who had shown himself all too ready to converse and gossip in whispers in the various periods of *attente* while the service was starting – somewhat to the surprise and irritation, I suspect, of the surrounding local politicians. I lost him in the crowd and then spotted him again. I broke off my conversation with Betty Easton, 'Why don't we go and have a curry?' He agreed.

On the way down to Mayflower Street we fell into step with an old trade union stalwart, Reg Curry, and his wife. They greeted me with the familiarity that comes from the secure knowledge of a condition of formal political hostility; but with David they were more reserved. 'You have lost weight David,' said Reg. DO brightened at the compliment. ' . . . it is because you deserted the Party that feeds you.' It quite spoilt the atmosphere and the four of us walked on in silence.

As soon as we were comfortably settled in the restaurant David launched into a great dissertation about his prospects, and that of the SDP.[1] To be beaten is agony, particularly when you thought victory was in the bag, but to be beaten by someone who you know, and everyone whose opinion you value knows, is inferior – that is really intolerable cruelty.

'I am blown,' he kept saying. 'I have had it.' He loathes the Liberals, loathes them more now than he does even his erstwhile colleagues on the extreme left of the Labour Party. At intervals he expressed his anxiety in Plymouth, admitted he was apprehensive about moving across to fight Janet, cursed himself again and again about having not fought a by-election immediately upon resigning from the Labour Party. David told me that he had been restrained by other SDP defectors who were uncertain about their own prospects if they did the same. This is of course a different tale from the excuse he gave me last year, which was that he could not afford to absent himself from the House of Commons for those critical months. David went on and on about how the Conservatives ought to have a general election this year. Volubly and persuasively he set out the plausible scenarios – the need to get public endorsement for further anti-trade union legislation; the need to avoid a pre-election blight on measures laid before Parliament next year, etc. But of course his real reasons are personal. If both the Alliance and the Labour Party are smashed, then David can play it long and rebuild the SDP independently of the Liberals,

---

[1] Owen had been defeated for the leadership of the SDP by Roy Jenkins.

but drawing heavily on the 'old' Labour Party. But if the election is put off for a year or eighteen months, the Labour Party might mend its fences in advance and the Liberals may become the dominant partner in the Alliance. David Owen will then be left with nothing, perhaps not even a seat in the House of Commons. What a nightmare for him, no wonder he looks haggard.

David talked about his immediate dilemma, which is whether to refuse to serve in the Shadow Cabinet and to refuse, perhaps, even a nominal role as a Shadow spokesman. Together we drafted letters to Roy Jenkins which would frighten him (because RJ still remains apprehensive of David), about how David would prefer to remain free to speak on any subject, how occasionally he (RJ!) might want David to deputise for him on economic subjects if RJ were away, and so forth.

At one point he started talking about me, said, 'You want to be careful though, you know Alan ...' I thought he was reverting to his old warning of last year when he told me that I could easily lose Sutton to an Alliance candidate. But no, he dismissed that idea completely – 'of course you will be all right.' What he had meant was that I should not accept a junior post in the Government, 'with your status, and reputation, as backbencher, it would be madness for you to go in as a junior under-secretary and do a two-year apprenticeship in an obscure post. You should insist on being made a Minister of State.' David told me how he had refused to go in as under-secretary when the Labour Government of 1974 was reformed, how Barbara Castle[1] had promised to give him Minister of State status in all but name, let him sit in on all consultations and so on and how in the fullness of time Harold Wilson had kept his word when he was moved to the Foreign Office.

I was delighted by all this, but when I told Jane she shrewdly pointed out that he was only doing to me what I regularly enjoy doing to him – flattering him with mildly fantastic compliments.

---

[1] Barbara Castle, MP for Blackburn 1945–79, was at the time Secretary of State for Social Services.

Saltwood   *Monday, 13 September*

Our last day before we set off on a very short motor tour, which, hopefully, will end in Zermatt. Still no news or mention of the reshuffle and I could not resist telephoning Jonathan Aitken again, bearing in mind that Michael Jopling was presently trying to get me to do something. JA now admitted that his source was Ian Gow himself, claimed that they had both got extremely inebriated at Jonathan's house in early August. But, and this *was* significant, JA said that he had recently run into Norman Lamont and asked him in jocular terms about his (NL's) prospects in the middle rank reshuffle. Alarmingly Norman Lamont had said, 'Apparently the whole thing is being held up because of Alan,' ie that some wanted me, others did not. It is really too vexing. I told Jonathan about Michael Jopling's request and he brilliantly advised me not just to carry out the instructions, but to copy my speech both to Jopling and Willie.

After putting the phone down I decided to go one better – for all I know this blasted reshuffle is being argued about at this very minute, before The Lady leaves for China – and send them both *advance* copies of what I was going to say, 'in case you want anything altered.'

Oh to be in the Citroen, wafting across France from one rosette to the next!

Cloisters   *Monday, 27 September*

I was sitting at my desk, first day back, when Tristan Garel-Jones walked through. He is *not* discreet. He is a good Whip because he is independent and has a nose for information, but he cannot resist the sound of his own voice. He said, but I think it a little simplistic, that the reshuffle had been deferred until January because of the need to make 'Notty' carry the can for the Falklands Enquiry. This is rather a bore as it means one has to be a good boy for the whole winter term, careful not to put a foot wrong, etc. Also I have got a nasty feeling that by the time New Year comes round things may have changed a good bit and the election may be so close that there will not be a reshuffle after all.

Cloisters   *Wednesday, 29 September*

I went today to Terry Lewin's[1] farewell party at the Admiralty building. I assumed that there would be a lot of politicians and a large crowd, but in fact there were few people in the room and practically no one I knew. Only four people spoke to me, but each in turn initiated the conversation and drew me aside from their predecessor. First, the Secretary of State, then the Chief of the General Staff (Bramall); the First Sea Lord (Leach); and finally the CDS.

It was a memorable little moment that, when the First Sea Lord, who had himself got rid of Bramall, and was complaining to me about the Secretary of State 'hanging on', was then himself similarly dismissed by the CDS, who came over, 'This looks a very naval corner . . .' and made plain his wish that Leach should leave us alone.

Terry Lewin was most interesting and indiscreet about future defence spending, the Falklands campaign, the National purpose and spoke frankly and genuinely. Not a bad bag for a backbencher, but what is the point?

Cloisters   *Wednesday, 13 October*

Plymouth City Council have been bothering me about their proposals to get Cattedown classified as an Enterprise Zone. God, how boring local government matters are! Like so many other tasks, the most notable and glaringly being my tax returns, I simply cannot bring myself to take action. But today, convulsively, I did so. I have to attend the quarterly meeting of the Executive Council in Plymouth and I know that it makes good feeling, and compensates for those very long periods when Janet Fookes is daily reported for her assiduous peering at cracked pavements and bent dustbin lids and I am not mentioned at all. So I, greatly to the detriment of our motoring schedule, spoke to the City Planning Office, rang the *Western Evening Herald* (who obligingly gave me a huge headline piece that evening, so that the grumpy members of the Executive could not have avoided seeing it) and sent a letter to Heseltine formally supporting their case.

At the last moment I thought I ought to take out an insurance

---

[1] Admiral of the Fleet Sir Terence Lewin, Chief of the Defence Staff, 1979–1982.

policy *in case* Michael is actually made Secretary of State for Defence. I enclosed a hand note saying how much I looked forward to it, working under him, etc. etc.

Very late we got into the little Renault and fought our way down through blinding rainstorms. I made a balls-up of getting on to the M3, getting lost in Kingston, and adding three-quarters of an hour to our time. On the way through we stopped at Mackenzie's Garage and I briefly drove the old $4\frac{1}{2}$. Very jolly.

Unfortunately I was not called. Huge numbers of colleagues wanted to catch The Lady on this her first day and the Speaker took no one from our bench.

Later that evening I popped into Michael Jopling's room. Perhaps he expected me to make another grumble about the Falklands visit,[1] however it was merely to tell him that I would be sending on reports of the meeting tomorrow of the 'Tory Immigration Group' and also of the '92' Dinner (at which committee nominations would be decided) but that these reports, for obvious reasons, would be unsigned and without attribution. I am but a cork bobbing about on the storm-tossed sea.

Cloisters   *Wednesday, 20 October*

An extremely full day. Dictating in the morning, then Foreign Affairs Questions. Francis Pym made a *deplorable* performance, answers far too long and mumbly. He is simply not the man he was. Has he been broken by The Lady? She used always to live in such private dread of him, but now the tables are turned.

At the end of questions I made my way to Committee Room 8, where the Defence Select Committee was taking evidence from the Task Force Commanders about their relations with the media.

Why have we all allowed ourselves to be conned into regarding this as a major issue? Many have seized on it as the only remaining angle from which to attack the Government, and thus The Lady, over the Falklands Campaign.

Also, there is the fact that the media, having this frightfully high

---

[1] AC had been disappointed not to be included in the first Government visit to the islands since the end of the war.

opinion of themselves, which they inflame by mutual massage, get dreadfully aggrieved when not accorded the respect which they think is their due. Not having been consulted at every stage about the Operation, not having been given a right of veto, and a right also to regale the audience with their opinions and interpretations on an unrestricted scale, they were resentful.

Mind you, I get the impression that there was a certain absence of tact in the way that they were treated by the Task Force Commanders – four journalists, including Gareth Parry of the *Guardian*, were taken into Carlos Water on 'D' Day and had their billets shifted from *Canberra* to an ammunition ship, then lay at anchor fully loaded for five days under air attack. When finally their pleas to be removed from this lethal target were allowed, the helicopter pilot took them to a lonely hillside overlooking Ajax Bay, the long abandoned site of 5 Brigade Command Headquarters, dumped them and clattered off, leaving them to make their own way without proper winter equipment to wherever took their fancy.

The Task Force Commanders sat in a row, Middleton (*Hermes*), Black (*Invincible*), Sandy Woodward, Jeremy Moore and Wilson, the Commander of 5 Brigade. All seemed formidable in the highest degree, clipped and authoritative. Wilson was the least impressive. With the others one can see why we won – a very different lot from some of their predecessors in World War II.

On the way in I had a chat with Robin Day. He said Heseltine could not go to Defence – 'his hair is too long'. A very good phrase, encapsulating all the reasons why it would be inappropriate.

I stayed on at the Defence Committee as long as I dared and then went along the corridor to a meeting which Lynda Chalker had organised – with David Howell bleakly sitting in, to explain to West Country MPs about projected road improvements. Naturally, being experienced politicians, we all realised that this was some kind of soft-sell approach to try and get us to shut up about heavy lorries. Everyone was in a combative frame of mind and as Lynda is so sweet natured and it would have been pointlessly cruel to have roughed her up, we vented our rage, led off by big Peter Emery, against the senior civil servants who did the 'presentation'.

This meeting, too, I had to leave early to go down to the asbestos protest in the Grand Committee Room. Place absolutely full, packed out, people standing blocking the doorway when I arrived (two minutes late, I was meant to be on the platform) and when I tried to edge past a huge livid barrack-room lawyer with pebble lenses and a raincoat, presumably a part-time flasher, he wouldn't give way. I was within an ace of cawdorising[1] him, but restricted myself to pushing past, *very* firmly, and just reached the platform in time.

I said my piece about asbestos and then had to move on to yet another engagement. This time one with greater promise, namely, the launching of Austin Mitchell's book, *Westminster Man*.[2] I snatched the last free copy, looked myself up in the index and found that I was mentioned no less than twelve times, more than any other MP. However, the atmosphere was soon spoiled when I got into a promising chat-up with a young blonde student at the LSE who ruined everything by asking if I had been at Oxford with her father. 'Possibly,' I said. 'When was that?' '1941' she answered. As I was at Oxford in 1951 and anyone with the slightest grasp of numeracy would have seen that to have been at Oxford in 1941 would make me 63, this was lowering.

Still low I was crossing New Palace Yard on my way to the '92' Dinner when Garel-Jones asked me if we could have a discussion '. . . Garel-Jones/Clark terms.' He had something to confide. I said I would meet him in the Lobby at the 10 o'clock vote. Gloomily I went on to the Dinner. Arriving late I was placed in starvation corner at the end of a very long table. Bad food, tepid beer, drunken and incompetent staff bumping and banging and sploshing sauce all over one's suit.

The awful thing is I really don't like the Right Wing, and this enlightenment is, I fear, mutual. The writing on the wall was last year when so many of them welched on me in the contest for the Defence Chair. George Gardiner who is, of course, sensible, put it down to jealousy. But that is too oversimplified because there is nothing to be jealous of, unless it is that gift of nature which makes me more intelligent than say, Sir Patrick Wall, or little Winston.

However, back in the Lobby Garel-Jones beckoned to me. He said that he had a special message from Jopling. A special message in the

---

[1] Earl Cawdor, father of the Clarks' friend Hugh, Viscount Emlyn, used to open Cawdor Castle once a year in the days before the stately home industry became established. Inevitably, a queue would form on such days and once the Earl, in passing to the front, had been accosted by a visitor who tried to restrain him, shouting, ''ere watch where you are going.' The Earl, without hesitation felled his visitor with a single blow to the jaw and went on through the gate without halting in his progress.

[2] AC appeared in the accompanying television series (see p. 171).

sense that it was not meant to be transmitted, but yet at the same time it was intended that I should hear of it. G-J more or less said that Jopling had undertaken to get me a job in the next reshuffle, we must do something for Alan, etc. After the vote I rang Jane and told her, but I said that I was not in the slightest degree elated by this. It is a what-of-it episode really. These undertakings are practically valueless. And if it was their intention to keep me quiet until January – well, that suits me fine as it conforms exactly with my own intentions.

Cloisters   *Tuesday, 26 October*

I was still in my flat at 11 o'clock this morning, washing up and pecking in a desultory way at housework. This always fills me with gloom – the cold empty chambers, the peeling wallpaper, the layers of dust and grease. Beautiful possessions surround one, but there is no warmth or vitality; the place is a dormitory only. I have not eaten a cooked meal there, or 'entertained', since 1974, when we gave the celebrated drinks party that is referred to in the chapters in George Gardiner's book about The Lady's accession.

Then the phone rang. I was in two minds about answering it. The telephone at Albany is nearly always bores or ill-wishers. It was the Chief Whip (the Chief Whip seems to be phoning me an awful lot at the moment). He told me that there was now a place in the Falklands delegation and would I like to go.

I could not refuse. 'When is it?' 'Tomorrow.' Christ! Apart from anything else this meant I would miss Andrew to whose return we had both been looking forward for weeks. I said I would have to talk with Jane, which I did and she said I 'must' go. I confirmed with Jopling and went straight round to the MoD where there was a briefing.

They had already started when I entered the room. Buck, who has been doing his best from the outset to keep me off the delegation, gave me what is known as an 'old-fashioned' look when I came in. They are a curious selection. Two knights, Hector Monro and John Biggs-Davison, Buck (nominally leader), myself and little Peter Viggers travelling, presumably, on a good-boy pass, and Member for Gosport. The Labour lot were somewhat more grizzled, if not actually elderly. Roy Mason (as a former Secretary of State for Defence and

Privy Councillor, he is the senior member of the delegation, though not, for Party reasons, its leader), Kevin McNamara, a shadow defence spokesman, Bruce George from the Select Committee, Dick Crawshaw from the Speaker's Panel, and a dear old boy whom I have noticed before, but to whom I have never spoken, David Young.[1]

There were three votes that evening, all quite unimportant, but the whips would not let me leave until they were over. I got away to Saltwood about 8.00 p.m. and spent the rest of the evening collecting my kit, warm clothes, etc. in a high state of excitement.

Ascension Island   *Thursday, 28 October*

We breakfasted at 7.30 a.m. and then spent about an hour looking at our beautiful eggshell white VC10 through the windows of the VIP lounge before being told that there would be another hour's delay as 'an oleo strut has collapsed' (!) I started spreading alarm and despondency, saying that it was at least a four-hour job to repair it, that there should then be proper taxi-ing trials and so on. The Air Commodore who was our temporary 'nanny' denied this.

Roy Mason and I had the two best seats, with room to stretch out our legs by the emergency door. I was benefiting, as I often do, from people muddling up my courtesy title as son of a peer of the realm with that of *Rt.* Hon. which of course denotes membership of the Privy Council and great seniority.

At intervals neat little WRAFs gave us delicious (by airline standards) meals, and at twenty to four p.m., after a very low approach, we landed at Dakar to emerge blinking on to a great white apron of concrete to the heat and glare and smells of tropical Africa.

At the top of the steps to the VIP lounge lay a beautiful cat, a perfect tiger in miniature. Not only her markings, but the very way in which she lay, was utterly different from Tabitha Twitchit in Chelsea. The MPs advanced clattering and stumbling up the steps and divided round the cat, who showed no emotion other than to bend back one ear.

---

[1] Richard Crawshaw, MP for Toxteth since 1964 (Labour 1964–81; SDP since 1981); David Young, Labour MP for Bolton E. since February 1974.

We were greeted by the Ambassador and a junior member of his staff, a serious, handsome youth, with a scar on his cheek, immaculately dressed in a pale suit. He talked intelligently about French West Africa and told me much that I didn't know. The inhabitants of Dakar are jet black but prosperous and amiable, and dress beautifully. The women wore wonderful silk headdresses and flowing robes and masses of tribal jewellery – not just crude spikes and rings through ears and noses, but elegantly in the French manner. The Ambassador said that the cooking was very good too, as is the case with all former French possessions. I would like to have spent longer there and was sorry to climb back into the VC10 and head south-west into the blue.

It was dark when we got to Ascension, after crossing the equator at 6.32 p.m. A marvellous scent, heat, sea spray and *pineti* entered our nostrils. Temperatures in the day time are in the high 80s, but every evening without fail the South-East Trades cool the Island and condense and deliver a little soft rain on the upper slopes of the Green Mountain, which dominates its centre.

An enormous airfield, and everywhere looming out of the darkness the shapes of resting aircraft – Vulcans, Victor tankers, Hercules upon Hercules, Phantoms, American C141s, that are still bringing in stores and ammunition direct from Florida. Lit from below from the orange strobe lights, the aura was one of menace and great power. Already we felt ourselves to be on the fringes of the War Zone.

Port Stanley   *Friday, 29 October*

We were woken at ten past three by an apologetic Air Marshal. I had slept badly as my bunk was immediately under the outlet of the air conditioning. Colder and colder it had got and I had spent the last hour curled in a ball with my head between my knees and shivering with a single blanket tucked in all round me.

Breakfast was delicious, beaming chefs on duty, splatting eggs into huge dishes of exploding fat. Sizzling bacon, bubbling baked beans – 'Open twenty-four hours a day,' it said. 'Last hot food for 4,000 miles.'

Then we were driving out to the Hercules, absolutely jammed with cargo up the centre of the fuselage with four ranks of side-facing seats on either side. The seats were webbing and the back bolt upright against a variety of spikes, taps, nuts and other protrusions. There was very little space, indeed, and those already established seemed not to welcome our arrival particularly, nor to be in any hurry to make room for us.

Just as we arrived on the outskirts of Port Stanley, I saw the doors of the nursery school open and out tumbled a lot of jolly fair-haired children in their anoraks, to be collected by their Mums. A completely English scene. We could not possibly have abandoned these people and packaged them up in some diplomatic deal. This has been a real war of liberation, not some dreary 'peace-keeping' effort on behalf of the UN, but a battle fought in obedience to a blood tie.

Our driver parked outside the Upland Goose and we trailed inside. The MPs, shabbily coughing and cigaretting, formed a queue outside the Reception hatch. I will never, under any circumstances, stand in a queue, so I chatted up some girls who were having tea at a table at the far end of the covered patio.

When the queue had dispersed I went to the Reception desk to claim my room. (Plainly if the reservations had been made there was no need to fuss or queue barge.) However, when I got to the desk it seemed that all the places had been allocated. Impossible, I remained calm.

I had noticed that the MPs were 'pairing off' and having to share rooms and thought perhaps that if I was the odd man I might get a room to myself. No, it was 104 I had to go to. Des King, the proprietor, guided me up to 104. Noises from within, spluttering and shufflings. We opened the door – and who should be my room mate, but Buck! Awkward, but not socially insurmountable.

Ascension Island   *Wednesday, 3 November*

From 22,000 feet the surface of the South Atlantic was rippled like the sand of a shallow tidal beach. But if I held an individual ripple in my gaze, I could watch it slowly alter shape and disintegrate into a thin white border that disappeared and blended into new patterns. With awe I realised that these were enormous waves, a giant swell that was rolling up the whole depth of the South Atlantic without interruption, the whole way from Diego Garcia, the Cape, or South Georgia itself. To have been visible to the naked eye from our altitude those rollers must have been seventy or eighty feet high. To our right were the great African cloud banks (I have never known good weather over Central Africa, invariably giant thunder heads), but Ascension Island was clear and blue.

Bleary and stubble-chinned we lurched out of the Hercules with our hand luggage. Senior RAF officers were ultra-creased and starched. Shorts, bleached stockings, chiselled tans, *they* had shaved twenty minutes earlier. In daylight I could see that the aerodrome consisted of two enormous runways in inverted 'V' formation pointing south into the alternative prevailing Trades. The centre of the 'V' was occupied by a knoll some 400 feet high of red volcanic strata – just as well that visibility was always perfect day and night – and our hosts immediately conducted us to the top of this knoll in a series of mini-buses to watch the scramble of another flight of Phantoms and their attendant tankers.

One by one the Victors lumbered down the runway. No fewer than seven were required to escort the two Phantoms to Port Stanley; three of the Victors would only be going half-way before topping up their colleagues who would give the last draft of 'motion lotion' in the latitude of the Argentine coast.

The first half of the runway is slightly uphill and the take-off of the tankers, loaded with fifteen tons of fuel, was painfully slow. Over the uphill stretch the Victors seemed hardly to be accelerating at all, then just in time, the gradient altered and at the very last moment they would rotate, and retract the undercarriage, though unable to make height until the thermals at the shoreline started to lift them. The 29 Squadron Phantoms roared down the runway side by side, showing off.

Our hosts told us with concealed – though not completely con-cealed – relish that our take-off had been delayed from 10.30 a.m. until 2.30 p.m., as the VC10 which was taking us back had had compass trouble on the way out and its arrival had been delayed. The statutory rest period for the crew made it impossible for us to take off until after lunch. Freezing fog was forecast for England and we might have to divert, they added.

Then to a delicious breakfast at the Ascension Chef, atmosphere very much better than the previous week when we had apprehensively toyed with our fried eggs at 3.15 a.m.

The Air Commodore then suggested that we should go on a

tour of the Island and there followed one of the most memorable experiences of the whole trip.

The mini-buses climbed away from the airfield into the foothills of the Green Mountain and the beginnings of vegetation could be detected. Dried-up, burnt-out stalks, without colour or leaf, except in little gullies where shelter from the sun had kept them green, rather like an Attenborough film of a desert awaiting the seasonal flood. But gradually, as we climbed, the vegetation became greener and thicker, brilliant and towering banks of hibiscus and bougainvillea crowded up to the edge of the roadside; dense greenery with fleshy leaves, nameless white and yellow blooms and petals and voluptuous curving ferns.

In the undergrowth one caught glimpses of Martin Johnson Heade[1] plumage. The gradient was very steep and often the mini-bus drivers had to reverse on the hairpins and hold bottom gear between swerves.

Then, quite suddenly, in this equatorial jungle, we drew up beside a perfect English vicarage of the Regency period. Everything was flawless, from the Georgian window panes, to the guttering, to the broken pediment over the arch that led into the separate kitchen garden. The lay-out of lodges and stables was precisely the same as the architect would have arranged on a hillside in Dorset in 1820. But of course the foliage that pressed around it was entirely different. And when I walked into the yard at the back to say hello to the pigs in their teak and granite sties, clouds of tropical birds flew up from the troughs.

This was the dwelling built for the Commander of the Marine Garrison that had been stationed on Ascension to help defend St Helena after Napoleon had been exiled there. All the materials and craftsmen had been brought out from Britain and the result was the most perfect country house south of the Tropic of Capricorn.

But our hosts would not allow us to linger and led us on foot through the kitchen gardens and on up the Green Mountain. Now, as in *Erewhon*, the vegetation started to change back, not to the red volcanic dust of the lower altitudes, but to a rough springy turf, gorse bushes and stunted blackthorn, a cold and penetrating mist, moisture running in rivulets everywhere. In the space of an hour we had moved

---

[1] AC knew his work well from *The Gems of Brazil* (see p. 232).

through 45° of Mercator from the tropics, the jungles to the vegetation and temperatures of the Moor around Tavistock.

The drive down the Green Mountain was a nightmare. Corporal Duffy, bandbox smart and sitting at attention, drove 'on his brakes' – and I mean *on* them. The only time he took his foot off the brake pedal (the mini-bus was loaded with an extra ton-and-a-half of humanity), was to accelerate downwards between the swerves, instead of using the gears to brake the mini-bus, and so steep was the gradient that it would overrun the rev. limit in second gear. He was actually changing up to a higher gear whenever he had the space. It was a matter of minutes before we all went over the edge. 'Don't change up,' I hissed, and actually put out my hand to hold the gear lever in second. Startled, he obeyed.

It had been suggested, and naturally welcomed by most of the delegation, that we should hang about on the balcony of the Exiles Club drinking and smoking and munching Club sandwiches, for the hour-and-a-half or so that remained before take-off. But I preferred to explore Georgetown and Kevin McNamara wanted to look at the Church, so we separated from our colleagues and drifted off on foot.

Just as I was about to turn down the hill into Georgetown quay I saw a white beach some half-mile away. I took a short cut and as I drew nearer could hear the thunder slap of those same giant rollers that I had watched from the Hercules crashing on to the sand.

'Do not whatever you do bathe,' had said the Air Marshal. 'The undertow is very dangerous and we lost quite a lot of personnel before we made it a Court Martial offence.' Court Martial offence! That made it even more irresistible.

The beach was deserted and I took off my clothes and went into the water. Perfectly incredible, the best bathe I have ever had, although the undertow *was* very very strong. It was dangerous to swim other than parallel with the beach, which meant one was rolled about and buffeted by the breakers.

I dried on my shirt and, towelled and full of white gritty sand, feeling marvellous, started back to the Exiles Club. On the way back I ran into two RAF erks who were goggle-faced. They said bathing was very dangerous and that sharks and Portuguese men-of-war came right up to the shore.

Letter to Michael Jopling   *4th November, 1982*

My dear Michael

Just a line to say how tremendously grateful I was for your including me on the Falklands visit.

It was without a doubt the most memorable and invigorating experience of my entire Parliamentary career. Within half an hour of arriving, as we came into Port Stanley, the Infants School was letting its pupils out to be collected by their Mums, and seeing all those dear little fair-haired children in their anoraks – exactly like any village in one's constituency – brought home more effectively than anything else could have done what exactly we were fighting for, and how impossible it would have been to have abandoned them to a foreign power. There is absolutely no question in my mind that this realisation is present in the minds of all personnel out there. Service morale is extremely high and practically everyone we spoke to remarked (a) on the distinction between saving our own people and 'mucking about in the Third World', and (b) on how the excitement of being in a War Zone made up for all the discomfort.

We visited and had time with RAF – flying personnel and Rapier crews – Infantry, Sappers, Artillerymen, Pioneers – and had one hectic day being transferred by Lynx from various Royal Navy ships on station, and found everyone working flat out and proud of the job they were doing (though this did not restrain their very understandable impulse to scare the shit out of us with low-flying practice firing!).

Yours etc

Alan Clark

This high point in AC's political career seems an appropriate moment to end this volume. Life and politics continues in the original published volume, 'Diaries', which opens in spring 1983.

ACKNOWLEDGEMENTS

This volume of Alan Clark's Diaries would not have been possible without the encouragement, first and foremost, of Jane Clark, to whom I am indebted.

My thanks, also, to James and Andrew Clark, who have, like their mother, answered my often ignorant questions. Following Alan's death in 1999, it was his long-time literary adviser, Michael Sissons, who first suggested that as his publisher at Weidenfeld & Nicolson for the original *Diaries* and his subsequent books, I should become the editor of this volume. I am grateful to him, and to the Clark family for their faith in me. It may be reassurance that I share the 13th as a birthdate (See Introduction, page xix, footnote 1).

Jane Clark invited me into Saltwood and gave unquestioning access to Alan's papers. She has also been a most generous host. Although the manuscript diaries are in a variety of bindings, as described in the Introduction, Alan also had a habit of jotting down entries on whatever was near to hand. This has required a diligent search. Even as this volume was about to go to press an early engagement diary surfaced and was found to contain unsuspected entries.

Jane was also an enormous help in deciphering Alan's script, particularly names of people and places, as well as in identification, not least of Alan's cars. But it was reassuring to learn that even Alan himself sometimes had trouble in reading his own handwriting.

I also particularly wish to acknowledge here my wife Sue, who put up with my absences during the transcription and editing of this volume. She, and our daughter Maria, sat at the keyboard on occasion as I deciphered an entry and dictated it to them. My thanks to each of them.

At Weidenfeld & Nicolson the forbearance of my colleagues who took the added strain when I was absent, has caused me no surprise, but I appreciate their support. I would especially single out Ben Buchan, who became my editor, Alice Chasey, our assistant, and our ace production team headed by Richard Hussey.

As that king of editors, the late Rupert Hart-Davis, once remarked, footnoting requires the arts of a detective and a network of supporters. I would like to thank:

Jonathan Aitken
Jane Birkett
Lynette Carr
Tim Heald
Simon Heffer
Michael Howard, MP
Peter Jay
Brian MacArthur
Douglas Matthews (and for his index)
Michael Ratcliffe
Andrew Roberts
Kenneth Rose
Graham Stewart
Hugo Vickers
Lord Weatherill
Alan Williams
David Willetts, MP
The staff of the London Library

Finally, and not least, let me thank Anthony Cheetham, chief executive of the Orion Publishing Group, who encouraged me 'to go for it'.

IT

INDEX

NOTE: Titles and ranks are generally the highest mentioned in the text

Yesterday, after getting back in the Susan car — from an early start we slept, was very nice; sort of what relaxation at being home. In the cold morning, could boys playing with terrain-cycle (now, expensive by forks and other low-pressure tyres). But didn't sleep very well; was woken by car coming up the drive (Jane was out), not dark a perhaps driving away again... or what? Got up, looked out — very wind — drizzle, pitch black, could see I scanned. No sign. could done a closed gate with fire.

Woken by Alpen at 6.30. Should of him to get back on him bed he wheezed, wouldn't. "I'll take them" said Jane, didn't move. Weak and fatigue I got up, dressed I went on the Alpen in the icy cold. Far too early for Reinman. With the kettle on I sat in bed. Jane under the beer. For sure were it didn't take so good or what, was it Alvanys Should day up bit of the immediate / anti-freeze; Jane slowly scratched Beady I clipped — what car of Mercers, only did Andrew have to go to Mercer, can held to be should me. As days, last down here of only start, took him down a 21 with, do fliers (sic) for removing canteen's notice fell hard at started a him road with, so all day. an alarm, let hens corn. left a bird loved at S. papers, but rose about 9.20. Eggs of breakfast he had for a finished early Susan's car; but in Alpen bothing in order to have Meyer to start with car. Here up to